User-Centred Requirements
for Software Engineering Environments

NATO ASI Series

Advanced Science Institutes Series

A series presenting the results of activities sponsored by the NATO Science Committee, which aims at the dissemination of advanced scientific and technological knowledge, with a view to strengthening links between scientific communities.

The Series is published by an international board of publishers in conjunction with the NATO Scientific Affairs Division

A Life Sciences B Physics	Plenum Publishing Corporation London and New York

C Mathematical and
   Physical Sciences
D Behavioural and
   Social Sciences
E Applied Sciences
	Kluwer Academic Publishers
	Dordrecht, Boston and London

F Computer and
   Systems Sciences
G Ecological Sciences
H Cell Biology
I Global Environmental
   Change
	Springer-Verlag
	Berlin Heidelberg New York
	London Paris Tokyo Hong Kong
	Barcelona Budapest

NATO-PCO DATABASE

The electronic index to the NATO ASI Series provides full bibliographical references (with keywords and/or abstracts) to more than 30 000 contributions from international scientists published in all sections of the NATO ASI Series. Access to the NATO-PCO DATABASE compiled by the NATO Publication Coordination Office is possible in two ways:

- via online FILE 128 (NATO-PCO DATABASE) hosted by ESRIN, Via Galileo Galilei, I-00044 Frascati, Italy.

- via CD-ROM "NATO Science & Technology Disk" with user-friendly retrieval software in English, French and German (© WTV GmbH and DATAWARE Technologies Inc. 1992).

The CD-ROM can be ordered through any member of the Board of Publishers or through NATO-PCO, Overijse, Belgium.

User-Centred Requirements for Software Engineering Environments

Edited by

David J. Gilmore

Department of Psychology, University of Nottingham
University Park, NG7 2RD Nottingham, UK

Russel L. Winder

Department of Computer Science, University College London
Gower Street, WC1E 6BT London, UK

Françoise Détienne

INRIA, Projet de Psychologie Ergonomique
pour l'Informatique
Domaine de Voluceau, Rocquencourt BP 105
F-78153 Le Chesnay Cedex, France

Springer-Verlag
Berlin Heidelberg NewYork London Paris Tokyo
Hong Kong Barcelona Budapest
Published in cooperation with NATO Scientific Affairs Division

Proceedings of the NATO Advanced Research Workshop on User-Centred Requirements for Software Engineering Environments held in Bonas, France, September 5–11, 1991

CR Subject Classification (1991): D.2, K.4

ISBN 978-3-642-08189-7

CIP data applied for.

© Springer-Verlag Berlin Heidelberg 2010
Printed in Germany

Contents

Introduction

The idea for this workshop originated when I came across and read Martin Zelkowitz's book on Requirements for Software Engineering Environments (the proceedings of a small workshop held at the University of Maryland in 1986). Although stimulated by the book I was also disappointed in that it didn't adequately address two important questions — "Whose requirements are these?" and "Will the environment which meets all these requirements be usable by software engineers?". And thus was the decision made to organise this workshop which would explicitly address these two questions.

As time went by setting things up, it became clear that our workshop would happen more than five years after the Maryland workshop and thus, at the same time as addressing the two questions above, this workshop would attempt to update the Zelkowitz approach. Hence the workshop acquired two halves, one dominated by discussion of what we already know about usability problems in software engineering and the other by discussion of existing solutions (technical and otherwise) to these problems. This scheme also provided a good format for bringing together those in the HCI community concerned with the human factors of software engineering and those building tools to solve acknowledged, but rarely understood problems.

In the original workshop the two halves were kept quite separate, in the hope (realistic as it turned out) that this would encourage interdisciplinary communication. It was decided to maintain this division in this proceedings, more because it reflects the actuality of the workshop than for any grander reason. Indeed, on reviewing the proceedings just before it went to press I began to suspect that this separation (reified in print) may inhibit cross-disciplinary communication. If any reader feels inclined to read only half this proceedings, I would exhort them to alternate their reading between the two halves rather than to overdose themselves on one approach.

Each half of the proceedings contains two themes, embodying different perspectives on the same approach to software engineering problems. These themes were sketched out in advance of the invitations to participate and later altered in response to the actual papers contributed. Each theme in the workshop consisted of a planned variety of papers — a review of the area's past, 3 research papers, a review of the area in relation to the other sections of the workshop and a discussion paper. However, since people met these workshop requirements in such varied ways, it was decided not to highlight this structure in this proceedings. A further reason for this decision was that a number of people contributed to the workshop by providing posters, which were outside the organised structure of the workshop, but which in many cases fitted the themes very well. To have reflected the organised structure in this proceedings would have separated the posters from the invited papers, an undesirable distinction, since this might imply an unjustified quality difference. Hence, the posters are included as chapters in the appropriate themes. This, plus the failure of some invited contributors to submit work for this proceedings, is why each theme has a different number of chapters.

Thus, this proceedings comprises 4 themes:

1. Design Activities and Representations for Design
2. Code Representations and Manipulation
3. Technological Solutions
4. The Impact of Design Methods and New Programming Paradigms

each theme comprising an introduction, a number of chapters and a discussion. In the workshop itself, half the time devoted to each theme was spent in discussion. As well as addressing issues raised by the workshop papers, the focus in most discussion groups was on fostering cross-disciplinary understanding. The workshop papers have been re-written to form chapters for this proceedings, taking into account relevant parts of the discussion. The discussions presented in this proceedings are "after the event" write-ups of the plenary sessions of the workshop, addressing the interdisciplinary issues not associated with particular workshop papers. It was felt that this approach was far more appropriate than trying to transcribe the discussions themselves.

The extent to which it is possible to capture a dynamic, real-time event in a static, printed proceedings is mainly a matter of many chance happenings and in the above I have tried to excuse the structure, coverage and content of this proceedings. Regardless of whether this proceedings succeeds in conveying the workshop to non-participants, it is fair to say that the workshop itself was a great success. Bringing together a range of nationalities, from a range of disciplines, with a range of personal objectives is always a risky business — the fact that we succeeded is due to many different factors, some of which I wish to record as a permanent account of our appreciation.

Firstly, one must, of course, thank NATO for providing the funding for bringing so many people together, including Robert Rist from Australia (who deserves extra credit for interrupting a teaching period to fly to Europe for a 5-day workshop and then flying straight back to Australia to continue his teaching responsibilities). Also, those participants who paid their own travel and workshop fees deserve acknowledgement of their vital role through their posters and their contributions towards the group discussions.

The workshop was held at the Chateau de Bonas (near Toulouse), a superb environment for such meetings, and a large amount of the credit for the workshop's success should go the environment they created for us, at the same time both work-directed and relaxing — talking shop around the swimming pool, or on the tennis court seemed both natural and inevitable. Furthermore, Claudie Thenault (from INRIA) dealt with the administrative aspects so efficiently that all there was left to do was talk shop or relax or do both together.

My thanks also go to all those who helped me put the workshop together in the first place — the administration was performed by Claudie Thenault and the scientific aspects were addressed by both the official and unofficial Organising Committees — in alphabetical order, Bill Curtis (Carnegie-Mellon University), Françoise Détienne (INRIA, Paris), Tim Dudley (Bell Northern Research), Thomas Green (MRC Applied Psychology Unit, Cambridge) and Marian Petre (Open University). Also, Russel Winder (University College, London) has proved invaluable in his understanding of sophisticated, document-processing technology and, thereby, getting all the contributions into camera-ready format.

Finally, as I write this introduction almost a year after the workshop I am acutely aware that by the time the book appears in bookshops and libraries it may already be beginning to show signs of age, so if anybody reading this feels that more is now known about the topic than occurs herein, I hope you will react as I did on reading Zelkowitz's book — organise the sequel!

David Gilmore
Department of Psychology, University of Nottingham

Theme 1: Design Activities and Representations for Design

Theme 1 Introduction

Early studies of programming were "human factors studies" using experimental paradigms to assess the usability of programming languages or tools. Evaluation of these languages and tools was performed according to performance criteria such as programming time and number of errors. However, no models of programming activities were developed for explaining observed differences of performance. Since the eighties, studies of programming have been characterized by the development of models and by the use of other cognitive paradigms such as the analysis of indirect traces of the activity like the verbal protocols approach. In addition, whereas earlier studies focused on processes mostly at the code manipulation level, more recently research studies have begun to focus on processes related to the design activity itself.

Software design problems have been described as 'ill-structured' or 'ill-defined' problems (Guindon, 1990b; Pennington & Grabowski, 1990; Visser & Hoc, 1990). Important features of design problems are:

- incomplete and ambiguous specification of goals;
- lack of a predetermined solution path;
- the need to integrate multiple knowledge domains (Specification and constraints come from various knowledge domains and have to be translated into a specific knowledge domain, the programming domain.);
- frequently conflicting constraints;
- ill- or un-defined criterion for testing any proposed solution where various different solutions are acceptable, one being possibly more satisfactory in one dimension, another in another dimension.

A number of limitations evident in most studies of programmers (Curtis, 1986; Soloway, 1986) arise from their focusing on "student programmers", programming-in-the-small, and from their conforming to prescriptive models from Software Engineering.

This theme covers topics such as models and empirical studies of design (planning, elaboration and evaluation), models of specification understanding, representation of design decisions and rationale, and individual and cooperative design. This theme introduction outlines how studies presented in the chapters overcome some of the limitations of previous studies of programmers. In the first chapter, different approaches to design are presented and discussed by Davies & Castell. The following chapters illustrate the shift of focus in design studies, from prescriptive to empirically-based models, from studies of students to studies of professional programmers and from individual to group studies. These new focuses are leading to the construction of descriptive/predictive models of the design activity and to the redefinition of the design task (the 'effective' design task), emphasizing, in particular, interactions between various aspects of Software Engineering.

Results from empirical studies of software design have questioned the validity of 'prescriptive models' of programming. One model which emerged from these studies is the 'opportunistic model' as opposed to the 'hierarchical model' of design. Whereas the hierarchical model can be qualified as a model of the 'prescribed' design task compatible with methods and tools developed in Software Engineering, the 'opportunistic model' is an empirically-based model of the activity, describing the actual behavior of the programmers/designers when they perform 'prescribed' design tasks. Such models have been developed in studies of professional programmers, illustrating the shift of focus from students' studies of students to studies of 'real' programmers dealing with complex tasks.

Such models are discussed in the chapters by Davies & Castell and Visser. Note that quite different 'opportunistic models' are presented in these chapters. Davies & Castell argue that program design is broadly top-down with local opportunistic episodes which are mainly caused by cognitive failures of working memory. Although Visser agrees that opportunistic episodes may be caused by the limitation of cognitive resources, the main difference with Davies & Castell's approach stems from the hypothesis that opportunistic deviations are controlled at a cognitive meta-level by criteria for evaluating the cognitive cost of alternative actions.

These different models reflect a shift not only from prescriptive to descriptive models of design but, furthermore, from descriptive to predictive models. As an illustration, Davies & Castell's model and Visser's model make quite different predictions on the likelihood of opportunistic deviations occurring due to the characteristics of the supporting environment.

Let us assume the environment allows the designer to work out (freely) a solution at different levels of abstraction and therefore provides an external memory of the solution in progress. According to Davies & Castell's model, it could be expected that the number of opportunistic deviations would decrease drastically because the working memory load is low and so less likely to cause cognitive failures. Visser's model makes quite different predictions. Even though the cognitive cost of alternative actions leading to the choice of the next action to execute may be affected by the availability of information on the worked out solution, other factors are important which may still lead the subject to deviate from an hierarchical plan because the cost of alternative actions is lower. For example, having a solution to a problem which may be exploited for other analogous problems may be more interesting from a cognitive cost viewpoint than sticking to a pre-existing plan.

An opportunistic model which has a distributed architecture is also discussed in the chapter by Simplício Filho to account for specification understanding. Very little is known of the cognitive mechanisms and knowledge involved in specification understanding as very few empirical studies have been conducted on this activity. Simplício Filho discusses mechanisms potentially involved in specification understanding, for example the importance of problem domain knowledge for hypothesis generation, the use of symbolic simulation for hypothesis verification and the importance of opportunistic deviations from a systematic approach. This leads him to specify elements of the support required for the specification understanding task.

Enriching models of design, like the ones discussed in the chapters by Davies & Castell and Visser, requires a psychological analysis of artifacts used by the designers in order to identify which conditions lead to the use of particular design strategies. In the chapter by Bellamy, a methodology is presented for analysing characteristics of artifacts which are relevant for the user activity. Her "strategy analysis" emphasizes the trade-offs between positive and negative psychological consequences of interface features.

Another shift in focus is from individual to collective studies. This is illustrated in the chapter by Strübing who questions the validity of the design task as it may be defined and studied in 'individual' empirical studies of programmers and defined in Software Engineering task models. The author places the emphasis on the characteristics of the 'effective' tasks of programming.

The notion of task may be defined as the goal(s), the means available, and the constraints in the execution of the task. The notions of 'prescribed' task and 'effective' task (Leplat & Hoc, 1983) reflect the differences between the task at it may be prescribed (in the documents, by the management, etc.) and the model of the task which is constructed by the operator. Activity analysis reveals which goals and conditions are in fact taken into account by the operator to carry out the task; this refers to the 'effective task' which is actually realized and which fits the subject's activity.

Strübing's sociological approach allows an analysis of the effective design task in collective work and challenges the Software Engineering view of the 'prescribed' programming task as being a separation between subtasks such as analysing the problem, designing, coding and maintenance. Interactions between programming subtasks are important. Furthermore, Strübing argues that each task is heterogeneous in itself and that there are additional tasks which are related to the social nature of programming such as negotiating and communicating.

These communicational aspects are most important in Reverse Engineering. As long as they remain in use, the products of design continue to evolve as modifications of the constructed programs are required. In the chapter by van Zuylen there are different views and representations for Reverse Engineering and a discussion of some links between results of empirical studies of design/comprehension and representations for design in the Reverse Engineering approach.

To conclude, the emphasis on the potential interactions between processes corresponding to various tasks challenges the distinction between design activities and representation for design as developed in Theme 1, and code representation and manipulation as presented in Theme 2. In the chapter by Détienne there is a discussion of these interactions. However, observations of professional programmers show that they use specific strategies to minimize some of these interactions because they are very costly to carry out, a position defended by Détienne. When solution reconstruction and revision is required in the design activity, she argues that instead of going from a detailed level to higher levels of abstraction, the programmers may use strategies to solve abstract-level-related problems at the code level, avoiding (as much as possible) changing the level of abstraction or, if the level of abstraction is changed, the programmers may employ strategies in order to do so in an economical way.

Françoise Détienne
Projet de Psychologie Ergonomique pour l'Informatique, INRIA

From Individuals to Groups Through Artifacts: The Changing Semantics of Design in Software Development

Simon P Davies[†] & Adrian M Castell[‡]

[†]Department of Psychology, University of Nottingham, Nottingham NG7 2RD, UK.
EMail: spd@psyc.nott.ac.uk

[‡]Information Technology Institute, University of Salford, Salford, Manchester M5 4WT, UK.
EMail: IT37@sysb.salford.ac.uk

Keywords: software design, problem solving.

1. Introduction

In this chapter we chart the changing semantics of software design. Our concerns focus upon the way in which the disciplines that have traditionally informed our understanding of the design process have framed modes of discourse about design. We are interested in questions relating to the way in which these diverse disciplines may interact in order to contribute to common design theory and practice. Adopting a broadly historical perspective we have identified four specific approaches to understanding the design activity and the products of design. These approaches have been chosen in order to provide a broad historical view of the changing scope and focus within software design.

We begin by reviewing studies of individual problem solving behaviour in software design. Next, we consider characterisations of prescriptive models of design as advocated by the software engineering community. We then move on to discuss more recent contributions derived from research into computer supported cooperative work (CSCW). Finally, we direct our attention to work in human–computer interaction (HCI) which has attempted to specify, among other things, representations for communicating design intentions and for analysing the products of design.

Each of these approaches embodies its own perspective upon design and the products of this activity. Consequently, we suggest that design cannot be uniquely characterised. Rather, we argue that design might be best understood as a nexus of issues which bear a specific relationship to the concerns of a particular discipline. Our analysis suggests that there are several important components to any particular characterisation of design. From our own perspective we have concentrated upon the following issues: how design is defined by each separate discipline, the scope of investigation or interest, the historical imperatives which have led to the development of these views, and finally, the way in which each of these disciplines may contribute to a theory of design and/or its practice. It is clear that any form of characterisation will be imprecise and prone to misrepresentation. However, we feel that our initial attempts in this regard provide a useful starting point from which we might attempt to chart the changing semantics of design.

Despite common strands in our analysis we believe that these different views of the design process may currently be irreconcilable. We suggest that each discipline's grounding in a specific form of analysis and discourse leads to a divergent set of perspectives and approaches based upon fundamentally different assumptions, core concerns and modes of enquiry. However, by characterising the perspective of each separate discipline we hope to provide the foundation for the development of a shared, or at least a partially shared, understanding of the design process.

Following Bowers (1991), one central theme of this chapter is concerned with the idea that these various design disciplines may exhibit particular forms of narrative about the nature of human activity and its products. Our concerns here stem from two primary observations. The first of these is that a 'rational' narrative may often be used to describe an 'irrational' process in order to mitigate or explain away that 'irrationality'. By using the term 'irrational' we do not mean to be disparaging, we merely wish to reflect upon the fact that the hegemony of certain design disciplines implies a 'rational' process. Our second observation is that narratives about the same activity or product may change depending upon the partners involved in the narrative or upon the stage in the design process when that narrative occurs. As a consequence, we argue that design cannot be subjected to analysis using the same methods and techniques commonly used to analyse other problem solving activities. Design takes place within a rich social context; individuals are taught to design, and deviations from the prescribed view of design can have negative implications. We wish to emphasise these observations since we believe that they may facilitate a common understanding of the design process and pose specific theoretical implications for each of the characterisations of design that we advance.

2. Implicit and Explicit Theories of Design Problem Solving

Recently, a significant number of empirical studies have begun to systematically explore the nature of design activities. Many of these studies detract from the basic hegemony of the software engineering community by proposing models of design which emphasise the heterachical nature of design decomposition and indicate the prevalence of opportunistic episodes in the design activity. In contrast, the software engineering community continues to foster a rigidly structured view of design. This endures in the face of many anomalies arising both from empirical studies of the design process and from practical experience of software development. The continued perpetration of this view is evident in current educational practice in software engineering training. Moreover, the development of tools and methodologies intended to support software design activities is still founded upon a top-down and highly structured understanding of design problem solving. It seems clear that basic research into the design process is not feeding back into prescriptive models of design, into education or into the development of tools to support designers.

2.1. The Established View

Simon (1962) was among the first to suggest that design should be considered a science. His view was that the science of design should be subject to formal laws and descriptions derived through empirical and theoretical analyses of design problem solving. According to Simon, the design process involves an attempt to understand the structure of the problem space by exploring the space of possible designs. In effect, design problem solving involves the stepwise and hierarchical decomposition of the problem space into cognitively manageable units. This view is reflected in Simon's approach to understanding human problem solving which suggests that problem solving is a focused process that starts from high-level goals which are successively refined into achievable actions. In addition, it is claimed that this process is hierarchically levelled. That is, plans or sub-goals are always fully expanded or refined at the same level of abstraction before the problem solver moves on to lower levels in the plan/goal hierarchy.

Such a view of design problem solving is clearly implicated in prescriptive accounts of the software design activity. For example, the major principle of structured design is that designers should define and compose data structures and types in a hierarchical fashion. According to this view, the designer is able implement the higher levels of a design and represent the lower levels by stubs which simulate their function in a simplified way. As the implementation of one level is completed, the designer can then move on to a lower level in the hierarchy and implement that in terms of its sub-levels.

A number of empirical studies have provided behavioural evidence which suggests that such a view of design problem solving might be broadly correct. For example, Jeffries et al. (1981) found that novice and expert programmers decomposed their designs in a top-down fashion — moving between progressive levels of detail until a particular part of the solution could be directly implemented in code. Adelson & Soloway (1985) provide additional support for the use of top-down design by experts working in both familiar and unfamiliar domains.

2.2. Challenging the Established View of Design Problem Solving

2.2.1. Opportunism

More recently an alternative view of the problem solving process has emerged. This view characterises problem solving as an opportunistically mediated, heterarchical processes (Hayes-Roth & Hayes-Roth, 1979). Here, in contrast to top-down models, problem solving is seen as a process where interim decisions in the problem space can lead to subsequent decisions at either higher or lower levels of abstraction in the problem decomposition hierarchy. At each point during the decomposition process the problem solver's current decisions and observations may suggest various opportunities for the development of solution steps. For instance, a decision about how to conduct an initially planned activity may highlight constraints on later activities, causing the problem solver to refocus attention on that part of the plan. In a similar way, low-level refinements to an abstract plan may suggest the need to replace or modify that plan.

A number of recent studies have highlighted the opportunistic nature of software design tasks (Guindon, 1990b; Visser, in this volume). For example, Guindon (1990b) has found that software designers often deviate from a top-down, stepwise refinement strategy and tend to mingle high and low-level decisions during a design session. Hence, designers may move from a high level of abstraction — for instance, making decisions about control structure (e.g. central vs. distributed) — to lower levels of abstraction, perhaps dealing with implementation issues. Guindon notes that the jumps between these different abstraction levels do not occur in a systematic fashion, as one might expect from hierarchically levelled models, but instead can occur at any point during the evolution of a design.

2.2.2. Problem Representation

Other studies (Siddiqi & Ratcliff, 1989) suggest similar deviations from a simple top-down model of program design and have questioned the basic adequacy of prescriptions stemming from the structured programming school, in particular the notion of functional/stepwise decomposition. For example, Siddiqi & Ratcliff (1989) found that subjects trained in structured programming do not carry out problem decomposition in manner which reflects a search for appropriate levels of abstraction in a specification, as would be expected if these subjects were rigorously applying structured programming techniques. Rather, their problem decomposition is guided largely by cues derived from the problem representation.

They describe two sources of cues; stimulus activated, where decomposition is motivated by content and surface characteristics of the problem specification, or knowledge activated, where decomposition is triggered by design experience. The latter would suggest a hierarchical problem decomposition strategy, if the subject had received prior training in program design. However the stimulus activated cues may suggest other decomposition strategies, and Siddiqi and Ratcliff have observed that on many occasions problem decomposition is triggered in this way and can often lead to simplistic non-hierarchically levelled decompositions.

Such studies suggest significant problems with hierarchically levelled, top-down characterisations of coding behaviour and software design. They suggest that designs are often constructed in a piecemeal fashion with frequent redesign and evaluation episodes and designers are frequently observed to move between different hierarchical levels at various points during the design process.

2.2.3. Accounting for Conflicting Evidence: Strategies, Verbalisation and Metacognition

One important issue that arises is how we might attempt to explain the range of different results found in previous investigations, and from this account for the dichotomy between top-down and opportunistic strategies. Substantial empirical data supports both views and as such it would be unreasonable to reject one model in favour of the other. However, these two strategies are often seen to be mutually exclusive, at least within the context of a given task. Hayes-Roth & Hayes-Roth (1979) suggest that some tasks are more suited to a top-down approach and others to the adoption of an opportunistic strategy. Additionally, Carroll et al. (1980) provide some empirical support for the idea that hierarchically structured problem representations lead to hierarchically clustered solutions. Hayes-Roth & Hayes-Roth claim that:

> "The question is no longer which model is correct, but rather, under what circumstances do planners bring alternative problem solving methods to bear?" (Hayes-Roth & Hayes-Roth, 1979, p.308)

They suggest that opportunistic methods are more appropriate for some tasks such as their errand-planning problem, while other problems will have a more obvious hierarchical structure and consequent will be suited to a top-down approach.

A different view is proposed by Davies (1991a). He presents a model of program design which attempts to integrate existing views by characterising program design tasks as broadly top-down with local opportunistic episodes. Davies reports an empirical study which suggests that behavioural regularities emerge during the program design process. These regularities appear to have clear top-down, hierarchical and goal driven characteristics. However, at many points in the evolution of a design, designers can be observed engaging in opportunistically directed activity. This can be contrasted with Hayes-Roth and Hayes-Roth's assumption that choice of strategy will be determined primarily by task characteristics. Rather, both strategies can clearly be seen to be evident in the context of a single task and the existence of opportunistic excursions does not rule out the possibility that the software design task can be broadly described as a top-down process.

There are a number of reasons for the prevalence of observed opportunistic episodes in previous studies of software design, and these highlight more general methodological problems. For example, such studies have used a small number of subjects and this makes it difficult to explore general statistical regularities in the design process. The validity of drawing implications from these studies for more general characterisations of design may be problematic when one considers the impact of individual differences on the adoption of particular problem solving methods and the intra-subject variation evident in a number of studies (Guindon, Krasner & Curtis, 1987). Also, conflicting views about the nature of the design activity might have arisen because previous studies may have described that same level of abstraction in different ways or different levels of abstraction in the same way.

Other work has indicated that the verbal behaviour of designers may not equate well with their actual behaviour. Davies (1992) has argued that the elicitation of concurrent verbal protocols during a design task may in fact *cause* opportunistic deviations from a top-down approach. This is based upon the commonly held assumption that opportunistic episodes arise from simple cognitive failures where information is lost from working memory. This suggests that those points in a design task which are cognitively taxing will be made more difficult when a designer has to articulate their problem solving behaviour. Moreover, the use of verbal protocols to characterise temporally bound events, such as a design decomposition, may have serious implications for the way in which such events are described. Davies (1992) reports an empirical study of a software design task which demonstrates that described behaviour elicited in the form of concurrent verbal protocols can differ significantly from observed behaviour. It is argued that this arises because of a tendency to linearise verbal descriptions of non-linear behaviour. This suggests that some care should be taken when using such a methodology to characterise events which have a significant temporal dimension such as software design.

In addition, it should be noted that software design is a semantically rich activity and that it may not be possible to disentangle 'pure' design behaviour from actual behaviour which is mediated by the designer's educational background and working practices. Parnas & Clements (1986) suggest that designers will often resort to a rational narrative in order to justify their adoption of a non-rational process. Hence, designers may document the design process and its products *as if* they had occurred in a systematic fashion.

Another difficulty concerns the nature of the problems that are generally considered appropriate for exploring software design. These problems rarely appear to display the sort of features that one would typically expect to exist in a non-trivial software development project; however, see Visser (1987) who presents an interesting longitudinal study of the design process. We wish to stress not so much the simplicity of the problems as this has been covered elsewhere, but would like to draw attention to their novelty. We feel that problems that typical designers have to deal with share many of the features of previous problems, and more importantly endure. That is designers are likely to be working on a particular problem or sub-components of that problem for some length of time. This suggests a familiarity with the problem that is profound and not captured in current lab-based research. Moreover, studying such an enduring process is not tractable given the methodologies and experimental techniques currently employed which typically fail to capture the important longitudinal features of this activity.

2.3. Forms of Narrative in Software Design

It appears that forms of narrative about software design may occur at several levels. At one level it could be argued that linguistic conventions lead to a tendency to structure verbalisations about an activity in a way that may not reflect the underlying form of that activity (Levelt, 1981). This is especially true of design where its temporal and process-based character make it particularly prone to mis-description Secondly, the effects of training and specific working practices may lead to a second order rationalisation whereby designers attempt to incorporate a sense of post hoc rationality into the design process. We suggest that these narratives may well affect the way in which design processes are described in the context of experimental studies. We believe that this may constitute a major methodological problem with cognitively-orientated studies of software design. It is difficult to see how such activities could be validly analysed using the methodological tools of cognitive psychology given its isolation from the social context of design.

The recent critique by Lave (1988) of information processing analyses of problem solving proposes a similar idea. Lave suggests that cognition should be studied in vivo as part of a world of cultural artifacts and social practices, rather than as a uniquely individual activity studied in the laboratory. In many ways design might be seen as being more fully located in a particular culture than many other problem solving activities. One reason for this is that design problem solving activities are formally prescribed whereas in other problem solving domains the problem solver is free to choose from a range of potentially useful strategies and techniques. Moreover, the prescription of 'acceptable' forms of design activity is formed by educational experience and work practice. Hence, it is very difficult to see how one might begin to study design in the laboratory in isolation from its social, organisational and educational context. Moreover, because of this rich social and educational context, it is not clear how studies of design activity may be straightforwardly equated with analyses of problem solving behaviour in other domains (Breuker, 1991).

Another major problem with studies of individual problem solving behaviour in design is that it is not clear how such studies might contribute to a theory of design in practice. In the main, such studies fail to provide any real feedback into the design process since they do not articulate requirements in a form which can be used by design practitioners. Moreover, suggestions for improving design infrequently match 'acceptable' management practice. In many cases studies of design that have emerged from the information processing paradigm have failed to provide any suggestions about the way in which the practice of design might be improved. We would argue that where such suggestions are made they are often incompatible with existing design practice or are presented in a form which is too vague to be of any real value.

One example of this can be found in Guindon's discussion of the way in which opportunistic processes might be supported by design environments. Guindon is one of the few authors to have made a serious attempt to suggest requirements for such environments based upon empirical study. However, these recommendations imply a view of the design process that is diametrically opposed to that held by the software engineering community. Evidence suggests that simply building new features into existing design methodologies is fraught with difficulty (Fowler et al., 1989) as a consequence seems clear that advocating a complete shift in the way in which design should be viewed is unlikely to be acceptable in any form. We argue that management of the software development process drives the development of new tools and that research into design will consequently have little real impact upon this process since it clearly has a different focus and is not concerned with commenting upon managerial practice.

Psychologists interested in design have traditionally been interested in contributing to theory rather than in building tools. However, this position appears to be changing. This is evident in the development of tools to support a range of design activities including collaborative decision making (Conklin & Begeman, 1988) and high-level design (Bloomfield & Ormerod, 1991). Anderson (1987) argues that only by building tools can one determine the adequacy of certain forms of psychological theory. Although Anderson is arguing specifically for the development of tools in the intelligent tutoring domain, his arguments are also applicable in the present context. We would argue that psychological theories of design may benefit positively from the adoption of this kind of approach. This is because the provision of a concrete instantiation of the theory tends to reduce the 'visibility gap' and more importantly it enables the testing and refinement of that theory to take place in an ecologically valid context.

We have attempted to stress the importance of contextualisation in interpreting human problem solving activities. Facets of this context such as its cultural location and the way in which the structuring of design activities reflect wider socio-technical concerns, underlie many of the difficulties we have identified. These play a significant role in the structuring of verbalisation and the development of different narratives rooted in particular design situations. Beyond this we have seen how these problems affect the choice of tools and techniques employed to study the design process and more importantly how the results of these experiments are used to develop theory and/or feed back into the design process itself.

3. Software Engineering

It is clear that a number of prominent software engineering methodologies incorporate implicit psychological theories about the nature of the design process. However, the software engineering community has been more interested in prescribing rather than describing design activities; see (van Zuylen, in this volume). In general, software engineering has articulated process models of software development whereby a set of initial requirements are transformed, thorough a number of stages, into an operational system. In principle, and if one takes this process model to its extreme, the transformation between requirements and specification should be error free if the process of transformation takes place as prescribed. However, this strict transformational view fails to take account of problem solving and creativity. The move towards structured development provided support for management by removing managerial hurdles such as unplanned and unpredictable designer creativity. There has been a tendency within software engineering to employ transformational structures from other disciplines. For example, the waterfall model reflects a manufacturing orientation and provides a visible control and monitoring structure for management. Moreover, these prescriptive approaches are further entrenched by the need to make the software development process compatible with certain software products (IPSE's, CASE tools, etc.), which in turn need to be compatible with existing process models.

In addition, there is an implicit supposition that design environments are composed of individuals following more or less prescribed tasks in well defined relationships with each other and, most importantly, independently. Creativity in design is not considered an issue emerging through global human interaction but is merely supported as local exchanges of information, more often than not related to forms of problem solving best characterised as 'fire-fighting' or to group activities embedded in the managerial process such as walkthroughs and milestone reviews.

Work within software engineering considering 'designing for designers', and the shift of attention to producing more sophisticated tool-kits have yet to demonstrate how they have benefited the products of design. We suggest that in fact they may have served to distract serious debate on the inputs, process and outputs of design. The critical questions centre around a shared understanding of what we need to do to support design and this problem is not addressed by providing 'better' technology such as CASE tools and multi-media applications to support ill-understood processes. The problems endure but become increasingly masked by the allure of the latest hardware and software; Strübing (in this volume) provides a useful overview of the social complexities of the design process.

While the use of formalisms and process models in software engineering reflects a strict managerial orientation for imposing control it bears little real relationship to the way in which design takes place. For example, Parnas & Clements (1986) argue that designers will frequently adopt a rational stance to describe their design behaviour. This is contrasted with their actual behaviour which is not seen to follow the prescribed approach. As we saw above, software designers may engage in different forms of narrative when describing the design process and it may be that the form of this narrative is at least partially dependent upon the partners in this narrative. Moreover, a recent study by Walz and her colleagues (Walz et al., 1987) showed that the level of agreement among designers reached its highest point when a deadline is approached and that after this short period of consensus the design team once again began to argue about design issues. This may suggest that attempting to capture the rationale for a particular design decision may be dependent upon the particular point at which that rationale is expressed. Software engineering has often neglected or overlooked the fact that the design of computer systems rarely involves a set of programmers working as single problem solvers in parallel with only a limited bandwidth of communications available to them. It sets up this over-characterised scenario precisely in order to justify the partitioning of the human activity system that results from the extension of the ideas to project management.

If one adopts this view it would appear that theoretical analyses of design behaviour will not feed back into design practice unless such analyses make specific concessions in terms of the way in which this activity is managed. There would seem to be little sense in advocating the adoption of tools and methods which give rise to radical changes in the way in which design is traditionally conceptualised. This is primarily because this conceptualisation is formed by the need to manage rather than by the need to understand the design process. Management orientation reflects a pragmatism which is expressed in the attitude that they are doing the best with what they have, given the demands under which they have to operate. If narratives between those studying design and those doing it, are to be initiated and sustained it is clear that the results of such studies need to be couched in a form which at least addresses these pragmatic demands. Software engineering environments are typically designed to support these pragmatic concerns and are not founded upon a theoretical understanding of the design process based upon empirical findings.

Moreover, such environments are evaluated in the context of the methods and techniques they are designed to support, rather than upon more wide ranging evaluation criteria. By the same token, psychologists have generally not felt it important or necessary to frame their results in a way which; meets with such management demands, recognises the importance of providing information in form which 'fits' existing work practices (Fowler et al., 1989) or is consonant with their training (Castell, 1986). Consequently, the way that psychological theory has moved into real world design has been slow and often limited to reference to human factors guide-lines (Smith & Mosier, 1986) with concern limited to the design of interfaces rather than systems. We suggest that these reasons, which in turn embody the deeper narrative structures previously discussed have led to the recognition of what Carroll & Kellogg (1989) suggest is the paradox of HCI applications leading HCI theory, with analyses performed on artifacts in advance of the development of any well-articulated theory.

4. Computer Supported Cooperative Work (CSCW)

We have seen over the last few years the emergence of CSCW as a recognised research discipline in its own right, and one which currently attracts much attention and funding. Better technology and the recognition that most office based work, not just design work, occurs through a sophisticated set of interactions between social agents, has led to a reformulation of research aims vis-a-vis software designers. This reformulation can be considered as a response to a strong economic imperative. Thus we are beginning to see a clear recognition of the importance of the organisational and social factors that underpin the software development process.

As the name suggests, here the remit of researchers of design is extended to include more than one individual and addresses notions of distributed cognition. However there is some debate in the community (Grudin, 1991) as to whether attention should be directed to the technology necessary to facilitate group interactions or to a better understanding of those human activity systems themselves. We regard this debate as one which characterises some of the essential points made in this chapter. Even moves towards some integration of the communities as proposed in the CSCW camp appear to have only masked enduring distinctions in what is considered to be the appropriate use of research output on design.

Given the explicit recognition of the role of groups in the design of software artifacts, it is not surprising that the social psychology of communications and decision making in small groups has been revisited and plundered by eager CSCW researchers (Bowers, 1991). However this has left them in a position of using and integrating this data to support arguments, make assertions and defend positions which are well outside the research philosophy which pervaded the original research. The problems with this sort of approach that we wish to stress are that the original work served to extend and develop theories within one discipline, whereas the results have been appropriated into another discipline revealing little about the development of theories in the latter. Research in social psychology has an explicit and defined relationship to theory, CSCW does not.

Similar sorts of criticisms can be made with respect to the contribution of other disciplines in the race to publish CSCW material. For example project support environments embody clear management principles while seeking to utilise research products of the currently influential conversational paradigm (Frohlich & Luff, 1989). The contribution of design within CSCW can now only be considered as annexed to a curious and pragmatic blend of existing theories applied to an ill-defined agenda, often exhibiting striking similarities with the structuring of design activities and managerial control mechanisms evident in software engineering.

Although concentration on shared problem solving and issues of roles and communication structures have been cited as explicit foci for CSCW in order to better understand the rich organisational context in which design occurs, the conception of what constitutes design held by practitioners and researchers from different disciplines, remain fundamentally polar. We concur with Bowers (1991) that such problems are rooted in the narratives provided by the contributory disciplines which paradoxically act as individual justifications while constituting boundaries to shared conceptions of design. Thus, although appearing to portend the establishment of a host of new feedback routes between theory and artifact, CSCW as yet appears to have contributed little either to the development of theories of design or practical support to the individuals engaged in design.

5. Claims Analysis and Design Rationale

The recognition that a great deal of software design is in fact re-design, ranging from reuse of knowledge of program fragments (Curtis, 1989a) through design templates to wider issues of criticality and constraints within the development process, has been partly responsible for the emergence of two views on the design process which we will examine briefly here. These views stress the capturing of high-level abstractions relating to either properties of successful artifacts or the underlying rationales for design decisions.

5.1. Design Rationale

'Design Rationale' (MacLean, Young & Moran, 1989) is an attempt to formulate an explicit representation of the reasons underlying particular design decisions which can be used to both support the communication of design intentions and facilitate argumentation surrounding the formulation of design issues. The two main problems that Design Rationale seeks to address are "what is an appropriate representation" and "how can this representation be used". MacLean, Young & Moran (1989) consider this representation as an explicit description of the design space which is divided into the decision space where alternative options are considered and an evaluation space which includes reasons for selecting between these options. Consequently they consider that this description is just as much a product of the design process as the artifact.

Hence the focus of this approach is on designers, but attention is directed towards not merely recording design decisions, but with codifying and structuring the reasons which underlie those decisions. It is suggested that an explicit representation of a Design Rationale should allow the designer to envisage a single design space in a more structured fashion and from this stems the idea that design alternatives can be compared with relative ease. Moreover, the recognition that breakdowns in design often occur because of cognitive limitations (Guindon, 1990b) also suggests that this form of structuring may be beneficial in terms of helping to avoid such breakdowns.

Design Rationale has been applied to interface design but it is claimed that it is applicable to more general design problems including organisational and technological issues. The focus on communications is explicit and is intended to mediate human–human interaction, but at least in its initial stages is limited to the interaction between members of the design team and psychologists. However, they believe that an approach which stresses preservation of the richness of the design process will lead to the development of an complex and unwieldy representation. They seek to aid the designer with the design task in areas where modelling techniques apply, while also helping to determine the parts of design where they do not apply.

The approach advocated by Design Rationale clearly accepts the need provide a representation which endures, in that it is anticipated that the representation will be of use during development between different stakeholders but also during redevelopment and between designers and users. However laudable this intention, it is not clear how it facilitates the integration and development of a shared understanding which must be a precursor to narrative rapprochement.

Following Parnas & Clements, MacLean, Young & Moran (1989), emphasise that "the content of Design Rationale is an idealisation of the design space" (p.248). This may be the case, but a deeper look at Parnas & Clements' work suggests that much of the description of the design task is a post hoc rationalisation, provided in a form that managers can assimilate comfortably. MacLean, Young & Moran use Parnas & Clement's work to bolster the idea that rationalisation may be seen to be a 'natural' process emerging from the design activity. However, Parnas & Clements' suggest that the rationales that their designers expressed were related to justifying their activities in terms of managerial demands that design should be a structured and rational process. It is not clear why the output of Design Rationale will necessarily be useful or usable since there are a variety of rationales that might potentially be derived, each existing for different narrative recipients.

Design Rationale does not appear to be concerned with testing or contributing to theories of design except in terms of its modelling components. Its primary aim is to construct better artifacts and as such it is open to similar criticisms levelled at Claims Analysis which we discuss below. In particular, the collection of information about the design of specific artifacts would not seem to be applicable to other artifacts without some specification of the mechanisms by which this might be achieved.

5.2. Claims Analysis

A complementary, yet rather different approach to representing design rationale has been promoted by Carroll and his colleagues (Carroll & Campbell, 1989; Bellamy, in this volume). Carroll suggests that designed artifacts embody implicit psychological theory and that this theory can be articulated in the form of claims about the artifact in terms of its support for intended tasks. Once again the emphasis here appears to be concerned with reuse. In particular, Claims Analysis fosters an evolutionary view of design which suggests that the best designed artifacts survive. As a consequence, it is suggested that one should attempt to embody the successful elements of extant designs in new products. Claims Analysis views design as an iterative process and promotes the idea that there is a reciprocal relationship between the articulation and re-articulation of psychological claims and the various iterations of a particular design.

Proponents of Claims Analysis utilise psychological theories merely in order to develop better artifacts, but do not believe that the knowledge gained in this process can in turn be used to extend and refine the psychological theories. This is because of the need to understand instances of artifact use as interactive processes of consensual interpretation and because the artifacts themselves embody implicit theories of Human–Computer Interaction. They point to serious shortcomings within academic psychology with its focus on narrow and artificial tasks, and human factors psychology which concentrates on simple and isolated performance measures which "rarely provide articulate direction in the design of artifacts" (Carroll & Campbell, 1989). This view appears at odds with that expressed by Anderson (1987) in which the very act of developing concrete instantiations of the theory (artifacts) facilitates the *explicit* testing of features of that theory, rather than driving the generation of a better designed artifact.

Those developing Claims Analysis have recognised that research has been led by the interpretation of interface innovations (Carroll & Kellogg, 1989) and seek to address this apparent paradox by adopting a more systematic approach to usability evaluations requiring a richer role for psychology in design while maintaining a focus on the design and interpretation of HCI artifacts. While we do not wish to suggest that a Claims Analysis approach will not meet these aims, our analysis has suggested that this *richer role* for psychology is crucially dependent on the narratives used by practitioners seeking to realise this role.

The primary focus of Claims Analysis is clearly related to improving the design of artifacts rather than providing support for group design processes. This can be contrasted with work on Design Rationale which, as we have seen, provides an explicit representation of design argumentation which is intended to be used by design teams. This raises problems with respect to the way in which Claims Analysis might be successfully incorporated into design practice. For example, it is not clear how the enhanced role for psychology promoted by Claims Analysis might be realised. As we have already seen, psychologists and software engineers adhere to fundamentally divergent interpretations of the design process. Hence it is difficult to see how psychologists could articulate these claims in a way that way that was acceptable to designers engaged in redesign. Consequently, any approach which posits a greater role for psychologists in this process must be clear about the means by which this might be effected. Indeed, it appears that this new mode of participation in design will require a redefinition of what we might traditionally consider the role of the psychologist to be. The setting up of such a role and the pragmatic difficulties specifying the nature of the deployment of such a person outside small-scale research teams will require an act of faith on the part of the development managers in terms of the possible benefits that may accrue.

Given the focus on existing artifacts, it appears that the scope for revising design decisions and postponing design closure are severely limited by the late stage in design at which Claims Analysis is intended to be employed. This is based on the assumption however that Claims Analysis is tackling real rather than notional artifacts. Although this may not be true, existing evidence (Bellamy & Carroll, 1990) is based upon analysis of existing artifacts such as programming environments. The lateness of the analysis may be acceptable for small scale problems but is problematic in terms of design-writ-large. Unlike Design Rationale, Claims Analysis considers design only with respect to usability issues. From a Design Rationale perspective, the artifact is considered as describing the set of options that are selected for the final design, which leaves, from a Claims Analysis point of view, other non-usability related concerns unconsidered.

Again, we can contrast the role for psychologists engaged in Claims Analysis, in which little consideration is given to the *methods* for communicating with and gaining the commitment of systems' designers, with the perspective emerging from CSCW which considers the important function of psychologists as agents participating in the rich context of real-world design. It seems clear that any rationale is bound temporally and contextually suggesting that there is no single rationale, and indeed that any rationale will change over time according the demands and constraints imposed by the particular development context. Gaining consensus from designers is a problematic activity and using a static rationale as a foundation for recording design decisions and facilitating communication is host to a range of potential problems.

6. Overall Themes

It is not surprising that given the changing semantics of design over time, the work that has emerged from any one perspective is not easily transferable, or meaningful to any other. If we adopt Anderson's view that the only way to progress is to encapsulate parts of that theory in a real-world implementation, then use that implementation to test and redefine the theory, it becomes apparent that these perspectives on design have only addressed *parts* of the feedback loop which is central to this notion. Moreover, if we sustain this analysis, then the divergence of these perspectives along the dimensions of evaluation and model-building are thrown into sharper relief. For example, software engineering has not been able to successfully employ what light psychologists have thrown onto design, precisely because their views of the world are so different. Only by refocussing attention on the contribution that these perspectives can make to the *explicit* refinement of theory, can we avoid further retrenchment of position and duplication of effort.

We have focussed on the contribution of cognitive psychology to our understanding of design in order to provide framework for our critique. This is because it provides a clear expression of the development of the different narratives that constitute the major concerns of this chapter. In particular we have concentrated upon those narratives provided by researchers attempting to grapple with the complexities of the processes involved in design, and the narratives of those who carry out design. We have seen that the tensions between these narratives have been expressed in a variety of ways.

At one extreme, the legacy of the information processing paradigm has left psychologists feeling unclear about how and why their work can be conveyed in a way that may improve and enhance human design activities. At the other extreme, we have seen a narrow transformational view extend to devalue contributions from psychology which cannot be easily applied. The middle ground is now becoming populated with researchers eager to apply their results to the messy environment of real world design, using techniques drawn from a variety of disciplines ranging from sociological analysis to the history of science. These approaches have found limited channels through which to apply their results and an emerging philosophical redesignation of design has spawned deeper methodological concerns about the processes they are seeking to explore.

Our aim is to encourage debate, and we have deliberately used characterisations in order to engender this. However, we hope that this is a debate in which the contributors may want to develop an awareness of the stories that they are telling themselves.

Planning and Organization in Expert Design Activities

Willemien Visser

Institut National de Recherche en Informatique et en Automatique (National Institute for Research on Computer Science and Automation), Projet de Psychologie Ergonomique pour l'Informatique (Ergonomics Psychology Project), Domaine de Voluceau, Rocquencourt BP105, 78153 Le Chesnay Cedex, France.

Tel: +33 1 39 63 52 09

Fax: +33 1 39 63 53 30

EMail: visser@psycho.inria.fr

The organization of actual design activities, even by experts and even in routine tasks, is not appropriately characterized by the retrieval of pre-existing plans; this organization is opportunistic. This position is defended through a discussion of an important number of empirical design studies. A major cause of this type of organization of design is that, even if expert designers possess plans which they may retrieve and use, they very often deviate from these plans in order for their activity to satisfy action-management constraints, the most important being cognitive economy.

Keywords: planning, organization, design activity, opportunistic organization, action management, control, cognitive cost, cognitive economy, routine task, non-routine task, expertise.

1. Introduction

This chapter defends the claim that, even for experts involved in routine design, retrieval of preexisting plans does not appropriately characterize the organization of their activity. The arguments that will be used are based on results from empirical studies showing that even the design activities of experts possessing plans are opportunistically organized because the designers often deviate from their plans in order for their activity to satisfy action-management constraints, the most important being cognitive economy.

In what follows, we first present the distinction between 'planning' and 'organization' and some hypotheses concerning, on the one hand, the relation between planning and the routine character of a task, and, on the other hand, the relation between planning and expertise. Next, Section 3 presents several empirical studies on design in different domains, each one showing one or more factors contributing to the opportunistic character of the organization of the activity. Section 4 resumes the presented results to draw conclusions about the opportunistic organization of design activities, even by experts, and even in routine tasks. Section 5 first discusses two points: the possible sources of the discrepancy between the studies leading to conclusions making the case for 'hierarchy' and those advocating 'opportunism', and the nature of preexisting plans. The chapter then concludes with a recapitulation of the different positions on the relation between the routine character of the task and the organization of the activity.

2. Planning and Organization: Definitions and Hypotheses

Hoc (1988a) considers a plan to be "a schematic and/or multilevel representation of an object (procedure or state), elaborated and/or used to guide activity". The anticipatory and schematic characteristics of a plan may guide a subject's activity in at least two ways:

- *Declarative plan: Structure of the result of the activity.* By showing the structure which the result — or an intermediary state — of the activity must have, a 'declarative plan' allows the states this activity must attain — or go through — to be anticipated.

- *Procedural plan:procedural plan Structure of the activity.* If a plan represents both the coordination between actions to be realized and elements of the control structure, it may guide the activity in that it provides a schematic representation of these actions and the order in which their execution has to take place.

Planning activity. In this text, the notion 'planning' will be used to refer to a subject's planning activity with respect to another, more global activity which it guides, here generally design. A distinction is introduced between designers' mental representations and the structure of their actual activity:

- *Plan.* This notion refers to the mental representations constructed or retrieved by designers in order to guide their design activity.

- *Organization.* This notion will be reserved for one of the results of the planning activity, i.e. the structure of the actual design activity such as it may be observed by an external observer.

Two forms of planning. Planning activities may roughly take two forms:

- *Plan retrieval* (comparable to schema instantiation). The designer may retrieve preexisting plans[1], i.e. representations which result from plan constructions in previous activities. If a plan is retrieved, it does not necessarily constitute the plan for the entire activity.

- *Plan construction* (possibly by using a preexisting plan as one of the components). If a plan is constructed, it is rarely constructed entirely before the activity that is planned.

Routine design. Various authors establish a distinction between 'routine' and 'non-routine' (or 'creative' or 'insightful' or 'innovative') design (Brown & Chandrasekaran, 1989; Kaplan & Simon, 1990; Mayer, 1989; Navinchandra, 1991). Given the rather imprecise character of their 'definitions', we will simply use the distinction 'routine'–'non-routine'.

Notice that the 'routine' or 'non-routine' character of a design task depends on the designer's knowledge of the 'problem' he is confronted with. A 'non-routine' task for one designer may constitute a 'routine' task for another designer. This second designer does not even need to

---

[1] 'Plan' and 'sub-plan' are relative notions (like 'problem' and 'subproblem'). Except if there is a risk of confusion, we will use the term 'plan' for representations which may constitute parts of larger representations.

proceed to 'problem solving' for the execution of the task: he can simply retrieve the required answer or a preexisting procedure leading to this answer.

The same remark might be made concerning the degree to which a designer may be considered 'expert' or 'novice'. Nevertheless, the characterization of a designer as 'expert' or 'novice' is often used more globally: designers with great experience in tasks in their domain are generally considered 'expert' (in the domain), whereas their colleagues who still have little experience in these tasks are considered to be 'novice' (in the domain).

In our discussion of the tasks examined in the studies presented in this chapter, we will thus use the distinction 'routine'–'non-routine'. We are not going to question an author's decision on this point, also because the studied tasks and subjects are rarely described in sufficient detail for such questioning. Concepts such as '(moderate) difficulty', 'novelty' and 'complexity' will be considered synonyms of 'non-routine'; 'familiarity' (of a task for a subject) as a synonym of 'routine'.

Planning and the routine character of the task. At first sight, the following 'naive' hypothesis could be thought to express the relation between the two forms of planning and routine vs. non-routine design:

- retrieval of preexisting plans would be sufficient for planning routine design tasks; whereas
- planning in the sense of plan construction would be supposed to characterize non-routine rather than routine design.

Planning and expertise. An analogous hypothesis, establishing a similar relation between planning and expertise, would be that:

- novices in a domain possess few preexisting plan structures, so their planning will tend to be constructive; whereas
- experts in a domain possess many preexisting plans, so they will tend to proceed by plan retrieval.

The data reviewed below impose, however, a revision of these hypotheses, leading to our stand:

Even for experts involved in routine design, retrieval of preexisting plans does not appropriately characterize the organization of their activity.

N.B. The dimension 'routine–non-routine tasks' may subsume the dimension of 'expertise'. In the rest of this text, we will continue to use the two dimensions, but the discussion will relate the routine–non-routine character of a task and the organization of the activity implemented in this task.

Planning as one of the component activities of design. Planning can be studied at several levels: as a problem-solving activity with its own components (in the case of plan construction), or as a component of another global task, such as design. Here it is considered as a component activity of design, next to the proper design-problem solving activities of solution development and solution evaluation — developed in (Visser, 1991b). The function of planning is then to organize and anticipate the actual problem-solving activity, especially concerning the definition, identification and/or choice of subproblems, the order in which these subproblems are to be handled, the strategies and knowledge sources to be used for solving them.

As soon as an activity becomes somewhat complex, i.e. as soon as it becomes a real 'problem solving' activity — such as the activity in real design tasks — a planning component generally appears. At a lower level of a global problem-solving activity, i.e. in particular stages, planning may sometimes be absent. When subproblems are solved by solution retrieval for example, the development of the solution does not involve several steps which require organization or anticipation (Visser, 1991b).

Design may itself be considered as a component of a more global task, such as programming. In this context, "design ... is often considered to be synonymous with planning, that is, laying out at some level of abstraction, the pieces of the solution and their interrelations" (Pennington & Grabowski, 1990) — see also (Visser, 1991a) who uses examples from three of her empirical design studies to present an analysis of design at three levels: the global organizational, the strategic, and the problem-solving process level.

To sum up, in this chapter 'planning' is analyzed as one of the component activities of the design activity; the notion 'plan' is used to refer to mental representations designers use in this planning activity, i.e. representations developed for guiding the course of action that they are going to follow (or suppose they are going to follow) in order to construct their design; and the notion 'organization' refers to the structure of their actual design activity.

3. Planning and Organization: Empirical Studies

An examination of the history of the research conducted on the organization of the activity in design tasks shows, globally, four stages: a first period in which the terms 'hierarchy' or 'opportunism' are not relevant, as they are not yet used; a second period in which several studies conclude that design is organized in a hierarchical way; a third period when the opportunistic character of design has been shown; a fourth period — in which we still are now — in which several researchers have started to qualify the 'conflict' between 'hierarchy' and 'opportunism'.

This section presents several empirical studies on various types of design domains (and one study on another type of ill-defined problem solving), each one showing one or more factors contributing to the opportunistic character of the organization of the activity. These studies will be presented according to the position the authors take on the 'conflict' between 'hierarchy' and 'opportunism'.

The claim defended in this chapter requires that one takes into consideration a factor which has not been considered in most studies, i.e. the evaluation of possible design actions with respect to their 'cognitive cost'. This factor will be presented briefly in the last part of this section and will be discussed in more detail in Section 4.

3.1. Before the 'Conflict'

The two studies presented in this section do not focus especially on the 'hierarchical'–'opportunism' dimension, but do, however, provide data relevant to this dimension.

An early empirical design study is that by Byrne (1977) on the 'planning of meals'. The observed activity mainly seems to be organized hierarchically, and most decisions with respect to the choice of a course (a meal component) are made in a top-down fashion. However, some deviations of the a priori plan structures are observed. In spite of a preexisting 'standard' plan for processing the subgoals of meal planning, Byrne observes 'goal reordering', generally leading to an order which allows goal satisfaction without any risk of backtracking. Byrne considers this the 'easiest' order (i.e. "[economizing] on effort").

One explanation could be that the 'standard' plan does not represent a procedural plan for the construction of a meal component, but a representation of the final result of the construction. So, next to its function in evaluating proposed components, this plan could serve as a declarative plan for the activity. Even if meal planning is "a familiar and practiced task" (Byrne, 1977, p.287), subjects would not seem to possess a preexisting procedural plan for it. Subjects would only be able to construct such a plan through their practice of the activity in a great number of tasks executed consecutively (such as the six tasks executed in the experiment).

Malhotra et al. (1980) studied restaurant design. They qualified the subjects' final designs by two different scores: 'originality', i.e. the amount of information present in a subject's design compared to the maximal amount of information that could have been present in the design, and 'practicality', i.e. the percentage of required goals satisfied. They also collected data on the design activity using questionnaires asking designers questions on their plan(s) and strategies.

The authors notice that "surprisingly, a majority of the subjects claimed to have designed top-down, to have planned their approach, and to have tackled the more difficult problems first. However, none of these self-reported strategy variables were correlated with [the scores of their final designs]. What was predictive of [these scores] were the subject's expressed goals" in terms of "having a design that was novel, imaginative and original" or rather "workable and practical" (Malhotra et al., 1980, p.127).

3.2. Hierarchy

Especially in the domain of software design, a certain number of studies have been conducted in order to examine how (rather than 'if' and, only if yes, 'how') designers organize their activity hierarchically. In their presentation of results, the authors insist on the hierarchical aspects of design, but generally notice some 'exceptions', presented as 'details' with respect to the general hierarchical organization.

Three studies are presented below. The first two are often referred to as 'the' software design studies showing the hierarchically structured character of software design. The second study could indeed be considered as showing that the design activity required by a non-routine software design task may be organized in a completely hierarchical manner by an expert. The confrontation of the results of this study, however, with those from other research conducted by the same authors leads us to introduce some nuances into this general conclusion.

Focusing on the control processes used in expert design of a page-keyed indexer software system, Jeffries et al. (1981) formulate the hypothesis that it is the mastery of decomposition that differentiates experts and novices in their design activity. Thus, central in the authors' data analysis is then the question of how subjects decompose the problem they have to solve and/or how they decompose their global problem-solving task.

The authors start their presentation of results asserting that "almost all subjects approached the problem with the same global control strategy", i.e. problem decomposition (Jeffries et al., 1981, p.270). In the Discussion, they assert that "experts expand sub-problems systematically, typically top-down, breadth-first" (Jeffries et al., 1981, p.280). A close reading of the paper shows, however, that this 'systematic' strategy has numerous 'exceptions'.

Only one expert out of four shows a systematic implementation of a top-down, breadth-first strategy. The other experts deviate more or less from this strategy. The authors present some examples of these 'exceptions': a designer may choose to deviate from the 'advocated order' when he realizes that a component has a known solution, is critical for success, or presents special difficulties.

Adelson & Soloway (1988) examined the design of an electronic mail system, a problem which was "similar to the types of problems [the] subjects had to deal with professionally", but leading to a 'novel' task, because "none of [the] designers had designed a solution to the problem previously". The interest of the study in the context of this chapter is that, in confrontation with a companion chapter (presented below), it allows the nature of the design activity to be related to the type of problem which is solved.

In the 1988 study, all three experts implement a breadth-first strategy. Repeatedly, until the design is complete, they try to achieve their top-level goal: Expand (Next level). "At any point in time, the resolved processing modules of the design were all defined at approximately the same level of detail." (Adelson & Soloway, 1988, p.187)

So, this study constitutes an example of a non-routine software design task by experts organizing their activity in a completely hierarchical way. Let us confront these results with those from other research conducted by the authors.

The Adelson & Soloway (1985) study examines several design problems, varying in their degree of "familiarity to the observed designers". An interesting observation in the context of our chapter has been made on an expert who solved two problems. The first was the design of an electronic mail system (EMS), which constituted for this designer a 'mixed' problem with respect to familiarity in that it concerned an 'unfamiliar object' in a 'familiar domain'. The second problem, the design of an interrupt handler, was globally 'familiar' to him: it concerned a 'familiar object' in a 'familiar domain'; but it included an 'unfamiliar' subproblem: the particular chip used as the interrupting device was 'unfamiliar'.

Once the designer had developed an abstract solution to the globally 'familiar' interrupt handler problem, "he turned his attention to the functionality of the [unfamiliar subproblem of the] chip" and explored it in detail. This differed from the way he handled the 'mixed' EMS problem, where "exploration was cut off sooner and postponed via the making of notes".

The authors explain this difference as the designer 'allowing' himself to deviate from 'systematic expansion' when he is familiar with a problem domain:

> "If the mental model is lost from working memory it can easily be
> reconstructed if it has been constructed frequently in the past. As a result,
> details can be explored ... and then the mental model can be reconstructed
> when the designer is ready to continue systematic expansion." (Adelson &
> Soloway, 1985, p.1358)

3.3. Opportunism

This section presents five studies in which the authors conclude that design activities are organized opportunistically.

The famous study by Hayes-Roth & Hayes-Roth (1979) on the design of errand plans, often used as 'the' reference for the opportunistic nature of planning, will not be detailed here.

The study by Voss et al. (1983) is not a study of design, but of another class of ill-defined problem solving activities, i.e. problem solving in the domain of the social sciences. It is included in our presentation as a study of 'ill-defined' problems which are different from design problems, but share many of their characteristics.

In this study, "experts did not show evidence of having a well-developed solution plan" (Voss et al., 1983, p.191). Subproblems were generated in two ways: they were either stated as part of a decomposition process or they were 'encountered' when "the implications of a proposed solution [were explored]. ... It is primarily the experts that generated subproblems via the second mechanism. ... Novice protocols are characterized by problem decomposition in which solutions are proposed for a number of relatively low-level subproblems." (Voss et al., 1983, p.193) Graduate students and 'non-expert experts' (i.e. advanced graduate students and political science faculty members not specialized in particular problem domains) formed a 'transition' between novice and expert performance.

Kant (1985), in her study of computational geometry algorithm design by graduate and undergraduate students, proposes the concept of a 'kernel idea': design generally starts by 'selecting and sticking' with an idea which is "quickly selected from those known to the designer ... [who] lays out the basic steps of the chosen idea and follows through with it unless the approach proves completely unfeasible" (Kant, 1985, p.1362). Even if the elaboration of the kernel idea proceeds by stepwise refinement, this "process is hardly one of pure top-down design". Refinement is brought about by difficulties arising during problem-solution development (missing steps, inconsistencies between parts of the algorithm). In addition, "if one aspect of the algorithm is a potential problem ..., then it is more likely to be expanded to ensure that the algorithm as a whole is feasible" (Kant, 1985, p.1366). "Often, the designers notice things about the sample figures that they were not looking for. When [this] turns out to be useful in developing their algorithm, [the author considers] that they have made a discovery. ... Discovery could be characterized as serendipitously satisfied goals" (Kant, 1985, p.1364). Refinement is also guided by evaluation in the form of "algorithm execution [exposing] opportunities for improvement or modification of an algorithm" (Kant, 1985, p.1363). Kant concludes:

> "In short, design processes are applied as appropriate. Control ... comes out of responding to the data and out of the problems and opportunities arising during execution." (Kant, 1985, p.1366)

Ullman, Dietterich & Staufer (1988), proposing a model for mechanical design, come to a similar conclusion:

> "The design process is controlled locally, at the episode and task level. The designer does not formulate and then execute a global design plan execution. Instead, a central concept is developed and gradually extended to accomplish the design goals." (Ullman, Dietterich & Staufer, 1988, p.36)

The authors notice that, firstly, designers progress from systematic to opportunistic behaviour as the design evolves and, secondly, they do not always keep their designs 'balanced'.

Little planning was observed by Ullman, Dietterich & Staufer (13% of the design 'episodes'):

> "[The observed] plans were usually rather short-range, near-term plans. Their main purpose seems to be to evaluate whether a proposed task is

worth performing at the current time. ... Plans, once formulated, were
not followed very exactly. Another hypothesis ... is that plans are formed
prior to tasks in which many distractions are possible. ... Such a plan
may provide a kind of defense against the possible distracting effects of
information that is going to be encountered during the next episode(s)."
(Ullman, Dietterich & Staufer, 1988, p.43)

The last study presented in this section is the study by Guindon, Krasner & Curtis (1987) on
design of the software to control lift movement. It is one of the two 'Second Workshop on
Empirical Studies of Programmers' papers which questioned the traditional software design
models (such as those by Jeffries et al. and Adelson & Soloway presented above, advocating
'hierarchy'). The other one was the Visser (1987) study which will be presented below (see
Section 3.4.2). Both papers made proposals for other models: Guindon, Krasner & Curtis in
terms of 'serendipitous' design, Visser in terms of 'opportunism'.

Guindon, Krasner & Curtis qualified design as 'serendipitous': even if the observed design
behaviour is interspersed with top-down decomposition episodes, control of problem solving
proceeded by recognition of partial solutions, at different levels of abstraction or detail, without
the designers having previously decomposed the problem into subproblems.

The recognition of solutions to subproblems at different levels of detail or abstraction,
often at another than that of the currently handled problem, may be triggered by familiar
aspects of the problem environment that happened to be focused on. Understanding and
elaborating the requirements through mental simulations often led to the sudden discovery
of new — added or inferred — requirements. This contributes to the 'serendipity' when the
corresponding solutions are developed immediately (rather than noted in order to be processed
later on). Examination of external solution representations also led to recognition of solutions
to subproblems before 'their turn'. The designers expanded their solutions by rapidly shifting
between different levels of abstraction and different parts of the solution decomposition
and by developing low-level partial solutions prior to a high-level decomposition. All the
'unbalanced' design activities taken together made up 52% of the total of design activities
(for the two designers under study in the analyses).

3.4. Hierarchy or Opportunism: (Only) a Question of Action-execution Knowledge or (Also) a Question of Action-management Knowledge?

In the introduction to this section on empirical studies we wrote that, after two consecutive
periods in which design was first supposed to be organized hierarchically and then considered
to have an opportunistic organization, we are now in a period in which researchers have
started to qualify the 'conflict' between 'hierarchy' and 'opportunism'. Before defending
our stand that, even if episodes guided by a top-down strategy may be observed in design
activities, opportunism is the general model for design, an author taking the opposite position
is presented.

Davies (1991a; Davies & Castell, in this volume) concludes that an opportunistic organization
holds only for local episodes, not for the global organization of the design activity. Indeed,
according to Davies (1991a), "a top-down hierarchically leveled approach" is the main global
design strategy adopted by experienced programmers. "While opportunistic episodes may
occur at any point in the evolution of a program" — Davies observes that they appear rather
as the task progresses than in early design stages — "the programming activity itself is
hierarchically structured and proceeds in a largely top-down fashion" (Davies, 1991a, p.173).

The main objection against the conclusion reached by Davies is that the top-down model may be considered as a special case of the opportunistic model, but not vice versa. This idea will be presented in more detail below.

Before presenting the last two series of studies by Rist (1990) and Visser (1987; Visser, 1990) who propose an opportunistic design model subsuming possible top-down oriented behaviours, our general approach to problem-solving is briefly introduced.

Modelling problem solving at two levels: Action-execution and Action-management. We distinguish the level of the actual design problem-solving actions (action execution) from the control level (action management) deciding on the priorities of these problem-solving actions. In a presentation of elements for a blackboard model of design, where the focus was on the control component, we proposed that these these two levels be articulated according to the following iterative sequence (Visser, 1990):

    i. Design knowledge: action proposal.

    ii. Control knowledge: action evaluation and selection.

    iii. Design knowledge: action execution.

    iv. Goto (i).

At the execution level, design problem-solving actions are proposed and executed; at the control level, the action proposals are evaluated and one action is selected for execution. The analysis of the data obtained in (Visser, 1990) led us to propose 'cognitive cost' as control's main action-selection criterion: if several action proposals are made, control will select the most 'economical' action.

3.4.1. Hierarchy or Opportunism: (Only) a Question of Action-execution Knowledge

In his study on very simple programming problems, Rist (1990) seeks to qualify the recently 'accepted' conclusion that design activities are opportunistically organized (see Section 3.3). He concludes that designers' activities may be organized hierarchically if these designers know the (schema of the) solution to the problem they are solving. However, if they do not, their activity will be organized opportunistically.

Rist analyzes very precisely and in great detail how the nature of design activity, such as its organization, depends on the knowledge available to the designer. He concludes:

> "If the designer could retrieve a known solution [a plan schema] to the
> problem, the solution was applied and the program was designed forward
> from the input and output, as each part of the solution was expanded in
> turn. If a solution could not be retrieved, it had to be created by designing
> backward from the goals of the problem. More precisely, it was created by
> a process of backward and bottom-up design from an initial sketchy solution
> or focal idea, that was expanded to define a complete solution. Interaction
> between the two approaches created the complex behaviour observed in the
> study." (Rist, 1990, p.307)

3.4.2. Hierarchy or Opportunism: (Also) a Question of Action-management Knowledge

Even if the conclusions of Rist's study may seem to concur with the stand taken in this chapter, there is an important difference.

Underlying our claim that, even for experts involved in routine design, retrieval of preexisting plans does not appropriately characterize the organization of their activity, is the idea that, in real design tasks, designers may often find it profitable to deviate from these plans. Indeed, even if they can and, in fact, do retrieve a known solution plan for their problem (which may be possible in routine design, as shown by the Rist study and as we will see below in the Visser studies), yet if they evaluate the cost of their possible actions ('cognitive' and other costs), as they will do in real design, and the action selected for execution will often be an action other than the one proposed by the plan.

It is not surprising that, like the authors of the studies presented in the previous sections, Rist did not take into account the action evaluation-and-selection. Indeed, this factor may be expected to make its appearance only in 'real' design, where questions of 'cost' acquire importance.

Two design studies that we carried out will be used to defend our claim. One was on specifications design (Visser, 1990), the other on software design (Visser, 1987). Visser (1988) globally presents the longitudinal study, composed of these two studies followed by a third one on the testing and debugging of the code; this third study is not discussed in the present chapter.

In the first study, an experienced mechanical engineer was observed throughout his definition of the functional specifications for the control part of a 'programmable controller' (a computer specialized in the control of industrial processes, here an automatic machine tool). The second study has been conducted on a rather experienced software engineer throughout his designing and coding of the software for the control part (whose specifications were those defined by the mechanical engineer). Both the software and the specification design tasks were globally 'routine' tasks, but there were subtasks having 'non-routine' characteristics.

In the first study (Visser, 1990), on the specifications design, we focused on the possible differences between the designer's mental representation of the organization of his activity, and the actual organization of this activity. So we asked the designer to describe his activity, explaining that we were interested in the actual organization, not in a rationalization of it, such as a linearization or any other type of structuring. He presented us with a description most appropriately represented by a 'hierarchically structured' plan[2]. So he possessed a complete solution schema for the specification problem.

This representation of his activity, i.e. a hierarchical action structure accompanied by a procedure which covers it, reflects a 'procedural plan'. The designer may have thought that he actually followed this plan, but our observations showed that he deviated from it whenever other possible actions, or local plans, that he perceived, were judged more 'interesting' from a cognitive economy viewpoint. The mental representational structure described by the designer was certainly a plan — even the main one — which guided his activity, but only as long as no 'cognitive-cost opportunities' arose, i.e. possibilities for actions which were more economical. When they did, the designer deviated from his plan.

We identified both the processes which, exploiting 'cognitive-cost opportunities', led to deviation-action proposals, and the control criteria used in order to select, from these proposals, the action to be executed. They will be presented in the next section.

---

[2] The plan is said to be 'hierarchically structured' and not 'hierarchical', to avoid confusion with 'hierarchical planning' as described by Sacerdoti (1974).

In the second study (Visser, 1987), we observed that the software designer, after one hour of planning, directly started to code (and continued for over four weeks). This coding was of course often interrupted for activities other than coding; it was intermixed with design actions (from planning to solution evaluation) but the interruptions were not systematic.

So, 'planning' in the 'design and coding stage' was 'local' and 'punctual'. It took place at varying problem-solving levels and concerned larger or smaller entities (e.g. at the design level, a function or a machining operation; at the coding level, a module or an instruction). The designer had a 'plan' inspired by the order of the modules in an example-program that he reused heavily, but he deviated from this plan if another order was judged more economical from the point of view of cognitive cost. Local deviation actions, or alternative local plans leading to more global deviations, were triggered by various processes. These processes may be analyzed in the same terms as those proposed for modelling the deviations observed on the mechanical designer involved in his specification task.

4. Cognitive-cost Opportunities

We propose that an activity may be said to be organized 'opportunistically' if the design actions do not follow a preexisting plan, but depend, at each moment t, on the evaluation of the actions proposed at t.

Which actions are proposed at a moment t depends on the data designers have at that moment: these data are mainly the designers' representation of the state of their design in progress (thus, the result of the preceding design actions), their knowledge (domain knowledge, design knowledge, more general problem-solving knowledge) and the information at their disposal and received from other sources (the client providing the requirements; technical documents; colleagues making remarks and suggestions or providing other information).

The evaluation of these proposed actions is based on action-selection criteria. The analysis of the data gathered on the specifications design task led us to propose 'cognitive economy' as control's main action-selection criterion: if several action proposals are made, control will select the most economical action.

Thus, ultimately it is the evaluation of the actions which are proposed as possible design actions which leads to an opportunistically organized activity. Ultimately, because if all these possible actions are proposed by a preexisting plan, the activity will be organized hierarchically. That is why we join Hayes-Roth & Hayes-Roth (1979) in considering the top-down model as a special case of the opportunistic model.

Hayes-Roth & Hayes-Roth propose that "one resolution of the apparent conflict between the [successive refinement model and the opportunistic model] would simply incorporate the top-down model as a special case of the opportunistic model" (Hayes-Roth & Hayes-Roth, 1979, p.307), "[because the top-down method] 'define and refine' is only one of many problem-solving methods adoptable in the framework of the opportunistic model. Thus, the question is no longer which model is correct, but rather, under what circumstances do planners bring alternative problem-solving methods to bear?" (Hayes-Roth & Hayes-Roth, 1979, p.308). We will take up this question below.

So, in order for an activity to be organized in an opportunistic, not hierarchical way (i.e. possibly with hierarchical episodes at a local level, but globally not hierarchical), there must be, next to a possible plan, other cognitive action-proposing knowledge sources.

After a short description of the control action-selection criteria, these action-proposing knowledge sources which exploit 'cognitive-cost opportunities' will be presented.

4.1. Cognitive Economy: The Main Control Action-selection Criterion

The main goal underlying the designers' 'choice' for the organization of their activity is supposed to be 'cognitive economy' (Visser, 1990) — see also (Byrne, 1977). At each step in the design process, control selects one action from those proposed. If an alternative-to-the-plan action is more profitable than the planned action from this cognitive economy viewpoint, designers abandon — possibly only temporarily — their plan.

Kant (1985) observes that the most difficult, most problematic problem-solution aspects are handled first, while Spohrer (personal communication quoted in (Rist, 1990)) suggests that either 'simplest-first' or 'hardest-first' orders are possible. Rist (1990) observes (or supposes?) that these 'more rational methods' are reserved to experts and that, before acquiring this expertise, novices tend to proceed by random selection.

In (Visser, 1990), we proposed a second action-selection criterion: 'importance' of the proposed design action. This criterion was suggested to play a role only when the designer has to choose between two, or more, actions at equal cost.

4.2. Cognitive Processes for Proposing Actions leading to an Opportunistically Organized Activity

According to the definition of 'opportunism' presented above, the main factors leading to alternative-to-the-plan design actions — and thus possibly to an opportunistically organized activity — stem from 'taking advantage of' the data available (or made available) to the designer, i.e. from processing of information, and of (permanent) knowledge and (temporary) design representations — cf. the role of 'interesting possibilities' suggested by Hayes-Roth & Hayes-Roth (1979), and that of 'discoveries' and 'good ideas' proposed by Kant (1985). Reformulating the six processes presented in (Visser, 1990), where more details and examples can be found, we identified five possible candidates for being 'taken advantage of':

- Information the designer is 'presented with':
    - by the client;
    - by a colleague;
    - 'by themselves' or by an information source when 'drifting'.

Different types of 'drifting' may be distinguished, according to:
    - the problem-solving stage in which drifting occurs; and
    - the source providing the information from which it occurs.

It may lead to phenomena described subjectively as "thinking of X", or "wanting to do Y now" because one is afraid of "forgetting it" otherwise.
    - Drifting may occur:
        - when the designer is looking for information required for the current design action, thus before he has identified it; or
        - once he has this information, but before he has used it for executing the current design action.
    - The designer may drift from information in an external information source, or from data processed in memory.

In all these cases, the designer comes to focus on information other than that required or used for the current design action.

- Information used for the current design action when considered from another viewpoint (e.g. for a designer involved in functional specification, consider information used for this functional specification task from its mechanical, i.e. physical, viewpoint).

- Information 'constructed' (or 'obtained') by

  — analyzing the problem specifications;

  — developing and evaluating solutions;

  — exploring the implications of a proposed solution — see (Guindon, 1990b; Kant, 1985; Voss et al., 1983).

- Activation-guiding relationships between mental representations of design objects (such as relationships of analogy, prerequisites, opposites and interaction). These relationships between mental representations may lead to switches between the design-object representations which are under focus. The 'goal reordering' observed by Byrne (1977) may be related to this process. In order to avoid the need for backtracking, the designer may process design components which are constrained by other components in such an order that the corresponding goals be satisfied without the risk of backtracking. In order to achieve this 'optimal' 'goal order', the design component representations must be related in memory and their relationships must be perceived and exploited by the designer.

- Available design procedures. A design solution procedure may be available because it has just been developed. The action proposal of taking advantage of such an available procedure may be selected by the control because it satisfies the 'cognitive economy' criterion: retrieving a procedure as one single chunk from memory is less expensive than having to develop it from pieces (later on, when it will no longer be available as a single chunk).

The previously described processes possibly lead to an opportunistically organized activity because, if the action they propose is selected, the activity does not follow a plan which may also be present in memory. Not following a plan is, however, not necessarily due to plan deviation. A designer may follow a plan, but skip an action proposed by this plan. This may occur when the planned design action is judged as being too 'difficult' — see for example (Jeffries et al., 1981; Kant, 1985; Ullman, Staufer & Dietterich, 1987) — or, more generally, when the planned action (P) is judged as costing too much, not compared to a currently proposed deviation action, but to P itself if executed later. This may occur, e.g. when the procedure for obtaining the information required by the planned action is judged as being too expensive (e.g. because the information is not available or is too expensive to obtain). In this case, P is postponed and a local plan is generally formed for re-proposing P, either as soon as the conditions leading to its postponement no longer prevail, or at a particular moment later in the design process.

This chapter started with a position which has been defended through the presentation of a considerable number of design studies: retrieval of preexisting plans does not appropriately characterize the organization of expert activity in routine design tasks. The data which have been presented and organized in this section have shown why and how design activity is organized opportunistically. As long as the activity is concept-driven, i.e. as long as a preexisting plan is used, this plan will be adapted, deviated from, and replaced by other guidance structures. However, design activity often is data-driven, when the activity is not, or no longer, guided by more or less abstract goals, but by the current data (information, design state, design knowledge and representations).

5. Discussion

The chapter closes with a recapitulation of the different positions on the relation between the routine character of a task and the organization of the corresponding activity. Before that final conclusion, two points will be discussed:

- Possible sources of the discrepancy between 'hierarchy' and 'opportunism' studies.
- The nature of preexisting plans.

Most early empirical design studies — besides, generally those in the domain of software design (Visser & Hoc, 1990) — have concluded that design activity follows hierarchically structured plans, which may be supposed to be retrieved and expanded in-situation. Later studies generally have shown otherwise. They showed design, like other ill-defined problem solving activities, to be opportunistically organized. The main 'proponents' of each 'side' have been presented in this chapter.

How can these apparently contradictory conclusions be explained? The difference may be due — at least to some extent — to the perspective the authors take on their data. Early design studies often stuck strongly to the normative viewpoint: design was supposed to proceed by top-down breadth-first decomposition as advocated by design methodologies (Carroll & Rosson, 1985). Psychologists know that the expectations held by a person influence their information processing — consequently, the researchers' expectations influence how they interpret the results of their experiments! The main reason seems to us, however, the type of design problems studied: more recent studies tended to use real (or realistic) design problems, whereas the problems which had been studied in earlier research were rather artificially restricted — but see also the recent studies by Rist (1990).

To make less counterintuitive that even in routine design, even for experts, and even if preexisting plans are available, plan retrieval does not provide the main guidance for the activity, one has to take into consideration the following point.

Design may be considered 'routine' if "both the available decisions and the computational processes used to take those decisions are known prior to the commencement of a design" (Gero, 1991, p.vii) and if "the outcomes are [also] known a priori" (Navinchandra, 1991, p.2). However, in real-life design, there are multiple 'opportunities' occurring during the design process which are generally not "known prior to the commencement of a design". They will influence which of 'the available decisions' is taken and which of 'the computational processes' is used. If one can 'afford' to deviate from possible preexisting, fixed plans — as does an expert (for reasons given below) — and if 'cognitive economy' is judged important, then it may be profitable to organize one's activity opportunistically (which may lead to plan deviation, if one uses a plan).

Preexisting plans are supposed to be only one of the knowledge structures which may propose actions on which the control next has to decide with respect to the course of action. Like other schemata, these plans may be useful from the viewpoint of 'cognitive economy' because executing an action for which such a memory representation is available may cost relatively little if all schema variables relevant for execution have constant or default values. But if other knowledge structures propose cognitively more economical actions, designers may deviate from their plan. This is especially true for experts, who may be supposed to possess — or else to be able to construct without any difficulty — a representation of their activity which allows them to resume their plan later on, when it once again becomes profitable to do so from the viewpoint of 'cognitive economy'.

To sum up the different hypotheses concerning the relation between the two 'dimensions' 'systematically-opportunistically organized activity' and 'routine–non-routine tasks' (subsuming the dimension of 'expertise'):

- *The 'naive' hypothesis*: the activity is organized systematically as long as the task has a routine character — cf. the observations by Davies (1991a) and by Ullman, Dietterich & Staufer (1988) that designers progress from systematic to opportunistic behaviour as the design evolves.

- *The 'realistic' hypothesis based on experience in the laboratory*: the activity becomes organized systematically as soon as the task becomes non-routine; cf. the suggestion by Adelson & Soloway (1985) that designers may 'allow' themselves to deviate from 'systematic expansion' when they know a problem domain very well; cf. the hypothesis formulated by Ullman, Dietterich & Staufer (1988) that plans are formed prior to tasks in which many distractions are possible, as a defense against these possible distractions.

- *The 'perverse' hypothesis based on experience in the 'real world'*: the activity can be organized systematically as long as the task has a routine character (plan retrieval is possible) and can be tried to be handled systematically as soon as the task becomes non-routine (for reasons of 'cognitive protection'), but often the activity will not be systematic because of constraints at the action-management level (especially 'cognitive economy') — cf. the studies by Visser.

Acknowledgement

The author wishes to thank Françoise Détienne for her help in the preparation of this chapter.

Views and Representations for Reverse Engineering

Henk J van Zuylen

Delft Hydraulics, P O Box 177, 2600 MH, Delft, The Netherlands.

Tel: +31 15 569353

Fax: +31 15 619674

EMail: henk.zuijlen@wldelft.nl

Reverse engineering is an activity which is often necessary in the software maintenance process. One of the main objectives is to comprehend relevant aspects of the program in order to understand where and how modifications can be made. Views on the program are important for understanding, reasoning, documentation and communication. The kind of views which is useful for software maintainers to support the understanding process are partly the same as those which are used in forward engineering. Since the operations on the views and the mental process in reverse engineering differ from forward engineering, reverse engineering imposes its own requirements on views, their representations as well as tools to generate these views.

[Part of this chapter has been published in the REDO compendium (van Zuylen, 1993).]

Keywords: reverse engineering, system development, maintenance, program comprehension, documentation, views.

1. Introduction

Most experienced software developers and managers involved in software engineering know that the development of new software is only the beginning of a process. Software evolves after a first delivery. It is assumed that no more than about 30% of the total cost of a system are used for the initial development. The remaining 70% are for maintenance. Although there are some doubts regarding the reliability of these figures (Foster, 1990), it is certain that software maintenance is an important issue.

The resources spent for maintenance are also difficult to estimate because it is often impossible to discriminate strictly between development and maintenance. Many 'new' systems are built on the basis of existing programs where either the source code or design concept are reused.

The amount of software in the world is rapidly growing. As long as this software is used and maintained, maintenance will also grow and will surpass (or even already surpassed) the work done on new development.

The importance of software maintenance is becoming more clear now. Efforts are made to develop methodologies (in the sense of 'meta-methods') suited to cover these activities. One of these attempts is the ESPRIT II project REDO. In this project tools and methods have been developed to support and improve the maintenance practice. The core of software maintenance appears to be *understanding*. Tools and methods for reverse engineering have to support this understanding process. The software engineer dealing with maintenance has to understand the program, the impact of the modifications he wants to make, the location where the modification should be made and the like. Documentation is useful, but seldom sufficiently reliable (Martin & McClure, 1985). The obvious assumption that documentation built up during the development of a system is useful or satisfactory for maintenance purpose, is dubious. In reality this documentation has another purpose.

In this chapter the problem of software maintenance is first discussed. It is explained that programs which are used and maintained for some time, must be upgraded from time to time. This upgrading starts with comprehension of the program. As a result of the comprehension the documentation can be (re)written.

The understanding of a program is done by ordering the different aspects in *views*: groups of aspects which have a mutual relationship and can be understood without referring too much to aspects outside the view. The data structure of a program and the control flow are examples of views. Views can be represented in different ways, for example in words, tables or diagrams. The kind of views which can be used to present the most important aspects of the program for the purpose of maintenance are analyzed. Finally a discussion is given of reverse engineering tools.

2. Maintenance and Reverse Engineering

Lehman & Belady (1985) formulated some laws for program development. The first two laws are:

1. A large program that is used, undergoes continuing change or becomes progressively less useful. The change process continues until it is judged more cost-effective to replace the system with a recreated version.

2. As a large program is continuously changed, its complexity, which reflects deteriorating structure, increases unless work is done to maintain or reduce it.

These laws confirm what most software engineers and managers dealing with maintenance of programs know from experience. The older the program becomes, the more maintenance has been done on the program and consequently the larger the maintenance costs become and the more effort is needed to modify the program. At a certain moment it is financially not wise to proceed without taking actions to improve the maintainability of the system. Apart from the effect of the second law there is the fact that many programs are difficult to maintain from the very beginning, because they have not been developed according to certain standards, do not have appropriate documentation or because the documentation was made only for the developers and has not been updated.

The maintainability of a program can be defined as the ease with which a program can be modified. Modification means corrections of errors such as deviations from the specifications, the change of functionality, the porting to other hardware and software environments and the optimization with respect to performance etc. The main problem in the modifying programs is to know, where the program code is to be changed and what the impact of the change is on the rest of the code. A well-known problem is the 'ripple-effect': when one function is modified, the use of certain variables is also changed. Since these variables are used in other modules of the program which perform other functions, also these modules should be modified. This, in turn, may affect the use of other variables etc. So the maintainer must be sure that he has followed all possible paths and has found all relevant data and functional dependencies.

Another maintainability problem is that certain functions are distributed over various parts of the program and, vice versa, that one module may have several functions.

The improvement of the maintainability can be realized by applying standards to existing source codes to ensure good programming. Such standards are for example:

- well-structured data, without redundancy of information;
- structured programs without unnecessary goto-constructions;
- each variable carries only one piece of information;
- dependency between data items implemented as separate functions;
- each functional requirement implemented in one or more distinct modules;
- each module has only one function.

Suppose that a program is relatively difficult to maintain. A strategic decision could be, that the maintainability has to be improved. The trigger for such decision could be for example a major maintenance request, a management review of the maintenance practice or a reorganization. For such a decision the program quality has to be assessed. Finally a decision has to be made either to leave the system as it is, to replace it by a vendor package, to discard it, to rebuild it, possibly with partial reuse of suited components, or to upgrade the system (Bennett, 1993).

In this decision process and especially after the decision, information has to be extracted from the program and its documentation, for instance about the quality of the code, its interfaces, data structure etc. There is no widely accepted name for these activities. In this chapter the term *reverse engineering* according to the definition given by Chikofsky & Cross (1990) will be used. They define:

> *Reverse Engineering* is the process of analyzing a subject system to identify the system components and their inter relationships, and to create representations of the system in another form or at higher levels of abstraction.

Reverse engineering does not change the subject system itself, it is mainly aimed at understanding. Changes which are made affect only the description of the system, not its function. However, a distinction between reverse engineering and re-engineering is often difficult to make. Reengineering is the implementation of a new version of the program. If, for instance, 'goto' constructions are replaced with 'if-then-else' and 'do-while', the description of the program will be better understandable. The function of the program should not be affected by this modification. It could even be possible that the compiler generates the same object code as with the old source in which the 'goto' construction still exists. Therefore, the term reverse engineering will be used in a loose sense in this chapter: also reengineering which does not change the functionality of the program is included in reverse engineering. The source code will be considered here as one of the specifications of the program. Changes in the specification without changes in the function are considered to be a part of reverse engineering.

The role of documentation in reverse engineering is twofold. Documentation is extracted (semi-)automatically from the existing program and used afterwards to understand it. Examples are cross-reference tables, call-graphs, data structures, compiler listings etc. Another role of documentation is the recording of the comprehension process. This documentation is built up semi-automatically during the reverse engineering process. An important part of the comprehension process is the writing of this documentation: the comprehension leads to a form of understanding that can be communicated by writing or drawing. These two aspects of reverse engineering are called *redocumentation* and *design recovery*. *Redocumentation* is the creation or revision of a semantically equivalent representation within the same relative abstraction level. *Design Recovery* is the process to identify higher level abstractions beyond those obtained directly by examining the system itself.

Reverse engineering is often applied in software maintenance. Although the term is only recently invented, the activities of reverse engineering have always been the core of maintenance. Since documentation is often absent, incomplete or out-of-date, much of the analysis has to be done from the source code and the observation of the program execution.

Reverse engineering as separate activity in software maintenance can be done in two ways. The first way aims at complete redocumentation and partial restructuring, the second one especially at comprehension, problem solving and partial redocumentation.

The first option starts from certain standards for programs regarding source code, data structures and documentation. The documentation is built up with the help of tools. Modifications are made to the source code to remove goto constructions and by replacing them with more structured alternatives. Other tools extract data structures from the source code and bring the data in some canonical form. The technical documentation is extracted from the source code by documentation tools. After these activities there is a standard documentation of the program and the source code has been improved such, that it satisfies some of the standards which are applied for new software.

Sometimes it is the purpose of this process to import an existing program into a CASE environment. Another possibility is, for example, that the program should satisfy certain contractual or legal requirements. This kind of reverse engineering can be done in a linear, more or less straightforward process, providing that the necessary tools are at hand.

The other way of reverse engineering is applied if the objective is to obtain partial knowledge about the programs, for instance the place and format of certain data in a file, the meaning of certain variables, the function of certain parts of the code. This kind of reverse engineering is less automatic, less straightforward and requires more knowledge and experience as the first one. In the following sections the emphasis is laid on the second kind of reverse engineering.

3. The Comprehension Process in Reverse Engineering

In the comprehension process, the software engineer has to use all kind of knowledge he has got already from the domain of the program, software engineering and about the language, the operating system, database management system etc. The knowledge can be distinguished in Shneiderman & Mayer (1979):

- *Syntactical knowledge*, facts and rules about the computer language, the operating system, the hardware. This knowledge includes the lexicon of the language, the meaning of the lexical elements and the grammatical rules, the program syntax. This knowledge is specific for a language and has a flat structure: there is no internal structure which connects the facts.

- *Semantic knowledge of software engineering*, contains the software engineer's knowledge of programming structures, data structures, algorithms, implementation schemes. The software engineer acquires this knowledge over a long time. The knowledge is for a great deal independent of the application domain, and, although language dependent, it may be transferred rather easily to other computer languages. This knowledge is level structured, that is: knowledge is grouped in patterns which contain subpatterns. For instance, the knowledge about the algorithm for matrix inversion may contain links to knowledge about accuracy of number representations. The strength of this semantic knowledge consists for a great deal of the existence of links between the knowledge elements.
A part of the software engineering knowledge consists of meta knowledge, that is knowledge about the knowledge and especially strategic knowledge about when to use certain knowledge.

- *Semantic knowledge about the domain*, knowledge which the software engineer has about the part of the world in which a program is used. This knowledge is independent of the programming language, software environment, hardware etc. It contains also knowledge about how computers, programs and certain software techniques are applied in a domain.

Software engineers must have a lot of knowledge of these three categories in order to work efficiently. Programmers starting in a new domain have to invest both a lot of time and effort before they become productive. An expert in one domain has to learn much low-level details and high-level goals, when he switches to a new domain.

In software engineering there is a tendency to employ always the same person for the maintenance of programs. It appears to be impractical, if not impossible, to transfer all relevant knowledge from one person to his successor. The role of documentation in the transfer of knowledge is restricted (Hoc et al., 1990; Martin & McClure, 1985). First of all, documentation is never complete in the sense that all relevant details are included. Common sense, basic knowledge about the domain and software engineering are not documented for each program again. Often authors of documentation assume that they and their readers have much common knowledge about the domain and software engineering. They emphasize aspects which they find important, but these aspects may be trivial for a reader. Authors also often 'forget' to supply information which is obvious for them, but which may be the key to the reader's understanding. Documentation which is available with a system has been written often during its development. Very little development documentation has been written with the purpose to support the understanding of the system after delivery. Often the software maintainer has to be careful in reading the development documentation. He has to realize that the purpose of the information may differ from the goals he has. This makes interpretation difficult (Winograd & Flores, 1986). On the other hand, documentation may be essential to get a quick understanding of the semantics of the program: why has the program been made, what is its function, for which users and in which environment has it been made. This means, that the high-level information from the documentation is more useful for knowledge transfer than the technical low-level information.

Experience and knowledge play an important role in the comprehension of a program. So novice software engineers will perform different compared to experts. Several studies have shown that the skill of experts to recognize, remember and structure the program code is superior to novices, unless very detailed information on statement level is involved — for example (Adelson, 1984). Another important fact is, that in practice there is a difference between software engineers who do maintenance and those who develop new programs. Often the people involved in maintenance have a less academic, more professional education or have got their training mainly in practice. Further, it seems to be common practice that junior software engineers get their first experience in a company by doing maintenance work. New systems are developed by people with a higher education, which means that they have developed more skills for abstraction, know more about theories and methods. Maybe this is not generally true, but in companies where the author had the chance to investigate this situation, this phenomenon had been consistently observed.

4. The Mental Representation of Software

Comprehension of a program means that a mental representation is created which represents some features of the program. There are many features or aspects of a program and even if someone knows the source code by hart, that does not mean that he understands the program. The software engineer doing reverse engineering has to understand the internal structure and the semantics of the program. Most of the semantics can be derived directly from the source code. Most programs contain a mixture of source code in a certain computer language, interaction with the environment, for example a database management system, a transaction processing system, an operating system, and calls to procedures which are external to the program such as user interface libraries. The semantics has to be found by combining the information from the language semantics with information from documentation of the software environment and the specification of libraries. We shall call all these aspects *software engineering knowledge* which is partly stored in the mind of the software engineer, partly stored in the documentation. The source code has to be interpreted, which means that the semantics must be determined by transforming the information from the source code and the software engineering knowledge into a representation of the semantics of the program. The process of creating this mental representation has been investigated by a few researchers. A rather likely model has been proposed by Gilmore (1990b). A slightly modified version is presented in Figure 1 (van Zuylen, 1993). It assumes that the reverse engineer develops a mental representation of what the program *should be*. This is the box in Figure 1 with the name *mental representation of the program*.

This model begins from an intuitive model, based on experience and some high level documentation, say a requirements document. A software engineer who studies a program which has to do payroll calculations knows, that the program probably has a certain structure, certain functions and uses certain information stored in some data structures. This model is gradually matched with the observations of the actual program. The software engineer develops a mental representation of what the program does, the *mental representation of the program*.

The process of understanding can be characterized by the generation of assumptions about how the problem should or could be solved by the program which is studied. This assumption can be stated as a hypothesis or as an assumed rule (Hale & Haworth, 1991). The software engineer will try to verify this assumption, to correct or to refine it. He can define a goal to do this, but this, in turn, may rise another problem that must be solved. The result is that both mental models match but afterwards new assumptions and new goals may come up.

The strategy will be a mixture of top-down and bottom-up procedures. Also a switching between breadth-first and depth-first is likely. The bottom-up process is described by Shneiderman (1980) and Basili & Mills (1982b). Such a process starts with statements

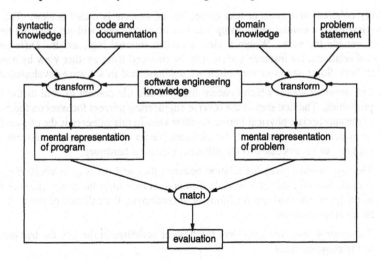

Figure 1: Inference structure for program comprehension

which are grouped together such that chunks are formed. After this a meaning is given to these chunks. Chunks of code are afterwards grouped together to form modules with a certain function etc. This process could be applied for small pieces of code, in order to obtain a partial mental model of the program. The top-down process is the one described by Brooks (1983) and Gilmore (1990b). The top-down process seems to be particularly suited for the generation of the *mental representation of the problem*.

Breadth-first and depth-first can be used for both mental representations. It is very likely that experienced software engineers have an opportunistic strategy for programming as well as for debugging (Pennington & Grabowski, 1990). They apparently apply a strategy in which they switch from a top-down to a bottom-up approach and vice versa, when that approach is more suitable. Further they collect their information from different views on the program.

The process of reverse engineering can be compared rather well with that of a medical clinic. Patients are brought in and examined by a specialist who, in most cases, has an intuitive idea what kinds of tests have to be done. He may even have an idea about the kind of problem. The tests confirm his assumption or give evidence which can be used to refine or reject the assumption, after which new assumptions are made, goals set and tests executed. Although this process may be called systematical, it does not fit in a single solution strategy. Much expertise is needed, apart from working hard in order to extract the information from the patient (or program).

5. Views

A computer program has many aspects. For example it can be seen:

- as an artifact formed by certain files;
- an architecture of program modules, data structures files and other hardware and software components;
- as an artifact which executes certain activities, shows certain behavior, etc.

A mutually coherent and more or less closed set of aspects is called a *view*. The aspects within a view have a mutual relationship and can be understood without referring too much to aspects outside the view. Within a view a certain internal logic exists. Different views have mutual relations, for instance a view may be deduced from another view by abstraction or specification. Some views as they often are distinguished in software development are:

- The *physical views*, which concern the files and file content as well as the physical properties. The first step of the reverse engineering process focusses on the collection of the appropriate physical items. Another view in this category is the physical system on which the program runs, the different pieces of hardware, the network and the assignment of processes to the different pieces of hardware.

- The *architecture* gives the relation between files and the way in which the program is made from the different module files and include files, the composition of the files in modules (for example functions or subroutines), the call tree of the modules and the overlay structure.

- The *control flow view* considers the flow of activities in the job, the transaction and in the program itself.

- The *data view* aims at all information about data, variables, external input and output files, databases.

- The *behavior view* contains the information about what the system does. Timing aspects and state transitions are parts of this view. Also the interactions between the system and the environment and users are part of this view. Further a declarative description of the system, for instance in terms of pre- and post-conditions and invariants may give a contribution to the behavior view.

- A program can be also considered as the product of a process. This view is called the *project process view*. This view contains information about the history of the system, the project in which the system has been developed, the management decisions and the resources used.

- Another view is the *domain view*. It contains all knowledge about the domain for which the program is used. Also the link between the program and the problems which it is supposed to solve, is a part of this view, for example the high level semantics of the program. Two aspects of this view which can be derived from a program are the user task and the business model.

- Finally, one may distinguish a *management view*. The information in this view concerns the project aspects of the development, introduction and maintenance of the system, the resources used and those necessary for the future, people involved, etc.

A software engineer has many views of a program. Some of these views have been discussed in literature, for instance by Olle et al. (1988). In terms of human understanding views play an important role. Knowledge about a subject consists of mutually linked views. The way people communicate and reason about these views depends on the character of these views as well as the kind of information which is contained in them. The fact that software engineering uses diagrams to represent many views shows that a spatial representation can be very useful to determine views, to reason about them, to recognize properties, etc. Some views — for instance the specification of the functions of the system — may be less suited for a graphical representation. A mathematical representation may be more appropriate because of its accuracy, precision and the possibility to formally verify certain properties.

The choice of an appropriate representation for the views depends on the purpose of the views. In forward engineering the identification of inconsistencies, conflicting requirements, conformance with other views and the requirements are important issues. The representations are used to breakdown the objects (functions, states or data) into smaller units.

The objectives in reverse engineering differ from forward engineering. Abstraction of higher order design views is an important objective, as well as the documentation and verification of assumptions about the system. The aggregation may be important too. For instance, if one starts with a call graph of a program, generated from the code, this may be transformed to a data flow diagram and a state transition diagram (not a simple task to do!). The data flow diagram may be transformed by 'chunking' the processes and hiding of internal data stores. The result may be a high level data flow diagram or context diagram (Yourdon, 1989).

This process as described is 'bottom up', which, at best should be done by reverse engineering tools. However, reality is that this process is not possible in an automatic way. If the process is executed with human intervention, the strict bottom up approach is less suited for experienced software engineers. They tend to start from some hypothesized high level view which they try to verify, as explained in the previous section with the code of the program, the system documentation, the user manual, the actual behavior of the program, etc. Drawing up new documentation may be a appropriate intermediate step to verify or adapt the hypothesized view.

5.1. A Comprehensive Classification Scheme for Views

The views described in the previous section still form a rather ad–hoc set of possible views. Essink (1986) defined a comprehensive scheme for views of a computer program. His scheme makes it possible to organize views, to identify where views are missing and how various views are related.

Essink's scheme is based on a two-dimensional space. One dimension is the level of abstraction, the other one on the aspect of the view. He distinguished four *levels of abstraction*:

1. *Object system model.* This is the model of the reality for which the program originally has been written. It contains the organizational processes, the business rules, the activities supported by the system. This model arises from reverse engineering of the code, when the functions of the system are abstracted. On the other hand, it is also a part of the mental model which the software engineer has of the domain. It defines the entities which from a part of the reality, the relevant knowledge about them, the possible states.

2. *The conceptual information model.* This is the model which makes the link between the domain entities and the data elements and functions of the program. In the development of a system, this model contains the logical structure of the data and the input and output interactions.

3. *The logical system model.* This is a description of an operational system. So the database content, the man-machine subsystem and the algorithms applied to the data together form this model.

4. *The implementation model.* This contains the physical data representation and the physical structure of the program.

The object system model is close to the domain problem for which the program is used. The implementation model is logically far away from the domain problem, but closely related to

Aspect	Levels of Abstraction			
	Object System Model	Conceptual Information System Model	Logical System	Implementation Model
Goal structure	1.1	2.1	3.1	4.1
Environmental interaction	1.2	2.2	3.2	4.2
Functional structure	1.3	2.3	3.3	4.3
Entity structure	1.4	2.4	3.4	4.4
Process structure	1.5	2.5	3.5	4.5
System dynamics	1.6	2.6	3.6	4.6
Allocation aspects	1.7	2.7	3.7	4.7
Realization considerations	1.8	2.8	3.8	4.8

Table 1: A framework for views and representations

the actual, operational system. The mental process to understand a program (the *problem model* as it was called) will often start on the object system level and go down to the implementation level. The mental model of the program (the *program model*) starts from the implementation level and goes up to the logical and possibly the conceptual level. The comprehension process may be characterized as *specification* (from object to conceptual level etc.), *abstraction* (deriving logical meaning from implementation aspects) and *matching*.

The second dimension of the classification scheme concerns the *aspect*. Essink (1986) derived them from systems theory:

1. The *goal structure*, the organization of elements to realize a goal.

2. The *environmental interaction*, the interface between a system and its environment.

3. The *functional structure* is the subdivision of the system into atomic functional units, which cannot be divided any more into smaller meaningful subunits.

4. The *entity structure*, the relations between entities and their properties. The entities are viewed as passive elements whose status can be seen as the result of active elements of the functional structure.

5. The *process structure* describes the transformation process.

6. The *system dynamics* is the adaption of the system in time to the changing situation in the environment.

7. The *allocational aspects* contain the equipment used to perform the process.

8. The *realization considerations* are the organizational and social constraints that play a role in the decisions made in the design process.

As one may observe from this scheme, it has been developed originally for the classification of views in forward engineering, views which are used to clarify design decisions, to reveal inconsistencies in requirements etc. The scheme is useful for a classification of reverse engineering views too, if one accepts that many categories will remain empty.

Realization considerations, for instance, can give useful information about a lot of technical decisions which are discovered in the code. If, for instance, a certain programmer was involved in the development of a system, traces may be found in the code of his style and preferences. In reverse engineering this background information, which fits in category 4.8 might be important. Generally speaking, one may say that categories 4.1 up to 4.7 have to be discovered in reverse engineering and that 4.8 may give useful background information.

Compilers and static analysis tools are able to derive views in category 4.2, 4.4 and 4.5 from the source code. The system dynamics of the implementation model could be studied from the source code, but there are several reasons to use at least debugging tools or just a study of the actual behavior of the system as a source of information.

The analysis of the functional structure of the implemented system can be done by the derivation of formal specifications from the code or by applying 'slicing' techniques (Stanley-Smith, 1993). Units with certain functions can be identified and their behavior can be expressed in a formal specification.

The goal structure, for example how the functions and data work together to realize a certain external behavior is not easily derived directly from the source code using tools. Here human experience and intuition is a useful source of information.

In the REDO project tools have been developed to fill the categories 4.2–4.6 to a certain extend. Views on a higher level of abstraction are difficult to generate with tools. Logical data models can be derived from physical datamodels, with some human interference. All other categories remain rather empty up to now. A data flow diagram could be generated from the code, which would fit in 3.5, but at this moment there is no tool which can do that completely automatically.

If we move further to the left, it becomes clear that the views of the *mental model of the program* become scarce. Here we find more views belonging to the *mental model of the problem*.

5.2. An Example: User Interfaces

As an example to illustrate the different views the user interaction in a program is considered. If one starts from the source code, first of all there is a view of all input and output statements which provide the communication with the user (screen, keyboard, mouse, etc.). This view fits in 4.2. If we make a list of variables which are involved in user interactions, with the text linked to them (field names in forms and names of topics in a menu), we get an entity structure (4.4). The control process in which the user interface is embedded, for instance the call–back functions or the decision tree in a more conventional user interface, is a view of the process structure (4.5).

The assignment of the output devices for the user interaction (mouse, keyboard, screen, files, etc.) can be allocated to category 4.7. If the user interface is adaptable to hardware, for example the quality of the screen resolution or colors, the keyboard, the existence and type of the mouse, the code corresponding to this part of the system represents the dynamics aspect (4.6).

Often the user interaction is implemented using library functions. These libraries are a part of the environment and the calls and parameters involved in these calls form category 4.2: environmental interaction.

On the logical level we can distinguish the same aspects, but here the *meaning* is considered more than merely the data, source code or other physical components. In category 3.2 the behavior of the external functions are considered, for instance, the behavior of windows of a certain kind, menus etc. In category 3.3 belong the description of the appearance of the screen, the windows, the menus, the keys. Category 3.4 contains the list of lexical dialogue elements, while the syntactical structure of the dialogue (the valid sequence of lexical elements) is a part of category 3.3 (Alexander, 1987). The system dynamics, for example in the form of state–transition diagrams, belong to group 3.5

As an exercise the reader can try to fill in the other categories. A few other relevant examples of views will be given below. On the Conceptual level, category 2.1 contains the *user task* as far as it concerns the operation and control of the program. The category 1.1 is again the user task, but here the task on domain level, for instance the task to solve a problem where the program can be used for. In 1.1 the task to write a thesis could be considered and in 2.1 the task to use a particular word processor.

In this way it is possible to find in each category views on the program or parts of the program. Not all categories are equally important. Sometimes a category can only be filled using much imagination. Still the scheme is useful to organize views and to verify whether one really covers all relevant aspects and levels of abstraction.

As a last example, the category 1.8 is considered: If a request exists to enhance a user interface or to replace it, one should verify whether this request solves the real problem. Often such requests hide a deeper problem. Then the problem with the user interface are only symptoms of the real problem such as the lack of functionality of the program or insufficient training for the users. Improving the user interface does not solve the real problem. Such an analysis fits in category 1.8.

5.3. Representations and Development Methods

The representation of a view is in fact the language in which the view can be documented, which can be used to reason about a view of the system or to communicate with other people about the system. Natural language in some cases is an appropriate representation, for example for the project process view. However due to the ambiguity it is less suited to describe aspects like the behavior of a system or the control flow.

Many representations have been developed in the last 30 years to be used in the development process of software. A few have been developed especially for existing programs, such as cross reference tables and other tables produced by compilers. Most representations have been developed, however, for the forward engineering process. They are a part of a design philosophy, method and process. In order to appreciate the differences between the different representations, it is important to know in which development method they are used and for which purpose. Some development methods are especially suited for real-time software, other for data processing software. This can be derived from the properties of the representations — see for instance (Essink, 1986; van't Veld, 1990).

Design representations have been developed to be used in forward engineering. This means that they support a stepwise definition of a goal and the identification of conflicting constraints in the requirements and the solution of these conflicts Visser & Hoc (1990). The suitability of these representation to express properties of an existing system and to support the process of extracting it from the code, is still unknown. The operations of the representation will differ in forward and reverse engineering. Forward engineering means specialization (filling in the details), conflict identification and solution and taking design decisions by choosing from the many possible ways to implement a function or requirement. Reverse engineering means reorganizing the representation, aggregating to another granularity, abstraction, standardizing, finding inconsistencies etc.

The representations of views were originally static: the views were printed or plotted on paper. With the case and reverse engineering tools the representations have become more dynamic. This means that views may be represented for example by the original source code, with some line marked in color, dependent on the request of the user. For instance, the user may ask for all statements which refer to a certain variable. Another example of a dynamic view is the representation of a part of the source code as a control flow diagram. The user can get the content of a node of the diagram by clicking on that node.

5.4. Granularity and Representation Format

The information in a view should be presented on the right level of granularity and in the appropriate format. This concept is determined by the size of the smallest entity which is distinguished in the view. On source code level the lowest level is the complete source code. A more coarse level of granularity only shows the control structure, by hiding the sequential statements. One step further gives only the module structure etc.

In some cases the change in granularity implies already a change towards a new view. For instance, when data flow diagrams are brought to a higher level of abstraction by combining different processes and hiding internal data stores, one may finally arrive at a context diagram (Yourdon, 1989).

Changes in the granularity are often useful in order to combine an overview (top-down) with low-level details. An example is the Turing Tool (Cordy, Eliot & Robertson, 1990), which can display the source code as modules, without showing the internal structure, while the user may ask for the details of the module if he wants, such as the control structure or the complete source. Another example is the static analyzer REPROBATE for Fortran, one of the reverse engineering tools developed in REDO (van Zuylen, 1993). The control structure of the modules is displayed as a graph. By clicking on a node, the user gets the content of the node (the source code of the module) displayed.

In the enumeration of the different representations of the views one may distinguish the following categories:

- text (make files, verbal description of the system, source code);
- numbers (quality and quantity measures, such as lines-of-code, budget, McCabe metrics);
- diagrams (entity-relationship diagram, context diagram, petri net);
- links between views and view elements.

Tables can be considered as text and/or numbers in a specific format and with specific semantics. In fact also diagrams have properties which are similar to a language. The objects in a diagram can be compared with the words in a language. The constraints on the connection between objects are a kind of lexical rules, while the layout can be used for both text and diagrams to structure the presented information and emphasize important elements. Much information is represented by the layout of the text (pretty printing), numbers (tables) and diagrams. The *semantics* of the representation is the interpretation of the elements, but also the links they have with other objects and the operations which are allowed.

A support system for reverse engineering should have facilities to store, edit and retrieve this kind of views and to present them in a natural way to the end-users. There are not many problems on an implementation level. Graphical object can be stored like text and manipulated in various ways. Hypertext techniques can be used to represent links between text, nodes or arcs of a diagram and/or statements or data definitions in the source code. The problem to be solved is how these representations should be accessed by the users, such that the diagrams are aesthetically and well structured, that the text is well formatted and the logic of the links is visible. For this problems several methods have been developed — see for example (Jakobs, 1993; Kamada, 1989). The problem which remains is how a software engineer involved in reverse engineering wants to use these views, for instance how a satisfactory task support can be realized. The first problem to be solved here, is how the task of reverse engineering can be described (or better prescribed).

5.5. Operations on Representations

An important issue in the choice of a representation is the question what kind of operations are possible on a representation. Natural language is a very general way to represent a view, but automatic operations of such a representation, definition of consistency rules and a check on inconsistencies are difficult to realize. Some relevant operations on a representation are:

- *Validation*: Evaluation of the software by means of the view to ensure that it complies with the requirements.

- *Verification*: Evaluation of a view to ensure that it is consistent with another view.

- *Aggregation*: A larger scale view of the system is obtained by clustering — see for example (Schwanke, Altucher & Platoff, 1989). Objects are grouped together into clusters and details internal to a cluster are removed. This can be done, for instance, with data flow diagrams, as the inverse process of decomposition. A strong coherence between components may be an indication that these components could be aggregated.

- *Decomposition*: The components are split up into subcomponents. An example is the separation of code into chunks which have little exchange of information and a definite function (sometimes referred to as 'objects'). Rotenstreich (1990) calls this "low cohesion elimination transformation".

- *Recomposition*: Rearrange the code or design components, such that new chunks are created which are each internally coherent and exchange data with each other (Rotenstreich, 1990).

- *Abstraction*: Some properties of the components are removed to hide details and to reveal the global structure. An example is to show only the control structure of a program or the call tree of the modules.

- *Specialization*: The reverse of abstraction: details are added to a global representation of a view.

- *Transformation*: Elements of one or more representations and relations between them are expressed in another form. In this process information may disappear and new information may be added. A simple transformation is the transition between the entity-relation diagram and the Warnier-Orr representation (Martin & McClure, 1985).

The operations mentioned above may form the bridge between various representations. The reverse development process has to be followed in some cases, but since the development process is only well understood on paper and less in practice (Hoc et al., 1990), the derivation of a new representation from existing ones is in most cases not a straight forward process.

6. The REDO Toolkit to Generate Views

Before a sensible abstraction of a view is possible, the source code has to be interpreted. Parsers are the basis of most reverse engineering tools. They contain the lexical rules of the programming language and a part of the semantics. Often the logical structure of the source code is transformed by a parser into a data structure, the 'parse tree'. The logical structure of a parse tree is for a great deal similar for different languages. It is possible to store programs for instance written in Cobol and Fortran in parse trees with similar structure. Most reverse engineering tools can do their work on the parse tree. When several tools are used then it could be a good decision to make this tree permanent and store it in a repository.

A browser on the source code which displays the source code in the granularity required by the user, displays in fact the parse tree down to a certain depth. A search for a certain construction in the program, for example all nested loops, can be implemented as a query on the repository. The user interface of the browser has to help the user to specify this query and translate the query into a form which can be executed by the database manager of the repository.

Browsers on the parse tree may represent the results of a query in the format of the original programming language but, depending on the abstraction level and the operations involved, a graphical representation (call graphs, control flow, data structures) or tables may be preferable.

Restructuring of the source code is done by manipulation of the tree subject to certain rules. Complexity measures can be defined as statistical properties of the parse tree and can be calculated by counting certain types of links and nodes.

The tools which parse the program and build up the parse tree, can be extended to interpret also job control language and interactions with the environment such as transaction processing systems, embedded SQL or user interface management systems.

Another approach in reverse engineering is, to interpret of the semantics of the source code. Here one has to surpass the representation from the parse tree. One has to identify what certain pieces of code do with parameters. The resulting view can be expressed as invariants (parameters and relations between parameters which remain unchanged in a certain module, preconditions and postconditions (conditions which exist before and after the execution of a module respectively). This approach may lead to a formal, mathematical description of the specification of the source code. In REDO tools have been developed to generate these descriptions semi-automatically.

Links between certain components are very important. Almost every programmer has the experience that he was browsing through a pile of compiler listings and had to use all his fingers to point to all lines of code he wanted to compare. In REDO an environment has been created which makes it possible to produce these links, store them in the repository and to display all pieces of information which are linked together. Logical links which exist in the source code, for instance between lines in which operations are performed on the same variable, can be made visible in the browser as a result of a query.

Another activity which is often carried out in software maintenance and which is supported by the REDO environment, is the making of notes. The character of notes may be:

- clarification — this may be stored afterwards as comment in the source code;
- questions;
- activities which still have to be done.

The last two kinds of notes can be collected for a task list or may be queried.

REDO aims at reverse engineering from the source code in a bottom-up way. Additionally to REDO standard CASE-environments can be used to build the views top-down. These views are, of course, the same as for forward engineering. Currently the CASE-tools do not have much possibilities to build these views from existing code or to verify these views with the actual program.

Other very useful tools to support the building of views are debuggers, dynamic analyzers and test environments. But there the main problem is that no links exist between these different tools. One single environment with one shared repository on which CASE-tools, reverse engineering tools, debuggers, test environments and dynamic analyzers work and where each tool can use the result from the other tools would considerably improve the possibilities for maintenance.

7. Discussion

Reverse engineering is a process apparently less clearly structured as forward engineering. In the latter the kind and role of documentation is much better defined. The same holds for the reverse engineering task. This chapter presents an analysis of a part of the reverse engineering process. The implications for tools are indicated.

Maintenance is a growing business. Some questions not fully discussed in this chapter may be important for the future of software maintenance:

- How to structure the most important part of maintenance, namely the comprehension process.
- Which views are most useful.
- What is the influence of the social status of maintenance.
  New methods and techniques are difficult to introduce in forward engineering. Since it is likely that the educational level of people working in forward engineering is higher than that of maintainers, it is also likely that here it will be even more difficult to introduce new methods in maintenance.
- How could one cope with the reluctance of software engineers in accepting the introduction of new methods.

In REDO *formal methods* are applied to maintenance. It is an interesting question whether such methods will be accepted by practitioners in maintenance. Introduction of more conventional methods in reverse engineering, will probably cause less problems.

Acknowledgement

This work is funded by ESPRIT project 2487, REDO, **Re**engineering, **D**ocumentation and Validation.

Strategy Analysis: An Approach to Psychological Analysis of Artifacts

R K E Bellamy

IBM T J Watson Research Center, P O Box 704, Yorktown Heights, NY 10958, USA.

EMail: rachel@watson.ibm.com

Designers look at and emulate existing good designs. Psychological theory can therefore best support design by explaining what makes existing tools good (Carroll, 1990). The chapter proposes an approach to explaining existing tools to designers called strategy analysis, based on claims analysis (Carroll & Kellogg, 1989). The chapter will describe a strategy analysis of Smalltalk/V.

Keywords: claims analysis, design methods, programming, Smalltalk.

1. Introduction

1.1. Claims Analysis

Claims analysis is a technique for expressing how, from a psychological perspective, a software artifact supports tasks. The representation consists of claims organised within a framework of interface techniques, e.g. metaphors, user levels, menu dimming, and Norman's psychological task analysis (Norman, 1986). Claims describe the psychological consequences of interface features and take the form: "interface feature has psychological consequence".

A claims analysis is composed of multiple claims, and it is the combination of claims made with respect to a particular task activity in Norman's task framework that determines the usability of the system. Carroll & Kellogg refer to this combinatorial effect as psychological over-determination. An artifact can be psychologically over-determined with respect to the task, both in terms of the breadth of coverage (how many of the task activities specified by Norman's task analysis are covered in the analysis), and in terms of the task depth (how many claims there are for each task activity in Norman's task analysis).

Carroll & Kellogg have developed a claims analysis for the error blocking technique used in 'Training Wheels' (Carroll & Carrithers, 1984). Training Wheels was designed to support users in learning text editing. It was based on the observation that novice users engaged in exploratory learning spent over half of their learning time trying to recover from error states. 'Training Wheels' blocks users from getting into such states. When a user selects a function that could lead to a non-recoverable error state, the system pops up a message telling the user that this function is not available to them. One of the claims in their analysis for the psychological task of evaluation is, *a reduced device space constrains hypothesis generation*. 'Training Wheels' constrains the device space by making certain operations unavailable. Because novice users are unable to perform these operations, they do not have to evaluate how they could use them to achieve task goals.

Carroll & Kellogg recognise that an analysis of all the system features and psychological claims of a tool is unnecessary, and that some claims are more important than others with respect to the tasks the system seeks to support. They suggest that it is the 'leading claims' that should be described by a claims analysis. However, they offer no definition of 'leading claim'. This makes it difficult to apply claims analysis as an evaluation technique, and to judge existing claims analyses in terms of coverage and explanatory power. For example, the original analysis of HyperCard (Carroll & Kellogg, 1989) was perhaps missing the most important claim embodied by that system: hanging code onto existing graphics is easier than developing the code first and then hanging graphics onto it.

A major advantage of claims analysis over other types of psychological analysis is that because it is based on analysing an artifact with respect to psychological theory and not on bringing an existing psychological theory to bear on understanding the use of an artifact, it can handle many types of psychological theory within one analysis. For example, in their analysis of HyperCard, Carroll & Kellogg mention both frustration and goal mapping: concepts which are treated very differently in the psychological literature and there is not a single psychological theory which addresses them both.

A problem with using claims analysis is that there is no methodology for producing a claims analysis. Without a methodology (which should include the definition of 'leading claim') claims analysis cannot be used systematically as a representation of how tools affect behaviour. Kellogg (1989) describes a method for extracting claims through empirical observation. She observed learners of HyperCard over a period of nine hours, and collected verbal protocols. The learning task was to develop something that would be of use to the subjects in their professional life. Using this method she was able to produce claims that were tied to particular observations of users interacting with the system, something that was missing from the original conception of claims analysis (Monk & Wright, 1991).

1.2. Strategy Analysis

Strategy analysis builds on claims analysis by providing a methodology, and an enhanced representation for claims. It seeks to use psychological analyses of artifacts to define a psychological theory describing the psychological characteristics of tools, with respect to how they affect planning. In particular it describes how the psychological consequences of a tool lead users to adopt particular strategies of tool use. To perform a strategy analysis, observations of expert task strategies are collected, and then claims analysis is used to explain how features of the tool interact with user cognition to determine these strategies. In this style of analysis, 'leading claims' are those which capture how the tool determines the observed strategies of use.

Explaining human–computer interaction by tying psychological explanations to specific observations of behaviour has also been suggested by Monk & Wright (1991). This is a particularly good approach for understanding how tools affect planning because it keeps the analysis of strategies of tool use tied to a coherent task context. Such an association is necessary to ensure that the scope of the psychological explanations developed are broad enough to explain human–computer interaction (Young & Barnard, 1987). Furthermore, it provides restrictions on the analysis that prevent it becoming infinitely detailed; only claims that explain the observed strategies are considered. Such restrictions were not provided by Norman's generic task analysis framework (Norman, 1986) which was used as an organising rubric for the claims in Carroll & Kellogg's claims analysis. Within Norman's framework all possible task behaviour supported by the artifact must be analysed, even if this behaviour is never observed when a user uses the tool.

The representations of claims used within strategy analysis differ from those used within Carroll & Kellogg's claims analysis. The notion of trade-offs has been introduced into claims, in the sense that an interface feature can (and does) have both positive and negative psychological consequences. The form of a claim is thus elaborated to become: 'interface feature has positive psychological consequence(s), *but has negative psychological consequence(s)'*. For example, a system feature may have the positive psychological consequence that it suggests ordering of actions, and a concomitant negative psychological consequence that it causes high working memory load. The use of trade-offs within claims emphasises that a particular interface feature can have both good and bad aspects with respect to a task. Such trade-offs are important, e.g. in determining whether a user chooses to use an external memory aid or not (Schönpflug, 1986a; Schönpflug, 1986b). One of the hardest parts of design is balancing the trade-offs amongst different system features. Strategy analysis focuses the analyst's attention on precisely such trade-offs.

1.3. Overview of Chapter

This chapter will describe a strategy analysis of Smalltalk/V (Hereafter Smalltalk will be used to refer to Smalltalk/V). Smalltalk is an interesting case for study, not only because it is one of the most mature examples of the relatively new paradigm of object-oriented programming languages, but also because it provides a dedicated programming support environment. Additional reasons for studying Smalltalk are:

- There is more than one strategy for developing a Smalltalk program.
- The system is big enough to impose a serious cognitive load on the programmer, so programmers are forced to make use of the facilities offered by the environment in order to be able to complete the task.
- A population of expert users was available.

The next section provides a brief description of the Smalltalk programming environment for those readers who are unfamiliar with it.

2. Smalltalk/V

Smalltalk is an object-oriented language with a dedicated programming environment. Object-oriented systems in general organise code in terms of classes and methods in the manner discussed in the previous section. An object-oriented program is built around messages being sent to instances of classes. A message encapsulates the name of a method, together with specified arguments; when sent to an instance of a class, the code for the method as defined in the class is executed.

The basic Smalltalk system provides a large library of classes and associated methods. Smalltalk programming consists largely of finding classes and methods within the hierarchy for reuse, understanding these methods, and adding new classes and methods to the hierarchy. The main system tool for supporting these activities is the Class Hierarchy Browser (Figure 1),

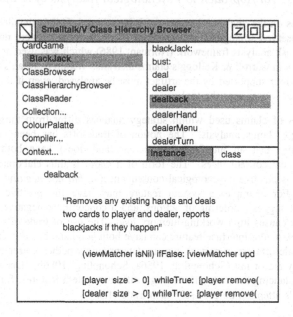

Figure 1:   The Smalltalk class hierarchy browser

which provides facilities for traversing the hierarchically organised list of classes. Selecting a class, for instance 'BlackJack', from the list of classes in the left pane causes the display of that class' description in the bottom pane, while its methods are listed in the right pane; selecting one of these methods, for instance 'dealback', results in the display of the method's text in the bottom pane of the Class Hierarchy Browser (this is the state of the system interaction illustrated in the figure).

The Class Hierarchy Browse provides a number of tools to help programmers in finding code that they want to reuse. One of these is the 'Senders' tool. Programmers can use this tool to trace chains of message sends; it helps them find all the methods in the class hierarchy which send the method they are interested in. To do this, the programmer simply selects the name of the method they are interested in, and a pop-up menu from which they select 'Senders' appears. A window opens which contains two window panes. The top pane contains a browsable list of method descriptors. Each item shows the method name and the class that contains the method. When the programmer selects a method descriptor in the top pane, the code for the method appears in the lower pane. The method text can be read and edited within this pane. However, the programmer does not have access to the hierarchical context, i.e. the class description and the description of other methods implemented in that class.

Aside from the Class Hierarchy Browser, Smalltalk provides two additional tools to support programming; the Inspector and the Debugger. The Inspector presents a view of an instance of a class at a given moment in code execution, and allows the current state of instance and class variables to be browsed. The Debugger is similar to standard program debuggers, it provides facilities for tracing an executing Smalltalk program. Within the Debugger, the current stack of methods, and the state of the object and its class and instance variables to which the method was sent, can be browsed.

3. A Strategy Analysis of Smalltalk

A strategy analysis commences with the collection of observations of the artifact in use. It is important to identify the characteristics of the users being observed, because users with different characteristics may behave differently when using the same artifact.

Subjects: Two expert Smalltalk programmers were subjects in this study; they were chosen because they were self-aware and reflective about doing object-oriented design. (This is in contrast to many Smalltalk programmers with a procedural background, who continue to use the language in a procedural style rather than exploiting its object-oriented features).

Task: The subjects were each asked to solve a simple problem using the Smalltalk language and environment. The task was to write a program that consulted a train timetable to find the last train to arrive before a stated time. It was found then to be non-trivial, demanding some problem-solving; however, it is still tractable in about one hour.

Procedure: The subjects were asked to talk aloud while solving the problem. In particular, they were asked to articulate how they were using the programming language and environment to solve the problem and develop the program. When the subjects fell silent, they were prompted to keep speaking. They could use any external aids such as the Smalltalk manual. The experimenter noted these episodes.

3.1. Method of Analysis

The data from the study was divided into individual *scenarios*. Each scenario corresponded to a *task strategy*, i.e. a concrete piece of goal-oriented behaviour. Figure 2 illustrates a scenario depicting a search strategy.

To understand exactly what it is about the system that determines task strategies, each of these scenarios was analysed to identify what aspects of the interaction between the user cognition and the environment promoted the behaviour in the scenario. Below, I describe the strategy analysis for the task of finding code. The strategies are described followed by an analysis of the claims for these strategies. The claims show how features of the environment and of the users cognition lead to the use of the observed strategies. This is not the full strategy analysis, but rather serves as an example.

3.2. Strategies for Finding Code

Smalltalk provides a class library because it aims to support reuse as a primary programming strategy (Goldberg, 1984). To be able to reuse code, programmers must first locate that code. Two search strategies that were observed were to browse the class hierarchy or to try to hypothesize the position of code on the basis of observing application functionality (see Table 1). Another strategy not obviously supported by the Smalltalk environment, but observed in the protocol study, was the use of the 'Senders' mechanism to find application code. To do this, a class is added to the hierarchy, e.g. 'DummyClass'. Class methods are then associated with it. The names of these methods refer to applications, e.g. chess. By placing this class and method in the code of other methods, e.g. 'DummyClass chess', the programmer can tag sets of methods as being part of an application. They can then use 'Senders' to find all the methods that have the method 'chess' as part of the method code.

Claim 1: A large number of examples provides multiple possible candidates for reuse, *but the larger the number the more difficult to find a specific example and users may be overwhelmed*.

Now let's look at Times. Now where are Times?

Scrolls the list to around 'T', and looks at the contents.

Hm, 'Time' doesn't seem to be here.

Goes to the top of the hierarchy and scans down.

I can't see anything that looks as if it would implement time. I'm sure it's here somewhere, must be a subclass of something. I can't be bothered to look at all the subclasses.

Next, let's look in the book and see if there's anything we missed.

Looks in manual under the class index.

Oh, it's a subclass of 'Magnitude'.

Goes to the browser and moves to around 'M'; finds 'Magnitude', double-clicks on it to access subclasses, scans the subclasses and sees the class 'Time'.

Figure 2:   A scenario for the goal "find the class 'Time'" (the recorded protocol is in plain text; the experimenter's notes are in italics)

The code library contains tens of classes and hundreds of methods. Thus, a programmer has multiple possible candidates for reuse. However, the larger the number of candidates to search, the harder it is to find a specific one. In the study, the programmers used the existing application to narrow the choice, by identifying a specific functionality to be searched for and then guessing the classes that implemented this functionality, and where those classes were located in the class hierarchy. However, it can be difficult to map application behaviour to specific classes and methods.

Claim 2:   Accessing structures by browsing supports serendipitous search and incidental learning of class and method names, *but distracts from the original task and can lead to disorientation.*

Smalltalk provides the class hierarchy browser to support organising and locating code in the class library. The browser supports scrolling through the list of classes as the primary strategy for locating code. As above, finding code using the class hierarchy browser is not easy in general. It was obvious from the study that the sheer size of the hierarchy makes navigation time consuming and confusing. One subject wanted to find the minimum of a list of times, and thought it would be defined in the class 'Time'. He went to the class 'Time' found <, but it took an argument. He decided this wasn't what he wanted, and scrolled to class 'Collection' to look for a minimum method there. Scrolled around the classes under class 'Collection' and couldn't find anything. Finally, he gave-up on browsing the hierarchy and looked in the book under minimum and still couldn't find anything, so decided to write his own method to find the minimum of a list. This example shows that, programmers get overwhelmed by the number of classes and methods, get lost in the hierarchy or forget their original goal as the task of navigating places too many demands on them.

Browsing is however not without its advantages, as when browsing programmers may happen across a useful class or method and this can reshape their solution constructively. For example, when looking for a 'minimum' method, the programmer came across the 'inject' method and

Browse hierarchy	Hypothesize location of classes by browsing existing applications	Use DummyClass and senders
(1) A large number of examples provides multiple opportunities for reuse, *but the larger the number the more difficult to find a specific example and users may be overwhelmed.*	(6) A functional hierarchy reduces the semantic distance from the domain to the code, *but there are multiple possible decompositions for any behaviour, other useful organisations are obscured, and user-defined decompositions can be difficult to understand.*	(8) Tagging code examples with a descriptor helps interpretation, *but having to remember to tag methods by hand increases working memory load, but user defined attribute names can be misleading.*
(2) Accessing structures by browsing supports serendipitous search and incidental learning of class and method names, *but distracts from the original task and can lead to disorientation.*	(7) The availability of code for demos and system tools encourages analysis of them as example applications, *but mapping from observed behaviour to code is difficult.*	(9) Reducing the amount of methods to be browsed prevents users being overwhelmed and distracted during search, *but it removes the opportunity for serendipitous search and incidental learning of the hierarchy.*
(3) A functional hierarchy reduces the semantic distance from the domain to the code, *but there are multiple possible decompositions for any behaviour, other useful organisations are obscured, and user-defined decompositions can be difficult to understand.*		
(4) Class and method names suggest class and method function, *but user-defined names can be misleading.*		
(5) Display structure can suggest interpretation of abstractions, *but the meaning structure must be readily perceptible.*		

Table 1: Psychological analysis of the strategies for locating code in the class library

decided to write 'minimum' using 'inject'. However, all too often programmers find that the search process is so complex that it is easier just to reinvent a class and method, thus adding to the size of the code library and making it even more difficult to find code in the future.

Claim 3: A functional hierarchy reduces the semantic distance from the domain to the code, *but there are multiple possible decompositions for any behaviour, other useful organisations are obscured, and user-defined decompositions can be difficult to understand.*

The functional hierarchy is supposed to aid code finding because hierarchical organizations are a 'natural' representation of categories (Rosson & Alpert, 1991). However, in Smalltalk you can assume that for any behaviour, there are multiple possible decompositions into classes and methods, and possible locations of classes in the functional hierarchy. Thus, there is no guarantee that the decomposition assumed by one programmer will match that assumed, or created, by another.

Claim 4: Class and method names suggest class and method function, *but user-defined names can be misleading.*

When scrolling through the hierarchy, the class name is the initial cue to the function of a class. This places considerable emphasis on the lexical semantics of class names. Good class names can provide useful information to enable the programmer to interpret the functionality represented by a class. The classes in the generic Smalltalk system do suggest naming conventions for associating names with the functionality represented by the class, for instance subclasses contain reference to their superclass, e.g. 'OrderedCollection' and 'IndexedCollection' are subclasses of 'Collection', 'GraphPane' and 'TextPane' are subclasses of 'Pane'; however there is no explicit support to help programmers choose meaningful names. The programmers in the study often invented class, method and argument names that were specific to the application being developed, rather than choosing general names. Application-specific names make it difficult to find classes and methods when they are to be used in different application contexts. One possible reason that programmers choose application specific names when developing code, is that this helps them remember what they are doing, and how classes and methods used in the application work together.

Like classes, the initial cue to the behaviour implemented by a method is the method selector. The arguments to the method are not part of this method description although arguments are conventionally used to indicate the types of objects passed in the arguments. When writing code, the programmer has to specify arguments as part of the method name, and thus the arguments are often a key component of the name and help identify the method's behaviour. One programmer in the study found an 'and:' method for the class boolean, and used it in his code. When the code was executed they got an error message, saying that 'and:' took a block as an argument. After some time they realized that there were two and methods, '&' and 'and', one took a single argument, and one a block. This was not obvious to them from scanning the method names, but may have been if the arguments had been indicated. Because finding methods is sometimes so difficult, people will often write another method when one with that behaviour already exists in the system.

Claim 5: Display structure can suggest interpretation of abstractions, *but the meaning structure must be readily perceptible.*

An additional cue to the function of a class which is available when scrolling through the list of classes is the class's position in the functional hierarchy. For example placing the class 'Process' under the class 'Collection' suggests that it contains a number of items, and you can perform operations on this whole collection of items, e.g. adding to the collection, iterating over it, and so forth. Although displaying classes in functional order is helpful, it can also be problematic as it disrupts the alphabetic ordering of classes. Thus, if the programmer knows the name of a class but not its functional relationship to other classes in the hierarchy, finding the class may be hard. This is not uncommon as the functional position of a class can sometimes seem counter-intuitive during search when the functionality of a class is not fully understood e.g. One of the subjects in the study failed to find the class 'Random', because he didn't think of looking under the class 'Magnitude' where it was located, and browsing through the hierarchy he failed to see it, because it was a number of levels down. Similarly, the position of class 'Symbol' under class 'Collection' may not be obvious until one realizes that the class 'Symbol' inherits functionality from the class 'String', and hence is a subclass of the class 'String' which, as a collection of characters, is one of the subclasses of the class 'Collection'.

The level of a class in the hierarchy is indicated in the display using indentation. Unfortunately, the indentation is not very large, and thus it can be difficult to perceive the exact level of a class. This is especially true in cases like 'Collection' subclasses, as the hierarchy here is deep, and there is not necessarily a superclass of class visible, thus programmers can't use a comparison of indentations in order to evaluate the level of a class.

Another problem with the inheritance representation used in the class hierarchy browser, is that classes deep in the hierarchy are hard to locate, especially as they are not always shown. The hierarchy supports programmers in hiding all subclasses of a selected class. Because of the difficulty in locating classes that are not at the first level in the hierarchy. Programmers were observed to promote a class to the first level, and copy all the methods it should have inherited to this level. For example, one of the subjects in the study created a class 'Timetable' under 'Object', although it was really a collection of train times, and could have usefully inherited much of the functionality of 'Collection's.

Claim 6: see Claim 3

Claim 7: The availability of code for demos and system tools encourages analysis of them as example applications, *but mapping from observed behaviour to code is difficult.*

One possible strategy is to hypothesize the functional location of code by observing examples of its use, for example describing the behaviour of one of the system tools, and then on the basis of this behavioural specification, looking for its implementation in the hierarchy. Instantiated examples of classes and methods suggest possibilities for reuse, however, given a particular application such as the 'Debugger', it can take hours as opposed to minutes to find the classes and methods implementing something like the jump function.

Claim 8: Tagging code examples with a descriptor helps interpretation, *but having to remember to tag methods by hand increases working memory load, but user defined attribute names can be misleading.*

The 'DummyClass' strategy has the usual problems for techniques that rely on user generated names as cues to meaning. The problem is that interpreting the meaning of these names is never straightforward, the same problem occurs for class and method names and is discussed above. Another problem for the 'DummyClass' strategy, observed in the study, is that it is difficult to remember to tag the methods appropriately, or even know what method tags will be useful a a later date. An advantage of the 'DummyClass' as a retrieval strategy is that programmers can see all the possible classifications to choose from during search, although obviously complex searches specifying more than one classification are not possible.

Claim 9: Reducing the amount to be browsed prevents users being overwhelmed and distracted during search, *but it removes the opportunity for serendipitous search and incidental learning of the hierarchy.*

Dummy methods provide a way of searching for application code, and thus reduce the number of candidates that must be searched to just those contained in an application. Thus if the programmer knows in which application the behaviour being searched for is located, they can then use the 'DummyClass' strategy which means they don't have to browse the whole hierarchy to find code. Reducing the number of examples to be browsed does however mean that programmers are less likely to accidently happen across a useful item.

4. Conclusions

This chapter has demonstrated how a strategy analysis can be used to understand how characteristics of a programming language and environment affects programming strategies. It has shown that strategy analysis can support the development of a detailed understanding of how the particular features of a tool have psychological consequences for user's programming strategies. Such an analysis is rich not only in the amount of detail, but also in the breadth of psychological theory that is brought to bear on the evaluation. Like claims analysis, any psychological theory can be used within a strategy analysis.

The trade-off representation used within strategy analysis is another important extension of Carroll & Kellogg's claims analysis. One of the reasons it is often difficult to evaluate a system is because system features are not all good or all bad, especially with respect to how well the system supports planning. For example, abstractions (such as the functional hierarchy in Smalltalk) reduce the semantic distance from the domain to the code, but although a particular abstraction may increase the ease of perceiving a particular structure, it can make the perception of other information structures more difficult (for instance, the functional hierarchy obscures the application structure of code). A second extension of claims analysis is the definition of 'leading claim' based on observed strategies of use. The leading claims of a tool are those psychological claims that can describe why a user of a tool adopts particular, observed, task strategies. Such a definition makes it possible to empirically validate the analysis, because any user should adopt the same strategies when given the same tool.

Although strategy analysis provides some necessary extensions to claims analysis, this chapter illustrates that there are still a number of problems with strategy analysis as currently formulated. One problem is that the observed behaviour captured by a scenario may be caused by something outside of the scenario; for example, something else on the user's mind could be interfering with their current activity. Individual differences will also affect programmers' behaviour and these are difficult to analyse within a strategy analysis. For example, different programmers may have had experience with very different systems, which influence their behaviour with the current system. This cannot be readily represented within the strategy analysis framework. A second problem with strategy analysis is that it has not fully solved the completeness problem inherent to claims analysis. The completeness problem stems from inability to judge whether a claims analysis is complete. Strategy analysis aims for completeness by taking observations of a tool in use as the data for analysis. However, there is no guarantee that the observed behaviour captures all possible uses of the tool, or even the most important ones.

Yet another problem inherent to claims analysis also carries through to strategy analysis: it is difficult to evaluate the correctness of an analysis. The claims represent the analyst's view of the psychological consequences of system features. Although this view is derived from psychological theory, in principle there is no guarantee either that the psychological theory is correct, or that it has been correctly applied in the analysis. Furthermore, because the representation of a claim does not allow reference to the particular psychological theory from which it is derived, it is difficult for external judgement to be made. Reference to the psychological theory from which a claim was derived within the analysis would perhaps provide a better basis from which to evaluate:

- Whether the original theory is correct.
- Whether it has been interpreted it correctly in analysing the observed strategies.

The representational adequacy of the strategy analysis framework is also questionable. It turns out that some important aspects of usability are difficult to represent in the terminology of claims — "system feature has positive psychological consequence(s), *but also has negative psychological consequence(s)*". An example would be the absence of a system feature having a negative psychological consequence: the lack of 'undo' for instance. Also, given the current representation of a claim, it is not easy to show the extent of the negative and positive effects of a system feature. Furthermore, strategy analysis offers no way of representing the extent of a positive or negative psychological consequence; for instance, consequences that cause hard errors, or prevent the user from continuing, are exceedingly negative and should be represented as such. If the representation could capture this, a generally applicable redesign technique would be to remove the most negative consequences, without removing the most positive ones. This, of course, may turn out to be an unrealistic and simplistic view of design; the point is that more work is needed to understand the nature and consequences of trade-offs.

Finally, the inevitable conclusion that further work is needed to develop strategy analysis as a methodology capable of systematic analysis of tools with respect to a psychology of tools and tasks.

Acknowledgements

This work was done while I was a pre-doctoral student working with Jack Carroll at IBM, T J Watson Research Center in New York. I would also like to thank Thomas Green for comments on this chapter.

Constraints on Design: Language, Environment and Code Representation

Françoise Détienne

Institut National de Recherche en Informatique et en Automatique (National Institute for Research on Computer Science and Automation), Projet de Psychologie Ergonomique pour l'Informatique (Ergonomics Psychology Project), Domaine de Voluceau, Rocquencourt BP 105, 78153 Le Chesnay Cedex, France.

Tel: +33 1 39 63 55 22

Fax: +33 1 39 63 53 30

EMail: detienne@psycho.inria.fr

This chapter will address the issue of interaction between code manipulation processes and design processes. We will first present some characteristics of the coding process considered as following the design phase. Although programming is now considered as opportunistically organized, it may consist nonetheless of a succession of planning processes and code generation processes at a microlevel. Second, we will present constraints (knowledge characteristics and language/environment characteristics) which lead the programmer to work at the code level although the worked out solution has not yet been evaluated or has been erroneously evaluated at higher levels of abstraction. Whereas this should lead to solution reconstruction and revision, we will argue that instead of going from a detailed level to higher levels of abstraction the programmers may use strategies to solve abstract-level-related problems at the code level, avoiding (as much as possible) changing the level of abstraction or, if the level of abstraction is changed, the programmers may employ strategies in order to do so in an economical way.

Keywords: design activity, strategy of design, coding mechanisms, abstraction levels.

1. Introduction

According to the waterfall and hierarchical models, programming includes a strict separation between the design stage and the coding stage. A solution was assumed to be fully developed and evaluated before the production of code. More recently, opportunistic models of programming have highlighted the deviations in programming activity from purely hierarchical models. These different models of programming will be briefly presented in Section 2. A parallel will be drawn with models of text production.

This chapter will address the issue of interaction between code manipulation processes and design processes. We will first, in Section 3, present some characteristics of the coding process considered as following the design phase. Although programming is now considered as being opportunistically organized, it may nonetheless consist of a succession of planning processes and code generation processes at a microlevel. Second, in Section 4, we will present constraints which lead the programmer to work at the code level although the worked out solution has not yet been evaluated or has been erroneously evaluated at higher levels of abstraction. Whereas this should lead to solution reconstruction and revision, we will argue that instead of going from a detailed level to higher levels of abstraction the programmers may use strategies to solve abstract-level-related problems at the code level, avoiding (as much as possible) changing the level of abstraction or, if the level of abstraction is changed, the programmers may employ strategies in order to do so in an economical way. This will be developed in Section 5.

2. Theoretical Approaches of Programming

According to the waterfall models of programming, the elaboration of a solution, at an abstract level, is assumed to be completed before translating. Furthermore, hierarchical models of programming (Adelson & Soloway, 1985) suppose that the solution is elaborated and evaluated completely at one level of abstraction before the elaboration starts at a more detailed level. So the elaboration of a solution is assumed to be complete before the solution is coded in a particular programming language.

In the same way, in text production studies, there is a distinction between processes such as planning and translating/reviewing. In Hayes & Flower's model on text production (Hayes & Flower, 1980), the planning process consists of generating ideas, organizing ideas and goal-setting subprocesses. The translating process acts under the guidance of the writing plan to produce language corresponding to information in the writer's memory. The function of the reviewing process, which consists of reading and editing subprocesses, is to improve the quality of the text produced by the translating process. It does this by detecting and correcting weaknesses in the text with respect to language conventions and accuracy of meaning, and by evaluating the extent to which the text accomplishes the writer's goals. The editing process consists of "edit for standard language convention, edit for accuracy of meaning, evaluate for reader understanding, evaluate for reader acceptance".

In programming, there is an evolution away from waterfall models and hierarchical models of design toward opportunistic models of design (Green, 1990a; Visser, in this volume) which highlight the importance of code manipulation processes interacting with design.

Code manipulation processes and design processes are increasingly being considered as interacting for different reasons (Pennington & Grabowski, 1990). The coding process has been shown to take place not only after the designing process; both processes are intrinsically related, a program being developed and worked out at different levels of abstraction and with different kinds of abstractions. Language constraints are taken into account in the design process even at high levels of abstraction. It has been shown that design consists partly of reusing solutions developed before; code reuse and so partly solution retrieval/code understanding are processes involved during design. Studies (Guindon, 1990b; Visser, 1987) highlight the deviations of empirical-based models of programming from a purely hierarchical model of programming.

Similarly, in text production, models highlight the opportunistic organization of the activity. Hayes & Flower (1980) show that the planning and translating/reviewing processes are not organized as a strict sequence from generating to editing. They observe that interruptions of other processes by editing and generating are frequent.

3. Coding as Translating

Although programming is now considered as being opportunistically organized, it may nonetheless consist of a succession of planning processes and code generation processes at a microlevel. To raise issues on the code generation process, an analogy will be drawn, whenever possible, between the coding process analysed in studies of programming and the translating process analysed in text production studies.

In text generation studies, translating/editing processes have been shown to involve linguistic decisions which would merit further analysis in the specific domain of programming. The issue of compatibility between mental structure and external structure of representation is addressed; translating as well as coding involves transforming an internal representation which has a given structure into an external representation which must conform to a structure depending on a particular language.

3.1. Linguistic Decisions

In text generation, cognitive studies are beginning to address the issue of the cognitive mechanisms underlying translating (Bisseret, 1990). In Artificial Intelligence, studies have been conducted on the translating process. Given a representation of ideas (semantic representation) which are organized in a certain way, how are these ideas translated into a linguistic form? This involves content decisions: what should be made explicit or remain implicit; in what order should the text be organized? This also involves linguistic decisions: decisions about lexical forms, syntactic forms, determining the order of the information, segmenting the text into sentences and grouping the text into paragraphs. All these decisions are dependent the one upon the other.

It is worth noting that these studies should be related to understanding studies in as much as the linguistic form affects the understanding process and that the representation the writer has of the future reader of the text surely affects the linguistic decisions made during translating.

In text production, the linear structure of a text is often constrained by the temporal structure of the story. In program production, it may be argued that most of the coding/translating processes are constrained by the notational structure of programming languages and by the functioning rules of the programming device. For instance, the linear structure of a program is highly constrained by the way the program should be executed in procedural languages (and less so with declarative languages). However, some linguistic decisions may also depend on the use of 'rules of programming discourse' such as those defined by Soloway & Ehrlich (1984). Furthermore, certain parts of the program such as comments and documentation are not constrained by the programming language.

As in text studies, the linguistic forms of programs have mostly been analysed in studies on the understanding process and on maintenance tasks. For example, studies show how the planliness[1] of programs affects the understanding process (Détienne & Soloway, 1990; Soloway & Ehrlich, 1984). Studies show that the lexical forms of variables, the types of

---

[1] In unplan-like programs, either the way the plans are composed is not prototypical or a plan is implemented with a value which is not prototypical. A way of constructing unplan-like programs is to construct programs that violate some rules of discourse.

comments or the structure of documentation affect the understanding process (Détienne, 1989). To date, few studies have been conducted on the processes involved in the construction of the linguistic form. Rist's study represents one of these few attempts (Rist, 1990).

Rist proposes a program design model which explains the variability of textual forms. For a given decomposition of the solution in terms of mental plans, merging decisions are taken to organize actions into segments of text. He distinguishes between merging actions on the basis of shared roles and merging actions on the basis of shared goals or shared data. Although these decisions to merge instances of the same plan depend on knowledge of language characteristics, they may also depend on rules of discourse the programmers have constructed from their experience. It may be assumed that the merging of actions which belong to different plans may be rejected because it violates a rule of discourse which ensures that "a statement of code should not perform different functions, particularly when these functions are parts of different plans". Remark that these merging decisions are particularly difficult to carry out in a correct way by novice programmers as has been shown in the studies of Spohrer, Soloway & Pope (1989).

3.2. Compatibility between Mental Structures and Notational Structures

Translating requires transforming an internal representation into a textual representation. In text production, the units of the internal representation are assumed to be semantic propositions and schemas although the textual units are language units like words and sentences. In programming, authors generally assume that the mental representation is structured in programming plans or schemas although this issue is controversial (Détienne, 1990a). Atwood & Ramsey (1978) assume that the units of the internal representation are propositions and Pennington (1987a) describes different abstractions which are more or less plan-like.

Code generation is affected by the compatibility between the structure of the mental representation (input) and the notational structure of the language in which the mental representation must be translated. Mental representations of programs are assumed to be composed of plans or schemas. As a model of the solution is elaborated, some parts of the plans are translated into the code so as to prevent working memory overload.

It can be assumed that the order of code generation deviates from the linear order of the program whenever there is a mismatch between characteristics of the mental structure and characteristics of the notational structure (Green, Bellamy & Parker, 1987). For instance, with Pascal notational structure, pieces of code which correspond to different programming plans have to be interleaved into programs. Although a programming plan constitutes a mental unit, textual forms representing one plan may have to be dispersed throughout the text because of the language notational structure. This should lead the programmer to generate code for one plan then generate code for another plan by inserting it into already written code either by going backward or forward into the text in progress. In fact, as will be shown in Section 5.2, the results are more complex; the choice of a coding strategy may depend on other characteristics of the language, making reconstruction or revision of the solution more or less easy.

It is worth noting that difficulties in code generation due to the incompatibility between mental structure and textual structure could be alleviated by an environment which allows the programmers to work at the plan level (Parker & Hendley, 1987).

4. Constraints for Working at the Code Level

In this section we present constraints leading the programmers to work at the code level although the correctness of the worked out solution has not been efficiently evaluated at higher levels of abstraction. We distinguish between the effects of the knowledge possessed/used by the programmers and the effects of language/environment characteristics.

4.1. Knowledge Characteristics

According to the waterfall models, the evaluation of a solution is performed at an abstract level before the translating process occurs. However, evaluating certain aspects of the solution is not always possible before translating. As noted by Green (1990a, p.119) "the waterfall models seem infeasible as a general technique because the consequences of higher level decisions cannot always be worked out fully until lower level ones are developed ...". In programming, a characteristic is that language constraints and system constraints (at least for most of the existing programming systems) must be taken into account so as to construct a solution even at high levels of abstraction and they must be integrated with other domain constraints.

Experienced programmers use knowledge structures which allow them to anticipate the implication of design decisions. A characteristic of experienced programmers is that they have constructed programming plans which are abstract structures representing solutions developed in the past and which depend to a greater or lesser degree on programming language and task domain. The use of a plan which guides the problem solving activity has a heuristic function because it provides the designer with a high level structure and the use of this structure saves him from dealing with too detailed an analysis of the situation in early phases of design. Validity rules may be associated with programming plans and can be used early in design so as to decide whether or not a selected plan is appropriate. Thus experienced programmers, at least for familiar problems, can anticipate problems which could stem from design decisions. Note that these structures could be used for solving familiar problems or, by analogy, for solving unfamiliar problems which may display features similar to known problems.

Novices cannot evaluate, at abstract levels, the correctness of a solution with regard to language constraints and other constraints. Novices often do not possess evaluation criteria for the appropriateness of plans: plans can be evaluated only when an implementation of them has been developed. At the code level, evaluation may come from external feedback, as tools are then available for testing and compiling/interpreting the code. Evaluation may also result from failure to implement a plan.

However, even for experts, a plan may be used as a working hypothesis which can be completely evaluated only on the basis of retroaction obtained during the activity driven by this plan and thus when a solution has been translated into the code. This is particularly true when experts solve unfamiliar problems or when they work with an unfamiliar language.

Judging a subproblem as particularly difficult may lead programmers to develop its solution in detail before dealing with other subproblems thereby leading them to deviate from a purely top-down balanced development of the global solution. When programmers develop the code, there are cycles of coding, evaluating and changing processes (Gray & Anderson, 1987). This is more likely to happen when a subproblem is not familiar, as the programmers have no compiled knowledge for solving it and solving implies more planning.

When working with an unfamiliar language, experienced programmers may not be able, at abstract levels, to evaluate the correctness of their plans and may evaluate the inappropriateness of a solution mostly at the code level. Studies about learning a second language, show how programming plans constructed with known languages are transferred and used in designing with a new language. Plans are developed and evaluated as inadequate mainly at the code level and failure to implement them leads to plan revision.

In inter-language studies transfer occurs between languages (Scholtz, in this volume). Plans of solution which had been elaborated with a source-language are transferred and guide the elaboration of solutions with a target-language. Scholtz & Wiedenbeck (1990) distinguish tactical planning, in which programmers manipulate abstract plans which express a local strategy or an algorithm for solving a problem which is still independent of programming language characteristics, and implementation planning in which code representations are manipulated and which mainly consists in translating 'tactical plans' into programming constructs specific to one language. Results show that programmers spend most of their time on syntax and implementation planning. The programmers often fail to implement their tactical plan. This leads to iteration between implementation planning and tactical planning which allow the programmers to modify or change tactical plans so as to be able to implement them successfully. Thus evaluating plans at the code level may lead them to return to a more abstract level in order to revise the plans. However, whenever subjects are able to translate these non adequate plans into programming language constructs, errors or 'inelegances' are produced revealing negative effects of transfer (Détienne, 1990b).

4.2. Language/Environment Characteristics

Constraints related to language/environment characteristics may lead the programmers to work at the code level whereas the correctness of the worked out solution has not been efficiently evaluated or must be reevaluated at higher levels of abstraction. First, the lack of tools for evaluating plans at high levels of abstraction and the availability of support for evaluating code mean that, in some situations, solutions may be evaluated mostly at the code level. Second, language and environment characteristics may lead the programmers to make a premature commitment, a part of a solution having to be developed in detail before it may be completely evaluated. Third, programming languages are often the only formalisms of representation reliably used for constructing external representations of solutions; so, in software reuse activities and in enhancement tasks, the programmers may be forced to work at the code level, in as much as the usable external representation of the to-be-enhanced or to-be-reused solution is developed mostly at this level.

In general, programming environments support mostly code editing. Plan editing is rarely supported although environments which allow the programmers to work at the plan level are starting to be developed (Parker & Hendley, 1987). Few tools are provided for evaluating plans at high levels of abstraction. Note that formal proofs of correctness methods are being developed in software engineering. Although these methods could theoretically allow designers to evaluate their solution before the coding phase, they do not yet seem to be usable for complex programs.

Language and environment characteristics may lead the programmers to take a decision before having all the necessary information. In this case, a part of the code must be developed in detail even though the programmers do not yet have the means to judge whether or not the solution chosen to be implemented is correct. These characteristics have been described by Green as leading to 'premature commitment'.

This can be illustrated by a study conducted by Détienne (1990b) in order to assess the usability of an object-oriented system, the O_2 system. With the O_2 language, a program is composed of two parts: a declarative part or model of classes which consists of the type specification, i.e. the names of classes, the types and names of attributes, the relations between classes and a procedural part which consists of the bodies of methods. In the version of the O_2 system which was assessed, it was not possible to use, in a method body, a class or an object which had not been completely specified in the declarative part beforehand. This constraint of order led the programmers to develop the declarative part first entailing premature commitment. Results highlighted that, at this stage of design, the programmers could not correctly anticipate the characteristics of classes which should be used in procedures. While developing the procedural part, the solution chosen previously concerning the characteristics of classes had then to be revised.

To a large extent, programming languages are often the only formalisms of representation reliably used for constructing external representations of solutions. Although other formalisms may also be used so as to document a program, the constructed representations are not always systematically updated when the program evolves.

Generally, designing a solution is not done from scratch. The designers retrieve past solutions in memory, for which they may have external representations, and they have to revise these source-solutions so as to ensure their correctness for solving the target-problem (the problem under study). External representations of source-solutions, formalized at the code level, are then used. Empirical studies show the importance of code reuse in the programming activity (Détienne, 1991a; Détienne, 1991b; Lange & Moher, 1989). Enhancement tasks or maintenance tasks are situations in which solutions have to be revised. The programmer often has the code as the only reliable external representation of the to-be-enhanced solution.

5. Mechanisms for Solving Abstract-level-related Problems at the Code Level

While manipulating code, problems which are related to abstract-level-information may arise. Abstract-level-related problems refer to the retrieval of solutions, the choice of a solution and the modification of a solution. For instance, testing a solution developed at the code level may lead to solution revision. Revising a solution involves the programmer partially reconstructing information used for designing this solution. Even when the solution was developed by the programmer himself, knowledge has not always been kept in working memory.

In this section, we will argue that, instead of going from one detailed level of abstraction to more abstract levels, the programmers may use strategies to solve abstract-level-related problems at the code level avoiding, as much as possible, changing the level of abstraction or, if the level of abstraction is changed, the programmers may employ strategies in order to do so in an economical way.

5.1. Anticipatory Mechanisms in Code Reuse

Some mechanisms involved in the elaboration of the solution have an anticipatory function concerning the future revision of the solution. First, the programmer may construct a representation of the solution which is operative for its potential future revision in a code reuse strategy. The effect of these anticipations will be to facilitate the coding of the reused solution; the programmer will use a constructed representation which distinguishes parts of code to be modified from parts of code which must remain unchanged and which specifies the kinds of modification to be made at the code level. Second, the programmer may choose a solution, from alternative solutions, by anticipating future problems so as to avoid as much as possible future solution revision in a reuse situation.

In a reuse situation, referred to as the 'new code reuse situation' by Détienne (1991a; Détienne, 1991b), the programmer develops a solution in a breadth-first manner; different solutions (various parts of a global solution) are evoked or elaborated which are then refined. The programmer judges that several solutions are instances of the same schema. One of the solutions is chosen as the one to be refined first and is thus given the status of 'source'. Other solutions are chosen to be developed by copying and modifying the source-solution code, and are given the status of 'target'.

In new code reuse episodes, target-solutions are elaborated from the source-solution representation and from the procedure constructed during the first instantiation of the schema. It has been highlighted in Détienne's study that the constructed representations of the source-solution, at different levels of abstraction, are operative in as much as, there is a discrimination between aspects of the solution which are constant and aspects of the solution which have to be changed. The programmers' attention is focused on differences between source and target, and the constructed representations are appropriate for elaborating the target-solution from the source-solution.

Analysis of protocol data suggests that anticipations, drawn during source-solution elaboration, allow the programmers to construct procedures for elaborating target-solution(s) from the source-solution. The input of such a procedure is a source-solution representation and its output is a target-solution representation. This procedure is elaborated at different levels of abstraction. At an abstract level, the source-solution representation and the target-solution representation are abstract and the procedure specifies modifications to be handled at an abstract level. At a detailed level, the source-solution representation and the target-solution representation are detailed and the procedure specifies modifications to be handled at the code level. Using the operative representation of the solution and the procedure will facilitate the coding process of the target-solutions and will avoid, during the target-solutions coding, reasoning at higher levels of abstraction on solution choice and solution modification.

The subject may judge the reusability of a solution under development for future (other) solutions development. In a new code reuse situation, refining the source-solution may imply choosing between alternative solutions and it could be expected that, in this reuse situation, this choice is influenced not only by the solutions' adequacy to the source-problem but also to the target-problem. More generally, the choice between alternative solutions may be influenced by the solution adequate to the problem under study and to future anticipated 'potential' problems. This could lead to the choice of a more 'standard' solution which would minimize modification mechanisms and so could avoid solution revision when code reuse is performed.

5.2. Coding Strategies

Green, Bellamy & Parker (1987) remark that, as the code is generated, the external representation is used by the programmer as an external memory. So code is generated then understood when further extending the solution. It is likely that the choice of a design strategy and coding strategy is made by experienced programmers so as to minimize the cost of future reconstruction/revision of elaborated solutions. First, in code reuse situations, the order of code generation may be chosen so as to manage in working memory, in a short period of time, a representation operative for code reuse. This strategy avoids reconstructing, revising and evaluating the solution at higher levels of abstraction. Second, the order of code generation may vary according to language characteristics which make revision and reconstruction more or less costly.

In new code reuse, reuse-in-a-row (elaborating and coding a source solution and different target-solutions successively without being interrupted by other activities) is a strategy which allows the management in working memory, during as short a period of time as possible, of relevant information for target-solution(s) elaboration. This may avoid overloading working memory and reconstructing a solution representation from source code. On the other hand, when reuse is scattered, i.e. interrupted by other activities, subjects should experience difficulty in managing, in working memory, information appropriate for the elaboration of target-solutions. It has been shown (Détienne, 1991a; Détienne, 1991b) that this causes errors which are 'omissions of changes'.

A shortcoming of the reuse-in-a-row strategy is that errors are caused by the propagation of source errors. Errors are propagated in that the target-solution correctness is rarely evaluated by programmers and that, processing repeated instantiation of a particular schema and repeated instantiation of a particular procedure tends to automate the solution coding process and so, to lower the level of control of the activity.

Reconstruction and revision mechanisms are more or less costly depending on languages and environment characteristics. Cognitive dimensions of the notational structure have been described by Green (1989) and this author has analysed how these dimensions affect the program writing activity. Reconstruction mechanisms are particularly costly when the language and the environment are not role-expressive, i.e. perceiving the purpose and the role of each program segment is not easy. Revision mechanisms are particularly costly when the language and the environment are viscous, i.e. hard to change.

In a study comparing coding behaviour in different programming languages, Green, Bellamy & Parker (1987) analysed non-linearity in code generation. Non-linearities occur when the order of code generation is different from the order of the text code. The authors remark that "departures from linear generation are significant. They increase mental workload, they risk omissions and oversights ...". Results show that programmers perform more backward jumps for Pascal than for Prolog. Although the use of both Pascal and Basic involves the interleaving of programming plans, the different writing strategies of programmers are interpreted as either minimizing the cost of modifying the code (for Pascal which is more viscous), or as minimizing the need to understand the code (for Basic which is less role-expressive).

5.3. Adjusting, at the Code Level, a Non-optimal Solution

While developing a solution at the code level, the programmer may judge this solution as non-optimal. Empirical studies show that, in this case, the programmer may prefer to stick with a non-optimal solution, preferring local adjustments at the code level instead of reconstructing information so as to revise the solution at more abstract levels.

In Hoc's study (Hoc, 1988b), language and environment characteristics led experienced programmers to adopt a depth-first strategy which consists of developing detailed coded parts of a solution even before experts can completely evaluate the appropriateness of these parts of the solution with regard to other problem parts. In Green's terms, language and environment cause premature commitment. Having to define a solution in detail before being able to evaluate its implications caused the production of non adequate solutions.

Solution revision, at abstract levels, was then avoided; experienced programmers kept non-optimal solutions with local adjustments. Solution revision may be too costly even for experienced programmers for several reasons. Firstly, subjects may not have kept information concerning previous design decisions in (internal and external) working memory and may have postponed problems which are relevant for carrying out the plan revision. This information may be difficult to reconstruct depending on the structure of information the subjects have at their disposal. Secondly, the revision may be too costly because the environment and/or the language are viscous, i.e. revision entails a lot of modifications which are not specifically related to the subjects' main goal while revising their plan.

In a one-subject study conducted by Lange & Moher (1989), the results highlight the importance of literal code reuse, i.e. literal copies employed without modification. Object-oriented programming languages have been designed to favour reuse by means of the inheritance property. However, the strategy of literal code reuse does not take advantage of this property. The programmer did not take full advantage of class hierarchy in order to reuse code by inheritance. Although the authors did not analyse the reasons for this striking result, it may be assumed that the programmer adopted a strategy which economized revision of the organization of classes. However, this strategy may make subsequent revision of the program particularly costly because modifying a part of the code acting as a source will also lead the subject to make changes in the targets.

In inter-language studies, we might expect the programmer to modify his solution when he has to solve a problem with quite different languages. Petre & Winder's (1988) results show that, on the contrary, programmers tend to keep the same solution which they translate in different languages. Although the authors interpret this result as demonstrating that a programming language has only a weak influence on the solution, an alternative interpretation is possible. Languages used were very different from one another so it is likely that appropriate solutions would be very different from one another depending on the language. However programmers may have chosen a strategy which minimizes the reconstruction of the solution for modifying it because reconstruction/revision was judged particularly costly. On the other hand, keeping the same solution (firstly developed) and translating it into a different language would be judged as less costly. In this situation, the programmers avoid revising solutions at high levels of abstraction, preferring to stick with a previously chosen solution and to adjust it at the code level according to various languages characteristics.

5.4. Trade-off between Solution Understanding and Code Modification/Evaluation

When the programmer has an external representation developed at the code level, which has to be modified, the representation of the solution should be constructed at abstract levels so as to perform solution modification. Studies on code reuse, in which this situation is analysed, show that the programmers may work at the code level using a generate/test strategy minimizing understanding processes. Modifications and feedback obtained from evaluation performed at the code level allow the source-solution to be adjusted, the programmer avoiding reconstructing a detailed representation of the source-solution. A study on enhancement task shows that the programmers may adopt a strategy for minimizing the understanding process being then more dependent on feedback obtained from testing/compiling the code.

In a study on object-oriented programming, Lange & Moher (1989) observed that, when reusing code, the programmer, who has a global representation of the program, avoids a detailed understanding of a reusable component. The subject's strategy is to change and test. Instead of understanding source-code in detail so as to modify it, she used plausible modifications with immediate testing. Interpreted execution was used to validate modifications.The authors note that testing was performed continuously, even when the methods were known to be incorrect. However, the authors remark that for the most difficult problem areas, the subject performs a symbolic execution.

Although Sutcliffe & Maiden's Study is on specification reuse (Sutcliffe & Maiden, 1990b), it provides insight into reuse mechanisms. These authors show that novices tend to copy rather than reason about the reusable source-specifications.

In an enhancement task, reconstruction processes can vary according to the programmers' chosen strategy. Programmers can adopt different understanding strategies which allow them to construct a mental representation which accounts for either the complete solution or part of the solution and which does or does not account for causal relations between program units. In an empirical study, Littman et al. (1986) distinguish two strategies for program understanding in an enhancement task. Some programmers use a systematic strategy: they trace data flow and control flow through the program in order to understand global program behaviour. They gather knowledge about the causal interactions of the program's functional components.

Other programmers use an as-needed strategy: they focus on local program behaviour in order to localize study of the program. They do not gather such causal knowledge and therefore fail to detect interaction among components of the program. They try to minimize the understanding of the program by localizing the parts of the program which must be changed and studying these parts only.

Empirical data show that there is a strong relationship between using a systematic approach to acquire knowledge about the program and modifying the program successfully. However, subjects were not allowed to test and debug their enhancements. As noted by the authors, it is likely that "programmers using the as-needed strategy may depend more heavily upon testing and debugging to learn about the program's structure than programmers using the systematic strategy."

6. Conclusion

In summary, we have presented constraints related to knowledge/language/environment characteristics which lead the programmers to work at the code level although the worked out solution has not yet been evaluated or has been erroneously evaluated at higher levels of abstraction. Whereas this should lead to solution reconstruction and revision, we have argued that instead of going from a detailed level to higher levels of abstraction the programmers may use strategies to solve abstract-level-related problems at the code level, avoiding (as much as possible) changing the level of abstraction or, if the level of abstraction is changed, the pro- grammers may employ strategies in order to do it in an economical way. These strategies allow the programmers to avoid processing solution reconstruction/revision mechanisms which are too costly because of existing languages/environments characteristics. While economical in this regard, these strategies have many drawbacks like the production of erroneous solutions by the propagation of source-code errors in code reuse or the production of non-optimal solutions.

Acknowledgement

Thanks to Willemien Visser for help in the preparation of this chapter.

Designing the Working Process — What Programmers Do Beside Programming

Jörg Strübing

Zentrum für Berufs- und Hochschulforschung, Gesamthochschule Kassel, Henschelstraße 4, D–34109 Kassel, Germany.

Tel: +49 (0)561 804 2415/3111

Fax: +49 (0)561 804 3301

This discussion presents, as a result of my own empirical studies, a description of software development as a social process with special problems and risks: vagueness of requirements, hierarchical and other organizational barriers, the necessity of negotiation and informal communication, heterogeneous tasks and so forth. This description is based on a model of cooperative creative work which understands programmers activities as subjective assimilation of constraints resulting from the materiality of the subject, given organizational structures, and the cultural differences between various groups as participating actors. Finally I discuss the problem of supplying this working process with adequate methods and tools.

Keywords: negotiativeness, heterogeneity, working process, software design, uncertainty, informal action.

1. Introduction

Up till now, talking in terms of science about software engineering has usually been the business of computer scientists for reasons of their technical expertise and of psychologists because of their expertise in questions of cognition and perception. Resulting from this 'division of labour', we find countless technological attempts to solve the obvious problems in software design and quite a few cognitive models to explain these problems.

Surprisingly, however, very few sociologists are concerned with these questions — even though designing software is a highly cooperative *social process*. Being a sociologist, I have found that the social process of working together in software project teams lacks analytical descriptions. Descriptions of "what is going on in such teams?" or "how do they deal with all those methods, tools, and all the other problems given to them by computer scientists?" or "what is their practice and what are their reasons to behave like they do?". The 'software crisis' is often discussed as resulting from 'human factors' or as a problem of 'software psychology' — but can it really be sufficiently explained in terms of inadequate cognitive models or individual lacks of programming expertise?

Attempting to answer these questions could lead us to a deeper understanding of programmers' 'shopfloor practice' and thereby perhaps to better solutions to the problems of software engineering. In the following discussion, I would like to present one attempt at an analytical description of the practice of cooperative creative work, in which I regard programming in terms of sociology. The findings presented are results of my empirical research during the last five years. I conducted two series of open-ended interviews, one with 10, the other with 25 software engineers chosen from a widespread sample, covering all qualification levels and dp-domains. These interviews served as an analytical reconstruction of programmers' real working processes.working process

After a few words on the analytical perspective which leads me through the empirical material, I would like to present three selected topics of programmers' practice: the first topic will be about individual organization of working steps; the second addresses the different practices of internal documentation and representation during the design process; and the third one deals with formal and informal structures of communication. Summarizing these findings I will then refer to what I see as the characteristic qualities and problems of programming work in general[1] and software designing work in particular. Finally, I come to some remarks on requirements for and problems with software engineering methods and tools.

This section is concerned with 'Design Activities and Representations for Design'. This may be useful for analytical purposes, but may involve the danger of preferring a view which abstracts over the perspective of everyday work which directs programmers in their daily task performance. In order to understand 'what they really do' we have to be aware of the fact that programming practice is much less a 'carrying out' of distinct tasks — as suggested by the conventional life-cycle-oriented models of the programming process — but a 'mixing up' and restructuring of all the various tasks to a new reality of work.

My analytical perspective tries to take this into account. The focus of my analytical interest is the 'doing' ('Tätigkeit') of programmers[2]. To 'perform' or to 'carry out' a task suggests a fully determined activity, whereas the term 'doing' refers to concepts of work, in which working is seen as a process of constant assimilation of given constraints, requirements, restrictions, and opportunities. Thus, 'doing' in this respect implicates acts of interpretation, redefinition and adaptive reconstruction of tasks.

For analyzing the 'doing' of working people — and here especially of programmers — we need some knowledge about the 'material' of their interpretational and reconstructional acts as well. This consists of different qualities. First, there is the *explicit* part of the task: instructions, prescribed methods, the structure of the organization represented in documents, contracts, and different hierarchical positions. Second, we find *implicit* aspects like informal norms and standards ('state of the art'), experience generated in the organization, non-documented knowledge about the project. The third aspect finally results from the *'materiality*

---

[1] As 'programming work' I regard the total amount of work to be done by programmers while producing programs. This includes the 'centre tasks' of design, coding, and at least a partial test of system components. Requirements analysis, the overall design, the overall test and maintenance duties are also belonging to what I call 'programming work' although not every programmer is in all cases involved in all of these tasks.

[2] I use the term 'doing' ('Tätigkeit') related to a theoretical concept for the analysis of work developed by a group of German social scientists — see (Projektgruppe Automation und Qualifikation, 1987). In their investigation they made a difference between the requirements of labour emerging from the productive forces, the tasks as they are formulated by the management, and the real activities of workers in the working process. I prefer the translation 'doing' instead of 'activity' because to me it sounds less abstract.

of the subject'[3]. This refers to a basic structure of the working process, underlying any action related to this subject. The 'materiality of the subject' cannot be put into effect by organizations, intentions or interests: if a CPU is based on binary logic, no matter what a software project wants to realize, every concept related to this CPU has to refer to it in terms of binary logic, otherwise it will not work[4].

The important point is that although formal and informal aspects of the organization and the task, as well as methods and tools, refer to the 'materiality of the subject', they also implicate other 'structures of relevance' ('Relevanzstrukturen'). The organization represents economic interests, a certain relation of power; methods and tools should ease programmers' daily burden — but they also serve as work control. This is how organizational structures and tasks can find themselves contradicting the 'materiality of the subject'. Such contradictory structures clash in the working process. In our case, it is the programmer who — at the risk of failure — has to find a synthesis or at least a 'modus vivendi'. This need to deal with conflicting structures, resources and requirements is both a constraint and an opportunity. Because the working process is not completely determined by constraints and 'hard' structures, programmers are not only *forced* but also *allowed* to design it themselves. Moreover, if the set of structures given by the organization, via norms, methods, and tools is not a sufficient base for structuring decisions other resources have to be taken into account, for example cultural background, individual skills and dispositions, and so forth.

To prove this thesis and to provide some evidence I would like to discuss three aspects of the design process: the relationship between, and the individual organization of, working steps; representations of design decisions; and the role of communication.

2. What Programmers Really Do

2.1. Organizing the Working Steps

Looking at the typical software design process[5], we can make out a set of different working steps to be done: requirement analysis, design specification, design, coding, testing, installation, documentation. Former concepts of software engineering which claim that these steps should be done and would be done successively, are obsolete — at least in the scientific discussion — see for example (Boehm, 1988). In fact we find various types of circular and iterative procedures in programming and it seems to be worth having a closer look.

Most programmers have first contact with their new project at some point along the requirement definition or early design phase. Sometimes they find at least rudimentary documents about application related requirements, sometimes there are only rough ideas or oral orders. The first thing they usually do is to start *'making'* their own task by reading documents, talking with people, and thinking together about the different requirements. Often this activity goes hand in hand with a horizontal division of labour. In 'making' the task as well as in collecting design ideas, there are different styles to be seen, which are related to the

---

[3] In the German sociological discussion, the idea of the 'materiality of the subject' and its implications for the working process was conceptualized by Ekardt, Hengstenberg & Löffler (1988).

[4] It is essential to point out that there are different 'materialities' in different fields. Programmers are experts of the constraints resulting from the 'materiality' of the programming field. The fact that they do not dispose of the 'materiality' of the application field often causes serious problems. Due to the matter of my empirical material I am only allowed to make statements about the programmers' perspective.

[5] Empirically we in fact find a huge variety of different types of software projects. For this purpose I will only talk about projects more generally.

type of problem they are dealing with (routine or non-routine, range of complexity) and also related to the individual preferences of the programmers: some like to communicate, while others gain their ideas sitting alone with a white piece of paper, staring holes into the wall.

In this phase, it often happens that programmers go to the machine and do some coding and testing. They do this for different reasons: one is that the complexity and the general uncertainty about the design problem requires a quick try-out of a sub-routine. This can be seen as a strategy of reducing complexity and uncertainty. If they fail with this sub-routine they find out early that it will be necessary to choose another approach, if it works properly they win at least a small but central 'island of certainty'. On the other hand it seems to be the attempt of re-installing something *sensuous* in this part of the mental work, to ease the understanding of the problem and to generate proper solutions. Also, this practice of '*mixing*' ('Durchmischung') is meant to be a break in the sometimes strenuous and severe phase of collecting and working out design ideas. We find similar strategies of 'mixing' also in other phases of the programming process.

The discussion of the variety of working process organization would remain incomplete if we did not talk about the embeddedness of the single programming process in the overall process of everyday work. At least in the cases I investigated, nearly all programmers were also involved in some aspects of maintenance work. This integration seems reasonable because, as the authors of a product, they are, in technical aspects, the only competent experts for maintenance tasks. In respect to the programming process of an actual project, the sudden appearance of maintenance calls are often rough interruptions of intensive mental processes (which is especially true for the phases of detecting bugs). In critical moments of their programming work, programmers sometimes apply strategies that minimize sources of disturbance. But the general dilemma remains: although they need the possibility of mental immersion, their sudden participation is also needed in heteronomous processes like the maintaining of 'old' programs in cases of actual disfunctionalities. Neither can they completely isolate themselves nor can they stay 'open' to all requests from 'outside'. They are forced to find a 'modus vivendi' with these two conflicting requirements.

So we can summarize that there is no certain structure of the working process in programming. Programmers (as individuals or in teams) are always forced to find their own appropriate mixture related to, the 'materiality of the subject' as well as to their individual dispositions like experience, self assurance etc., expressed in their working styles.

2.2. Representation of Design Decisions and Ideas

The objectification of design ideas by written texts or graphical visualizations is an important means for individuals to save their ideas against sudden interruptions, it helps to span the mental distances especially in complex design tasks, and it seems to be a useful technique in achieving commitments: ideas get a certain concretion by being laid down in, for example diagrams or sketches. Beyond that, in cooperative working structures, visual representations of design ideas acquire a second set of functions: they are useful, and in some cases obviously necessary, to explain those ideas to the cooperants in a team, for example to make arrangements about common interfaces or to discuss sources of failures. Finally, a third set of functions is maintaining a documentation of the project progress independent of the author as an insurance against cancellation and as a mediation of design information in very large projects.

Software engineering methods provide programmers with many different diagram techniques, each with some level of structuredness and formality. But it is interesting to note that programmers apparently do not make constant use of them. Instead of working with those proper and clear tools and their helpful definiteness, they seem to prefer tiny pieces of worn-out paper on which they note obscure signs or draw incomprehensible figures. The reasons for this behaviour should be obvious. The more structured and clear a diagram technique is, the more information and certainty about the structure as a whole is required: names have to be found in order to conform to the company's standards, the place of a sub-routine in an overall structure has to be defined, etc. It is true that these functions have to be fulfilled before finishing a project, but we should be aware that the notes of programmers during design phases are not intended to serve the third of the above mentioned purposes. Instead of being a subject-independent objectification, expressed in a system of standardized general expressions, programmers' notes are meant to be somewhat like a *'sketchy-explanation-to-oneself'* ('skizzenhafte Selbstverständigung'): in their concrete work programmers only need a support for their brain and a *temporary* visual representation as a sort of projection board to lure out additional ideas and possibilities.

The formalization of scripts has no special benefits to the immediate working process, and in fact the programmers I talked to usually handled the internal representation of their design ideas and decisions dependent on what I labelled 'materiality of the subject'. For 'handy' everyday design problems and in smaller project teams, they do not take the effort of formalized notations in structured diagrams upon themselves. The limited purposes of this kind of documentation would not justify the expenditure of clarifying all details with definiteness. This, they only spend on problems of some complexity, where they need clear, structured and well defined diagrams in order to understand what is going on. More precisely, all the 'obviousnesses' underlying a program design need not be explicitly expressed in temporary representations of everyday designs. Only if a problem reaches a certain level of complexity or if it is a completely new approach, does a standard activity become unobvious and needs to be brought to mind.

We all know the 'documentation problem' in general as a tricky one. There are at least two further aspects worth mentioning. Firstly, the problem of inconsistency of comments in the headline: the recommended way of documenting the source code during the coding session is to put a short text in the head of every section or sub-routine which explains the structure and the functions of this part of the program. If programmers do not often make use of this way of documentation, it is less a question of laziness but rather a lack of practical use. Although made for supporting maintenance activities, the maintaining programmers can never be sure that the text is really consistent with the actual source code, because often alterations in the code (e.g. during debugging sessions) are made without adjusting the text passages.

Secondly, to write a customers documentation is not exactly the programmers' most preferred task. There are apparently two reasons for this aversion: One is an organizational reason, caused by the necessity of optimal exploitation of labour resources under conditions of a competitive profit system; new projects are started while documentation still needs to be done for the preceding ones. The other reason has something to do with programmer's subjective preferences resulting from their professional self definition: they usually do not define themselves as writers but as special types of technicians. This aspect of self definition may also have some influence on the above discussed aversion to writing complete and formalized documentation of design decisions.

2.3. Communication and Negotiation

Although the quantity and quality of communication needed and practised in software projects naturally differs with the huge variety of organizational structures in which programming work is embedded, there are some aspects to discuss in general. When asking programmers how and in which form they receive the requirements for the system to design, they remarkably often answered that they usually do not have real user-contact before starting the design work. The requirements are given to them by marketing experts, organizers, or by their superiors. If there are documents about requirement specifications at all, they are usually incomplete or with serious misconceptions and very often important parts of the task are handed over by acclamation. The necessity of 'making' their own task is mainly a communicational job. To understand the specific problem with this job we have to recall, in short, the way requirements reach the programmer's desk. Initially, formulations of the actual problem are commonly undertaken somewhere between the future users and their superiors. This description — often in terms of the 'application world' — will be handed over to organizers and the management. Suppose another company realizes the concept, managers of both sides will come to terms about a frame of conditions and the problem will be a matter of discussion between organizers of the customers side and the system analysts from the software company's marketing division. The results — more or less concrete and consistent requirements — will be given to the programming team, but not without passing the desk of the executives in the programming division.

Thus, there are a lot of very different departments and responsibilities involved with this communication process. Even if we only think of information in a technical sense, it is inevitable that what reaches the programmer will seriously differ from what users thought would have been handed over. The different instances appear as kinds of 'filters' between future users and the authors of their system. Filters may be useful for purposes of 'cleaning' the information of seemingly irrelevant 'particles', but sometimes the essence gets lost as well. As I pointed out above, information was spoken of in a merely technical sense or, more precisely, as if it would be something technical. However, the process we are dealing with actually consists mainly of 'negotiations' about how to reconcile the different, and in some aspects antagonistic, interests of the groups participating in the design process. So the requirement definition is fundamentally a *political process* and its result is a political product with all the inherent consequences[6].

With regard to the communicational aspect of programming, this means that all the requirement information programmers receive has a 'certain aspect of uncertainty' (which results from one basic aspect of the 'materiality' of design, its general contingency): requirements are compromises as the result of a particular constellation of power, they reflect for example the different extent of influence management and works councils can exert on the reorganization of working processes related to a new system. Programmers are part of this constellation in two respects: they certainly have their own particular interests (for example, to get an interesting project in which they can realize something ambitious in a technical respect); and they are the ones with responsibility for the 'runability' and the functioning of the resulting product.

Thus, what programmers do while 'making' their task is negotiating — and this action runs through the whole programming process: negotiations with their managers about the time

---

[6] Friedrich Weltz et al. found out a lot about this aspect. They use the German expression 'innerbetriebliche Handlungskonstellationen' — see (Weltz & Lullies, 1983) and (Weltz, Lullies & Ortmann, 1991).

frame, with the marketing division about the 'realizability' of functions, with system designers about mistakes discovered in the operating system, and so on. In this they have to be aware of their double perspective as self-interested actors and at the same time advocates of what I called 'materiality of the subject'.

Thinking of the above described functionally and hierarchically 'filtered' communication process, raises the question of reorganizing this process to support more direct interaction between users and programmers. Asking my interviewees, I received, at first glance, surprising answers. Although all of them expressed their discomfort with the hierarchical influence and the lack of information in the communication structure and resulting misconceptions in design specifications, they did not agree to the proposed solution of enhanced direct communication. The reason is that apart from the disfunction, the existing communication structure is a shelter against an *'unspecific claiming'* ('unspezifische Inanspruchnahme') by users and other non-technical participants. Programmers do not always get the information they need, but at least they would have less disturbance for irrelevant reasons; the existing communication structure functions in this regard as *'ambivalent filters'*. This should not keep us from thinking about the reorganization of communication, but we have to realize the inevitability of these two conflicting functions, which are just one more indicator of the heterogeneity of requirements to be fulfilled in the programming process. Although a constant flow of information and a permanent process of bargaining is necessary, programming requires mental immersion as well.

3. Conclusions

3.1. Peculiarities of the Programming Process

After this discussion of the three exemplary topics of programmers' design activities, I would like to pick up the 'red thread' again to stress some more general aspects characterizing the peculiarities of the programming process before discussing a few conclusions about the use of and problems with methods and tools. The first point to mention is that programming is a task consisting of very heterogeneous activities and requirements. *'Heterogeneity'* is to be found at different levels:

- Even the working steps are heterogeneous in themselves and require very different capabilities and competencies as to be seen in the design task with its conflict between communicational needs and the necessity of mental immersion. The relation between the single working steps also contains heterogeneity, if we compare, for example, the creativity needed in some parts of design activity and the meticulousness indispensable for successful coding.

- The second level of heterogeneity lies in the tension between given organizations, methods, and tools on one hand and practical requirements on the other (e.g. the conflicts between hierarchical structures in organizations and the necessity of free information flow for fitting programs). This aspect of heterogeneity is closely attached to the tension between the 'materiality of the subject' and aspects like organizational interests in control over the labour process and the 'logic of commercialization' ('Verwertungslogik').

- A third level of heterogeneity is formed by the divergent interests existing in a field with such an amount of participants coming from different 'sides' and acting with different goals. The process of programming has to bring those different perspectives together in one definite product whose advocates are the programmers.

- Finally, and related to the just mentioned aspect, heterogeneity appears in the, often very different, cultures of the various fields and communicational and work-related styles. For example, application programmers have to bring together at least the mentality of bank clerks with the 'structures of relevance' of their own field.

Besides heterogeneity we have to talk about the basic fact of 'uncertainty' underlying the programming process in general and the design work especially. As far as I have explored this problem, there are at least two major sources of uncertainty:

The first is that bringing forth anything new is a *creative work* in which the requirements and the results cannot be anticipated completely. It is true that a lot of software solutions are not in any or all regards new, and certainly there is an aspect of routine in design work as well, but the fact remains that the 'nature' of design consists of the creation of something new and no matter what routines can be established, there is always an important part of creative work remaining — and this is why companies pay programmers.

The second source is the uncertainty resulting from the growing *complexity* of application problems and their technical solutions. Although binary logic is, in principle, the most clear and unequivocal matter we can imagine, the sum of small logic structures bears 'monsters' of at least seeming irrationality. With the growing range of complexity it becomes more and more evident that programmers cannot be capable of overviewing all environmental factors and all internal feedback implemented in the structure as a whole. So system reactions seem to be irrational, and programmers cannot foresee later results of combining certain structures to a new one. This is to be seen most clearly in large systems or in networks.

'Uncertainty' results in 'indefiniteness' ('Unbestimmtheit') of software tasks. Uncertainty hinders the formulation of complete job orders. This is a general feature of nearly all types of work, but my thesis is that, in programming work, this problem appears in a special intensity that allows us to claim uncertainty as a constituent quality of programming. This lack of definiteness has to be filled with the programmer's own risky assumptions and decisions. For purposes of reducing risk, programmers are forced to initiate searching and clearing activities by *'negotiating'* with other participants. Thus the *communicational character* of programming work is not simply an additional effect of cooperation in large projects but the consequence of programming's inherent lack of definiteness. As communication is ubiquitous in cooperative work, we could better call *'negotiativeness'* another constitutional attribute of programming work.

One of the typical 'silent conflicts' in software companies is that the hierarchical distribution of responsibilities and spheres of competence does not fit with the necessities of the working process. The consequence often seems to be *'informal action'*: programmers do, for example, some unofficial bargaining with competent users apart from official communication channels, just to keep the project going on successfully. Curtis, Krasner & Iscoe (1988) called this 'boundary spanning', but more in a sense of 'bridging' an informational gap. I consider it noteworthy that the underlying problem is a conflict between formal competence and actual skills and experience.

Thus 'heterogeneity' and 'uncertainty' result in a double consequence for programmers: they are *forced* to take over the initiative and they *have the chance* to take responsibility and to bring their own personality to both the design of a software product as well as the design of the working process. On the other hand this twofold challenge to programmers causes situations in which work tends to break through the established boundaries between work and private life. Remarkably often, programmers described situations in which they — especially while under high pressure of project progress — found solutions under the shower or in sleepless nights (maybe 'under the lamppost' — see (Curtis et al., 1987)). To have paper and pencil at hand in such situations appears to them as a professional matter of course.

If my thesis about the 'negotiativeness' of programming work and the importance of programmer's subjective contribution to this work makes some sense, programming should be discussed in regard to its *cultural aspect*: what preferences do programmers have and what are their cultural sources? What about divergent disciplinary cultures of the various groups and organizations involved in negotiating relations? These questions are not the subject of my considerations here but they should be mentioned as suggestions for further discussions (Strübing, 1993).

3.2. What Tools Cannot Achieve

Based on the proceeding statements, the question of good methods and tools should be: How to serve programmer's self-responsibility and risky 'doing', and furthermore, are methods and tools the solution to obvious problems?

First of all I would like to state that between the *intended* use of software tools designed by software engineering experts and their *real* use lies a gap deep enough to swallow up a large amount of ill-begotten software and mis-spent money. For example, the CASE tools idea to assist and lead programmers during the whole programming process seems not to be of much practical relevance — high selling rates of these tools do not indicate the contrary: it is the company who invests in CASE tools and the programmer who does not use them as indicated. When my interviewees referred to their practice with tools I got the impression that they use them only partially and only in some cases. For example, they use Nassi–Shneiderman Diagrams to get a tricky design problem structured but never would they put every programming task into such a diagram. In their talks they usually reflect very clearly the informality which lies in such a practice; they refer to the official way of using tools in terms of offending a company's norm.

The main problem with the use of tools appears to be the *tendency of formalization* inherent to software tools. They require a 'definiteness' of structuring and labelling and thereby cause such a high amount of work just to serve the tool, that programmers often decide to avoid their usage. Additionally, software tools require the constant use of computers and although programming deals with computers as a subject, not all programmers prefer to do all their work with computers. It is inevitable for coding and testing, but large parts of design work can be done with paper and pencil — and a lot of my interviewees prefer to do so.

But it would be idealistic to think of tools as made only to serve the comfort of programmers: CASE tools and tools to support the documentation serve essentially the company's purposes of making software work more person-independently and to standardize processes as well as products. Though this may be important for managing large software projects, it nevertheless ignores the characteristics of programming work. In a word, I would say that programming work has certain inherent *boundaries against standardization*. One of which is the forcing relation to the 'materiality' of the various subjects and another is the close attachment of the programming process to the (unstandardizable) personality of programmers. We should accept the fact that programming is the work of 'authors' rather than of 'clerks'. This difference should be reflected in the tool discussion. It is astonishing to me, although maybe knowing software engineering it shouldn't be, that every time software engineering is asked to propose solutions for more effective programming processes it bears a *technical* approach: a method, a tool, a machine. My thesis is, on the contrary, that better solutions can be found by thinking about communicational skills, structures of cooperation, altered hierarchies, and so on.

To summarize: 'uncertainty', 'heterogeneity', 'negotiativeness', and 'informal action' are — and this may be the most general conclusion — inevitable attributes of programming work. They have to be taken into account, otherwise any programming process will fail. Although the organization often does not adequately deal with these basic qualities, most programmers do, because of their direct and daily experience of both: the 'materiality of the subject', and the short-comings of organizations as well as of methods and tools. The result is a double reality: the one represented in formal structures and official relations and the other one of the programmers' informal 'muddling through'.

Modelling Cognitive Behaviour in Specification Understanding

Francisco C Simplício Filho

Imperial College, Department of Computing, 180 Queen's Gate, London SW7 2BZ, UK.
EMail: fcs@doc.ic.ac.uk

Embrapa, DIN, W3 Norte Parque Rural, Brasília, CEP:70770, Brasil.
EMail: fcs@sede.embrapa.br

Understanding complex and unfamiliar domains is a demanding task performed in most software development projects. Specifications play an important role in achieving and sharing this understanding among project members; specifications are used as a tool for understanding. Little is known about this activity. This chapter examines the modelling of cognitive behaviour in the activity of specification understanding. It focuses on the control mechanisms that guide the understander in deciding what to pursue and which parts of the specification to work on next. It reviews relevant models of understanding in the related activities of program understanding and design, and extend them in order to identify the key features of specification understanding. This chapter concludes that the activity is best described in terms of a distributed control architecture, where competing sources of knowledge and different strategies of application of knowledge can be controlled in a systematic or opportunistic way. Based on these features some requirements for providing suitable assistance tools are discussed. It is suggested that symbolic simulation, alone, may not provide enough support to specification understanding. It requires additional assistance to deal with opportunistic behaviour.

Keywords: specification understanding, cognitive behaviour, opportunistic behaviour, design, program understanding.

1. Introduction

Specification is one of the most important phases of software development and is becoming still more important, as software engineering progresses towards more automated and productive processes of software development. In addition, specification plays an important cognitive role. Specifications are used as a tool for understanding. As pointed out by Turski & Maibaum (1987), the key to the specification's role is twofold: precision and understanding. Specification is a process of achieving common understanding at a suitable level of precision. In contrast with formal methods research, which focuses on precision, our work focuses on the complementary issue of understanding.

Specification understanding plays a much more important role in software engineering than has commonly been thought. Using a given specification to achieve understanding is rarely seen as a significant activity. However, it is real and usual in many activities such as design, programming, inspection, maintenance and reuse. The comprehension of specifications generated automatically from programs has been pointed out as an open problem in reverse engineering. Indeed, there is little use in exhorting software designers to expend effort in building good specifications if they can not be understood. Research in specification understanding may also contribute to other areas of research related to large and complex software development. First, it may contribute to meeting the challenge (Soloway, 1986) of bridging the gap between 'programming-in-the-small' and 'programming-in-the-large'. Since specifications are abstractions (Maibaum, 1986) and abstractions are important means for coping with complexity, it is reasonable to suggest that specification understanding is an important component of the distinction between these two programming extremes. Second, research in specification understanding may help formal methods to scale up to practical industrial software development. There is a considerable amount of work in formally based specifications. However, currently these techniques, which are tractable in small academic demonstrations, do not scale up well to practical industrial software development (Finkelstein, 1989). We suggest that, in general, formal specifications do not characterize real world abstractions in a form that aids human understanding. Research in specification understanding may provide a basis for a better match between the understanders requirements and the 'mechanically oriented' formal specification.

Many issues in how people understand specifications seem intimately related to human cognitive or problem solving limitations. Suitable tools and techniques may help to overcome some of them (Guindon & Curtis, 1986). However, a detailed comprehension of the cognitive requirements of specification understanding is essential for placing the development of such tools on a sound engineering footing (Newell & Card, 1985).

2. Issues in Specification Understanding

A central feature of understanding is that the explicit content of a discourse is usually only a blue print for an underlying state-of-affairs (Johnson-Laird, 1989). This blueprint relies on the understander to complete the missing details. People are seldom aware of these additional inferences though they may show up subsequently in recalling discourse (Clark, 1977). These inferences may depend on general knowledge, but their conclusions are usually only derivable from an underlying understanding. At issue here, is whether this individual underlying understanding is relevant to the role of the specification as a tool for sharing understanding.

We devised the following example to illustrate that even the use of formal notations cannot entirely avoid different understandings. It also illustrates that different understandings may exert substantial influence over the subsequent developments. The theory of abstract data-type specification has been one of the key concepts in providing an intuitive formal account of computation. A common criticism of this theory is that the axioms that define the types are rather arbitrary; that is, a single type may be defined by different specifications. de Queiroz & Maibaum (1989) proposed a formal framework extending the data-type formalism. They introduce a single linguistic framework which, instead of allowing an arbitrary number of axioms for each type, provides a calculable principle to determine when there are enough. Based on this framework different types may be compared.

The theory of Lisp lists and the theory of Stacks are presented by the formalism. From them, it can be proved that lists and stacks are the same structure. It is claimed that the more intuitively appealing semantic view of the proposed formalism can make artificial distinctions disappear, such as the distinction between what seem two instances of the same data structure. The operations that define their theories are equivalent:

Emptystack = Nillist
Push(a,b) = Cons(a,b)
Top(s) = Car(s)
Pop(s) = Cdr(s)

In contrast, we suggest that the representation that constitutes a specification is not the only product of the process of specification building. It also involves understanding in individual terms. For most people, stacks and lists are different. However, stacks and lists are analogous and some of their analogous aspects are exposed by their specification in the proposed formalism. The formalism reveals the operational aspect but ignores others. For example, if stacks and lists were the same structure, the following judgment should be true for both of them: a stack becomes higher after adding a new element to it. The judgment holds for stacks but not for lists. It includes a 'spatial' aspect, not captured by the formalism.

Most significant however, is the fact that, although they are the same structure, lists and stacks have experienced simultaneous but quite different developments. The notion of stacks has been applied in arithmetic evaluation, implementation of programming languages and stack-oriented computer architectures. Lists, on the other hand, have become the core notion for the development of symbolic processing, being applied in programming languages, computer architectures and many symbolic applications. This is a testimony to the significant influence that different understanding may exert. Could the symbolic processing applications be developed based on the notion of stacks? Since they are the same structure, the answer is yes. But actually they were not. The different understanding underlying stacks and lists favour different applications. To focus on specific aspects is not wrong. Abstractions like these are relevant components of how we perceive and are able to interact intelligently with the world (Winograd & Flores, 1986). But it is wrong to assume that other aspects are 'artificial' as suggested by de Queiroz & Maibaum.

3. Cognitive Behaviour in Specification Understanding

Current research on modelling understanding tends to focus on the development of specialized representations. This approach focuses on the knowledge held by the understander, its structure and its relationships. Representations like 'plans' (Détienne & Soloway, 1990) and 'design schemas' (Guindon, 1990a; Soloway & Ehrlich, 1984), to name a few, offer different, but related constructs to describe different organizations of the understander's knowledge (Brooks, 1990). The assumption is that an increase in the information that can be captured in machine processable forms improves our ability to automate parts of specification construction, understanding and evolution. A major problem with theories of understanding based on knowledge representation is their incompleteness. As pointed out by Winograd & Flores (1986) the background knowledge cannot be represented as a set of explicit propositions. The overwhelming nature of knowledge may make it difficult, impossible perhaps, to construct a complete explicit representation. However, knowledge organization is not everything; the mechanisms that use knowledge are equally relevant. A scientific account of how knowledge is acquired, retained, and used in interpreting the world does not necessarily call for a complete specification of all knowledge (Johnson-Laird, 1989). In order to understand how knowledge is used, research focuses on the cognitive behaviour, in particular focuses on the control mechanisms that produce the behaviour and guide the understander in deciding what to pursue and which parts of the problem to work on next. Models of these dynamic processes are in their infancy and are the subject of our particular attention. The emphasis is on assisting the activity of understanding rather than automating it.

Divergent models of cognitive behaviour in the activity of program understanding have been proposed. Three contributions are particularly relevant to this chapter: Brooks (1983), Letovsky (1986) and Détienne & Soloway (1990). Important differences in the way that their models explain the process of understanding arise from the way in which they see this process as being 'driven'. According to Brooks, understanding starts with the generation of primary hypotheses, as a tool for reducing the problem space to a manageable level, and progresses toward their verification. Letovsky, by contrast, suggests that it starts with information gathering which leads to questions, which lead to conjectures as an attempt to answer questions. Détienne & Soloway, in their turn, propose that the process is driven by goals. Cognitive strategies are selected and used according to the goals achieved by each strategy in response to expectation failures. In Simplício (1991) we have reviewed these models in detail and have suggested that they can be looked at in other terms. The process of understanding can be described in terms of data-driven or theory-driven models, as reflecting a classical dilemma in philosophy of science about what comes first: the observation that leads to the theory or the theory that leads to a focused observation. In the theory-driven models, the understanding process starts with a formation of hypotheses and progresses towards their verification by observation. The Brooks' model describes program understanding as theory-driven. Letovsky model describes it as data-driven. It starts with information gathering, the observation, which leads to questions, which lead to conjectures and so on. Détienne & Soloway introduce a goal-driven approach. The selection and use of strategies are guided by the goal achieved by them. However, no single approach is complete by itself and raises different open issues. For example:

- In the theory-driven approach, where do the hypotheses come from?
- In the data-driven approach, what should be observed in the data, since the observation is not constrained by a theory?
- In the goal-driven approach, how do you know the goals are achieved, in other words, how do you specify goals in advance and verify them later on?

In conclusion, we assume that several processes often alternate or even blend together.

Other models have been proposed to account for cognitive behaviour during design. Current studies, for example, Visser (1990) and Guindon (1990b), have observed that designers do not follow a strict order of activities and suggest that prescriptive models, such as the top-down approach, cannot fully explain the behaviour of understanding. The designer often abandons the prescribed action to perform a deviation, that is, an alternate action. Guindon (1990b) suggests that such deviations are not due to inadequate application of the top-down model, but they are natural consequences of the ill-structuredness of the problem being solved. Problem solving behaviour in this cases seem best characterized as 'opportunistic'. Guindon discuss two possible models to account for the opportunistic behaviour in design: blackboard architecture and ACT*. On one side, opportunistic planning has been modelled with a blackboard architecture (Hayes-Roth & Hayes-Roth, 1979). On the other side, according to Anderson (1983) behaviour which appears to violate hierarchical planning may actually be due to simple failures of working memory; some goals may be simply forgotten while the designer is looking for details. So, opportunistic behaviour can also be accounted for in the ACT*. The two models can make behaviourally equivalent predictions. However, it is speculated that these models would suggest different ways of supporting software designers. Anderson would insist on a process with hierarchical goal structure. The blackboard model would insist on supporting flexible and easily organizable goal structures, thus in line with Guindon's conclusions.

We support the hypothesis that cognitive behaviour is best described in terms of a distributed architecture which may be seen as a generalization of blackboard architectures. First, if problem solving is understood in terms of goals and the plans to achieve them, then we have to consider that goals may be highly dynamic and a product of the understander's active interaction with the environment. There is no known way to anticipate goals accurately. New goals may be generated from existing ones. For example, a new goal may generate the further goals of determining whether it has been achieved and recording what was accomplished. Second, some behaviours seem not to be fully determined by goals but rather by underlying psychological mechanisms. For example, cognitive processes may be interrupted by unanticipated events like the understander recalling from memory a related specification segment. So, while some cognitive processes are undertaking particular activities, others should be monitoring the memory and the environment for information that might cause these activities to be interrupted. This points to a distributed model of cooperating concurrent processes. So, a proper model of the cognitive behaviour should assume that the understander deals with a dynamic set of goals, alternates several strategies, and is based on underlying concurrent mechanisms. However, such a model has yet to be developed.

4. Key Features of Specification Understanding

The review above shows that currently no single model addresses all the activity of specification understanding. This conclusion is compatible with Soloway (1986) and Brooks (1990). However, so far, the activity can be characterized by the following key features:

- The activity includes the interacting processes of hypothesis generation and hypothesis verification. The first deals with the evocation of representations from the understander memory and the second deals with the activation of cognitive processes that can lead to the integration of observations into the evoked representation.

- Hypothesis generation depends on the understander knowledge about the problem domain. When the understander deals with unfamiliar domains, the lack of this knowledge often leads to incomplete or unsuccessful hypotheses.

- Hypothesis verification relies mostly on the cognitive process of symbolic simulation, which is used for simulation of scenarios in the problem domain.

- Simulation of scenarios is the main source of recognition of opportunities for applying knowledge to other situations.

- The activity combines several strategies of application of knowledge, in particular data-driven, theory-driven and goal-driven strategies.

- There is no evidence for a general and objective mechanism of selection of cognitive actions, and consequently, no general linking structure between partial solutions.

- About half of the behaviour of the activity is not systematic and in unfamiliar situations the behaviour is best characterized as opportunistic in which deviations from a systematic approach and drifting from partial solutions in a sequence of associated partial solutions can be expected.

5. Implications for Tool Support

The features above provide some basis for discussing how to support the activity of specification understanding. Since the activity involves hypothesis generation and verification both processes should be supported. However, to provide direct support to hypothesis generation may be difficult. It relies on the understander knowledge and skills and may be influenced by other levels of psychological mechanisms, such as motivation or stress. The answer may be to provide an indirect support. Hypothesis generation and verification are interdependent. Failings in generating good hypotheses are counteracted by verifying them. These are arguments for tools able to support mainly hypothesis verification. Since the domain knowledge plays a relevant role in hypothesis verification, this is an argument in favour of knowledge based specifications and against abstract specifications. In addition, opportunistic behaviour usually leads from one partial solution to another, in a sequence of associated partial solutions. This suggests that tools should be able to deal with arbitrary parts of a given specification and that the building of associations between partial solutions is an important area to support. The understander may prefer to verify partial solutions in an associated familiar domain. Keeping the associations may help to provide fast access to associated solutions and new insights for less experienced understanders.

A crucial issue here is whether opportunistic behaviour should be avoided or supported. Opportunistic behaviour has been broadly described as an ineffective approach, an approach that is difficult to perform and to control, and an approach likely to produce incorrect solutions (Guindon, 1990b). However, empirical studies have shown that about half of the problem solving behaviour has been characterized as opportunistic. Thus, it cannot be regarded as noise, or inadequate applications of a systematic approach. Rather, this considerable proportion together with the models of the activity discussed above suggest that opportunistic behaviour is a legitimate and expected cognitive behaviour. Attempting to support it seems more realistic. Some issues arise when we combine the decision of supporting both hypothesis verification and opportunistic behaviour. It seems clear that simulation of scenarios in the problem domain should be supported, particularly with symbolic simulation tools. However, contrary to the expectation that simulation tools would directly help understanding, we argue that their use may result in more opportunistic behaviour. Mental simulation is the main source of recognition of opportunities of application of knowledge to other contexts. The more exercise in a particular simulation, the more it becomes a source of consistent knowledge and the more other related knowledge is activated from the understander memory. This suggests that tools for symbolic simulation, graphics and logic animation tend to increase the need for supporting opportunistic behaviour. Without it, possible advantages with the use of animation tools may be wasted either with frequent drifting and deviations or with the constraints imposed on the understander.

6. Conclusion

This chapter has reviewed some representative models of cognitive behaviour in program understanding and design and discussed how they contribute to modeling the activity of specification understanding. In particular, we have focused on the cognitive control mechanisms. From these models some key features and requirements of the activity have been identified. We conclude that the activity is best characterized in terms of a distributed control architecture in which concurrent sources of knowledge and several strategies of application of knowledge can be controlled in either a systematic or opportunistic way. However, a detailed model based on this approach is yet to be developed. Based on the key features we suggest that both hypothesis verification and opportunistic behaviour are important areas to support. We also suggest that without combined support, the possible advantages in the use of animation tools may be wasted either because of frequent deviations or constraints imposed on the understanding activity.

Acknowledgements

I would like to thank Anthony Finkelstein and Thomas Maibaum for their comments in earlier versions of this chapter. The author is supported by grants from Embrapa and CNPq.

Theme 1 Discussion Report

1. Introduction

The workshop's first session titled 'Design Activities and Representations for Design' covered a large number of topics and approaches. There were talks from computer scientists as well as from software psychologists and from a sociologist. The areas covered in this theme ranged from an overview of the different and changing patterns of addressing the 'problem of problem solving' (Davies & Castell), via empirical reports dealing with strategies in programming practice and their underlying constraints (Détienne, Strübing, Visser), to suggestions for software 'redesigning' (Bellamy), and 'reverse engineering' (van Zuylen). Not all of these aspects found themselves reflected in the final discussion, which rather focused on a couple of questions derived from the concluding talk about design of the working process.

2. The Questions

There were four questions given to the discussion groups:

1. A lot of problems in programming work are closely attached to the complexity of tasks and the growing size of large projects. Are there any ideas how to reduce, if not the level of complexity of tasks, at least the size of projects so as to remove the problem of marginal utility in large projects?

2. One important aspect of the task of designing software is communication and — even more important — negotiation, although it is neither part of the job descriptions nor taught in programmer's training. If the competence of 'boundary spanning' is not to remain the domain of a few exceptional programmers, what can be done to strengthen programmer's competence in these 'political' processes?

3. In software engineering methods, tool conceptions, and organization of work there seem to exist conflicting definitions of what programmers should be seen as: Are they 'authors' or 'clerks'? Do we need the programmer for their unique, creative contribution in programming or do we want them to be interchangeable workers doing standardized routine jobs? Which of the alternatives or which different concept is to be prefered and what could this mean for organization, methods, and tools?

4. Although made *by* software experts *for* software experts, a lot of tools seem to be costly academic exercises rather than a pragmatic support for programmer's everyday work. Organizational structures like hierarchies and areas of competence often appear unfitted to deal with the requirements resulting from the task, but it appears that software designers usually have a more appropriate practice. This raises the question

of what could be a proper means to benefit from their knowledge when thinking about methods and tools?

The different discussion groups did not try to answer all these questions but usually chose only one or two aspects or themes found within the questions. In this report I will concentrate on the main themes of the various discussions without outlining the discussion process of every single group. While reflecting the discussions of this first session, I couldn't resist adding my own personal comments and remarks. To underline the intention that these comments are neither censorship nor a later correction of the discussion, they appear in italics to separate them from the main report.

3. The Discussion

3.1. Authors, Clerks and the Question of Creativity

The first topic in the discussion focused on the concept of 'the programmer' and what might be the best definition of the role. One attempt to answer the question was to investigate the type of tasks programming work consists of. It was argued that if a task is mere mechanical routine it would be better done by machines such as compilers rather than by programmers, so the conclusion was that at least some *intellectual* effort will always be necessary. No answer could be found to the question of whether *creativity* is also an inevitable feature of programming tasks. In a second attempt to answer the question, the discussants approached the problem by describing it in terms of the well known house-building metaphor: If building a system was like building a house, who would be the architect, who the building contractor, and who the bricklayer? By discussing this metaphor, it turned out that the label 'programmer' seems to be of little use. While the system architects were seen as more comparable with real architects, system engineers were seen as having more similarity with building contractors, because both have to translate specifications into feasible implementations. Finally, the correspondence of the bricklayers task — which has been described as dealing with the minutiæ — was found in the mechanical transformation process undertaken by the compiler. Creativity in this respect would be concentrated mainly in the system architects' task, whereas the system engineer would need less and the creativity necessary to find solutions for compiler problems would be part of the architectural task of compiler writers.

I fear the house-building metaphor is of little use for discussions about the type(s) of work in programming or in system building as a whole, since it suggests the existence of the same structure of division of labour in the 'modern' type of work represented in programming as is practised in the more 'traditional' work of building houses. There seems to be a lot of similarities between the architects' work of designing a building and the work of designing an edp-system, but there is a significant difference as well, architects designing houses wouldn't usually lay bricks whereas software designers very often combine their design work with at least some parts of 'laying program-bricks'. What the discussion labelled 'system engineering' deals with architectural tasks as well and a strict segregation between design and implementation — at least in industrial practice in Germany — does not exist.

3.2. Negotiation

As a second focus, there was a discussion about the importance of negotiation in programming work. It was stressed that negotiation means more than communication: it requires an evening out of divergent interests — which is different from just transmitting information. The need for negotiation was seen as resulting from the various sources of contingency in the programming process. Even the mere translation of different terms from one 'world' to the other involves negotiation: it is not only to prove that the same sense is shared but to recognize the underlying claims and politics inherent in these terms and to bring them to a suitable solution which can be objectified in an edp-system.

The task of negotiating is made more difficult by feelings of ownership as they usually result from creating ideas. To match different approaches or concepts of a future system requires not just compromises but also a cut back on at least parts of ones own design to serve a common product.

Negotiation itself is not a task of special difficulty, such skills are found in various professions. The problem in programming work derives from the gap between the high amount of negotiation work required in programming projects and the role of programmers as it is conceptualized in, for example, job descriptions, programming courses and computer science teaching. Often programming seems to be nothing but a *technical* job. The discussion underlined the need to change this role to make the required skills in negotiation explicit.

The discussion also addressed the issue of whether technical solutions to the negotiation task are feasible. Although CSCW tools were seen as a way in the direction of a better support for communication in groups, it was pointed out that for real negotiation problems there are no technical solutions in sight.

3.3. Design Tools

In a third approach, the discussion turned to a more pragmatic attempt of outlining a concept for an ideal tool to support programmers' design work. The general conclusion was to demand a type of 'sketching tool' with the following main features:

- *Provisionality*: The possibility of being vague or uncommitted, but still able to express some idea.

- *Abstraction*: A way of being precise at one point and yet to abstract over detail in other parts.

- *Behaviour*: A design produced with such a tool must give a faithful impression of the final product. Although prototyping tools approach this ideal, they are not sufficient since they do not allow abstractional provisionality.

- *Clarity*: The design should serve the basic needs of reasoning and evaluation by being understandable by the designer and by other designers whose work may be affected by it, but it need not necessarily be communicable to users.

- *Demonstrability*: Although it is not necessary to make the notated design understandable to the user, its provisional result should be demonstrable to the user.

Because Christmas is near [1] *I would like to add one more desirable feature to this 'list of things one would like': An ideal sketching tool should be handy enough so as not to force the programmers to invest too much work just in serving the needs of the tool instead of bringing forward the design itself.*

Knowing that a tool like this is not in sight, the discussion group demanded at least the supply of software design work with good templates which could express complex generalities, with some possibility of recording design ideas and delineating the design space to improve programmers' understanding of the problem.

---

[1] At the time of writing, anyway — eds.

4. Conclusion

These were three main topics covered in the session's final discussion. Limited time did not allow the group to address more of the underlying structural problems of programming work and led to a quite quick move to more pragmatic tool suggestions. At any rate, the result of the negotiation discussion should have shown that tools cannot be the answer to all problems in programmers' design work.

Jörg Strübing
Zentrum für Berufs- und Hochschulforschung, Gesamthochschule Kassel

Theme 2: Code Representation and Manipulation

Theme 2 Introduction

This theme includes chapters covering what is probably considered to be the established perspective on studies of programming skills. The focus is on coding behaviour and on the nature of programming languages, in so far as they support coding behaviour.

The main function of this theme is to convey a clear flavour of the type of work which has already been conducted, and to raise some remaining questions about coding behaviour which are still to be answered. The previous theme has addressed a growing concern with psychological skills used in program design and this theme is a partner in aiming to air the whole range of issues in relation to programming skills.

The opening chapter by Gilmore presents a psychological task analysis of the use of programming notations. There is a common belief that notations make little difference for expert programmers, but there is little or no evidence for such an argument — the error rates in software engineering do not suggest that notational slips are a trivial matter. This chapter assumes that software engineers who have to use some of their thinking capacity to deal with poor notations will pay less attention to the functionality and usability of the software being designed. Whereas many previous papers on this topic have stated that notation matters, this chapter tries to present a clear statement of how notations are used.

From such a general chapter, the second chapter by Patel et al. provides a contrast in offering a detailed evaluation of different notations for presenting program trace information. The key feature of their evaluation is the inclusion of different question types such that they can evaluate the different tracer notations in respect of different types of information. It might appear inevitable that they can reach no firm conclusions, since each tracer seems to support at least one type of information better than the others. However, the strength of this is that it leads to an improvement in our understanding of the rich variety of information structures present in software and serves to remind us of the criticality of supporting access to all these structures, not just one of them.

The next chapter by Teasley et al. relates notational features to the development of expertise. Although the property of role-expressiveness has not been well-defined in the literature, they use it to good effect, emphasizing that notational properties have knock-on effects throughout programming skill development. This is clearly an area which deserves more attention.

A common problem for novice software engineers (and their employers) is the fact that they have been taught languages other than that which they must use in employment. The chapter by Scholtz reviews studies on the transfer of skills between programming languages, with particular attention to the question of what this tells us about the way that people represent (mentally) their knowledge about programming languages. Her review comes to the conclusion that the evidence supports plan- or schema-based theories of programming knowledge.

A full definition of these theories can be found in the next chapter by Rist which presents one of the most detailed formalizations of a plan-based approach to programming knowledge. Remarkably, in doing so he also touches on one of the key issues — namely that systems must present multiple representations of programming information. Rist's thesis is that the program plan is common to all programming paradigms and thus provides a central description from which other representations can be generated.

The chapter by Waddington provides a review of the preceding contributions in the context of the need for reverse engineering tools. This concern with reverse engineering can be reflected back onto the chapter by van Zuylen in Theme 1. Waddington concludes that the usability of reverse engineering tools could be improved if their design took more account of what is known about the ways in which human experts comprehend code in the absence of design information.

The final chapter in this theme, by Monk et al., presents a sceptical view of this area which asks why designers are still using recognizably bad notations, despite all the best efforts of researchers to encourage them to use new well-designed notations. Although based on interviews with only six practitioners, the chapter provides an excellent reminder of the reflexivity of much of the research described in this proceedings — namely that whilst we might be concerned with the usability of tools and notations in software engineering, software engineers are more concerned with the apparent lack of usability of our research. The chapter also suggests some research issues which are yet to be addressed.

David Gilmore
Department of Psychology, University of Nottingham

Does the Notation Matter?

David Gilmore

Department of Psychology, University of Nottingham, Nottingham NG7 2RD, UK.

Tel: +44 (0)602 515287

EMail: dg@psyc.nott.ac.uk

Although the early focus in the study of psychological issues in computer programming was on the cognitive ergonomics of programming notations, there appears to be a growing feeling that the notation is of little importance now.

One reason for this is that the research lacks face validity, being inherently limited in the range of languages studied, in the subjects sampled and in the size and nature of the materials used. Many of the studies are regularly interpreted as criticisms of particular languages or features (e.g. the GOTO studies and the novice Prolog studies). Furthermore any principles articulated from these studies have often appeared to be limited in their generality.

This chapter will briefly look at some of this research, and present some of these principles. However, the central part of this chapter will examine ways of developing these principles into concepts more generalizable and more focussed. These developments will involve an examination of the psychological tasks which users must perform with notations. Six such tasks will be described, which although not being principles, may encourage more focussed research which could itself lead to the development of principles.

Another reason for lack of concern about notations is that design activity has become a greater focus of attention, compared with coding activities. The tasks described are, therefore, also intended to apply to notations used for representing design.

In conclusion, this chapter suggests that much of the research on coding behaviour could be viewed most usefully as research on the use of notations, which, regardless of any technological developments, will always be required in the software engineering process.

Keywords: notation, programming language design, naturalness, visual programming, program visualization, mental representations, perceptual processing, programming plan, beacons, connectedness, dynamic behaviour, role-expressiveness, variable naming, discrimination.

1. Is There any Argument?

Of course the programming notation matters — could anyone possibly want to argue with the suggestion that it does not? The literature on programming language design and use is littered

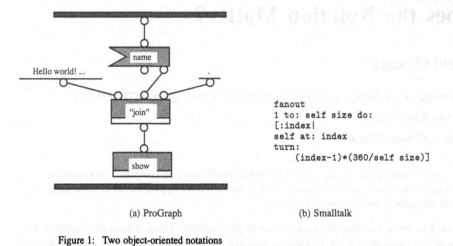

```
fanout
1 to: self size do:
[:index|
self at: index
turn:
        (index-1)*(360/self size)]
```

(a) ProGraph   (b) Smalltalk

Figure 1: Two object-oriented notations

with claims and counter-claims about the naturalness and the ease of use of various languages and paradigms (the current favourites being object-oriented and graphical languages). The very existence of these claims might suggest that people are only too aware that the notation matters. On the other hand the ease with which many people dismiss these claims could be used to argue that many people believe that notation does not matter.

However, the promotion of new paradigms and new languages is often based on claims about their mapping onto a natural language of thought, or a natural perception of the world. Thus, Booch (1986) writes that:

> "Perhaps the greatest strength of an object-oriented approach to development
> is that it offers a mechanism that captures a model of the real world."
> (Booch, 1986, p.220)

But, although these claims are being made about the paradigm, there are many different notations for object-oriented programming. For an extreme example consider ProGraph (a graphical language) and Smalltalk (see Figure 1). Here we can see that the claims relate more to the paradigm than to the notation — perhaps the implication is, in fact, that the notation does not matter as long as you have the right paradigm.

For a different example, consider the claims of visual programming, which often rely on the cliché that *a picture is worth a thousand words*. For example, Shu (1988) writes (in words) that:

> "Pictures are more powerful than words as a means of communication.
> Pictures aid understanding and remembering." (Shu, 1988, p.7)

Neither of these claims relates to the graphical notation and neither does the author seriously address the issue of whether these claims apply to all pictures, or just to some visual representations. Again we can examine the difference between ProGraph (Figure 1(a) above) and a Nassi–Shneiderman diagram — Figure 2, taken from (Shu, 1988). Note that these claims

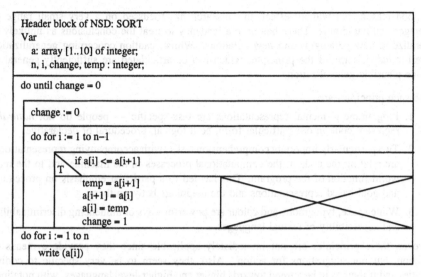

Figure 2: A Nassi–Shniederman diagram — from (Shu, 1988)

are orthogonal to claims about conventional programming paradigms (i.e. visual programming can be applied to many different computational models). Thus, Shu is making claims for a notational paradigm, based, I would argue, on a very one-dimensional view of human information processing.

The distinction between visual programming and program visualization (Baecker & Marcus, 1990) is useful here — visual programming is a notational paradigm, whereas program visualization is a technique for making programs more accessible and more informative. It is the latter which is the concern of this chapter, with the intention that the conclusions should apply across all notational and computational paradigms.

2. A Brief Historical Overview

Numerous studies have been performed on language constructs, programming styles and the problems that novices have in a particular language. I do not have space here to describe them in any detail; see (Hoc et al., 1990) for a more thorough review.

Most of the studies were performed in response to claims made about good programming practice, the nature of programming skills and the psychological processes involved in programming. Thus, the suggestion that GOTOs should be avoided led to studies on the design of conditional statements, whilst the claim that logic-programming reflected the natural language of thought gave rise to studies of novices learning Prolog.

In most cases, the research demonstrated that the claims were overstating their case, and rarely did the research offer a simple, coherent solution to any particular problem. Nevertheless, this style of research has continued, focussing increasingly on programmers' knowledge about their programs and asking questions about how environments and notations can best support those skills which programmers possess.

For good reason, but with ill effect, this research has focussed on a very small range of languages and paradigms. There has been a tendency to treat the conclusions as unlikely to generalize to new paradigms and new notations. Whilst, caution concerning generalization is well-founded, some of the principles which can be articulated are sufficiently general to provide plausible generalization.

Three such principles are:

1. Programmers' mental representations are task-specific — people do not *naturally* represent code in one particular form, be it logical, procedural or declarative.

2. Two particularly important comprehension tasks (with accompanying representations) are relating the code to the computational processes in the machine and to the real-world function of the program. This has led to a particular emphasis on procedural and goal-based representations and the mappings between them.

3. White space, typography and colour are powerful ways of influencing discriminability and accessibility of textual languages.

However, these principles are not immediately applicable since they provide a means of reflection, but not suggestions for action. Also, they seem to be very specific to coding activities and if there is to be a trend towards higher and higher-level languages, with notations for representing designs and design decisions, then it is necessary to find alternative ways of articulating these principles.

One possibility is to examine the psychological tasks which must be performed with notations, in contrast to the above principles which emphasize programming tasks. In the rest of this chapter I shall attempt to describe some of the important psychological tasks which notations need to support. These tasks are derived predominantly from the above three principles and from intuition, rather than from direct empirical evidence.

3. Psychological Tasks when Processing Notations

3.1. Discriminations Required with Notations

There are a variety of discriminations which notation-users need to be able to make readily and easily. Notation designers need to ensure that these are supported, though the relative importance of each may vary according to the programming context. As with all such human factors decisions there may be numerous methods for supporting different discriminations (e.g. through revised notational design, or through tools to support discrimination).

These discriminations are:

- symbol;
- location;
- action;
- function.

Symbol Discriminations

These are the low-level discriminations which make it easier to read/construct programs in the notation. Each of these discriminations may be of two types (the first of these is the one usually focussed upon by designers, but both are equally important):

1. Discrimination from the general background.

2. Discrimination from something of a similar appearance, but contrasting semantics.

An obvious example is the bracket in Lisp, which can be extraordinarily difficult to perceive precisely in a heavily nested structure. This is a classic example of discrimination from something of similar (*identical*) appearance. The brackets within Lisp, although of the same notational meaning (most of the time), actually exist in pairs, where discriminations about which bracket is paired with which bracket are important. This is also the classic example for tools in the environment supporting the discrimination.

An example of discrimination from the general background is the semi-colon in Pascal, which serves a critical role in the notation's syntax, but whose presence or absence can be tricky to perceive. This situation is not helped by the fact that the function of the semi-colon is not one which a novice programmer readily comprehends. There are two problems here — one involves a poor choice of symbol, whilst the other involves the poor notational structure, which requires a symbol at all. Thus, we have a small, tricky-to-perceive symbol, which fulfils an obscure computational function. It is not surprising that many mistakes occur.

Another example, less well-known, but with serious effects is the use of round and square brackets within the language POP11. As one would expect these occur in pairs, and they can be nested inside each other. However, the precise meaning of round brackets within square brackets is different from that outside square brackets. In order to perceive correct usage, or to perceive the structure represented it is necessary to discriminate other structures around the one of current interest. As in the Pascal example above, this problem is compounded by the fact that many novice programmers do not have a good conceptual grasp of the reason for more than one bracketing symbol, and thus they commonly regard the brackets as interchangeable. The contention here is that, if the symbols were more readily discriminable, then comprehending and debugging code would be easier, and maybe the conceptual difficulties would be reduced.

Two general rules which might be drawn are that:

• the discriminability of a symbol within a notation should be commensurate with its syntactic significance; and

• a symbol should have only one conceptual function in a notation.

Although these examples are old and familiar, their relevance to current software engineering issues are easily overlooked. For example, graphical and object-oriented languages generally require the notation to support a very wide range of different functions, increasing the difficulty of applying the above rule.

Example 1: ProGraph

ProGraph is a Macintosh programming environment, which is object-oriented and graphical. In this example, I wish to focus on the graphical component, though the object-oriented nature makes the language richer in terms of the number of concepts which the notation must support.

Figure 1(a) showed an example ProGraph routine, illustrating three different *symbols* which need to be learned (the *get attribute*, *string* and *system method*). Note the use of small perceptual changes (e.g. the use of a small white bar along the bottom of the box, indicating a system defined method). These small changes relate to semantic differences, rather than syntactic. Thus, although all such boxes refer to different sorts of methods, the small syntactic change tells the system where to look for this method. For example, in order to detect the difference between 'sum-pos' and 'sum_pos' one has to notice these small perceptual changes.

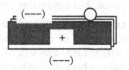 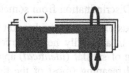

(a) Construct for adding a number
to each element in a list.

(b) Construct for adding together
all the positive elements in a list
(using local routine sum–pos).

(c) Control annotations for conditionals – representing next case,
continue, terminate, finish and fail respectively (on failure). The X
can be replaced by a tick for each action to occur on success.

Figure 3: Some of the symbols used in ProGraph

Other examples are given in Figure 3. These examples not only reveal the large range of different symbols used in ProGraph, but they also illustrate the problem of relating symbol discrimination to semantics. In Figure 3(a) the output of the construct is a list, whereas in Figure 3(b) it is a number (probably — depending upon the input to the loop node). In Figure 3(c) the shape, symbol and presence of a bar all contribute to the precise meaning of the command.

In a graphical language the use of different symbols is essential and the choice is much greater than for textual languages, but the problem arises of ensuring that appropriate discriminations between the symbols can be made.

Example 2: Baecker & Marcus' Presentation of C

ProGraph illustrates the potential problem of multiple constructs very effectively. However, traditional textual programs find it difficult to represent such a range of constructs except through the use of subtle notational differences. This means that textual programs create more considerable problems of discrimination, even to the extent that comments and program may be distinguishable only by small syntactic cues (e.g. an different type of bracket, or a particular number or combination of existing symbols).

The work of Baecker & Marcus on the typography of C programs has made a significant attempt to try and reduce these problems. Using a variety of perceptual cues (e.g. highlighting, bold, enlarged characters, italic characters, bold lines and white space they increase the general discriminability of the various components of a C program. An example is given in Figure 4.

Summary

These examples reveal the high symbolic overload which can occur in notations which contain multiple syntactic constructs. The problem can be avoided by minimizing the number of syntactic constructs (e.g. Lisp), but this has the problem that most of the remaining tasks to be described rely on efficient symbol discrimination.

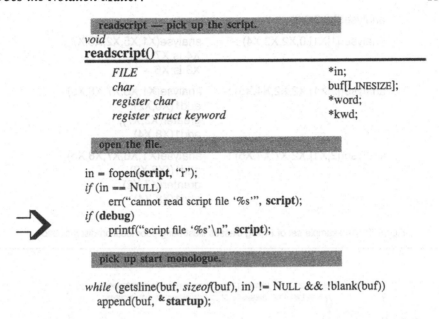

```
readscript — pick up the script.
void
readscript()
         FILE                                    *in;
         char                                    buf[LINESIZE];
         register char                           *word;
         register struct keyword                 *kwd;

open the file.

in = fopen(script, "r");
if (in == NULL)
        err("cannot read script file '%s'", script);
if (debug)
        printf("script file '%s'\n", script);

pick up start monologue.

while (getsline(buf, sizeof(buf), in) != NULL && !blank(buf))
        append(buf, &startup);
```

Figure 4: An example C program — from (Baecker & Marcus, 1990)

Furthermore, although it might seem as though symbol discrimination is a minor factor in real software engineering, it is worth commenting that it has been demonstrated that chess masters can perform basic perceptual processing of a chessboard (e.g. counting pawns) significantly faster than average players (Saariluoma, 1991), suggesting that their skill is more than knowledge or memory.

Location Discrimination

In many programming tasks there is a need to examine numerous parts of the program simultaneously. An important discrimination which supports this activity is location discrimination, in which programmers need to be able to recognize the part of the program which they are interested in.

In textual languages this activity can be supported by the existence of a variety of keywords and through the use of white space. In Prolog, for example, a set of program clauses are, by their very nature similar to each other, and often the Prolog system will convert the variable names to standard internal representations. The effect of this is to produce programs like that shown in Figure 5. In this program it is difficult to readily discriminate clause 3 from clause 4, even when one is aware the difference between them at an action or function level.

In graphical notations, location discrimination will often depend more heavily on the particular programmer and whether they lay out the program in a way which aids discrimination. However, there do seem to be some features which might support such discrimination. One of these is the use of multiple, discriminable symbols. Another is the ability to place entities in varied spatial relationships to each other, since it gives rise to greater variety in the eventual program. The use of just one spatial relationship between entities may make location discrimination hard.

```
analyse([],0,0,0,0).

analyse([1|X1],0,X2,X3,X4) :-      analyse(X1,X5,X2,X6,X7),
                                   X4 is X7 + 1,
                                   X3 is X6 + 1.

analyse([2|X1],X2,X2,X4,X5) :-     analyse(X1,X6,X7,X8,X5),
                                   add1(X6,X2),
                                   greater(X2,X7),
                                   add1(X8,X4).

analyse([2|X1],X2,X7,X4,X5) :-     analyse(X1,X6,X7,X8,X5),
                                   add1((X6,X2),
                                   greater(X7,X2),
                                   add1(X8,X4).
```

Figure 5: An example set of Prolog classes illustrating poor location discrimination

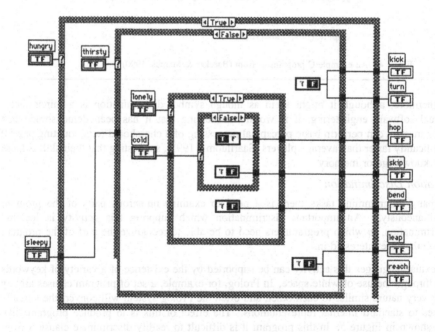

Figure 6: LabView representation of a (partial) conditional statement

For example, consider the representation used by LabView for conditional statements (see Figure 6). In this representation nested conditionals are displayed using enclosure, which means that different cases for the same conditional (and different conditionals) are going to look very similar. The critical distinguishing features are the labels on each of the boxes and the nature of the internal connections.

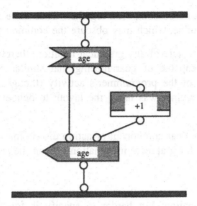

Figure 7: An example of updating an attribute in ProGraph

An interesting property of object-oriented systems is their lack of support for location discrimination, since the programmer is encouraged to divide the tasks up into many small modules, with many similar modules occurring in different places. This aspect has many advantages in relation to the general software engineering process, but we should be alerted to the need for software engineering environments to support the act of identifying where in the program one is examining; cf. the Cognitive Browser (Green et al., 1992).

Graphical cues are the most effective way of supporting location discrimination. Colour can be readily perceived, discriminated and remembered, and whilst greys and white space may be less easily remembered they can be perceived and discriminated with reasonable ease.

Action Discrimination

This reflects the ease with which the action being performed by a piece of code can be appreciated by a programmer. In its simplest terms it is the speed with which the action embedded in a program statement can be perceived. It is important to distinguish between perceiving the action of a statement (or set of statements) and the function of the set of statements (in real-world terms), which is described below.

Once more I wish to take ProGraph as an example, since this supports action discrimination, but not necessarily function discrimination. A common task in object-oriented programming (a *programming plan*, maybe) is to access and update the value of some attribute of a particular instance of a class. This action gives rise to a particular pattern within the ProGraph method which is illustrated in Figure 7.

Although Figure 7 shows the most simple version of this routine, the perceptual pattern is quite easy to recognize even when cluttered by other actions in the same method. However, although the action is readily appreciated, the general function is obscured by the absence of any indication of the calling procedure, or of the type of object whose age is being increased.

This example would make it appear that graphical notations must naturally support action discrimination, since they inherently create more patterns than textual notations. However, this advantage is not guaranteed since there are often no rules given about how the elements of a graphical notation should be composed together. Thus there may be an infinite number of versions of the same routine, which may obscure the common perceptual pattern.

One potentially important feature of any graphical notation, therefore, is an intelligent 'tidy-up' command, which is capable of guaranteeing that similar routines are laid out in a similar fashion regardless of the programmer's activity (though this would, of course, be frustrating when the programmer was using the layout to deliberately indicate a difference from normality).

Symbol discrimination is a clear component of action discrimination, though it depends also upon a consistency of use for graphical information and on the set of symbols having some psychological validity.

Function Discrimination

Similar to action discrimination, but harder to specify is function discrimination. This feature of a notation is closely related to the feature which we have previously termed *role-expressiveness* (Gilmore & Green, 1988). The principles of programming language design described earlier emphasized the importance of the comprehension of both machine level actions (action discrimination — see above) and the real-world problem domain. Discriminating the mapping between code and the problem domain can be labelled as function discrimination and can been supported through the use of 'beacons' (Brooks, 1983; Green, 1989; Wiedenbeck, 1986c), through the use of meaningful names (for methods, functions, variables, etc.) and through the provision of contextual information (i.e. increasing the amount of the program visible at one time).

Providing a large chunk of context may support function discrimination (presuming the notation supports action discrimination), since more actions of the program can be seen together, enabling a broader perspective on the program's function. It is here where Pascal would score more highly than many recent modular, graphical or OOPs notations which are poor at providing the contextual information for an action. Indeed, the very nature of modularity often ensures that contextual information is not provided.

The use of meaningful names is an interesting solution, since provision of function-related names should improve function discrimination, but probably at the expense of action discrimination, whereas machine-related names should improve action discrimination, but at the expense of function discrimination. Yet the provision of multiple names for variables (functions, etc.) brings with the probability of impairment in the other kinds of discriminations. This is a good example of the way that these various factors trade-off one against the other in the design of good notations — just as with systems, notational design requires a good grasp of the user, their knowledge and their tasks.

3.2. Recognition of Connectedness

Besides the above discriminations, there are at least two other important tasks which good programming notations must support. One is the recognition of connectedness, whilst the second is the perception of the static-dynamic mappings. Both of these is, in part, related to these discriminations, but not in a wholly general way.

Most notations emphasize one information structure at the expense of others, which means that elements of these other structures become disconnected spatially, despite their potentially important relationships. A good feature for a notation is to support the recognition of these *secondary* connections.

Clayton-Lewis' *Nopumpg* (Version 1) provides an example of how connectedness can be obscured. In *Nopumpg*, lines are described by five, spreadsheet-like cells, representing the x- and y-coordinates of the two ends and the visibility of the line (*on* or *off*). Each of these five cells can be moved or hidden independently, breaking the connections both between each of the five cells and between them and the line. Even in quite small *Nopumpg* programs this quite rapidly creates a considerable lack of comprehensibility.

3.3. Static–Dynamic Mappings

A vital component of programming is understanding how the static representation on the page is translated into dynamic activity. This task is especially important when considering the tasks of testing and debugging. Indeed it is highly probable (though I know of no evidence) that the criticality of this task explains the continued dominance of the procedural paradigm and the strong preference which novices show for languages which have a simple mapping from the static to the dynamic.

Unfortunately, there have been practically no studies of the process by which programmers extract the dynamics of program behaviour from the static program code. The most common demonstration is that complex machine models (as in languages such as Prolog) make the mapping much harder. The emphasis of most of these studies has been on mechanisms for displaying program behaviour clearly, but there has been very little interest in the mapping from the code to this new display. An exception to this is the work of du Boulay et al. (Patel, Taylor & du Boulay, in this volume).

4. Summary

The tasks presented are all necessary in the mental processing of any programming notation, regardless of paradigm, though the relative importance of each may vary according to both the paradigm and programming activity.

If one considers non-coding activities (such as recording design decisions) then many of the tasks are still relevant. For example, symbol and location discrimination will be important for all notations, as is the recognition of connectedness.

This list of notational tasks is preliminary and is capable of further expansion and clarification. Nevertheless, it offers a clearer perspective on the role of notational features and it allows the articulation of a more precise set of guidelines for notation designers:

1. Use many discriminable symbols, with each symbol representing a psychologically coherent construct.

2. Try to ensure that large semantic differences between the constructs are represented by large symbolic differences, and small by small.

3. Provide facilities for colour and white space to be attached to symbols.

4. Provide support for appreciating the overall context of any visible chunk of notation.

Acknowledgements

ProGraph is a trademark of the Gunakara Sun Systems Ltd. LabView is a trademark of National Instruments Inc.

The Effect of the Mental Representation of Programming Knowledge on Transfer

Jean Scholtz

Computer Science Department, Portland State University, P O Box 751, CMPS Portland, Oregon 97207-0751, USA.

Tel: +1 503 725 4103

Fax: +1 503 725 3211

EMail: jean@cs.pdx.edu

Programmers are often called upon to develop programs in several languages. At times they need to learn another language with little or no formal training. Studies in psychology of programming have looked at the representations of programming knowledge that are used during program development. These studies are reviewed here and are examined to see what effect these representations have on the process of transfer to another language.

Keywords: implementation plans, knowledge representation, plan creation, plan retrieval, plan knowledge, schema, semantic knowledge, strategic plans, syntactic knowledge, tactical plans, transfer.

1. Introduction

In order to successfully generate a computer program a programmer must possess several different types of knowledge. This knowledge includes problem solving techniques, domain knowledge and knowledge about a programming language. In this chapter various representations for each of these categories are discussed and studies which show how these representations are used in programming are reviewed. Domain knowledge is not discussed in this chapter. The studies that have been conducted in programming design have concentrated on programming and problem solving knowledge. A motivation for examining knowledge representation concerns the ability of programmers to switch between programming languages. Is knowledge representation a factor that hinders or facilitates this process? The research that has been done on knowledge representation of programming languages is examined and analyzed for implications concerning the effect on transfer to another language.

2. Problem Solving

Constructing a computer program to solve a certain problem requires that the programmer possess the problem solving skills to determine the procedure needed to arrive at a solution. It is not necessary that the programmer actually solve the problem. It is only necessary for the programmer to be able to accurately specify the procedures that must be carried out in order for a solution to be obtained. Problem solving skills in the area of computer programming involve taking a textual specification of what the program is to do and turning that into a working program.

In terms of human cognitive processes, Newell & Simon (1972) conclude several character-istics pertinent to programming activities:

1. The human information processing system is serial and consists of input, output, long term, short term, and external memories.

2. Long term memory is unlimited in capacity, organized associatively and contains stimulus configurations organized in chunks.

So if one is using a "decompose into smaller problems" heuristic, the serial processing characteristic implies that the subgoals generated along the way must be stored either in short term memory or in external memory. The organization of long term memory implies that heuristic methods might be chunked together and explicit design methods might be chunked together. Newell & Simon find evidence for goal-directed activity in the human information processing system.

Studies of programming activities support this goal-directed behavior. That is, programmers have been observed to generate subgoals and attempt to solve these in a serial fashion. If they are unsuccessful at solving a particular problem using one method they will attempt another. Furthermore, programmers manage to keep track of what they have attempted and do not repeat futile attempts.

Guindon (1990a) finds evidence for three different types of problem solving in programming: use of explicit design methodologies, use of heuristics and use of criteria to evaluate possible solutions. Use of explicit design methodologies would use a known means such as Jackson System Development method in order to develop a problem solution. Heuristic methods are more general and, therefore, weaker. These might involve a rule such as "decompose the problem until it consists of smaller problems for which there is a known solution". The third strategy is to use a set of criteria to guide the search through the problem space. The assumption is that the problem space consists of all possible solutions to the problem and that problem solving is a search through this space for a likely candidate (Newell & Simon, 1972). A criteria such as "the program must be highly efficient" would help eliminate solutions from the search space.

Ratcliff & Siddiqi (1985) conducted several experiments that showed the effect of training upon selection of a design methodology. Subjects were asked to design a program for a traffic survey. The authors found that two solutions types predominated: a non Jackson-like solution and a Jackson-like solution. The Jackson-like solution reflected more accurately the logical structure of the data. In the first experiment, 91% of the 106 solutions classified were the non Jackson solution. A second experiment used subjects who had received training in Jackson Structured Programming. In this experiment the percentage of subjects using a non Jackson-like solution was reduced to 55.2%. The authors speculate that use of the Jackson-like solution did not predominate due to the limited nature of the skill and experience subjects had with Jackson Design. However, this study showed that a small amount of training in a particular design method could drastically alter the type of solutions produced.

Hoc (1981) examined problem solving by looking at the direction of the approach used in the design. A prospective approach or forward plan is exhibited if intermediary steps are defined using the input data and modifying it to achieve the desired output. A retrospective approach or backwards search is the definition of intermediary results from the final output, going backward toward the input data. In experiments students of two different methods of design, one advocating a prospective approach and the other a retrospective approach, were asked to produce a program to solve a problem in which the output was not a good guide to the correct solution. The retrospective approach did indeed show more errors. The structures of the subgoals indicated that a prospective approach at this level was used in many instances, regardless of which design methodologies the students had been taught. Hence, the nature of the problem was used as a criterion for selecting an appropriate methodology, overruling the design training in some instances.

Rist (1991b) found that previous knowledge of solutions also affected the development of program design. Subjects who already knew a solution or algorithm for this particular program merely retrieved it in a forward fashion from memory. However, subjects who did not possess the solution were forced to do problem solving. In these instances, subjects focused on the key or kernel element in the plan. Once that had been solved, subjects worked both backward and forward from the kernel to produce the full plan. Rist found that forward and top-down expression of plans increased with expertise. These studies have shown support for the various problem solving strategies identified by Guindon. Moreover, the selection of these strategies was shown to be affected by training, problem type and previous programming experience. In some instances, the selection of the strategy was made solely on the basis of training or previous experience. In other cases, the characteristics of the problem influenced the selection. The representation of problem solving knowledge appears to transfer adequately once an appropriate strategy has been selected.

3. Programming Knowledge

What kind of knowledge does an experienced programmer have about a particular programming language and about programming in general? There are, in fact, many levels of knowledge that one could have about a programming language. At the most basic level, one has an understanding of the syntax of the language. That is, how to produce sentences that belong to the language. This requires knowledge of the grammar rules of any given programming language. Syntactic knowledge alone is not sufficient. Knowing only syntax would allow a programmer to construct a 'correct' but, nonetheless, meaningless sentence. Knowledge beyond this is semantic knowledge or knowledge of the function of the various constructs in the language. Although complete semantic knowledge of a programming language constitutes a large body of knowledge, it would still be difficult to construct a correct program knowing only syntax and semantics. A higher level of knowledge about a programming language concerns mapping a procedure to solve a problem into a sequence of programming language statements that will accomplish this. This activity of program development is referred to as planning.

In examining the representations of programming knowledge, studies on program comprehension as well as program generation will be reviewed. The same mental representation should suffice for use in either direction. In comprehension, a programmer takes code and tries to map it to a representation. In composition, the representation is used to generate code. In both cases, slots in the representation framework are filled with specific values from the code. Therefore, no distinction will be made in this chapter between studies of comprehension and composition.

Soloway et al. (1984) looked at plan knowledge as a function of programmer expertise. They defined a plan as "a procedure or strategy in which the key elements of the process have been abstracted and represented explicitly". Plan knowledge was classified as strategic, tactical, and implementation. Strategic plans are global, language independent plans. Tactical plans are language independent and specify a local strategy for solving a problem. Implementation plans are language dependent and specify how to carry out tactical plans given the constructs available in the target language. Figure 1 shows a possible hierarchy in plan knowledge proposed by Soloway et al. Each plan is described in a frame based representation.

Strategic plans have many different tactical plans that could be used in different instances. The same is true of the relation between tactical and implementation plans. Studies by Soloway et al. showed the existence of plan knowledge but also showed that less experienced programmers had difficulties in selecting an appropriate plan.

Rist (1991b) hypothesized that novice programmers do not have plan knowledge and must create it while more advanced programmers are able to simply retrieve and reuse plan knowledge from long term memory. Rist identifies three parts to all plans: input or initialization, calculation and output. Plan creation can be seen in a backward and bottom-up expansion; that is, first the code for calculation is generated, followed by input or initialization. Plan retrieval, however, would result in a top-down, forward expansion of initialization or input, followed by calculation. Rist found that both novices and intermediate programmers retrieve as well as create plans. Novices, however, add only one part to a basic plan at a time. Likewise, only one basic plan at a time is added to a complex plan. Intermediates are able to retrieve and use plans for simple problems with little planning activity. But for more difficult problems, intermediates are also forced to design the code for the focal portion of the problem first. Hence, as the difficulty of the problem increases, the amount of retrieval decreases even for more experienced users.

Davies (1989) investigated the amount of plan structure knowledge with respect to expertise. He found that intermediates and experts used the same number of plan structures. Moreover, the number of plans used was not dependent on language. Subjects writing in Pascal and *BASIC* used the same number of plan structures in each language. However, Davies found that the way in which intermediates and experts combined the plans was significantly different. Experts tended to make a greater number of inter-plan jumps while intermediates used more intra-plan jumps. Experts, therefore, generated more cohesive code that was loosely coupled independent of the language.

Robertson & Yu (1990) also found plan knowledge to be independent of language. Programs were written in Pascal and Fortran that instantiated the same plans. Subjects were asked to segment program code in one experiment and to sort program descriptions in a second experiment. Results from both experiments showed that abstract programming plans form the basis for organizing programs.

Davies (1990b) further showed that the development of appropriate selection rules and program discourse rules separates the novice and more experienced programmers. So while novices are capable of both creating and retrieving plans, they often use plans which are inappropriate and violate discourse rules.

Gilmore (1990a) noted the existence of plans but questioned how important that knowledge is compared to an understanding of how and when to use that knowledge. He reviewed studies

Strategic

Frame:	read/process looping strategy
Description:	specifies structure of loop
Strategy:	loop
	get a value
	process
	end loop

Tactical

Frame:	indefinite loop plan
Description:	loop until no more values are present,
	processing each value
Variables:	new value
Set up:	NA
Action in body:	test, read, process

Implementation

Frame:	while loop plan
Language:	Pascal
Description:	an indefinite loop to process input
Code:	`while not eof() do`

```
while not eof() do
begin
  readln(newvalue) ;
  process(newvalue)
end
```

Figure 1: An example of strategic, tactical and implementation plans

showing instances where the task or the requirements of the language take precedence over plan knowledge.

The schema-based approach (Détienne, 1990a) showed the use of plan-like structures which are instantiated during the comprehension process. These schema can be used in either top-down or bottom-up comprehension methods. That is, a programmer could retrieve from memory a schema based on hypothesis and then attempt to match that schema to the actual code by filling in missing slots in the framework. In the case of unusual or difficult programs, the schema-based approach supports a bottom-up or hand simulation approach. In this model, a programmer determines the functionality of the program from the code and in the process develops the schema.

In summary, a reasonable case has been made for the use of plan knowledge along with a higher order knowledge of which plans to select and how to combine plans within a more complex problem. These studies have shown that plan knowledge exists at all levels of programming expertise. Likewise, plan knowledge was shown to exist independent of language. Additional knowledge about selecting and combining plans was shown to be a component of expertise in programming.

4. Transfer Studies

Having presented the representation of knowledge used in programming, it remains to determine what portion of that knowledge, if any, will transfer to a new programming environment. Petre (1990) states that "programming languages can either hinder or facilitate expression of a solution but the language does not strongly influence the nature of solution strategy". She goes on to say "just about everyone knows someone who can write Fortran in

Language	Initial	Final	Ideal Final
Ada	80.7%	74.2%	66.7%
Icon	69.4%	27.8%	0%

Table 1: Percentage of tactical algorithms that were Pascal oriented

any language". Petre found that experts developed abstract models of solutions using a private pseudo language. She found that experts were resistant to a change of algorithm and that changing to another language did not force them to change unless they encountered failure in implementation. Programmers tended to take an abstract solution and bend the programming language in order to implement it.

Katz (1991) looked at transfer between Pascal and Lisp. Experiments were conducted with subjects writing two different versions of a program, one in Pascal and one in Lisp. The experiment was balanced so that half of the subjects first wrote in Pascal and half first wrote in Lisp. Two solution methods were used: a nested strategy implemented using nested conditionals and a separate strategy implemented using a series of conditionals. Katz found that subjects using Pascal first tended to favor the separate strategy (90% of the subjects used that strategy) while subjects using Lisp were equally divided on the method selected. This suggests that the characteristics of the language may have been used as a criterion for selecting the strategy.

In this study Katz also asked subjects to write the same program in the other language. He then compared the Lisp and the Pascal version of the programs. Of the 19 programs, the same strategy was used on both version in 14 cases. In this instance the previous selection of a strategy overruled the language effect. Katz also used an accuracy measure to assess transfer and found that subjects' programs were more complete on the second version. However, there was not a correlation between strategy transfer and accuracy. Programs that were more complete on the second version did not always use the same strategy as in the first version. Katz asserts that these two transfer measures examine different types of knowledge transfer. Accuracy transfer measures transfer of specific subgoals used in the versions while the strategy measure examines transfer of subgoal organization.

Scholtz (1989) recorded protocols from experienced subjects as they went about encoding a problem in one of two unfamiliar languages (Ada or Icon). These protocols were examined with respect to the initial algorithm used by the subjects. The problem that subjects were given was decomposed into six subgoals and in each the initial algorithm that subjects developed was examined to see if it reflected any of the characteristics of the new language or if it was a typical Pascal-like algorithm. For example, one subgoal was to reverse a line of text. Subjects working in Icon could do this by applying a built-in reverse function to a string data structure. A Pascal-like approach would be to take an array of characters and switch elements within it. Table 2 shows the results of this analysis. The ideal percentage shows the actual percentile of algorithms out of a total of 36 in which a Pascal-like solution would be appropriate. Although both Ada and Icon subjects initially used many Pascal-like algorithms, they did find more language appropriate algorithms during development. This necessitated many changes to the initial code.

Another way to examine the effect of transferring this knowledge is to look at the type of changes that subjects made during program development. Scholtz & Wiedenbeck (1992)

	High-level	Algorithm-level	Detailed-level
Ada	4 (0.67)	3 (0.50)	69 (11.50)
Icon	23 (3.83)	23 (3.83)	44 (7.33)
Pascal	1 (0.33)	1 (0.33)	27 (9.00)

Table 2: Changes at three levels of program development

Method	Intermediate	Expert
Long Term Memory	72.6%	32.3%
Focused Documentation Search	24.2%	44.1%
Opportunistic Documentation Search	3%	7.6%
Short Term Memory	0%	5.9%

Table 3: Percentage of algorithms arrived at by each method

looked at the number of changes the subjects made at three different levels: high-level, algorithm level and detailed level. High-level schemas correspond to Soloway's strategic or global plans, algorithm-level changes are a revision of a local strategy and detailed-level changes are syntax or semantic coding changes. Table 2 shows these results in absolute numbers and the number of changes per subject. The Pascal control group consisted of only three subjects compared to six subjects in both the Ada and Icon groups.

Ada is more similar to Pascal in that the same tactical algorithms suffice. Icon, on the other hand, is a string oriented language and while some of the same tactical algorithms suffice, their implementation is very difficult and more prone to error. Subjects needed to make many adaptations to their algorithms in order to produce working solutions. In particular, Icon subjects made many changes at the high-level and algorithm-level.

Also relevant to the transfer process is the assessment of how the initial algorithm for each subproblem was produced. The protocol data from Scholtz (1989) was analyzed to determine whether subjects initial plan was retrieved from memory or based on language characteristics. The following classifications were used:

- Long Term Memory — subjects, without any reference to language documentation, produced a familiar algorithm.

- Focused Documentation Search — subjects consulted the documentation with the express purpose of locating a plan for a particular subgoal.

- Opportunistic Documentation Search — subjects, while scanning the documentation for some other purpose, found a more suitable plan for a subgoal.

- Short Term Memory — subjects reused what they had learned in implementing prior subgoals.

Table 3 shows the results of this classification broken down by expertise.

Experts were better at looking at the documentation and determining a new method. Less experienced subjects were much more likely to attempt to implement a familiar algorithm regardless of the language constructs being used. Again, this illustrates an increase, dependent on expertise, of knowledge about how and when to use plan knowledge.

5. Summary

These studies present evidence for plan-like or schema-based knowledge and for several types of problem solving methodology. These knowledge representations appear to be accessible and useful in the numerous programming environments in which these studies were run. These studies also present evidence that shows this type of knowledge is not the primary differential between levels of expertise. Procedural knowledge about problem solving methodology and plan use is an important factor in developing successful programs. These studies indicate that this type of knowledge is lacking at the less experienced levels

The studies examined in this chapter deal mainly with procedural or functional languages. Studies are just evolving that examine concurrent and object-oriented languages. What results will examination of the transfer to these types of languages yield? One speculation is that attempts to use inappropriate plans and strategies will result in many futile attempts to arrive at a solution, or even worse, severely convoluted programs in which these plans were implemented. As the studies reviewed here have pointed out, there is a higher level knowledge needed: the knowledge to choose the appropriate technique for the given circumstances. As programmers use languages that are more distant from their familiar languages, this selection knowledge will become increasingly important. Programmers need to have a way to assess the similarity of a new language and to evaluate what kind of representations from a prior language will easily transfer.

The research reviewed here shows that problem solving strategies are more independent of the target language than they should be. Language characteristics are not always used to evaluate solutions but they should be. The type of language and its characteristics should be a guide to the programmer searching the problem space at each level of knowledge. This guiding knowledge should be embodied in training materials and in tools designed to aid more experienced programmers in transferring to a new language.

Textual Tree (Prolog) Tracer: An Experimental Evaluation

Mukesh J Patel, Chris Taylor[†] & Benedict du Boulay

School of Cognitive and Computing Sciences, The University of Sussex, Falmer, Brighton BN1 9QH, UK.

Tel: +44 (0)273 606755

Fax: +44 (0)273 671320

EMail: bend@cogs.sussex.ac.uk

[†]Department of Computer Science, City University, Northumberland Square, London EC1V 0HB, UK.

We report the findings of the effect of Prolog trace outputs' format and information content on simple Prolog problem solving performance of novice Prolog programmers. In this study trace outputs based on Transparent Prolog Machine (TPM*), Spy (based on Byrd Box) and Textual Tree Tracer (TTT) are evaluated for effectiveness in providing information about Prolog program execution; the last one is a new (prototype) tracer developed at The University of Sussex which was designed to partly overcome some of the shortcoming of other tracers including those evaluated in a previous similar study. Subjects (n = 13) solved simple Prolog programming problems with the aid of a trace output from one of the tracers. The results show that there was little overall difference between TTT and TPM* based trace outputs. Analysis of responses reveal relative strengths of TTT and confirm the relative usefulness of TPM* trace outputs observed in the previous study. Implications of similarities and differences of findings from both studies are discussed, as are issues related to the effect of format (or notation) on access to information and subjects' comprehension of Prolog.

Keywords: Transparent Prolog Machine, Spy, Byrd Box, Textual Tree Tracer.

1. Introduction

The overall aim of this experimental study, together with a much larger similar study (Patel, du Boulay & Taylor, 1991a; Patel, du Boulay & Taylor, 1991b), was to evaluate the usefulness of different Prolog program trace outputs for solving simple problems associated with novice debugging activity. Prolog is a complex and powerful programming language. Certain key aspects of Prolog remain *implicit* (or 'hidden') during program execution. Prolog tracers are designed to provide information about hidden features such as flow of control, and therefore can be particularly useful to Prolog learners. The hidden mechanisms of Prolog can be described or explained (or traced) in more than one way with different *perspectives* emphasising different aspects, such as variable binding, flow of control, recursion, search space, etc. (Pain & Bundy, 1987). Often it is not possible to present information about all aspects both simultaneously and equally clearly. This is partly because of the nature of the language; emphasis on one aspect, such as flow of control, often precludes the possibility of emphasis on other aspects without loss of clarity. Format or notation (Gilmore, in this volume), for example textual or graphic, acts as further constraint on information representation. For example, a perspective focusing on the flow of control in program execution can be presented as an AND/OR tree either as a top down (graphic) tree (Eisenstadt, Brayshaw & Paine, 1991) or a left to right sideways (textual) tree as in TTT (Taylor, du Boulay & Patel, 1991).

Perspective and format interact with the information content in a trace output. On a strictly formal basis, information on program execution cannot vary across tracer; all tracers generally provide the *minimum* information necessary for reconstructing the whole 'story' of a program's execution, assuming one has an adequate grasp of the underlying logic and access to the source code. However, the level of detail and explicitness of information can vary between different tracers. Together, perspective, format and level of detail and explicitness determine ease of *access* to information which in turn determines their usefulness. The task and the level of user expertise as well as user interface also play a role in determining overall usefulness of help tools such as Prolog tracers.

The major factors that determine the relative usefulness of different tracer outputs are described and discussed in greater detail in a previous study (Patel, du Boulay & Taylor, 1991b) in which three different types of *static* trace output were evaluated. The first was Spy (or Byrd Box), which provides basic traces with very limited explicit information in a textual format not always easy to comprehend (Byrd, 1980). The second, Transparent Prolog Machine (TPM*), is an *idealised* version (hence the '*') of a commercial product (TPM-CDL) based on the original TPM tracer designed by Eisenstadt, Brayshaw & Paine (1991) which graphically displays flow of control and backtracking as an AND/OR tree. The third, Enhanced Prolog Tracers for Beginners (EPTB), a textual tracer developed by Dichev & du Boulay (1989) designed to overcome some of the obvious shortcomings of the Spy tracer. The findings of this study show that not all these factors are equally important and that different combinations of perspective, format and level of detail determine trace outputs' relative usefulness in Prolog problem solving. Detailed analysis of the data further confirmed the correlation between ease of access and problem solving performance. For example, the adverse effect of the limitation of a graphic format AND/OR tree representation of flow of control on amount of textual detail was evident in novices' problem solving performance. The results served to emphasis the crucial tutorial role that Prolog tracers can play during the early learning stages. It also provided insights into how different aspects of perspective, format and level of detail can be blended in order to minimise the tension between them (and therefore, reduce the possibility of undermining the novices' uncertain grasp of Prolog).

Taylor, du Boulay & Patel (1991) describe a number of strengths and weaknesses of EPTB, TPM-CDL and Spy (Byrd box) tracers. Consideration of these together with some of the findings of the previous evaluative study has led to the conception of the Textual Tree tracer (TTT). It incorporates a number of the better features of existing tracers, whilst avoiding some of their shortcomings, together with some novel features. The present study was designed to evaluate the usefulness of a TTT (as compared with Spy and TPM*) trace outputs. TTT is currently under development, and exists only as a partially constructed prototype and its design features are still evolving. All three tracers are described in more detail in the next section.

Note that these trace outputs were evaluated as static representations in a non-interactive mode. In each case an appropriate screen dump of the relevant trace output was shown in its entirety, so users could not 'grow' the trace nor add or delete information from it. Thus, variation between method of control between tracers was eliminated. Our intention was not to examine the tracers 'in the round' but to focus on the influence of format and level of detail in *static* trace outputs based on Spy, TPM* and TTT tracers on the clarity and accessibility of information.

More specifically, this chapter focuses on TTT's performance *vis-a-vis* our set of stimuli problems which are similar to the ones used in the previous study. Given this similarity in the problem solving task we also expected to confirm previous findings of the relative usefulness of TPM* and Spy trace outputs. So the results presented here are also of general methodological interest; it provides data which allows us to compare the results of this and the previous evaluative studies. The combined findings of both experiments help to clarify the nature and scope of programming help tool evaluations. Further, it is possible to interpret these findings with a great deal of confidence because it is possible to identify the reasons for differences in the findings of both studies.

In the following sections Spy and TPM* Tracers are briefly described, followed by a more detailed account of TTT which is the main focus of this chapter. A general introduction to Prolog can be found in (Bratko, 1990) and a description of research into using and learning Prolog in (Brna, Pain & du Boulay, 1990; Pain, Brna & du Boulay, 1991).

1.1. Spy Type Trace Output

Spy is a very basic linear textual tool and is included in this study because subjects were familiar with it. The version used in this study did not show system goals. This tracer provides most of the basic information necessary for programming or debugging in Prolog, but much of it is implicit. In particular, the relationship between the source code and the trace output is not as clearly displayed as it is in TPM* and TTT, which are both designed to overcome some of the obvious shortcomings of Spy. In the previous evaluation study Spy trace outputs were not nearly as helpful as TPM* or EPTB in the problem solving task. In the present study it was not expected to perform any better than TTT. A simple program and query with its Spy trace is shown in Figure 1.

1.2. TPM* Type Trace Output

The TPM* (Transparent Prolog Machine) is a tracing tool which makes use of a modified and extended AND/OR tree representation, known as the 'AORTA' representation. The TPM-CDL version is an interesting illustration of the use of graphical representation in tracers. However, the tracer suffers from a number of drawbacks which considerably limit its usefulness in practice — see (Taylor, du Boulay & Patel, 1991) for more a detailed discussion. Trace outputs used in this study are based on an *idealised* version of TPM-CDL, which are free of these drawbacks evident during interactive use. There are now other versions of TPM available, particularly one for the Macintosh, which offer significant improvements over TPM-CDL — see for example (Eisenstadt, Brayshaw & Paine, 1991). Further, the outputs used in this study were significantly modified to include all the relevant details otherwise optionally selected by the user. The spatial layout of TPM* provides a great deal of information at a glance, particularly on the flow of control and search space. A TPM* trace output also looks a lot less cluttered compared to TTT. Overall it gains in clarity by exploiting some of the advantages of graphic format outlined above. However, the display of argument instantiations makes it

```
    s(b).
    r(b).

    p(X):-
      q(X),
      r(X).
    p(c).

    q(a).
    q(X):-
      s(X).

    ?- p(Y).
    ** (1) Call : p(_1)?
    ** (2) Call : q(_1)?
    ** (2) Exit : q(a)?
    ** (3) Call : r(a)?
    ** (3) Fail : r(a)?
    ** (2) Redo : q(a)?
    ** (4) Call : s(_1)?
    ** (4) Exit : s(b)?
    ** (2) Exit : q(b)?
    ** (5) Call : r(b)?
    ** (5) Exit : r(b)?
    ** (1) Exit : p(b)?
    Y = b?
    yes
```

Figure 1: A simple program and query with its Spy trace

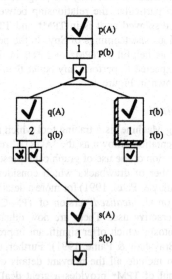

Figure 2: A TPM* trace output for the same program as shown in Figure 1

```
***1: p(Y)    1S
 |1     Y = b
 ***2: q(Y)    1SFb/2S
 |1     Y # a
 |2     Y = b
  ****4: s(Y)   1S
  |1     Y = b
 ***3: r(a)    Fm
 ***5: r(b)    1S
yes
```

Figure 3: A TTT trace output for the same program as shown in Figure 1

difficult to see the bindings that variables have obtained, particularly in the case of large data structures such as lists. This constraint is a direct consequence of the format of the tracer. The use of a graphical representation of AND/OR trees restricts the screen space available for augmenting with information about predicates with a large numbers of arguments, or variables with long names. This problem can be overcome by including a scrolling facility but the display of essentially textual information is still poor compared to more conventional textual tracers such as EPTB, TTT and Spy. A TPM* trace output for the same program as shown in Figure 1 is shown in Figure 2.

1.3. TTT Type Trace Output

TTT is a textual, non-linear tracer. It uses a *sideways tree* notation relying on text rather than graphics with the 'root node' at the top left, branches growing towards the right, and new subtrees of a node being added below any previous subtrees of that node. Immediate subcalls of a call are shown indented by one character width from the left-hand edge of the trace with respect to that call. Like the EPTB, it also shows clause matching and retrying events, distinguishes several failure modes, and provides detailed more explicit information about variable bindings. The last are presented with variable names used in the program code, on a couple of lines below the relevant (numbered) call line. The results of the previous study confirms the benefit of a high degree of explicitness (at least for the present experimental task).

Unlike Spy, and like TPM*, the information about a particular call is *localised* in and around the line showing that call in TTT notation. In Spy notation the outcome of a call is indicated by other lines (e.g. 'exit', 'redo' or 'fail' lines) which are typically some way further down the trace, usually separated by information about intervening sub-calls and calls. Without line indentation it is difficult to match pairs of 'call' lines with a corresponding 'exit' or 'fail' lines. In the TTT notation, each line showing a call includes a 'status field', which gives information about the clause number (if any) matching a call, together with an indication of the successes or failures of the clause. The status fields include all relevant information of previous executions of clauses; its a record of the history of the execution of a program concisely presented on one line in tandem with clause call matching (or not) information. A TTT trace output for the same program as shown in Figure 1 is shown in Figure 3.

In comparison with TTT notation, TPM*'s graphic AND/OR tree representation of the overall structure of the computation is more clear. However, in practice for non-trivial programs the graphics take up too much display space severely limiting presentation of other relevant (textual) information (though very large unannotated AND/OR trees can be displayed).

Normally, extra information is displayed in separate subwindows which is not convenient for information about calls to recursive list-processing procedures with long lists. TTT's sideways tree representation is intended to make it easier to correlate the trace output with the program clauses, and also allows more space in which to display the arguments of calls, whilst retaining the structural clarity that a tree representation provides.

At the time of the experiment the tracer had not been fully implemented. So trace outputs were constructed by hand, but given the static nature of the task this difference is of no significance to findings reported here. As regards TTT trace outputs evaluated in this experiment, their chief weaknesses are their cluttered look. Also traces are typically lengthy as a result of more detailed information described above. The elongated nature of its notation makes it difficult to clearly perceive the *overall structure* of a computation and the flow of control, particularly when backtracking is involved. In the final implementation of the TTT, considerable use will be made of default restrictions to curb the amount of trace output produced, with further information being shown only on request, so that traces will typically be kept very short, and bugs should be quickly located by a breadth-first top-down search of the trace tree. Indeed, the compactness of the TTT's trace output will be one of its most useful features. Overall, TTT traces will be shorter than Spy traces — particularly when backtracking is involved — and yet be far more informative. However, this advantage is unapparent in the present non-interactive study, in which only complete static traces were evaluated, and in which the degree of detail shown was much greater than would be usual in normal default mode operation.

2. Information, Format and Experimental Task

Apart from the effect of perspective, how do trace outputs vary in terms of overall information content? In this context, the term *information* is used in a specific way; it refers to information about when, how and which clauses are matched, how variables are bound to (and unbound from) values at particular points, and the overall flow of control, including backtracking, together with the success or failure of goals. Information about the operations of a Prolog program, that is, the states it passes through, the variable bindings at each important step and the amount of backtracking involved, is useful in understanding and debugging Prolog programs. Trace outputs vary in terms of the exact nature of information provided. The variation can be due to the level of detail. For example, the Spy trace does not indicate which clause of a predicate is being used at any point, whereas TTT and TPM* do. Spy refers to program variables by their internal names such as '_405', while TPM-CDL systematically labels variables with letters, and unlike both, TTT and later versions of TPM use the names chosen by the programmer appended with a numerical subscript to distinguish between copies. Though all three methods serve the same function, they are not equally efficient in providing relevant information for the sorts of problems that were used in this evaluative study.

For the purpose of this study it was assumed that the three tracers provide the minimal — and in the case of Spy this could be very minimal indeed — information, and that any main differences in their usefulness is due to format and *access* to information. More realistically, it is obvious that in most cases there would be some interaction between format and information content, and so any explanation of helpfulness of tracers would have to give an account of such an interaction. But our strong assumption of information equivalence is justified because the stimuli problems were designed and tested to ensure a fair evaluation of similar features of each tracer's judged useful for well-defined specific tasks. Further, the same rigour in designing the task material enabled us to clearly pinpoint the source of such interaction. Overall, we assume that apart from the perspective, the two main determiners of differences between tracers are format and the level of detail and explicitness of information about executed programs.

Further, trace outputs have different degrees of explicit information. For example, information about number of sub-goals of a clause can be highly implicit, as in a Spy trace, or fairly explicit, as in TPM* (as long as the clause succeeds), and in TTT (independent of whether the clause succeeds or not). While, it is not difficult to provide exemplars to define our notion of level of detail and explicitness of information, in reality these two aspects are often closely inter-related. However, this is not a serious drawback as long as it is clear that whatever level of detail and the degree of information explicitness, its the effect on access that determines a trace output's usefulness. Thus, it follows that simply having more detailed or explicit information does not increase usefulness, because too much detail can be hindrance in some cases. This tension between being explicit and overwhelming the user with 'unnecessary' details (or redundant information) is an important determiner of ease of access to information and therefore tracer usefulness. Hence, one of the questions that this study addresses is the amount and sort of information that is useful to novice programmers.

To recap, assuming that the information content of tracers was similar for all relevant aspects of Prolog, but that they varied in terms of access to information, how would this affect users' ability to solve Prolog problems? Leaving aside the effect of perspective on information access, it is probable that the more explicit the information, the quicker a subject would be able locate it. In this study, the task required subjects to study trace outputs in order to solve problems. Typically, they would have to work out whether a particular clause was matched on not or whether it affected the execution of another part of the program. These problems required the subjects to make inferences based on trace output. It was assumed that the more explicit the relevant information, the fewer inferences necessary, and therefore less time spent on solving the problem. However, according to this line of argument there would be no reason for ease of access to information to affect *accuracy* of response; all things being equal, a subject would be able to solve the same problem with different trace outputs though it might take her varying amounts of time. Therefore, any significant differences in response accuracy would have to be accounted for in terms of the effect of format and perspective. Such an account would strongly suggest that the choice of format and perspective had important implications for human cognitive processes.

3. Method

3.1. Design

The trace output evaluation task was presented on a workstation as part of an automated process including a learning and a trial phase. The stimuli consisted of five problems, divided into two groups which were roughly determined by aspects of Prolog on which their solutions depended. Group 1 included three very simple problems which could be solved with information on backtracking, clauses tried and undefined predicates. By contrast, solution to the remaining two problems in the second group depended (to a certain extent) on information about recursion, system goals, goals with variables, and list manipulation. An example of a problem from group 2 is given in the Appendix. Each problem was presented three times, once with each trace output. Care was taken to disguise similarity between question across different trace output types as is evident from the appended examples. This was done by altering words and phrases of problems, as well as program code names of definitions and variables. The disguised problems were tested in a pilot study before being selected for the problem stimuli set.

All subjects were given detailed instructions on TTT and TPM* type trace outputs after which they had to pass a criterion test designed to check their comprehension of these trace outputs. Subjects who were not able to reach the criterion of correct responses were excluded from the main evaluation study. The experiment was a within subject design: all subjects attempted to solve all the stimuli problems. Problems were presented in a pseudo random order; no problem was allowed to be followed by another of the same type but with a different trace. Subjects responded by picking a response from a multiple choice set. Data on time taken to solve a problem as well as the chosen response were collected.

3.2. Subjects

13 undergraduate novice Prolog programmers at Sussex University *completed* the problem solving task, and were paid for taking part in both parts of the experiment.

3.3. Procedure

The instructions and problem solving task were presented on Sun workstations in three stages. The entire process was self-administered by the subject, who responded by pressing a few keys on the keyboard. Following the preliminary instructions explaining the aim of the study and the nature of the problem solving task, subjects were given a tutorial on non-interactive, modified trace outputs based on TPM* and TTT tracers. Descriptions of various features of both type of trace outputs assumed a basic understanding of Spy trace outputs. Subjects who felt that they had an inadequate understanding of Spy tracers therefore did not take any further part in the study. In the next stage subjects were required to pass a criterion test designed to ensure that they had the necessary understanding of TPM* and TTT to be able to attempt solving the problems. The criterion test had 11 questions on various features of both tracers, and subjects had to get at least 9 correct in order to proceed to the main part of the experimental task. Subjects were allowed three attempts to reach this criterion. Following every response, subjects were given a short feedback explanation. Those who failed to meet to criterion did not take part in the rest of the study. This procedure ensured that only subjects with an adequate understanding of Prolog as well as TPM* and TTT were included in the results reported here.

The third stage was the main problem solving task. Each problem was presented as a multiple choice question (with the order of choices randomised) which the subjects were requested to read through before pressing a key to see the accompanying multiple-choice answers and trace output. This enabled us to collect data on time spent reading the question separately from time spent trying to solve the problem with the aid of a trace output. Subjects picked a response which they had to confirm by pressing an appropriate key which ensured the possibility of altering unintended responses. Response data were recorded, but subjects were given no feedback on them. The order of presentation was as random as possible and avoided presenting the same question (but with different trace outputs) consecutively. Subjects were asked to complete the task as fast and as accurately as possible.

3.4. Results

Solution times (ST) ANOVA was carried out with subjects as the random factor and Trace Output (3 levels) and Problem (5 levels) as fixed factors. All solution time data is included in the analysis. There was no significant main effect of trace output, indicating that differences in overall mean solution times are not significantly affected by tracer type (see Table 1). There is a significant main effect of problems, $F(4, 48) = 20.96$, $p \leq 0.001$. Given the variance in level of difficulty of problems this effect was expected; subjects took varying length of time attempting to solve different problems.

| Problem | Group 1 | | | Group 2 | | |
Trace	1	2	3	4	5	Mean
TPM*	52.7	69.7	67.9	74.5	155.0	84.0
Spy	66.4	115.0	55.8	109.4	152.4	100.0
TTT	52.1	85.5	115.5	64.0	170.5	97.5
Mean	57.1	90.4	79.7	82.6	159.3	—

Table 1: Times (secs.) of all problem by trace (n = 13)

| Problem | Group 1 | | | Group 2 | | |
Trace	1	2	3	4	5	Mean
TPM*	54.3	76.9	72.5	83.0	161.4	85.9
Spy	66.4	153.7	59.6	171.2	193.7	97.3
TTT	57.5	106.2	119.8	72.9	162.2	101.1
Mean	59.5	105.8	87.5	81.7	166.8	—

Table 2: Times (secs.) of correctly solved problem by trace (n = 13)

| Problem | Group 1 | | | Group 2 | | |
Trace	1	2	3	4	5	Mean
TPM*	85	77	85	46	62	71
Spy	100	46	62	8	23	48
TTT	77	54	92	85	62	74
Mean	87	59	78	46	49	—

Table 3: Percentage correct response by problem and trace (n = 13)

The interaction between problem and trace type was marginally significant, $F(8, 96) = 1.85$, $p \leq 0.1$. Overall, the combined effect of trace output and problem displays no particular trend. The effect of difference in format of trace outputs is not consistent across different questions. Table 2 shows solution times of correctly solved problems. As would be expected the means are generally higher but no different in trend from those based on all solution times (given in Table 1). Correct solution to problems presented with Spy traces take the longest in all expect one problem; however, unlike the rest, Problem 2 is solved fasted with the Spy trace). Compared to TPM*, solutions to problems presented with TTT trace outputs take longer in Problems 1, 2, 3 and 5. We will return to a more detailed analysis of these effects after presenting the response data analysis of variance.

An ANOVA similar to that of solution time data was carried out on the responses themselves. There is a significant main effect of problems, $F(4, 48) = 8.43$, $p \leq 0.001$, which corresponds to differences in solution times reflecting the varying level of difficulty of problems. On average subjects found Group 1 problems easier to solve. There is also a significant main effect of tracers, $F(2, 12) = 14.00$, $p \leq 0.001$.

There is a significant interaction between tracer and problem, $F(8, 96) = 3.08$, $p \leq 0.01$. Apart from Problem 1, correct responses varied significantly according to the accompanying trace output. The pattern of differences between problems solved with Spy traces is similar to that observed in the earlier study (Patel, du Boulay & Taylor, 1991a; Patel, du Boulay & Taylor, 1991b) where it was evaluated in comparison with TPM* and another textual (non-tree) Prolog tracer, EPTB (Extended Prolog Tracer for Beginners); the same is true for TPM* except that these percentages are consistently lower than those observed in a previous study. These similarities suggest that the effect of differences in trace format are independent of the specific experimental task and consistent across different combinations of Prolog trace outputs.

Apart from Problem 1, Spy trace outputs are the least helpful in solving these problems; the above average mean solution times do not seem to aid correct solutions. Even when trying hard, subjects encounter difficulties in solving problems (particularly, Problem 4) with Spy. Problems 1 and 2 are solved by more subjects with TPM* traces than with TTT; the reverse is the case for the remaining problems. This is quite interesting because they both emphasise the same Prolog perspective but in different formats. Though subjects take longer to solve Problems 3 and 5 with TTT traces (compared to TPM*), the responses are more likely to be correct (unlike Spy). Next we consider differences in solution times and correct responses in more detail.

3.5. Details of Trace Output and Problem Interaction

Here we attempt to account for these differences by relating each problem with information availability or access in each trace. Essentially, the following will highlight the nature of compatibility of problems with trace outputs. Without doubt the problems (and the experimental design) could not possibly have tested all aspects of each tracer adequately. Apart from the complexity of such a task, our experimental design precluded any interactive assessment. The following is a diagnostic analysis aimed at a more descriptive account of the nature of the interaction between problems and traces outputs; in particular it aims to provide a more detailed explanation of TTT trace outputs effect on problem solving performance. Similarly detailed accounts of the effects of TPM* and Spy were reported in the previous study and therefore will not repeated here except where appropriate in illuminating our focus on the effect TTT format and perspective on problem solving performance.

Problem 1: To solve this simple problem, subjects had to work out how often a particular procedure is called. To ensure that subjects used the trace output, it was presented without the program. Correct response were relatively high for all trace outputs. Spy traces scored better than either the TPM* or TTT probably because of explicit reference to 'call' whenever the relevant clauses are called during execution. This information was no less clear in TPM* or TTT except that there are no explicit references to 'calls' in either. Further, in the TTT format calls to procedures may have been confused with clauses displayed for the same procedure; extra information not available in Spy traces. More detailed notations in TPM* and TTT traces may be a hindrance for solving this type of simple problem.

Problem 2: This problem, also presented without the program used to generate the traces, required subjects to find out how many times a subgoal of a particular clause had been called. Again not a very difficult problem but one that serves to highlight one major shortcoming of Spy traces; the lack of explicit information about the number of calls to subgoals. Though the mean solution times of TPM* and TTT traces were similar, TTT trace was less helpful in solving this problem. It seems that the layout of information about clauses, clause numbers and calls to subgoals is potentially confusing in the TTT format. This may have led to miscounting subgoals which accounts for most of the errors.

Problem 3: To solve this problem subjects had to pick a false statement from a choice of four. The problem was presented without the program and with traces of the same program as for Problems 1 and 2. The correct answer was that it was false that a particular call succeeds. Other options (all true) included whether the first clause of a particular procedure had more than two subgoals, whether the second clause of the same procedure had exactly three subgoals, and whether a particular clause was tried. TTT and TPM* format traces were better than Spy at enabling subjects to solve this problem. However, TTT required nearly twice as long as TPM* trace outputs. The main reason being that to a generally cluttered format together with the unclear layout of TTT seems to more time to verify the true options and confirm the false one. Spy's poor performance is accounted for by its less explicit representation of information about clauses, and its non-localised display of the outcome (that is, success or failure) of calls. In the Spy format, the outcome of a call is shown by means of an "Exit" or "Fail" line, which may be some way further down the trace than the corresponding "Call" line, separated by several lines pertaining to subgoals, subgoals of subgoals, and so on.

Problem 4: This problem was presented with the program clauses corresponding to the trace. To solve it subjects had to work out the number of times a clause of a particular procedure had been invoked. Trace outputs based on TTT format performed better than TPM* format in helping the solve this problem. TTT's significantly better performance reflects the clarity of its representation of this information; the status (goal) line against the relevant clause number provides a summary of every invocation of the clause (number), which is all that is necessary to solve this problem. Unlike solutions to Problems 1 and 2, the confusing representation of information about calls to subgoals does not have an adverse effect on problem solving performance. The main reason for the TPM* high error score is the less explicit nature of some clause matching; in our static traces only the most recent clause number which matched a call is shown explicitly, and, Spy performed as badly as expected because of its highly implicit representation of clause matching information.

Problem 5: To solve this problem subjects had to work out from the trace how often a clause of a particular procedure was invoked. The problem was presented with the relevant program code. Solution with a TTT trace output, though more accurate, took slightly longer than that with TPM* traces. The overall lower means reflect the respective shortcomings of both types of trace outputs. As in the case of Problem 4, TPM* obscures information about previous invocations. And the general clutter and its consequent potential for confusion in the TTT format partly accounts for the overall below average performance. Correct solutions with a Spy trace output took the longest and is the least accurate; once again the main reason being the implicit representation of information about clause matching.

4. Discussion

Broadly speaking the limitations of perspective and format (notation) of Spy tracer together with the noted spareness of explicit information about certain key aspects of Prolog is once again evident from findings reported here. The overall pattern of differences in solution times and response errors for Spy trace outputs were similar to those observed in the previous study. Similarly, bearing in mind that this study involved a much smaller group of subjects, TPM* trace results more or less replicate the trends observed in the previous studies. However there are some notable dissimilarities which we presume are due to individual differences and therefore not indicative about any general properties of the trace output. The rest of discussion will be confined to TTT trace outputs' performance in this evaluative task.

Compared to EPTB's above average performance in the previous evaluative study, TTT trace outputs did not perform nearly as well. From the detailed analysis the reason for this outcome is not very clear. For example, it is not possible to explain the errors in the same way as TPM* ones can be, that is the resulting confusion due to the graphic format representation obscuring 'historical' information about program execution (equivalent to the status field in TTT traces). More generally, it seems that the particular order in which information about clause numbering, clause calls and variable binding was not very clear. While solutions to all problems relied on this sort of information, it was not possible to pinpoint the exact effect of this cluttered representation (with its potential for confusion) on the basis of response results to a particular question. But comparing the differences in performance of EPTB and TTT traces seems to suggest that some of the information in TTT format trace output was not very clear. As in EPTB, the TTT traces used in the experiment, explicitly showed the syntactic form of each called clause and the corresponding instantiation of the clause head matching against a goal and the resultant variable bindings. In addition, the number identifying a clause was given on a line preceding the one with the information about the relevant clause. Further, we suspect that the inclusion of a lot of details — again not a serious problem in EPTB trace output notations though it resulted in longer solution times — was superfluous for the problem solving task and may have ended up being a hindrance. So the advantage of localised information on particular clauses was dissipated by the lack of clarity in the TTT trace outputs. At the time of the experiment, the prototype version had not been implemented. So trace outputs were artificially constructed which accounted for part of the cluttered look and 'feel' of the notation, and inevitably some errors crept in though their effect on performance was negligible since solutions to none of the stimuli problems depended on such errors in the trace. However, there is no direct evidence of this in response data reported here.

With this in mind the latest version a prototype TTT tracer has undergone a number of changes since it was experimentally evaluated. The trace notation in the latest version is a lot simpler, clearer and concise (compact). Many of these improvements have been based on the experimental findings of both evaluative studies. In the final version, the program code clauses will be displayed in a separate *database window*, which will include explicit clause numbers. It will also provide details on calls to subgoals (if any) of each clause suitably indented to coincide with indentation of lines in the main trace. Thus the clutter due to details about clause matches etc., will be shifted into a separate window.

Acknowledgements

This work was supported by a grant from the UK Joint Research Council Initiative in Cognitive Science/HCI. The experimental work was conducted using the POPLOG programming environment.

Appendix A.

This section includes Spy, TPM* and TTT questions and screen dumps for question 4. In each case the question is shown together with the answer choices. The correct answer choice is starred.

```
SPY Question 4

Suppose the goal

?- trundle([7,11], [5,7,10,12], L).

is evaluated against the program

trundle([], _, []).
trundle(_, [], []).
trundle([X|Xs], [X|Ys], [X|Zs]):-
    trundle(Xs, Ys, Zs).
trundle([X|Xs], [Y|Ys], Zs):-
    X < Y, trundle(Xs, [Y|Ys], Zs).
trundle([X|Xs], [Y|Ys], Zs):-
    X > Y, trundle([X|Xs], Ys, Zs).


From the trace you are shown, how many times does the head of
the 4th clause of "trundle" match a call to "trundle"?

Once / Three times* / Four times / Not at all
```

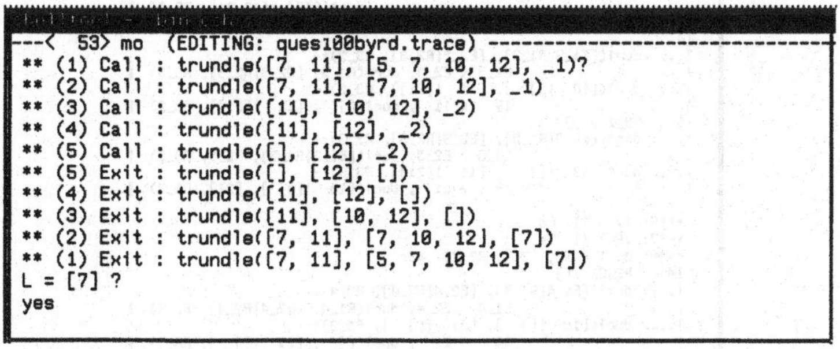

```
---< 53> mo  (EDITING: ques100byrd.trace) ----------------------------
** (1) Call : trundle([7, 11], [5, 7, 10, 12], _1)?
** (2) Call : trundle([7, 11], [7, 10, 12], _1)
** (3) Call : trundle([11], [10, 12], _2)
** (4) Call : trundle([11], [12], _2)
** (5) Call : trundle([], [12], _2)
** (5) Exit : trundle([], [12], [])
** (4) Exit : trundle([11], [12], [])
** (3) Exit : trundle([11], [10, 12], [])
** (2) Exit : trundle([7, 11], [7, 10, 12], [7])
** (1) Exit : trundle([7, 11], [5, 7, 10, 12], [7])
L = [7] ?
yes
```

Figure 4: SPY Question 4

TTT Question 4

The procedure durl is defined as follows. What is the number of times that its 4th clause is invoked (whether successfully or not) when the following goal is evaluated:

?- durl([1,19], [0,1,11,21], A).

```
1  durl([], _, []).
2  durl(_, [], []).
3  durl([E|R1], [E|R2], [E|R3]):-
     durl(R1, R2, R3).
4  durl([E1|R1], [E2|R2], R3):-
     E1 < E2,
     durl(R1, [E2|R2], R3).
5  durl([E1|R1], [E2|R2], R3):-
     E1 > E2,
     durl([E1|R1], R2, R3).
```

Once / Thrice* / Four times / Never

```
---< 53> ved ques100ttt.pic1.src  (EDITING: ques100ttt.pic1.src) --|
***1: durl([1,19], [0,1,11,21], A)  4Fg/5Sr
|4
|.... durl([E1_1|R1_1], [E2_1|R2_1        ], R3_1):-
|              E1_1 < E2_1, durl(R1_1, [E2_1|R2_1        ], R3_1) |
|.... durl([1   |[19]], [0   |[1,11,21]], A   ):-
|              1    < 0  , durl([19], [0   |[1,11,21]], A   ) |
|5    A = [1]
|.... durl([E1_1|R1_1], [E2_1|R2_1        ], R3_1):-
|              E1_1 > E2_1, durl([E1_1|R1_1], R2_1      , R3_1) |
|.... durl([1   |[19]], [0   |[1,11,21]], A   ):-
|              1    > 0  , durl([1   |[19]], [1,11,21], A   ) |
***2: 1 < 0  Fs
***3: 1 > 0  Ss
***4: durl([1,19], [1,11,21], A)  3Sr
|3    A = [1]
|.... durl([E_2|R1_2], [E_2|R2_2   ], [E_2|R3_2]):-
|              durl(R1_2, R2_2      , R3_2) |
|.... durl([1  | [19]], [1  |[11,21]], [1  |R3_2]):-
|              durl([19], [11,21], R3_2) |
***5: durl([19], [11,21], R3_2)  4Fg/5Sr
|4
|.... durl([E1_3|R1_3], [E2_3|R2_3], R3_3):-
|              E1_3 < E2_3, durl(R1_3, [E2_3|R2_3], R3_3) |
|.... durl([19  |[]   ], [11  |[21]], R3_2):-
|              19   < 11 , durl([]   , [11  |[21]], R3_2) |
|5    R3_2 = []
|.... durl([E1_3|R1_3], [E2_3|R2_3], R3_3):-
|              E1_3 > E2_3, durl([E1_3|R1_3], R2_3, R3_3) |
|.... durl([19  |[]   ], [11  |[21]], R3_2):-
|              19   > 11 , durl([19  |[] ], [21], R3_2) |
***6: 19 < 11  Fs
***7: 19 > 11  Ss
***8: durl([19], [21], R3_2)  4Sr
|4    R3_2 = []
|.... durl([E1_4|R1_4], [E2_4|R2_4], R3_4):-
|              E1_4 < E2_4, durl(R1_4, [E2_4|R2_4], R3_4) |
|.... durl([19  |[]   ], [21  |[] ], R3_2):-
|              19   < 21 , durl([]   , [21  |[] ], R3_2) |
***9: 19 < 21  Ss
**10: durl([], [21], R3_2)  1Sf
|1    R3_2 = []
|.... durl([], _5   , []).
|.... durl([], [21], []).
yes
```

Figure 5: TTT Question 4

TPM Question 4

Let "zwysick" be defined by the following five clauses.

```
zwysick([], _, []).
zwysick(_, [], []).
zwysick([A|P], [A|Q], [A|R]):-
    zwysick(P, Q, R).
zwysick([A|P], [B|Q], R):-
    A < B, zwysick(P, [B|Q], R).
zwysick([A|P], [B|Q], R):-
    A > B, zwysick([A|P], Q, R).
```

What is the number of invocations (successful or otherwise) of the 4th clause when the following goal is computed?

?- zwysick([3,7], [2,3,5,8], I).

One / Three* / Four / None

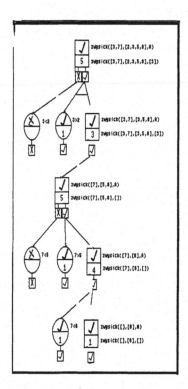

Figure 6: TPM* Question 4

TPM Question 4

Let "myslicK" be defined by the following five clauses:

```
myslicK([], []).
myslicK(_, []).
myslicK([A|B], [A|R]):-
    myslicK(B, R).
myslicK([A|T], [B|R]):-
    A < B, myslicK(T, [B|R]), R):-
myslicK([A|T], [B|R]):-
    A > B, myslicK([A|T], [], R).
```

What is the number of invocations (successful or otherwise)
of the 4th clause when the following goal is computed?

```
?- myslicK([3,7], [2,3,8,9], []).
```

one / three / four / None

Figure 6. TPM - Question 4

Longitudinal Studies of the Relation of Programmer Expertise and Role-expressiveness to Program Comprehension

Barbee Teasley, Laura Marie Leventhal, Keith Instone & Diane Schertler Rohlman

Computer Science Department, Bowling Green State University, Bowling Green, Ohio 43403, USA.
Tel: +1 419 372 2337

Fax: +1 419 372 8061

EMail: teasley@cs.bgsu.edu

Theories of expert program comprehension generally fall into one of two categories: bottom-up or top-down. While evidence exists to support both types of theories, we propose that Gilmore & Green's concept of role-expressiveness may explain certain contradictory findings.

This chapter describes three longitudinal experiments which examined the development of sensitivity to role-expressiveness. We found that after only 3 months of programming experience, novices were sensitive to coarse-grained role-expressive cues. This sensitivity appears to increase across a span of 3 years. Subjects did not show sensitivity to fine-grained differences in role-expressiveness across the span of the study, although they did perform differentially based on subtle differences in algorithms. We conclude that role-expressiveness is related to top-down comprehension, and that utilization of role-expressiveness is a component of programmer expertise.

Keywords: program comprehension, expertise, role-expressiveness, longitudinal method.

1. Introduction

Program comprehension is a crucial skill for software engineers and programmers. Comprehension is involved in nearly every phase of the software life cycle, including coding, debugging, testing and program maintenance. As an example of the importance of program comprehension in software engineering practices, Basili & Selby (1987) studied the effectiveness of different testing strategies. They found that professional programmers, using a code-reading testing strategy, found more errors than professionals who used either functional or structural testing.

Program comprehension has also been an active area of interest in the psychology of programming. Much of the existing research has focused on describing the processes involved in comprehension. In addition, the role of expertise in comprehension has been widely explored. From this body of research, two contradictory positions regarding the interaction of comprehension and expertise have emerged. The first position states that as programmers acquire greater expertise, they tend to comprehend procedural and operational information in the early stages of comprehension and functional information in the later stages. Thus, comprehension by experts can be characterized as a bottom-up process. The second position postulates that as programmers acquire greater expertise, they tend to comprehend functional information in the early stages of comprehension and/or to use functional knowledge as a basis of comprehension. From this position, comprehension by experts can be characterized as a top-down process.

1.1. Bottom-up Comprehension Models

Early models of comprehension suggested that program comprehension is a bottom-up, incremental process. In these models, a programmer first understands individual lines of code and procedural information about a program. Next, aggregates of small numbers of lines are comprehended. Only after comprehending the aggregates does the programmer begin to comprehend the program's function — for example (Basili & Mills, 1982a; Shneiderman & Mayer, 1979).

More recent support for bottom-up comprehension by experts comes from Pennington (1987a; Pennington, 1987b). She has proposed that programmers have various kinds of information available after studying program text. These different types of knowledge have different mental representations. Programmers' comprehension typically is based on program structure knowledge, and is achieved "bottom up". In her model, comprehension is built up from a recognition of operations, through control flow and understanding of local purpose to an understanding of program function.

In one study, Pennington had expert programmers read eight 15-line program segments written in Cobol or Fortran for a short period of time. They then answered a series of true-false questions on the segments, followed by free-recall of the segment. The study-test sequence was repeated three times in a row for each of the eight program segments. A recognition test followed each block of three trials. She found that subjects made the most errors on questions concerning functional information and fewer on those related to the procedural information. She concluded that comprehension of the lower levels of knowledge precedes understanding of program functions.

1.2. Top-down Comprehension Models

Considerable support for a top-down process of comprehension has also emerged. Broadly speaking, the top-down position states that as programmers acquire greater expertise, they tend to comprehend function information earlier in the process of comprehension.

In Brooks' top-down model of program comprehension (Brooks, 1983), programmers comprehend by initially developing a high-level hypothesis about the program function. Next, the comprehender attempts to verify her/his hypothesis by searching the program for supporting evidence in the form of certain objects and operations. In this search process, comprehenders focus on cues that convey information about program function. These cues take a stereotypical form and may or may not correspond to a line of code. Brooks refers to these cues as *beacons*, and cites as an example a swap of values as a beacon for sorting an array.

Recent work by Wiedenbeck (1986a; Wiedenbeck, 1986b; Wiedenbeck, 1991) supports the position that expert programmers comprehend functionally and use beacons to guide comprehension. She defines beacons as "any surface feature of a program which strongly points to the program's function". For example, in Wiedenbeck (to appear), four experiments were carried out to study the role of beacons in programmers' initial formation of knowledge of program function. She found that the presence of a beacon made a program easier for experienced programmers to describe its function and to recall after brief exposure, even when the specific program containing the beacon was previously unfamiliar to the programmer. In addition, beacons which were inappropriately placed in a program lead to "false comprehension" of the program's function. False comprehension occurred when a strong misleading beacon was present. In this situation programmers tended to use the beacon to form their initial idea of a program's function and to largely ignore other information which contradicted it. As a whole, the results of Wiedenbeck's work suggests that beacons may play an important role in the initial high-level comprehension of programs.

The work of Soloway and his colleagues (Rist, 1986; Soloway & Ehrlich, 1984; Soloway, Ehrlich & Bonar, 1982; Soloway et al., 1982) is also consistent with the notion that experts comprehend functionally. For example, Soloway & Ehrlich (1984) studied the effects of various violations in stereotypical program structures on program comprehension. Subjects were asked to fill in missing lines in programs. They reasoned that subjects would be able to respond correctly only if they had comprehended the function of the programs. For experts, programs which used stereotypical structures lead to better performance than programs which did not. A similar but smaller effect was found for novices.

Additional support for the notion that expert comprehension is functionally-oriented comes from Adelson (1984). In Adelson's study expert and novice programmers were given programs accompanied by flow charts to study. In some cases the flow chart described the functions of the program without revealing the underlying logic. In other cases, the flow chart described the step-by-step operation without describing the program's functions. The subjects were then asked questions about both the function of and operational features of programs. Expert programmers were superior in their ability to answer questions about the functions of a program after being given the program and a operationally-oriented flow chart to study. Surprisingly, novices were actually better than the experts in their ability to answer questions about how a program worked after being given the program and a functionally-oriented flow chart. However, experts were better overall when the content of the question matched the type of flowchart that had been studied. Adelson speculates that experts, given an experimenter-induced set toward functional understanding, formed representations that no longer included the details of operation. Novices, on the other hand, tend to form representations that include both sorts of information.

A number of comprehension studies comparing experts and novices have used a methodology involving the free recall of scrambled vs. meaningful stimulus materials — for example (Chase & Simon, 1973; de Groot, 1965). Typically, experiments using the de Groot methodology find that experts and novices recall about the same amount of scrambled material, but experts recall much more of the meaningful material than do novices. For example, McKeithen et al. (1981) found that novices were equally inept at reconstructing either a scrambled or meaningful Algol program. Experts and intermediates, however, were able to recall the meaningful program much better than the scrambled program. They also found that the programming statements recalled by experts were based on their role in the program and tended to be chunked together, while novices recalled statements based on the first letter of the statement and other non-programming considerations. Other researchers have found similar effects — for example (Adelson, 1981; Robertson et al., 1990; Schmidt, 1986). These studies consistently indicate that experts' comprehension is based on program function.

Using similar methodology, studies from a number of domains besides programming have demonstrated that experts' comprehension is functionally-based. Some examples include: electrical circuitry (Egan & Schwartz, 1979), chess (Chase & Simon, 1973), basketball (Allard, Graham & Paarsalu, 1980), and volleyball (Allard & Starkes, 1980). The cross-disciplinary nature of this finding makes it all the more persuasive as a true phenomenon related to expertise.

1.3. Role-expressiveness as a Factor in Comprehension

It is apparent that convincing evidence exists to support both the top-down and bottom-up models of comprehension among experts. One explanation for the contradictions may be that characteristics of the stimulus materials, in combination with expertise, influence the way programs are comprehended. Gilmore & Green (Gilmore, 1986; Gilmore & Green, 1988; Green, 1989) have suggested that the *role-expressiveness* of programming notations may affect comprehension. In their definition, notations whose functions are easy to comprehend are said to be role-expressive. Role-expressive notations provide easily-discriminable perceptual cues about function. Pascal is an example of a highly role-expressive language, because its use of key words and scope markers may provide beacons or cues which guide perception and comprehension. When a program has a low level of role-expressiveness, distinctive cues are not as apparent and determining the functional role of a particular component in a program may be difficult. Gilmore & Green have described three components of role-expressiveness. The first component is discriminability: whether the notation makes portions of code easily discriminable. The second component is statement-structure matching: Does the notation facilitate the discovery of the relationship between the statement and its role within the program, independent of the problem being solved? The third component is statement-task mapping: whether the notation aids understanding of the task role of statements.

The notion that role-expressive notations aid in the comprehension of function is supported by Gilmore & Green (1987; Gilmore & Green, 1988). In these studies color-highlighting was used to identify those program segments which performed critical program functions. They found that in Pascal, a language whose constructs are highly role-expressive, color-highlighting improved comprehension of program function. However, in BASIC programs, a language low in role-expressiveness, color-highlighting had little effect on comprehension of program function. Further support comes from Green (1977), in which it was shown that control constructs can influence comprehensibility, and from Gilmore & Green (1984), in which the effects of language syntax on comprehension were studied. In addition, Curtis et al. (1979) found that comprehension can be influenced by the number of identifiers and number of statements.

The concept of role-expressiveness provides a possible explanation for some of the apparent contradictions in the comprehension literature. It follows that program comprehension should be top-down and functionally-oriented when the program is presented in notation that is role-expressive; that is, when the program contains rich cues about function. When a program is presented in notation that is not role-expressive and provides only limited cues about function, comprehension should be more procedural or line-by-line. As an example of how role-expressiveness might explain previous findings, consider Pennington's studies. Pennington used Cobol and Fortran programs as the stimulus materials. Neither

Cobol nor Fortran could be considered to be highly role-expressive. That Pennington's subjects comprehended procedural information more readily than functional information is consistent with the hypothesized effects of low role-expressiveness. Mynatt (1990), in contrast, used Pennington's methodology in a study of the effect of variable naming on program comprehension for novices. Subjects studied small Pascal programs for short periods and then answered true/false questions testing their comprehension of operational, control flow, state and functional knowledge. For half of the programs variable names related to the function of the program were used. In the remaining programs nonsense variable names were used. Unlike Pennington, Mynatt found that comprehension for almost all types of knowledge was equal. The one exception was that functional knowledge was significantly poorer for the programs using nonsense variable names. Because Pascal is a role-expressive language, Mynatt's findings are congruent with the idea of role-expressiveness. It appears that stylistically correct Pascal makes different sorts of knowledge, including functionality, equally accessible. However, when poor variable names (names low in role-expressiveness) were used, the comprehension of function was reduced.

Role-expressiveness as an operational concept also explains the robustness of the de Groot recall paradigm. The scrambled programs used in this methodology can be considered to be devoid of almost all useful notational cues. Whatever cues are embedded in the statement-level notation of the language provide useless or misleading functional information in the scrambled program. The meaningful programs, on the other hand, allow the subjects to take advantage of whatever role-expressive perceptual cues the language and programs offer.

1.4. Why Role-expressiveness Instead of Plans?

One of the more pervasive contemporary theories of program comprehension is *programming plans*. While role-expressiveness as a theoretical paradigm can be consistent with a theory of plans, it is a viable theoretical approach in its own right. In this section, we discuss why we have focused on role-expressiveness as a theoretical approach.

The concept of programming plans is based on the plan-goal concept from text comprehension — for example (Bower, Black & Turner, 1979; Shank & Abelson, 1977). It has been developed and modified by Soloway and his colleagues (Soloway & Ehrlich, 1984; Soloway, Ehrlich & Bonar, 1982; Soloway et al., 1982) and extended by Rist (1986). The plans paradigm hypothesizes that experts have many programming plans and that plans guide program comprehension and generation. Work based on the plans concept predicts that programs which do not follow an expected plan structure should be more difficult for experts to comprehend and that expert programmers differ from novice programmers in terms of their plan knowledge.

In practice, the concept of plans has proven difficult to standardize and to operationalize — see for example (Gilmore, 1990a). Definitions range from a description of a stereotypical structure (Soloway & Ehrlich, 1984) to many types of plans (Rist, 1986) to a more schematic, scaffolding structure (Détienne & Soloway, 1990), and in fact may be mislabelled entirely (Ormerod, 1990). For example, in Davies' overview of the literature on plans (Davies, 1990a), he makes the point that there are apparently two prevailing views of plans: "plans as natural artifacts" and "plans as notational artifacts". In the first view, "plans are natural strategies that characterize the cognitive representation of a program and the programming activity of the expert programmer ... [and] ... represent the 'deep structure' of the programming problem" (Davies, 1990a, p.463). In the "plans as notational artifacts" view, plans are "artifacts both of a particular language and the structure that this language imposes on the programmer via the constraints of its specific notation" (Davies, 1990a, p.463). Soloway and his colleagues apparently assume a combination of the two views of plans (Détienne, 1990a). Wiedenbeck's work on beacons, on the other hand, could be interpreted as looking at "plans as notational artifacts".

Recent experimental work has challenged the pervasiveness and even the utility of plans as a psychological concept in program comprehension. Leventhal (1987) used a program-completion procedure, identical to Soloway & Ehrlich, to study comprehension of iterative structures which either did or did not contain plan violations, by subjects with different levels of programming expertise. Unlike Soloway & Ehrlich, Leventhal found that subjects were not affected by plan violations, regardless of their level of expertise. However, the different algorithms used had a significant effect on comprehension across groups and she did find an increase in ability across three increasing levels of expertise. Leventhal speculates that the more familiar or typical algorithms were the most readily comprehended. Subjects' interest level (affect) for each program they saw was also measured. Overall, subjects found programs containing plan violations marginally more interesting than those not containing violations. This effect was largest for the novices. Taken together these results suggest that for iterative structures in Pascal, plan violations are less important to comprehension than the algorithm structure, and that expertise is related to an increased ability to comprehend a variety of algorithmic structures.

Gilmore & Green (1988) found that Pascal programmers were able to benefit from visual cues to plan structure when performing a debugging task. However, BASIC programmers were unable to benefit from the visual cues on a similar task. They inferred that the BASIC programmers were not employing a plan-based representation of the program, but relied more on control flow information. They concluded that "plans as a natural artifact" do not generalize across different programming languages. If this is in fact so, then plans become a much less interesting theoretical construct. Davies (1990a), on the other hand, reports two experiments which show that BASIC programmers who had received training in design were better able to detect plan-related bugs, utilize plan-related cues in finding bugs and recall plan-related lines of code. Although these findings challenge Gilmore & Green's conclusion that programming plans are not utilized by BASIC programmers, Davies suggests that programming plans are useful constructs *only* for those programmers who possess design-related skills.

1.5. Our Research Questions

The Gilmore & Green model does not specifically speak to the effects of both role-expressiveness and programmer expertise on comprehension. While the theory suggests that comprehension in the presence of role-expressive notation should be functional, it does not differentiate between the comprehension of experts and non-experts. Therefore, an open question is "How is comprehension affected by variations in role-expressiveness and subject expertise?" In addition, within the Gilmore & Green model, there is an open question concerning what degree of richness of cues is required to trigger the hypothesized effect for experts and novices.

We hypothesized that the ability to detect and to use role-expressive cues to comprehend function is affected by programmer expertise level. Programmers who are more expert and are in the presence of role-expressive cues should comprehend functionally because they "see" the role-expressive cues. Experts given programs with few or misleading notational cues should tend to comprehend procedural information more readily. Programmers who are less expert should not utilize the role-expressive notations as readily. Thus these programmers

		Role-expressiveness: Low	Role-expressiveness: High
Programmer Expertise	Low	Limited Comprehension	Comprehension is Primarily Procedural
	High	Comprehension is Primarily Procedural	Comprehension is Primarily Functional

Figure 1: The hypothesized relationship between levels of role-expressiveness and programmer expertise as related to program comprehension.

should be unaffected by the presence or absence or role-expressive cues and should tend to comprehend procedural information more readily. Our hypotheses are summarized in the grid shown in Figure 1.

To test our hypotheses, three experiments were conducted. These experiments considered the effects of both the role-expressiveness of stimulus materials and programmers' expertise on comprehension tasks. In the first two studies, the difference in numbers of role-expressive cues in the materials was extreme. In the third study, the differences were small. We had no *a priori* expectations about the effects of small variations of role-expressiveness on comprehension.

A particularly important aspect of these studies is that they used a longitudinal methodology to explore the role of subject expertise. The same subjects were repeatedly tested over periods as long as two years. The following section discusses the relevance of using a longitudinal approach.

1.6. Why Use a Longitudinal Methodology?

Traditionally, studies of the interaction of expertise and program comprehension have used a between-subjects model, where the subjects are divided into two groups: experts and novices. The focus of such studies is on the differences between the two groups. The traditional approach has two apparent limitations. First, what constitutes an expert and a novice is determined by each experimenter, making it difficult to make more than superficial cross-study and cross-disciplinary comparisons of experiments. One experimenter may pick practicing programmers with 5 or more years or experience as "experts", while a second might label graduate students in computer science as "experts". Secondly, this approach suggests that expertise is a dimension that has two discrete states: expert or novice. In fact, expertise is not discrete, but continuous. If expertise is assumed to be discrete, the dynamic changes that occur as a programmer becomes more expert are ignored.

An alternative approach, advocated by Pea & Kurland (1984) and Whiteside & Wixon (1985), is to focus on the *development* of expert behaviors. This approach has the strength that the same subjects can be compared to themselves at different levels of expertise. In addition, a more fine-grained understanding of what characterizes high and low-level expertise behavior is possible. Some research has been done on the acquisition of computer science and programming skills using longitudinal approaches. For example, Campbell (1989; Campbell, 1990) has looked at the acquisition of Smalltalk programming skills and Segal, Ahmad & Rogers (1989) studied acquisition of syntax in Algol. Doane, Pellegrino & Klatzky (1990) studied the acquisition of expertise in UNIX. Anderson, Farrell & Sauers (1984) performed an intense protocol study of three subjects learning to program in Lisp. Pirolli & Anderson (1985) studied two adult novices and an 8-year old child learning to write recursive functions in Lisp, LOGO and other recursive languages.

As the review of the program comprehension literature above suggests, a number of consistent differences have been found between experts and novices. However, we need to know as well about how the differences develop. It might be supposed, for example, that acquisition of expertise is more or less monotonic: each new thing learned adds a little bit to one's ability to perform. However, it has been shown in a number of domains that performance can actually decrease temporarily during the process of skill acquisition — for example (Bowerman, 1982; Karmiloff-Smith, 1979; Karmiloff-Smith & Inhelder, 1974; Klahr, 1982; Richards & Siegler, 1982; Stavy et al., 1982; Strauss & Stavy, 1982). We felt that the longitudinal methodology would provide an opportunity to learn about the process of skill acquisition in program comprehension.

2. Experiment 1

In Experiment 1, our goal was to evaluate the interaction of changing levels of expertise on the comprehension of highly role-expressive programs versus programs with low levels of role-expressiveness. Our method was based on the de Groot paradigm of recall of scrambled versus meaningful program source code. The meaningful programs, which were written in traditional, textbook Pascal style, were highly role-expressive. The scrambled programs were low in role-expressiveness because they contained few useful cues about program function.

Subjects were recruited from among first-year computer science majors taking their first computer science course at the university. These subjects were tested after 4 months, when they had completed their first course; a second time after an additional 4 months, when they had completed their second computer science course; and a third and final time after 8 additional months, when they had completed at least their third computer science course. Although between-subject studies using the de Groot method have looked at a wider range of expertise, we expected that the subjects would do consistently better at recalling the meaningful programs compared to the scrambled programs. This prediction stemmed from two assumptions: first, that programs in an unscrambled form present many more functional cues than do scrambled programs, and hence are more role-expressive; and second, even novice programmers should be somewhat sensitive to role-expressiveness. However, we had no predictions regarding the rate or direction of changes across time.

2.1. Subjects

Twenty-four subjects originally began the study. Seven dropped out between training and Iteration 1; 3 dropped between Iterations 1 and 2, and 3 more between Iterations 2 and 3. The drop-outs were due to a change in major, dropping out of school, or personal preference. Three females and eight males participated in all 3 iterations of this study. The students initially were computer science majors who had taken no computer science courses. By Iteration 1 of the study the students had completed an introductory course in Pascal programming. By Iteration 2 of the study the students had completed a second course in Pascal programming.

The Meaningful Procedure

```
procedure Burgandy (var Table : IntArray;
                        SizeArray : integer);

var
        MinPosition, MinItem : integer;
        I , J : integer;

begin

        for I := 1 to SizeArray - 1 do
                begin
                        MinItem := Table[I];
                        MinPosition := I;
                        for J := I+1 to SizeArray do
                                if (Table[I] < MinItem) then
                                        begin
                                                MinItem := Table[I];
                                                MinPosition := J
                                        end;

                        Table[MinPosition] := Table[I];
                        Table[I] := MinItem
                end
end;
```

The Scrambled Procedure

```
        Sum : real;
                var YearDone : boolean);
var
                FirstYear, LastYear : YearRange;

end;
        writeln ('Year', 'Total' :13);

begin
                begin
                        SumByYear[CurYear] := Sum
                end;
        YearDone := true
        CurYear : YearRange;

        for CurYear := FirstYear to LastYear do
        writeln ('Total Sales by Year');
                for CurMonth := Jan to Dec do
                writeln (CurYear, Sum);
                Sum := 0.0;
        CurMonth : Month;
                                Sum := Sum + Sales [CurYear, CurMonth];
procedure Scarlet   (var Sales : SalesArray;
                var SumByYear : YearArray;
```

Figure 2: The two Pascal procedures used in Experiment 1

By Iteration 3 of the study the students had completed an introductory course in assembler language and C++ programming. The program recall task was part of a larger set of tasks which included Experiment 3 as well. Subjects received $10.00 for each iteration.

2.2. Materials

The materials consisted of two Pascal procedures, shown in Figure 2. Procedure Burgandy was a selection sort and consisted of twenty lines of code. Procedure Scarlet was a two-dimensional array traversal that consisted of twenty-one lines of code. The main processing for both procedures consists of two nested *for* loops. A scrambled version of Scarlet was created by randomly ordering all lines, including blank lines, from the original version. Unscrambled Scarlet and Burgandy had been previously pilot-tested for equivalence. The versions of Burgandy and Scarlet used for Iteration 2 had different variable names, but were otherwise the same and had been pilot-tested previously for equivalence.

2.3. Procedure

Each subject participated in a training session and 3 iterations. The training and iterations took place at the beginning of each of the four main semesters of two consecutive academic years. Each session was held during the second or third week of the semester, depending on the academic calendar.

In the training session subjects were trained on the free recall procedure. They were given a small meaningful program to study for 3 minutes followed by free recall for 5 minutes. For each of the 3 iterations of the study, the subjects received one scrambled procedure and one meaningful procedure. The subjects were allowed to study each procedure for 3 minutes. Then they were given 5 minutes to write down as much of the procedure as they could remember. The process was then repeated for the second procedure. The subjects were instructed to write down as many lines of the procedure as they could recall in the same order as they had appeared. They were told that exact recall was required. The order of presentation was counterbalanced.

2.4. Scoring

Each subject's recall was coded into a performance score. A performance score was calculated as the sum of a content score and an ordering score.

To determine the content score, each line of code in the original was matched with the line from the subject's response which best resembled the original line. Any lines which could not be matched were not considered for the content scores: no bonus or penalty was assigned. For each original line of code, a score of 0 to 3 was assigned using the following scale:

0	not reproduced at all
1	partially correct: semantic error
2	mostly correct: syntactic error
3	perfect reproduction

The most common partially correct errors were incomplete lines and incorrect array subscripts. Misspelled variables names were also common (and worth a 2). The overall content score was the mean of the content scores for all of the lines, and could range from 0 to 3.

The ordering score was designed to measure how well the subject remembered the structure of the procedure. So as to not unduly penalize those subjects who had recalled fewer lines, the ordering score only considered those lines which the subject remembered, i.e. those lines which received a 1, 2 or 3 in the content phase of the grading. Pre-order and post-order scores were assigned for each recalled line. A particular recalled line received a pre-order score of 1 if the proper line preceded it on the page and a 0 otherwise. The same line was also given a post-order score: 1 if the following line was correct and a 0 otherwise. The original first line received a 1 for pre-order if it appeared first on the page; the original last line earned a 1 for post-order if it was the last line on the page. Any extraneous lines were considered incorrect when calculating the the pre and post-order scores. The sum of the pre and post-order scores

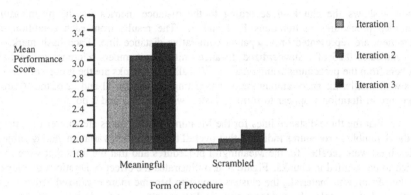

Figure 3: Mean performance score as a function of the form of the procedure for the
three iterations of Experiment 1

were averaged over the number of correct lines. Thus, the final ordering score for one subject
could range from 0 to 2 and can best be described as "how well the subject ordered only
what s/he remembered".

The performance score for each subject was the sum of the content and ordering scores.
Performance scores could range from 0 to 5.

Although blank lines used for visual spacing in the meaningful procedures were also included
in the scrambled versions, they were not considered in any way in scoring the data.

2.5. Results

The results are illustrated in Figure 3. The mean performance score for the meaningful and
scrambled versions of the procedures is plotted for each of the three iterations. Analysis of
variance showed that, as expected, performance was much better on the meaningful procedures
than the scrambled ones, $F(1, 10) = 75.1$, $p < 0.0001$. There was also a marginal effect
of Iteration, $F(2, 20) = 3.3$, $p < 0.057$. Overall, performance improved with Iterations.
Inspection of the bars in Figure 3 suggests that Iteration had a much smaller effect on
the scrambled procedures than the meaningful procedures. This conjecture is supported by
planned comparisons performed on separate analyses of the scrambled and meaningful data.
There were no pairwise significant differences among the three iterations on the Scrambled
procedures. However, there was a significant difference between Iterations 1 and 3 on the
Meaningful procedures (Scheffe $F = 3.8$, $p < 0.05$).

To determine what, if any, groupings of code the subjects used for recall, a metric was
developed for evaluating chunking of lines of recalled code. First, the mean performance
scores for all subjects for each line of the original version of the procedure were calculated
and the standard deviation of these means from the grand mean was computed. Next, a
standardized measure of distance between successive lines of the original procedure was
calculated by computing the number of standard deviations between the pairs of lines. It
is assumed that small distances indicate chunking: all lines in the chunk were recalled at
similar performance levels. Larger distances indicate no chunking: the lines were recalled
with dissimilar performance levels.

Figure 4 shows the chunking according to the distance metrics for the meaningful and scrambled procedures in Iterations 1, 2 and 3. The results from each condition of the experiment are represented on a separate cumulative distance line. Each hash mark on the lines indicates 0.25 of a standardized distance unit. The numbers reference sequential line numbers from the procedures being recalled. Visually, the chunks are the groups of successive lines with smaller distances among them. For example, lines 10, 11 and 12 of the Meaningful procedure in Iteration 1 appear to form a cluster, while lines 1 and 2 do not.

The fact that the three distance lines for the Meaningful procedures are shorter than the three for the Scrambled procedures indicates that overall there was less variation among subjects in which lines were recalled for the Meaningful procedures and that the lines that were recalled tended to be recalled in chunks. Figure 3 also illustrates the effect of iterations on clustering. For the Meaningful materials, the clusters appear to become more organized across the three iterations. For example, observe the pattern of distance measures for lines 9 to 18. These lines are approximately equally spaced in Iteration 1, have more internal clusters in Iteration 2, and become a tight cluster in Iteration 3. These nine statements form the body of the main *for* loop in the stimulus materials. For the Scrambled materials, there are no particular interpretable patterns in the changes among clusters across iterations.

It also appears that the chunks formed in the Meaningful procedures are based on integrated semantic units, and that these units become more complex across the three iterations. For example, the chunk in Iteration 1 of statements 11 and 12 comprises the initialization of a variable, I, and then the use of that variable in the inner *for* statement. In Iteration 2 the same chunk is expanded to include the *if* statement that follows, and by Iteration 3, the chunk includes the entire body of the outer *for* loop. Taken together, these results replicate findings based on between-subjects designs: meaningful materials produce more clustering during recall and the clusters are based on meaningful units.

2.6. Discussion

Prior research using between-subjects designs has shown that the de Groot method is a powerful indicator of expert/novice differences, suggesting that expert subjects are more sensitive to gross differences in role-expressiveness than novices. Our results indicate that developing novices are sensitive to coarse-grained differences in cues. Across the three iterations of meaningful procedures, subjects improved their recall performance. More interestingly, their patterns of recall became more functionally-oriented. Across the three iterations, there appeared to be decreases in the number of separate chunks, increases in the size of chunks and increases in the meaningfulness of the chunks. The scrambled procedures show no such changes. These results suggest that even after one introductory, university-level computer science course novices are indeed sensitive to role-expressive cues in Pascal and their comprehension becomes more functionally-oriented. Disrupting most of those cues by scrambling the program causes severe decrements in recall performance.

In addition, it appears that across the time-span covered by the experiment, subjects showed a monotonic improvement on recall of the role-expressive materials.

3. Experiment 2

Experiment 1 clearly indicates that increasing expertise leads to increased sensitivity to role-expressive features of Pascal. In addition, the results indicated that the de Groot methodology worked well at detecting subtle developmental changes. The subjects used in Experiment 1

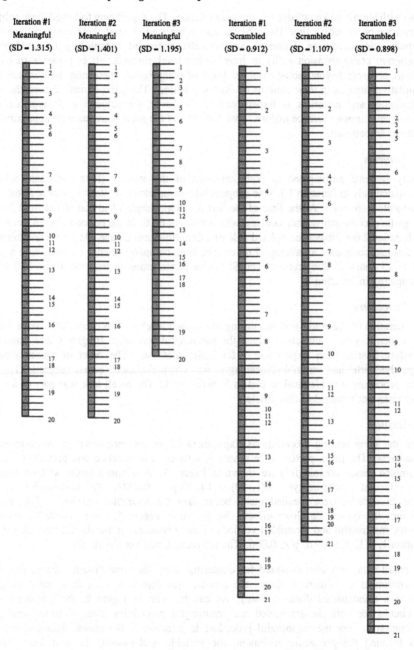

Figure 4: Clustering in recall of meaningful and scrambled versions of the procedures used in iterations 1, 2 and 3 of Experiment 1. Numbers represent lines from procedures. Each hash mark equals 0.25 standardized distance units.

began with almost no knowledge of computer science. The experiment followed these subjects for two years, at which time the subjects had completed at least three basic college-level computer science courses. However, we were also interested in exploring the development of program comprehension skills in intermediate-level students. It is possible that once students progress beyond some minimal level of competence, there may be qualitative or quantitative changes in their patterns of skill acquisition. Thus, Experiment 2 used the same methodology and materials as Experiment 1. However, the subjects were approximately junior-level computer science majors. Two iterations of the study were run with approximately 5 months in between.

3.1. Subjects

Twenty students participated in both iterations of the study. (Five additional subjects participated only in Iteration 1.) Nine subjects who completed both iterations were female and 11 subjects were male. At the time of the first iteration, subjects had completed from 3 to 13 college-level computer science courses, with a mean of 6.16. In the period between Iteration 1 and Iteration 2 the subjects completed at least a data structures course. At the second iteration, subjects had completed an average 7.68 college-level computer science courses, with a range of 4 to 15 courses. Subjects received $8.00 for participating in Iteration 1 and $10.00 for participating in Iteration 2.

3.2. Procedure

Each iteration of the study was run during the second week of two consecutive semesters in one academic year. Subjects received the meaningful procedure Burgandy and scrambled procedure Scarlet from Experiment 1 for both iterations. The order of presentation of Burgundy/Scarlet and scrambled/meaningful was counterbalanced across subjects. The rest of the procedure was identical to that in Experiment 1. The recall task was part of a larger set of tasks not reported in this article.

3.3. Results

Using the same scoring procedure as Experiment 1, performance scores were obtained for all subjects. The mean performance scores as a function of iteration and procedure version (scrambled versus meaningful) are shown in Figure 5. A within-subjects ANOVA found a main effect of procedure type, $F(1, 20) = 141.8$, $p < 0.0001$. The meaningful versions of the procedures were recalled much better than the scrambled versions. This finding replicates the typical de Groot effect. As shown in Figure 5, subjects recalled more of both the meaningful and scrambled versions of the procedures in Iteration 2 than they did in Iteration 1, $F(1, 20) = 9.6$, $p < 0.006$. The interaction was not significant.

The recall data were also analyzed for clustering using the same distance metric described in Experiment 1. Figure 6 shows the results. (In Figure 6, each hash mark indicates 0.25 of a standardized distance unit.) As can be seen in Figure 6, the composition of the chunks for both the scrambled and meaningful procedures changed from Iteration 1 to Iteration 2. For the meaningful procedure in Iteration 1, the chunks included the two lines forming the *procedure* statement, the variable declarations, the first four lines of the outside *for* loop, three lines inside the body of the inside *for* loop, and two lines at the end of the outside *for* loop. In the Iteration 2 meaningful procedure, the chunks included the two lines forming the *procedure* statement, some of the variable declarations and the first *begin* statement, and most of the nested *for* loops. The chunks that were recalled from the meaningful procedures in Iteration 1 appeared to consist of non-executable

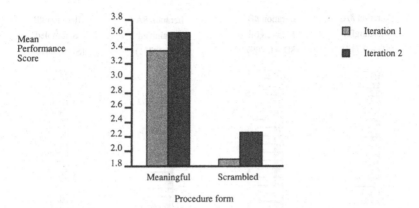

Figure 5: Mean performance scores on recall of scrambled and meaningful procedures in
Iterations 1 and 2 of Experiment 2

statements, such as the *procedure* statement and variable declarations.   The executable
statements which were chunked accomplish only small operations, such as initialization or
movement of data within the array. However, in Iteration 2 the major chunk consisted of
the main operational part of the procedure — the nested *for* loops which accomplish the
sorting.

Chunking also occurred in the recall of the scrambled procedures. Like the chunks for the
Iteration 1 meaningful procedure, the Iteration 1 scrambled chunks consisted of small sets
of either executable or nonexecutable statements. In the typical outcome using a de Groot
procedure, such as Experiment 1, there would be no improvement on the recall of scrambled
material with increased expertise. However, in Iteration 2 subjects apparently were trying to
group larger, potentially legitimate sets of statements. Most noticeably, the subjects chunked
a few consecutive random lines that happened to resemble a nested *for* loop structure. This
artifactual chunk was probably mainly responsible for the improved performance on the
scrambled procedures in Iteration 2.

3.4. Discussion

The results of Experiment 2 are consistent with the results of Experiment 1. They suggest
that subjects with increasing expertise levels are increasingly sensitive to variations in
role-expressiveness.   In this study, the subjects recalled more functionally-related groups
of statements after the end of one semester than they had at the beginning.   Thus, as
in Experiment 1, subjects comprehended progressively more functionally with increasing
expertise in the program with a high level of role-expressiveness. However, in the program
with minimal role-expressiveness, subjects did not improve functional recall, except perhaps
as an unanticipated artifact of the materials.

It is interesting to compare the performance scores of subjects on Experiment 1 and
Experiment 2 on the meaningful materials, as shown in Figures 3 and 5, respectively. Although
comparing within-subject scores to between-subject scores, these figures combined suggest a
consistent pattern of approximately 0.2 points improvement across each semester on the task.
One can conclude that comprehension, as measured in the low role-expressiveness (scrambled)

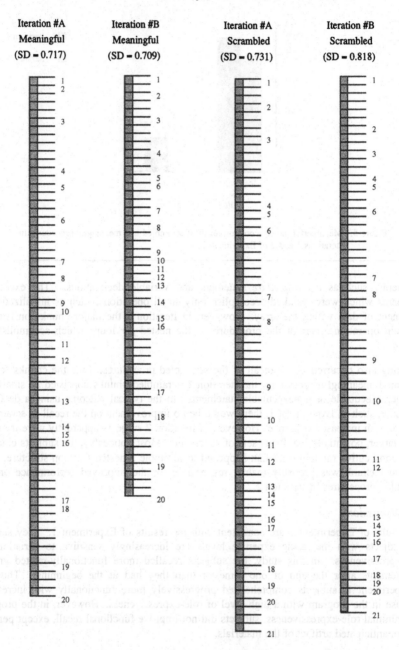

Figure 6: Chunking in recall of meaningful and scrambled versions of the procedures
used in Iterations 1 and 2 of Experiment 2. Numbers represent consecutive lines
from the procedures. Each hash mark equals 0.25 standardized distance units.

vs. high role-expressive (meaningful) program paradigm, does become increasingly more oriented to program function. The pattern of skill acquisition on this task appears to be both monotonic and linear.

4. Experiment 3

The de Groot procedure was used in Experiments 1 and 2 to show that increasing expertise in computing results in an increased ability to use role-expressiveness in a program comprehension task. Another focus of our work was to explore the quantity of role-expressive cues necessary to produce changes in comprehension of function. In Experiments 1 and 2 the meaningful programs contained many functional cues and the scrambled programs contained few and misleading cues. In Experiment 3, we wished to explore the effect of more fine-grained differences in the role-expressiveness of programming notations, in the context of varying expertise. To increase the potential generalizability of our results, the measurable complexity of programs was varied using the program-completion paradigm.

Experiment 3 again used a longitudinal approach. The subjects were the same ones involved in Experiment 1, and the data were collected within the same sessions. Thus the experiment sampled their performance three times at approximately one-semester intervals.

4.1. Materials

The materials were derived from those used in Leventhal (1987) and Soloway & Ehrlich (1984) and consisted of two pairs of complete Pascal programs that each solved a particular problem. The two pairs of programs differed in cyclomatic complexity (McCabe, 1976). For Problem 1, the McCabe complexity was 2 and for Problem 2, 3. Each program had two workable solutions. One solution, the normal, used Pascal constructs in their normal, textbook-style ways. The other solution, the unusual, used Pascal constructs in stylistically unusual ways that violated the typical role-expressiveness of the constructs.

The two problem types and the associated Pascal constructs were as follows:

> *Problem 1 — Executing a loop a fixed number of times.* In Pascal, the normal solution to the problem of executing a loop a fixed number of times involves using a *for* statement. A *for* is used because a loop counter is maintained automatically and the end condition is automatically checked. An unusual solution to this problem involves using a *while* statement. If a *while* is used a loop counter must be explicitly maintained. The programs to solve Problem 1 had a cyclomatic complexity of 2.

> *Problem 2 — Executing a loop body one or fewer times (conditional statement).* When a body of statements is to be executed one or fewer times, the convention in Pascal (the normal solution) is to use an *if* statement. If the condition specified in the *if* statement is true, the statements in the body of the *if* will be executed. If the condition is false, the statements will not be executed. A *while* statement can also be used in this situation (the unusual solution). In the condition specified in the *while* is true, the statement body is executed. If the condition is false, the statement body does not execute. However, with a *while* the condition is checked again following execution of the statement body, unlike the *if*. If the condition is still true, the statement body executes again. The statement body continues to be executed until the condition becomes false. In order to cause the statement body to be executed one time only, the condition must be changed to false within the body the first time the body is executed. The programs to solve Problem 2 had cyclomatic complexity of 3.

To limit practice effects, each pair of programs had two instantiations. The two instantiations were identical to each other in every way except for the variable names. To implement the program-completion procedure, one line of code was taken from the loop body of each program. By using two versions of each pair of programs and two orders for the task, at each iteration there were four possible combinations of materials.

4.2. Procedure

The experiment was conducted in three iterations in combination with the final three iterations of Experiment 1. At each iteration of the current task, subjects received a total of four programs: two of each problem type (1 and 2), and within each type, one normal and one unusual solution. To limit the effects of order, two random orders of the materials were used. Half of the subjects received Order 1 during the odd-numbered iterations of the study and received Order 2 during the even-numbered iteration of the study. The other half of the subjects received Order 2 during the odd-numbered iterations of the study and received Order 1 during the even-numbered iteration of the study.

The task used computerized presentation and data collection on a Macintosh computer, using HyperCard. Subjects were initially shown a screen with a description of the task, task directions and a Done button. Subjects were instructed to Fill in the blank line with the piece of code, which in their opinion, best completed the program. When subjects had read and understood the directions, they clicked on the Done button using the mouse. Then they were presented with consecutive screens containing the programs. Subjects entered their answer from the keyboard and clicked the mouse on the Done button when they were finished. After they completed the four programs, they saw a thank you screen. The task took about 30 minutes to complete.

Subjects completed a training task before they began the task for data collection in the first iteration of the experiment. The directions and procedures for the training task were in every way identical to the directions and procedures for the real task.

This task was part of a larger set of tasks, including Experiment 1. Subjects received $10.00 for each iteration.

5. Results

The accuracy of the subjects' responses was scored according to the following scheme:

0   no response was made
1   a response was made, but it did not rate a score of 2, 3 or 4
2   a response was made; some values were assigned to the proper variables
3   a response was made; some values were assigned to the proper variables, and the response was semantically correct
4   a response was made; some values were assigned to the proper variables; the response was semantically correct and the syntax of the response was correct

5.1. Data Analysis

The mean accuracy scores for all conditions of the experiment are shown in Figure 7. The results for Problem 1 (loop executes a fixed number of times), including both the normal and unusual versions, are shown in the left half of the figure. The three bars within one adjacent group of bars represent the three iterations. The results for Problem 2 (loop one or fewer times) are shown in the right half of the figure.

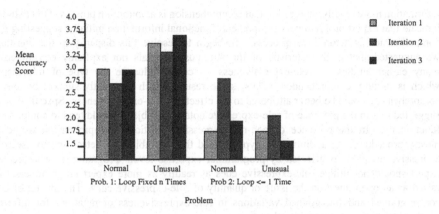

Figure 7:   Mean accuracy scores as a function of problem and use of role-expressive notation for the three iterations of Experiment 3

An analysis of variance showed there was no significant effect of varying role-expressiveness ($F < 1.3$). There was a significant main effect of problem type, $F(1, 10) = 18.3$, $p < 0.01$. The problem with the higher McCabe complexity metric (Problem 2) produced poorer performance. There was also a significant interaction of these two factors, $F(1, 10) = 8.1$, $p < 0.02$. For Problem 1, the unusual solution consistently produced better performance than the normal solution across all three iterations. For Problem 2, the normal solution produced equal or better performance than the unusual solution on the three iterations. These outcomes parallel those found by Leventhal (1987) using a between-subjects design. That is, it appears that problem type is a more influential factor in program comprehension for beginning computer science students than subtle variations in role-expressiveness.

5.2. Discussion

Experiment 3 examined the interaction of increasing expertise, fine-grained variations in role-expressiveness and small differences in algorithm. No main effect was found for role-expressiveness. This result suggests that forms that computer science educators and experts consider to be more role-expressive are not experienced in this way by first and second-year students. However, there were significant differences due to variations in problem type. This suggests that variations in the measurable complexity of the underlying algorithm may have affected the subjects' comprehension, although the programs were quite similar in length and other surface features. In addition, there were no significant main effects or interactions due to expertise. The patterns of performance, as shown in Figure 7, are clearly non-monotonic. The non-monotonic nature of the patterns makes it difficult to infer whether subjects would have in fact been differentially sensitive to fine-grained changes in the role-expressiveness of cues over a longer skill acquisition period.

6. General Discussion

6.1. Summary of Results

Previous studies of program comprehension have shown two apparently conflicting patterns of comprehension. In some cases, expert programmers appeared to comprehend procedural information more readily, suggesting that comprehension is a bottom-up process. Other studies indicate that expert programmers comprehend functional information initially, suggesting that comprehension is a top-down process. To begin to resolve this disparity in the literature, we suggested that a characteristic of the stimulus materials not explicitly considered in many earlier studies — role-expressiveness — could influence the type of information which is initially comprehended. Thus, some results which apparently support bottom-up comprehension could be better attributed to the effects of role-expressiveness. Specifically, we suggested that in the presence of role-expressive notations subjects would tend to comprehend functionally. In the presence of non-role-expressive notations, comprehension would be mostly procedural. In addition, we hypothesized that the ability to detect and to use role-expressive notations is affected by programmer expertise level. Programmers who are less expert should not utilize role-expressive cues as readily as more expert programmers. We raised as an open question the issue of quantity of role-expressive cues. The impact of both coarse-grained and fine-grained variations in role-expressiveness of notations for different levels of expertise was considered.

To test these hypotheses, we conducted three studies of program comprehension which varied both the role-expressiveness of stimulus materials and programmer's expertise using a longitudinal methodology. The experimental materials were written in Pascal, a language that is highly role-expressive. It appears that the de Groot procedure used in Experiments 1 and 2 successfully measured the effects of disrupting role-expressiveness in a broad and coarse-grained way. In Experiment 3, where fine-grained differences in role-expressiveness were made, the results suggested that what computer science experts called "role-expressive" is not uniformly experienced as such by beginning computer science students.

6.2. Assessment of the Longitudinal Methodology

A meta-issue related to the experiments described here was to assess the feasibility of the longitudinal method in exploring the development of expertise in program comprehension. Most research in expertise has used between-subjects designs. While such research indicates that differences do exist between experts and novices in certain skills, it does not show the pattern of acquisition. In order to have a complete understanding of expertise, it is important to understand its developmental cycle. Although there are special concerns associated with longitudinal methods, our experiments demonstrate that longitudinal research can be successfully carried out in this domain. In addition, phenomena which appear in a within-subjects experiment may not be detectable in a between-subjects design. In the third experiment, there were no significant quantitative effects due to expertise. However, non-monotonic development patterns were observed. Whether these patterns are an accurate reflection of development is a question for further research.

One issue that surfaces in doing longitudinal experiments is that of practice effects. For example, was it possible on Experiment 1 that the improved performance observed across the three iterations was simply the result of increased familiarity with the task? We believe that in these experiments practice effects were not a significant factor. Our conclusions are supported by at least three considerations. First, in Experiments 1 and 3 different versions of the materials were used at each iteration, so that the subjects did not become practiced on the specific contents of the procedures. Second, if the results of the experiments were due to practice effects, one must conclude that practice differentially affected performance on the tasks, independent of the manipulations of role-expressiveness. This seems unlikely considering that in the example of Experiment 1, performance on the role-expressive (meaningful) procedures improved significantly, while performance on the low role-expressive (scrambled) procedures did not. Third, our results on all three experiments were consistent with prior research on novice/expert differences using a between-subjects design, where no practice effects can operate.

6.3. Conclusions

The results of these studies, taken together, confirm our hypothesis that in the presence of notational cues of function, more experienced programmers tend to comprehend function. In situations of low role-expressiveness, more experienced programmers tend to comprehend less functional detail; while in situations of no useful notational cues, they typically have only minimal comprehension. In contrast, less expert subjects in the presence of high role-expressiveness apparently cannot use the information from the notation to comprehend function and tend to comprehend only procedural information. Novices, in situations of no role-expressiveness (e.g. scrambled programs) may not comprehend at all. However, at least for low-expertise subjects, fine-grained differences in role-expressiveness may not be as critical to comprehension as differences in complexity.

It appears that the role-expressiveness of notations is an important aspect of program comprehension and should be included in any complete theory of program comprehension. In addition, we believe that our results suggest that comprehension involves many more variables than have been considered historically as an integrated group. Past research has considered programmer knowledge structures, expertise, notational cues, and other issues. We feel that the time has come to consider program comprehension from an ecological perspective and to explore its interactions with environmental aspects as well as programmer variables.

Search Through Multiple Representations

Robert S Rist

School of Computing Sciences, University of Technology, P O Box 123, Broadway, Sydney, Australia 2007.
Tel: +61 (0)2 330 1849

EMail: rist@socs.uts.edu.au

*A program is an artifact, a machine designed for a purpose. It can be viewed from a causal perspective, in which actions are executed in temporal order. In this view, the **structure** of the solution is analyzed, and questions about **how** the code works are paramount. A program can also be viewed from a functional perspective, in which actions are connected by plan dependencies to form plans or functions. In this view, the structure of the **problem** is analyzed, and questions about **why** an action exists are paramount.*

An algorithm to derive plan structure from program code is given, allowing a formal definition of a program plan. A single plan structure can be derived from programs that achieve the same goal, but are organised differently. A single plan structure can be derived from programs that use the same plans, but are written in procedural, functional, or object-oriented languages.

Keywords: programming plan, structure, representation, searching.

1. Introduction

There seem to be three main ways to view a program: as a sequence of instructions, a set of plans, and a series of modifications to data. These three perspectives lead to the definition of procedural, functional, and object-oriented (OO) languages. Procedural analysis chunks code into a series of adjacent units: programs, routines, loops, initialisations, and so on. Functional analysis groups code into a set of plans, where the actions in a plan may or may not be adjacent to each other. Object-oriented analysis groups together the code that manipulates or refers to the same data. The three representations provide different information about a program.

The three approaches may be seen as different uses of an underlying plan structure. A plan is a series of actions that achieve a goal. Plan structure shows the plan dependencies (Sacerdoti, 1975) between actions; in programming, an action is a line of code. This structure defines a set of piecewise dependencies between the actions in a plan; logically, some plans can be executed in parallel. A serial computer, however, requires that all the actions be placed in one, single order. To impose a single, linear order on the actions, two steps are needed after the plan has been defined. First, the piecewise constraints on action ordering have to be combined by a process of constraint propagation (Stefik, 1981). A single ordering for the lines of code is usually not defined after this process. The remaining 'unordered' lines of code then have to be placed in some order for serial execution, on the basis of similarity or modularity (Rist, 1990).

Plan structure shows which lines of code implement a goal or subgoal of the program; the ultimate goals are defined by the problem specification. It is found by starting from the program goals (outputs), and tracing back along the data and control flow. The resulting acyclic, directed graph is the plan structure of the program; each node in the graph is a single line of code. A plan is a branch of this structure, and defines the code that achieves a goal. It shows the code that implements each problem goal, but does not specify how these actions are serially ordered.

If a decision is made to group the code in plan chunks (actions that lie in the same branch of the graph), then the global organization of the code is functional. If a decision is made to group the code into sequential steps (such as input, calculate, output), then the global organization is procedural. If a decision is made to group the code based on the changes to the data, then the global organization is object-oriented. In each case, the decision defines what is a module, and organises the same plans into a different modular structure.

Each of the three bases for organizing the code define a particular program structure, but are not limited to that purpose. Essentially, they define different ways to view, interrogate or search the code. Program design and understanding can thus be seen as search tasks. Top-down design searches for, retrieves, and expands sequential code chunks; a systematic or strategic approach to understanding uses sequential module structure to 'map out' the macrostructure of the code. Goal-driven design searches for, retrieves, and expands plans, then places the code in some sequential order; detailed program understanding maps out the microstructure of the code, which can be defined as the plan structure. Object-oriented design starts with a piece of data, identifies the plans that change or use the data, then collects the relevant code into a module; in program understanding, the data is used to search for the relevant plans.

2. Deep vs. Surface Structure

The surface structure of a program is the view seen by the computer: a series of actions executed in order. The actions may be grouped in various ways, such as routines, loops, and blocks of code, that reflect the syntactic structure of the program. There are many "equivalent" programs for the same specification, however. Consider a program that calculates the area of a simple house, defined as a rectangle with a prism (roof) on top. Three programs that implement this specification are shown in Table 1. In the table, the variable names have been abbreviated: w means width of the house, 1 means length, h means height of the box or rectangle part, and ah means height of the attic or prism.

Plan structure is built by starting with the program goals, and tracing back through the data and control flow in the code. The plan structure of the first two programs is shown to the left of Figure 1; lines show the data dependencies between actions. The length must be read before either volume is calculated; the box height must be read before the box volume can be found; the attic height must be read before the attic volume can be found. There is no ordering constraint, though, on whether the box or attic height is read in first; either is possible. Plan structure shows the piecewise dependencies between lines of code, and ignores the global linear order.

```
read (w, l, h);          read (w, l, h);          read (w, l);
read (ah);               box := w * l * h;        floor := w * l;
box := w * l * h;        read (ah);               read (h);
attic := 0.5 * w * l * ah;  attic := 0.5 * w * l * ah;  box := floor * h;
vol := box + attic;      vol := box + attic;      read (ah);
write (vol);             write (vol);             attic := 0.5 * floor * ah;
                                                  vol := box + attic;
                                                  write (vol);
```

Table 1: Three surface structures for the House program: procedural, functional, and object organisations

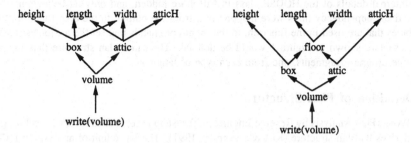

Figure 1: Deep or plan structure for the House programs

If a decision is made to group syntactically similar code together (input, calculate, output), then the first program is produced. If a decision is made to group code that implements the same plan together (here, each of the basic calculations), then the second program is produced. The plan structure of the third program is different, because information has been added to the solution. A new concept has been defined, that of the floor, which creates a program with more structure. The same plan underlies all three programs, but they differ in the way that the actions in the plan have been grouped and merged. The algorithm discussed in this chapter shows how to derive the plan structure from a given program, and abstract out the solution ordering, but the ability to equate alternate plan organizations or merging has not yet been implemented.

The House program above is written in a procedural language, Pascal. It is instructive to rewrite the program in functional (Lisp) and object-oriented (Eiffel) languages. The three code fragments are shown in Table 2. At the left is a procedural version, which has been merged as far as possible. There is a range of surface structures that can be defined by merging statements; here the reads have all been merged, the assignments have all been merged, and the resultant single calculation has been merged into the write statement. In the middle is the Lisp version, in which the individual read functions have been replaced for clarity; each variable has to be read in. At the right is the Eiffel version, consisting of an object declaration, and three executable parts. The first line of executable code creates the object by setting the attributes (data values) for the object: width, length, box height, and attic height. The second part is a function that calculates and returns the volume, and the third part is an output statement to show the area.

The procedural version was merged along the plan structure links, from the output, to the calculations; the *read* statements could not be merged with the output, because in Pascal a

```
                                                                 myHouse: HOUSE
read(w, 1, h, ah);                                               myHouse.Create;
write(w*1*h+0.5*w*1*ah);    (print(+(* w 1 h)(* 0.5 w 1 ah)))    putreal(myHouse.volume);
```

Table 2:   Three implementations of the same plan: procedural, functional, and object
languages

---

read is a procedure. It can change the value of its parameters, but does not return a value
like a function. Thus, the values cannot be used instantly within the formula, as is possible
in Lisp. The Lisp version can read and use the values instantly, because *read* is a function in
Lisp; in this case, the code fragment is defined by completely merging along the plan links.
The internal details of the HOUSE class in Eiffel are hidden, and only its behaviour is seen
here. If the dependency links were mapped out, from the output, to the area function, to the
attributes that are used in the function, to the input commands that set the attributes, then the
plan structure shown in Figure 1 would be defined. The same plan structure thus underlies
all three program fragments, one from each type of language.

3. Definition of Plan Structure

The PARE (Plan Analysis by Reverse Engineering) system accepts an arbitrary Pascal program,
and derives its plan structure (Rist & Bevemyr, 1991). The basic unit of analysis in PARE is
a line of code. Lines are connected by data and control flow links. A line of code has four
slots that connect it to other lines of code:

```
lineOfCode :use  :obey
           :make :control
```

The content of each of these slots is zero or more lines of code; more formally, pointers to
objects that represent a line of code. A line can use no data (such as prompts and labels),
or one or more data values; similarly, it can make no (write, if, while), one (calculation,
function), or more (procedure) data values. A line can obey no, or one line; it can control no,
one, or many other lines. The plan structure is created by scanning backward up the code,
so only :use and :obey (pointing away from the goal) links need to be created. The :make
and :control links are symmetric relations to these, but are not currently used by PARE.

The basic method is to start with each goal (output) in the code, and trace back through the
data and control flow links; first the data links from a line of code are followed, then the
control links. The product of this tracing process is a directed acyclic graph, with a single
root. Joins are quite common, when two lines obey the same line, or use the same data
value. When a join occurs, the tracing process terminates (all further links from that node are
already defined) at that node, and recursively resumes at the last missing link. If a program
has several outputs, then the tracing process is repeated for each goal. The complete plan
structure is a directed acyclic graph, with multiple roots, one root for each goal.

The focus of the algorithm consists of a single, recursive routine, that links first the data flow
into the line, then the control flow into the line; a simplified version of the CLOS code for
the routine is shown below. For each line of code, the routine first finds all lines that produce
or make data that is used by this line; this is done by the *findData* routine. It stores pointers
to these lines, then calls the link routine on each of the producers. Recursion continues until
a terminal is reached. The routine then finds any line that controls the current line using
the *findControl* routine, stores the pointer, then calls the link routine on the controlling line.
Linking (recursion) stops when a terminal is reached, or when the line of code has already

been processed; this is tested by seeing if the :use and :obey slots already contain links. In this way, links are found and stored from each line of code to the lines that produce data for it, or control it, for every line that is used in the program. Lines of code that are not used in any plan are not linked.

```
(defmethod link ((l lineOfCode))
    (cond ((not (slot-boundp l :use))
                (setf (use l) (findData l))
                (dolist (line (use l) (link line))) )
          ((not (slot-boundp l :obey))
                (setf (obey l) (findControl l))
                (link (obey l)) ) ) )
```

Usually, PARE only has to search for these links above the current line in the program, but there are three special cases. *Alternate data flows* are created by if and loop statements. The value existing before the object may or may not be the same as the value after the object. Statements in a *loop* may use data values produced before the loop, or within it. A line within a loop has to search first up to the top of the loop, then from the bottom of the loop to that line, then above the loop itself, to find a producer. When a *routine* (function or procedure) is found, both the plan structure in the calling module, and the structure within the routine, must be built. The plan structure in the calling module depends on the type of parameter passed. A call by value uses a value, but makes nothing; it has no output data flow. A call by reference uses a value, and makes a value; it has data flow both into and out of the parameter. Every output (function value or call by reference) is used as a root to build a new plan structure in the routine.

4. An Example Analysis

To illustrate plan structure, I will use the classic Noah problem. The problem statement is: "Write a program that shows the *average* and *maximum* rainfall for a period; the end of the period is signalled by an input value of -99". A solution program is shown in Table 3; input error checking and output formatting are omitted for clarity. My remarks refer to this small program, but can be applied to arbitrarily large and complex programs.

There are two goals specified in the problem statement, two values that must be output: the average and maximum rainfall values. The rest of the program is required purely to create and display these two values. The lines of code that define the plan for each goal may be found by tracing back from the outputs along the data and control flow links in the solution. Plan tracing begins with the last write statement, in this case for the *average* value. The plan structure for the *average* goal is shown to the left of Figure 2; details of its derivation are given in Rist & Bevemyr (1991). In the figure, single arrows indicate dataflow, double arrows indicate control flow and the arrows with no terminal indicate a join to a line of code shown elsewhere; prompts and labels are omitted for clarity.

The plan structure for the maximum plan is shown to the right of Figure 2. The plan accepts one data flow (rainfall, shown by a double arrow) and produces one data flow (the maximum rainfall). Because much of the loop control and data structure was already built when tracing the average plan, the maximum plan graph does not include them. The algorithm allows the plan to be cleanly and automatically separated from its context.

5. Plans and Constraint Propagation

A plan is a branch of the plan structure, including the root. The structure of a basic plan may be described as IC*O, an initialization (I) followed by zero or more calculations or

```
1.   program Noah (input, output);
2.   const endValue = -99;
3.   var sum, rain, day, max: integer;
4.        average: real;
5.   begin
6.        sum := 0;
7.        max := 0;
8.        day := 0;
9.        write ('Enter rainfall for day ', (day + 1), ': ');
10.       readln (rain);
11.       while rain <> endValue do begin
12.            day := day + 1;
13.            sum := sum + rain;
14.            if rain > max then max := rain;
15.            write ('Enter rainfall for day ', (day + 1), ': ');
16.            readln (rain);
17.            end;
18.       writeln ('The largest rainfall was ', max);
19.       average := 0.0;
20.       if day > 0 then average := sum/day;
21.       writeln ('The average rainfall was ', average);
22.  end.
```

Table 3: A program to solve the Average problem

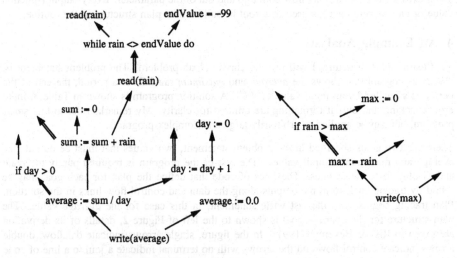

Figure 2: Plan structure for the Average plan

changes (C) to the variable, followed by an output or use (O) of that variable. A complex plan is formed by combining basic plans; a complex plan is just a larger branch of the plan structure.

There are five basic plans in the program code: the read loop, sum, count, average, and max plans, shown in Table 4. To transform these plans into a program, the lines of code must be placed in a single linear order. The plan structure defines piecewise dependencies of data and control flow, but the constraints do not define a single execution order.

	Sum	**Count**	**Max**
I	sum := 0.0	day := 0	max := 0
C	sum := sum + rain	day := day + 1	if rain > max then max := rain
O	use sum	use day	write (max)

	Read loop	**Average**
I	read (rain)	average := 0.0
C	read (rain)	if day > 0 then average := sum/day
O	while rain <> endValue do	write (average)

Table 4: Plans used in the Noah program

	Sum, count, max	**Read loop**
I	before loop	before loop
C	inside loop	at bottom of loop
O	inside or after loop	loop control

Table 5: Ordering constraints on plan actions

The default constraints on the ordering of plan actions are that a data value must be produced before it can be used, and a controlling line (if, case, while) precedes the controlled line; the repeat statement is a special case. Thus, the initialization precedes the calculation, and the calculation precedes the use, in execution order; execution order usually corresponds to listing order. Extra constraints on the locations of the plan actions are shown in Table 5; the average plan requires no extra constraints. Given the code in each plan and these constraints, it is a trivial exercise to produce a program using constraint propagation. In practice, programmers usually code the loop as the first plan during design, and other plans are added one at a time.

A plan is a branch of the plan structure, including the root. If the corresponding code is written out as a program, it defines a plan to produce the root value. The structure of a basic plan may be described as IC*O, an initialization followed by zero or more calculations or changes to the variable, followed by an output or use of that variable. A complex plan is formed by combining basic plans (Rist, 1991b). A complex plan is just a larger branch of the plan structure. This definition of a basic plan is very similar to Weiser's program 'slice' (Weiser, 1984), but the notion of plan structure is missing from that earlier work.

A plan schema is a known solution to a common programming problem (Soloway, Bonar & Ehrlich, 1983). Some parts of a plan will correspond to plan schemas, while other parts that are unique or unusual will not be schemas; only common or repeated plans are stored in memory as schemas. Plan schemas in general seem to be terminal branches, which can be isolated, analyzed, and stored easily. Some plans will be schemas, and some will not. Some plans will have their actions adjacent in execution order, and some will not.

A plan schema can now be precisely defined as the plan, plus the constraints on the plan actions, plus the serial ordering of the plan actions. The creation and propagation of a plan is a long, tricky, and error-prone process. Once the plan has been defined and placed in a program, however, the whole structure can be retrieved as a chunk with little effort. It is far easier to recall a solution than to derive one from first principles, even if the retrieved solution is incorrect for the problem! Once the schema has been stored, the knowledge representation can be searched via the plan links (data, control, or both), and via the serial order of plan slots.

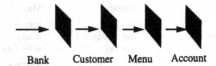

Bank   Customer   Menu   Account

Figure 3:   A client chart for the bank system, showing which classes use other classes

6. Plans in Object-oriented Languages

The plan structure for an object-oriented (OO) system can be found using the same method that PARE uses for procedural code, but the details are considerably more complex; the system has to search the many classes that make up an OO system, rather than just a single program. Such an analysis reveals that plans and objects are orthogonal: one plan can use many objects, and one object can take part in many plans. In real life, this is no surprise — a plan to make an omelete uses eggs, ham, spices, and so on; eggs can be omeleted, boiled, scrambled, and so on. The formalism of plan structure makes the result clear in OO programming.

Consider an OO system that models an automatic teller machine (ATM) in a bank. The main objects in the system would be a BANK, that contains a set of CUSTOMERs. A CUSTOMER has a set of ACCOUNTs, such as SAVINGS and CHEQUE accounts. The ACCOUNT would have a MENU as a system interface, so that the user could input commands and queries. Such a system is shown in Figure 3; arrows indicate that the class to the left uses routines defined in the class to the right. In Eiffel, this is called a client chart.

Assume that a user wishes to withdraw money from her account. To do this, she would first enter her customer identifier into the ATM; this is usually done by pushing a card into a slot in the ATM. The BANK would validate it, and use it to look up the particular CUSTOMER. The CUSTOMER module would then ask for a password or PIN, and transfer control to the MENU. The MENU would ask for the type of account, and the action on that account; assume that the user chooses the cheque account, and enters 'W' to withdraw money. The MENU system would validate the input, then call a routine in the account to actually change the account balance. The action that directly implements the goal is a small piece of code in the ACCOUNT class; it is the focus of the plan (Rist, 1989). Everything else in the system is added to allow this code to work at the right time, in the right way. The plan structure can be derived by tracing out the plan dependency links (data and control flow) from the focus to the terminals, as discussed above. The resulting plan has fragments of code in each of the other classes.

Of course, there are other things that can be done with an account. A customer might wish to deposit money, transfer money between accounts, or display the balance of the account. A bank teller might wish to add interest to an account, or find the total amount of savings invested in the bank. These become goals of the system, and plans to implement the goals are defined. Each plan would use the classes discussed above, and probably others as well.

The overall object structure of a system has been captured by data flow diagrams, and underlies many analysis techniques such as the Jackson System Development method. The detailed object structure is captured by object-oriented programming, which organizes the code so it is placed with the data. The strength of OOP is in fact its explicit separation between plans and data. On the analysis given here, it is suggested that plans and objects are orthogonal and should be explicitly separated. One plan can use many objects, one object can take part in many plans. Many accounts of OO design begin with a definition of the object. This analysis indicates that an object is defined by the plans in which it takes part. Design based on tracing out plans seems to be an intuitive and powerful heuristic used by programmers, logically prior to the definition of the behaviour of an object.

7. Design

Plan structure provides a single representation that can capture many design strategies. The most obvious of these is plan-based design, in which planning begins with the goal, moves up the data links to the focus, and then supporting actions are added as required; this strategy is detailed in (Rist, 1989; Rist, 1991a; Rist, 1991b). Such design proceeds backward from the goal, and is based on plan retrieval and expansion. Code can be added to remote parts of the program at any time, as unforeseen goals are noticed and plan links traced out from these new.(sub-)goals. Novice programming often appears to be chaotic, as new chunks of code are generated and added to disparate parts of a program, but can be understood by following the microstructure given by plan dependencies. Novices are often forced to use this strategy, because they do not know, and thus cannot retrieve, a previous solution. Experts often choose this strategy, because they know that the dependencies flow back from the goals, not forward from the input. Experts may develop the plan backward mentally and verbally, then code the program from first line to the last (Rist, 1991b), or code the most important (key or focal) parts of the program first and add the details later (Davies, 1991b). One way to describe this pattern of behaviour is that experts trace out the plan structure in a breadth-first order, whereas novices favor a depth-first search of the structure, reducing the load on working memory.

Expert programmers typically show a pattern of top-down code design, in which a schema is retrieved and implemented in schema or execution order, because they have a large corpus of stored schemas. Each slot in the schema is expanded in order, from the first to the last. This pattern of problem-solving has been known for decades and embodied in the design of early programming languages (Green, 1990a). Top-down design begins with an abstract solution schema, which is then refined by filling slots in the schema. The final solution maps directly onto a module chart for the code. Expert designers appear to use a balanced, breadth-first development of the program modules (Adelson & Soloway, 1985; Jeffries et al., 1981), where novices are said to use a depth-first development strategy. Top-down design is a winning strategy as long as the slots can be filled with schemas. When a schema cannot be retrieved and must be created, top-down design breaks down and is (temporarily) replaced by bottom-up design. Much of the time, this bottom-up design is based on plan dependencies. As has been shown, the plan structure of a program can be as easily mapped as the module structure, and also defines a tree structure. Plan structure does not echo the module structure, however, unless we have a functional organisation or a functional language. It covers the program, but groups the code in plan chunks, not in execution-time chunks.

Another common design strategy is to start with the input, and develop the code forward from the input, by looking to see where and how the input is used (Ratcliff & Siddiqi, 1985); this may be termed data-driven design. Design is forward, but not abstract. As design proceeds by tracing out the main data flow, the need for other data and control flows is noticed, and these are added around the major data flow. Formally, design traces out the :make links, then :use, :control, and :obey links are added as required. Such a strategy appears similar to top-down design, but there is little global guidance because the structure of the solution is not known.

The basic data in any study of design is the order in which parts of the solution were generated. This order is then used to infer the design strategy, as discussed for top-down and backward or plan-based design. The fact that code is generated out of sequence, and added to remote parts of the program, has recently been used as evidence for opportunistic design. The model of plan-based design given here makes it clear that a deviation from top-down design, by itself, does not differentiate between plan-based and opportunistic design.

8. Understanding

To understand a program, a programmer builds up a mental model of what the program does, and how it does it. The two main strategies used to understand a program are systematic and as-needed strategies (Littman et al., 1986). A systematic strategy comprises tracing data and control flow through the program, in order to understand its global behaviour, where an as-needed strategy operates by working out local program behaviour as the need arises.

A systematic strategy is only feasible when there is little time pressure, and the programmer can spend the time to understand all of the program. In program maintenance, a programmer wishes to understand only as much of the code as is needed to make the modification; whatever the rest of the program does is irrelevant to the modification task, and can be avoided. Such a strategy was seen by Koenemann & Robertson (1991), who found that programmers followed a pragmatic as-needed strategy when they had to modify a large and complex program.

Program understanding is not an end in itself; a program is usually understood as a prelude to being modified. The modification is usually defined as a change to the goals of the program; either a new goal is added, a previous goal is removed, or the operation of a plan is changed in some way. Following Pennington (1987a) and Koenemann & Robertson (1991), I will assume that the understanding process is driven by the need to identify and understand the plans in the code, both as plans and as executable actions. The understanding task is then to locate, identify, and simulate the plans that are relevant for the current modification.

Koenemann identifies three kinds of data that are relevant in program understanding. First, there is the set of code that is directly relevant to the modification. Second, there is intermediate relevant code, that includes those code segments that are perceived to interact with the directly relevant code. Third, there is strategic knowledge, that guides the comprehension or search process, such as module calling charts.

8.1. Strategic Knowledge

Given a large program to modify, the first task of the programmer is strategic, to find out roughly where the relevant code is located in the program. This may be done using information about the macrostructure of the program, such as module charts or the sequence of routine calls in the main program. The problem with using module charts to locate the relevant code is that there are many bases for deciding on what is a module, only some of which localise plans.

Consider the fragment of code shown in Table 6. This fragment is the first part of a program that plays the game of Hangman (Rist, 1991b). It consists of four initializations, and could thus be stored as a single chunk, an initialization module. To understand why this code is needed, it is necessary to describe the plans in which it is used. In Hangman, the player has to guess an unknown word, one letter at at time. Before each guess, the part of the word that has been guessed so far is shown to the user. Guessing continues until the word has

```
1.  i := 0;
2.  repeat
3.      i := i + 1;
4.      read (word[i]);
5.  until eoln;
6.  length := i;
7.  for i := 1 to length do
8.      guessed[i] := '-';
9.  wrong := 0;
```

Table 6: Initializations for the Hangman program

been guessed, or seven wrong guesses have been made. The code initialises the word to be guessed, the length of the word, the guessed array, and the count of wrong guesses. When a letter is guessed, it is stored in the guessed array, so the guesses so far can be displayed.

Chunks of adjacent code define the macrostructure of a program (Robertson & Yu, 1990). There are four chunks in the code shown above, lines 1–5, 6, 7–8, and 9; a line can be drawn between any of these chunks to define a module, and the remainder placed in the same module as the code to handle the guesses. If the line is drawn after the first chunk, that module could be labelled 'read the word'. If the line is drawn after the second chunk, a better label would be 'initialise the word', because the length is no part of reading in the word. If the line is drawn after the third chunk, the module could be labelled 'initialise the words'. If the line is drawn after the last chunk, then some generic label such as 'initialise' is required, because the module does not do a single thing; it does not even initialise objects of the same type. Note that there is only one necessary ordering on these four chunks: the word must be read before the length can be set. Apart from that, no ordering is imposed on the chunks by the plan structure of the code.

8.2. Tactical Knowledge

Once the rough location of the relevant code has been found from the module or sequential structure, that code has to be understood in detail. Pennington notes that at this stage, detailed control and data flow are the main concerns of the programmer. There are two ways to interpret this description, however, from the perspectives of causal (machine) and reason (artifact) analysis. As has been demonstrated, plan structure is control and data flow, viewed from the goal. A plan (reason) analysis looks at one plan at a time, and ignores the irrelevant code. A causal analysis takes a section of code and executes or simulates all the code in that section, no matter how many different plans are involved.

A detailed analysis of the behaviour seen at this stage is provided by Letovsky (1986), who develops a taxonomy of questions that are asked by programmers. He describes five main question types: why, how, what, whether, and discrepancy questions. *Why* questions can be answered by searching the plan structure, toward the goal; they are questions either about the goal itself, or about how the plan implements the goal. *How* questions can be answered by searching the plan structure away from the goal; they ask about the detailed plans by which a goal is achieved. *What* questions take an object or variable, and ask for the plan or plans in which that object is used. *Whether* questions ask for more detail about what a routine does, detail about the plans in the routine. They are a form of how questions, in which the programmer has to select between possible explanations. *Discrepancy* questions arise when there is conflicting information about something.

Given only the normal sequential information about the code — modules, listing order, and an execution trace — these questions are difficult to answer. They involve tracing through the code, looking for some section of code that is relevant to answering the question, then working out how the pieces of code fit together. The relevant code may be close to where the question is asked, or may be far away in the program listing. The result of answering these questions is knowledge about the function of the code. Given the plan structure as an explicit graph, the questions would be easily answered.

9. Conclusions

This chapter has contrasted two ways of looking at program code. The causal or temporal structure of a program has received most attention in the past, and a plethora of tools and notations have been developed to test and show how the code executes. Actually, some tools have shown the listing order where other tools concentrate on the execution order, but these two dimensions are usually equivalent. The functional and object structures of program code have not received anywhere near as much attention.

The functional or plan structure can now be algorithmically defined, and tools built to display and use this structure. From the principled definition of plan structure, several insights have emerged. First, plans often do not correspond to adjacent chunks of code. Second, the location of the actions in a plan can vary widely, depending on the choice of the individual programmer. Third, the definition of a module may, or may not, be functionally (plan) based; a module groups 'similar' code together, and there are many ways to define similarity.

The major contribution of the chapter is its definition and application of plan structure. This chapter has attempted to give a principled definition of a plan, and to show how plans interact with other important views of a program. Programmers do not adopt a single approach to design or understanding; a program is too complex to allow it. Instead, they engage in a opportunistic, as-needed search through multiple representations in both program design and understanding. They see a program as an artifact, a machine designed to achieve some purpose. A program does not have a structure: it can be seen from many perspectives. The most important of these seem to be the causal, reason, and object structures of a program.

User-Centered Requirements for Reverse Engineering Tools

Ray Waddington

Information Technology Development Branch, Atomic Energy of Canada Ltd Research,
Chalk River Laboratories, Chalk River, Ontario, Canada K0J 1J0.

The most recent genre of software engineering environments — and that predicted for the future of software development — comprises a collection of Computer Aided Software Engineering (CASE) tools. Most CASE tools available today are targeted at forward engineering, which is the engineering of new software. Yet most software costs are accounted for by maintenance of existing software. In contrast to forward engineering, reverse engineering is the engineering of old software: the process begins (usually) with the source code of an already implemented (and possibly maintained) application. The products of reverse engineering are recovered design documents in the form of structure charts, dataflow diagrams and the like.

Psychologists have studied how expert programmers understand source code — and typically how they do so in the absence of any form of design documentation. Reverse engineering is, in principle, the automation of source code comprehension in the absence of design documentation. This chapter reviews the current state of reverse engineering technology and the current level of psychological understanding of the cognitive processes involved in source code comprehension. It proposes a matching of psychological and software engineering research with a view to the improved design of reverse engineering CASE tools.

Keywords: reverse engineering, CASE, programming plan, psychology of programming.

1. Introduction

It appears that much software engineering in the near future will be performed in Computer Aided Software Engineering (CASE) environments. Most commercially available CASE tools today are of somewhat limited applicability. This is because they are targeted at forward engineering — the production of new software, using structured analysis, design and programming techniques, frequently on the assumption of following a 'waterfall' software process model. How accurately these factors model software engineering practice depends on the organization using the technology. McClure (1989) and others — see articles in (Spurr & Layzell, 1990) — have documented the commercial success of this type of software engineering in many companies.

Whilst the degree of new software production varies greatly among companies, it is the goal of many commercial software producers to be able to reuse existing software. Indeed, one form of software reuse that many companies practice is maintenance. How much time a commercial software producer spends on maintenance is a contentious issue. The most often reported statistic in the literature today is 80% of its time.

Reverse engineering tools are among the most useful in software maintenance. Reverse engineering itself is a relatively new subdiscipline, and there are few commercially marketed products. Successful results have been reported in limited contexts only: usually the reverse engineered code has been Cobol code, and the application has been targeted in a narrow, well understood domain, such as financial transaction processing. Completely automatic reverse engineering is a future goal, whose feasibility has not yet been demonstrated.

This chapter discusses current research trends in reverse engineering and the psychological study of programming. It proposes ways in which the psychological study of programming can contribute to the design of the next generation of reverse engineering tools.

2. Reverse Engineering Today

Re-engineering is a process commonly undertaken during perfective maintenance (Bohner, 1990), and is also suited to the requirements of adaptive maintenance. It involves two stages: first, taking an existing software artifact and working backward from the source code to regenerate its design, and, second, working forward from the recovered design to produce a modified version of the original software artifact. The first of these two stages is called reverse engineering. Reverse engineering is one of the most recent subdisciplines of software engineering. There are few commercially marketed reverse engineering tools — most of these are applicable only to the Cobol programming language. (Interestingly, Cobol itself enjoys a noticeable absence in current trends in forward engineering CASE technology — e.g. (Schussel, 1990).)

The most general principle behind reverse engineering is to begin with products from one phase of a software lifecycle and from them generate the products of the previous phase (Chikofsky & Cross, 1990). In practice this has meant beginning with source-level code (usually in Cobol), and generating design products in the representations of structured design techniques. Examples of these representations are data dictionaries, process specifications, module descriptions, entity-relationship diagrams, structure charts, module and variable tables, and so on. There are no principled reasons why the recovered design products could not be based in other representations. Those of structured design have been chosen in the past, partly because of the familiarity of structured methods and partly because they allow the forward engineering stage of reengineering to be undertaken using appropriate CASE technology (Martin, 1991).

Broadly speaking there are two classes of products from reverse engineering tools: to do with code and data (Martin, 1991), although most currently available tools produce both types of representation, rather than strictly one or the other. Four factors may be used to characterize reverse engineering tools (Bohner, 1990):

- *Abstraction*: different tools generate design representations of higher or lower levels of abstraction.
- *Completeness*: different tools capture more or less design information in a particular representation format.
- *Interactivity*: different tools allow/require more or less user intervention.
- *Direction*: some tools allow forward and reverse engineering, others allow only reverse engineering.

3. Experts' Representations of Source Code

In terms of programming subtasks reverse engineering is most appropriately associated with program comprehension. Section 2 showed how today's reverse engineering tools attempt to support software comprehension. According to Martin (1991, p.395): "The best way of representing and manipulating structured code is with an action diagram." In other words, Martin's claim is that the most appropriate reverse engineering tools will be ones that represent design in terms of action diagrams. (Note that this claim is made explicitly for *structured* code; see Bush (1985) for a detailed qualification of the term 'structured' as well as a demonstration that any unstructured program can be transformed into a structured equivalent.) He does not attempt to justify this claim, and evidence from the psychological study of programming can currently neither confirm nor refute it. However, psychological theories of how expert programmers mentally represent programs suggest how such tools should most appropriately represent design.

This section briefly surveys the main, current theoretical accounts of how expert programmers mentally represent software. It then discusses the implications of these accounts for reverse engineering tools.

3.1. Program Slices

Weiser (1982) has proposed that expert programmers automatically 'slice' programs when debugging them. A 'slice' is a fragment of program code which is a subset of the original program (and hence is usually smaller). It contains those statements of the program that would be visited in order for control to reach a given place in the program. Weiser asked experienced programmers to debug ALGOL-W programs. After the debugging phase, subjects were presented with modified code fragments and asked to rate, on a scale of 1–4, how sure they were that that fragment had appeared in the original program. Among these code fragments were a program 'slice' that was relevant to the bug in the program, and a contiguous program chunk that contained the erroneous statement. The modifications made were syntactic so that if a fragment were recognized, this was likely to be from semantic knowledge of the program. Weiser found no difference in the accuracy with which his subjects recognized 'slices' and contiguous chunks. Hence he proposed that programmers mentally 'slice' programs when debugging them. Although associated with debugging in Weiser's experiment, slicing is clearly applied during the comprehension, as opposed to diagnosis, phase of debugging.

3.2. Beacons

Brooks (1983) has proposed a theory of program comprehension that views the task as one of hypothesis formation and verification — see also (Letovsky, 1986). This mixed top-down/bottom-up process relies on the presence of so-called program beacons, which are critical in guiding the expert in program comprehension. Beacons are key features of code that an expert would expect to find in the code, based on their hypothesis of how the code works. For example, Wiedenbeck (1986c) tested Brook's example that in a program that performed a sort (she actually used a Pascal procedure to perform a Shellsort), the beacon would be the part of the code that did the swapping. She found that after being allowed just 3 minutes to study a 23-line procedure expert programmers recalled the three 'beacon' lines significantly better than novices. It seems that expert mental representation of software, then, comprises beacons.

3.3. Programming Plans

The most powerful, most widely researched, and the most contentious theory of programming expertise has been proposed by Soloway and others (Pennington, 1987a; Rist, 1986; Soloway & Ehrlich, 1984). Plans are (Soloway & Ehrlich, 1984, p.595) "... program fragments that represent stereotypical action sequences in programming, e.g. a RUNNING TOTAL LOOP PLAN, an ITEM SEARCH LOOP PLAN." 'Plans' are supposed to be a language-independent representation of expert programming knowledge. However, Gilmore & Green (1988) did not find any evidence that BASIC programmers used the 'plans' that Pascal programmers used. They suggested that 'plans' may not exist outside Pascal. In contrast, Robertson & Yu (1990; Yu & Robertson, 1988) found that programmers partitioned equivalent Pascal and Fortran programs into the same 'plan' structure. More recently, Davies (1990a) extended Gilmore & Green's observations by repeating their experimental procedure on expert BASIC programmers — who had received formal training in structured design methods. He found that, for those who had received such training, 'plans' appeared to be a meaningful feature of BASIC programs.

Each of theses studies has looked at procedural programming languages. However, Bellamy & Gilmore (1990) looked at logic programming in Prolog. A further issue that plan theory must address is that of the paradigm independence of programming plans — are they universal not only across languages within the same paradigm, but also across paradigms? Bellamy and Gilmore found equivocal evidence for the existence of plan structures in the code of Prolog programmers. Our own recent work (Shah & Waddington, 1991) attempts to address the issue of transfer of plan structures to different models of concurrent programming.

4. Current Research Trends in Reverse Engineering Tools

Of all the expert representational strategies discussed in Section 3, only programming 'plans' have been applied to reverse engineering tools. Perhaps the best known example is in the Programmer's Apprentice project (Rich & Waters, 1990). Rich & Wills (1990) describe a technique for recognizing a program's design from its source code. Their approach is based on a library of 'clichés'. (Although the terminology is different, 'clichés' are essentially the same as the programming 'plans' discussed in Section 3.) Both the program to be recognized and the 'clichés' themselves are represented in a formal, graphical notation (the plan calculus). A graph parsing algorithm is then applied to this representation to produce a design tree of recognized 'clichés'. Finally, the library 'clichés' that are present at the leaves of the tree can be matched back to the source code to generate natural language documentation.

Rich & Wills (1990) identify five difficulties of design recognition based on 'clichés' (some of which have been acknowledged by other researchers in this field):

- *Syntactic variation*: the same program function can be realized in a variety of ways within the same language.

- *Non-contiguousness*: 'clichés' ('plans') are often delocalized in a program — see also (Letovsky & Soloway, 1985; Soloway et al., 1988).

- *Implementation variation*: the same design abstraction (e.g. an abstract data type) can be implemented in different ways.

- *Overlapping implementations*: one part of a program may at once 'belong' to many 'clichés'. This is especially true when code has been highly optimized, as it often is in embedded, real-time software, for example.

- *Unrecognizable code*: since programs are not composed of 100% 'clichés', this approach has to be extended to allow partial recognition of 'clichés'.

They have been able to demonstrate considerable success in 'cliché' recognition for small size programs; they concede, however, that this approach in its present form will not scale up to programs of the size currently being maintained with the aid of commercial reverse engineering tools. This issue is considered again in Section 5.

A 'plan' like approach is also described by Harandi & Ning (1990). Whereas Rich & Wills (1990) are clear that "our goal is not to mimic the human *process* of 'cliché' recognition", Harandi & Ning's Program Analysis Tool (PAT) is based directly in their proposed model of expert program comprehension. PAT has a very different architecture from that of the Programmer's Apprentice, which reflects a different view of the structure and content of 'plan' knowledge, as well as a different philosophy of the kind of support that can and should be provided to program maintainers.

PAT also has a library of programming 'plans', formally represented in a plan definition language. In PAT's view of expert programming knowledge, 'plans' are associated with program events. These events are such things as statements, algorithms, data structures, etc. They have been classified by Harandi and Ning into an object-oriented class hierarchy. Here, for example, a program-event (the base class) is a superclass of an algorithm event, which is a superclass of a sort event, and three levels down is the specialization of a bubble-sort-map. 'Plans' also contain textual slots that are filled with information regarding the 'plan's' intended function. These are used for output, as discussed below.

During understanding, source code is first parsed into a collection of program events. The programming 'plans' are also parsed into production rules and stored in a plan base. These rules test for the existence of low-level events in the code and assert the existence of new, higher-level events. For example, in understanding a program containing a decremental (descending step) FOR-LOOP, a rule is fired that asserts the consequent existence of a DEC-COUNTER event. The process is then one of iterative inference, matching the test part of the plan based production rules to the event base generated from both the program and previous rule firing. The final event to be asserted is a top-level such as a bubble sorting algorithm. PAT's architecture includes a truth maintenance system, which tracks the firing of plan rules. After understanding has arrived at a final program event, this history of recognized events is combined with the textual slots stored as part of each 'plan'. The result is a natural language documentation of the original program, with an explanation of how each part (statement, variable, etc.) of the program contributes to its total function. The level of detail here is greater than that of the Programmer's Apprentice.

5. Conclusions: Requirements for Future Psychological Research and its Application to Reverse Engineering Tools

Despite the on-going theoretical debate about the psychological validity of programming 'plans', clearly something akin to these is useful in building the next generation of reverse engineering tools. How much of reverse engineering can be accomplished by 'plans' alone is unclear, since the successful application of 'plan' based tools has not been demonstrated for commercial size software. The Programmer's Apprentice 'cliché' library currently holds just a few dozen 'clichés', whereas PAT contains a few dozen 'plans'. It is not clear how many 'plans' an expert programmer holds, but estimates place the figure at 50,000 to 100,000.

A major problem with current psychological theories of 'plans' is that there is no established operational method for identifying them — but see (Rist, in this volume). In the past, proposers of 'plans' have invented them and then attempted to show their existence experimentally. Whilst this is a psychologically valid methodology, it is not a practical agenda for populating a commercial 'plan' library with the tens of thousands of 'plans'. Both Rich & Wills (1990) and Harandi & Ning (1990) have suggested that the problem might be overcome by incorporating some learning mechanism in a future tool, such that when it fails to interpret code according to known 'plans' it learns the 'plan' based interpretation of that code and stores this for future recognition of the same plan. Although psychologists have shown that one component of the development of programming expertise is the acquisition of programming 'plans', they have not yet addressed the issue of how 'plans' are learned. This is an area where psychology might contribute to the successful next enhancement of a tool like PAT or the Programmer's Apprentice.

A second problem with psychological theories of 'plans' is this: What knowledge do they capture? Section 4 showed that two independent workers used the same basic idea of 'plans'; yet in each case the knowledge they contained, and their role in comprehension, was different. In addition, neither of these two accounts of their content is consistent with that proposed in the psychological theories. Furthermore, these theories are themselves sometimes contradictory: whereas Soloway & Ehrlich (1984) claim that 'plans' are fragments of *code* meaningful to *expert* programmers, Pennington & Grabowski (1990) describe them as a mental representation of *design*; Bonar & Liffick (1990) use them as an *intermediary between design and code to help novice* programmers. The user of a reverse engineering tool probably doesn't care much for these esoterisms. However, if a mechanized understander purports to give the expert user the same design information they would seek themselves, it ought to work better if it is using the same knowledge to do this. A strong challenge to psychological theorists is to resolve these issues. An indication of the apparent inconsistencies of the different approaches to 'plan' theory can be seen in Table 1.

Even if the status of 'plans' is resolved, the 'plan' based approach will not likely solve the whole problems of reverse engineering. In any case, note that neither PAT nor the Programmer's Apprentice can be claimed strictly to be reverse engineering tools in their present form, since the format of their output is not directly compatible with any forward engineering tools. They are closer to re-documentation tools. Rich & Wills (1990) propose an extension of their approach which is a mixture of top-down and bottom-up processing. For example, they consider that human understanding proceeds by making high-level conjectures based on superficial analyses of code, which then direct bottom-up 'plan' based reasoning. This is similar to the beacon theory described in Section 3. Wiedenbeck (1986c) suggests, however, that the understanding given from beacons is not sufficient by itself for modification. Perhaps the kind of information gleaned from beacons is sufficient only for the *as-needed* strategy of understanding described by Littman et al. (1986). They found that those subjects who formed a superficial understanding of a program (using the *as-needed* strategy) did not acquire a detailed enough mental model of the causal interactions of program parts to succeed in a maintenance task. Here is another area where psychological research can contribute by investigating precisely how superficial top-down and detailed bottom-up human understanding proceed together, and how this process might be applied automatically.

Research along similar lines has offered design recovery as the next evolution of reverse engineering. Design recovery is based on the premise that the source code alone does not contain all the original design information — see also (Bachman, 1988). It therefore uses

	Rich & Waters	Johnson & Soloway	Pennington & Grabowski	Bonar & Liffick	Harandi & Ning	Rist
System	Programmers' Apprentice	Proust	†	BridgeTalk	Program Analysis Tool	Plan Analysis for Reverse Engineering
Lifecycle Stage(s) Addressed	Requirements Design Implementation Modification	Implementation	Design	Bridge between Design and Implementation	Modification	Modification
Algorithmic or Data Structure Plans	Both	Algorithmic	†	Algorithmic	Both	Algorithmic based on control and data flow
Novice or Expert Knowledge in Plans	Expert	Expert	Expert	Expert	Expert	Expert
Expert or Novice User of System	Expert	Novice	†	Either	Presumably Expert	Presumably Expert
Forward or Reverse Engineering	Both	Forward	Both	Forward	Reverse	Reverse
Type of Knowledge Represented in Plan Structures	Stereotypic Code Fragments Documentation Information	Stereotypic Code Fragments	Design Knowledge	Stereotypic Code Fragments	Stereotypic Code Fragments Documentation Information	Stereotypic Code Fragments

Table 1: Use of plans in software engineering. † These authors present a theoretical discussion — not an actual system.

more inputs than reverse engineering — in particular, any design documentation that may still exist, as well as more informal information such as personal experience and general knowledge about the domain in a domain model. The products of design recovery are also more general than those of reverse engineering (Bohner, 1990). In short design recovery attempts to support maintenance programmers by helping them understand fully what a program does and how it works. It is here that psychological work can have its greatest impact on future software tools. Ultimately, the expert must have a multitude of possible perspectives of any piece of code; the four mentioned in Section 3 are just some of those that have been proposed in the literature. The expert must also have a range of strategies for using these views as appropriate. It is up to psychologists to complete what is currently just a fragmentary picture of experts' full range of abilities.

Why Industry Doesn't Use the Wonderful Notations We Researchers Have Given Them to Reason About Their Designs

Andrew Monk, Martin Curry & Peter Wright

Department of Psychology, University of York, York YO1 5DD, UK.

Tel: +44 (0)904 433148

EMail: AM1@york.ac.uk

Software design is a complex problem, and the designer needs some way of structuring and reasoning about that problem if it is to be solved effectively. Various abstractions and formalisms have been proposed by the research community using diagrammatic and mathematically based notations. While industry has recognised the potential benefit of using these notations to abstract, and hence reason more clearly about, a design their uptake has been disappointing.

This chapter is based on interviews with six designers working for a large UK defence contractor. The conclusions drawn are summarised as five 'obstacles' to the use of formal notations in practical design situations. They are:

- *Learning to use a notation to the point where productive work can be done represents a considerable investment on the part of the designer.*

- *There is rarely any procedural guidance about how a notation should be used.*

- *The use of formal notations is labour intensive and may become impractical with large or even medium scale projects.*

- *The notations available may not be suitable for modelling the aspects of the system of most interest to the designer.*

- *Specifications are continually changing, at the time of requirements specification, during the process of design and after implementation.*

Keywords: specification, formal methods, notation, software design.

1. Who Was Interviewed?

The site visited was that of a major UK defence contractor who have an interest in the application of formal methods. Designers at the site were familiar with the use of MASCOT and CORE. They were interested in exploring more mathematical notations such as VDM

(Jones, 1986), Z (Spivey, 1988), and OBJ (Goguen & Tardon, 1979) and diagrammatic notations, e.g. statecharts (Harel, 1988).

The interviewees were probably better qualified and more mathematically oriented than is the norm in the software industry. All had a degree in mathematics, engineering or computer science, one had a PhD in physics. The site at which they worked had a research orientation and was primarily concerned with software related to defence contracts. The background and situation of the interviewees should have made them unusually sympathetic to formal and semi-formal notations, yet all six felt there were serious problems which prevented their use in real design tasks. Some had experience of mathematically based notations others diagrammatic or tabular notations.

2. Obstacles

Obstacle 1: Learning.

Learning to use a notation to the point where productive work can be done represents a considerable investment on the part of the designer.

Just as learning the elements of a programming language is easy but learning to use it productively may take many months, so learning to apply a notation effectively may take some time (see Quote 1 & 2). It is not reasonable to expect someone to learn several very different notations or to change the notations that they use on a regular basis (see Quote 3).

> Quote 1: "It was probably six months or so, before I felt happy enough to start suggesting modifications myself rather than just taking what was given."

> Quote 2: "It takes years, perhaps, to get up to the top (MASCOT) level ..."

> Quote 3: "One tends to find that people have a natural ... inertia ... once they have tried, or have been told to use, certain methods ... that's it, they are **the** methods and nothing else ... means anything, or shall be used ..."

Obstacle 2: Coordination.

There is rarely any procedural guidance about how a notation should be used.

Commonly, researchers who develop formal notations believe that their task only extends to providing the basic facilities for reasoning and that the manner in which the notation is applied is up to the individual. However, guidance about how to use a notation helps to reduce the investment needed to use it (Obstacle 1). Perhaps more importantly, unguided use of a notation will result in very idiosyncratic representations (see Quote 4).

A notation can only be used to communicate the work of one individual or group to another if the way that notation is used is standardised. This is one of the purposes of a software design methodology such as SSADM (Downs, Clare & Coe, 1988) or JSD (Jackson, 1986). To date, formal notations have not been integrated into software design methodologies. However, until they are, the use of formal notations is unlikely to be supported by management.

> Quote 4: "I made a conscious decision that I wouldn't ... go and read CORE spec's or too much about it until I'd made up my own mind, because

that was part of my research ... when I did actually have a look at CORE specs that had been written, by that time I had developed my own views and philosophy, I realised that the CORE spec's that I had been producing were not going to look the same as the ones that other people had produced because I had different views on it."

Obstacle 3: Scale.

The use of formal notations is labour intensive and may become impractical with large or even medium scale projects.

Concern was expressed as to the adequacy of any particular formalism for proving things about development projects of realistic scale (see Quotes 5 and 6). Proof is only one of the benefits claimed for formal notations. They have also been proposed as:

- as a medium for communicating design solutions to others; and
- tools for thought.

However, notations often do not scale up gracefully so that the specification becomes unmanageable, even for these purposes, as it becomes larger.

> Quote 5: "Just taking a simple three line exercise took quite a long time to actually prove, to actually try to prove a ... large system ... (will) just take too long to do unless you get really automated tools."

> Quote 6: "You can do part of a project with them, like if you can determine ... where you've got your problems, you can formally prove that bit but you could never prove a system like XXXXX. It's just too big. It would take you a couple of decades."

Obstacle 4: Scope.

The notations available may not be suitable for modelling the aspects of the system of most interest to the designer.

The work at this site was to develop multi-processor systems for real-time applications, thus concurrency and timing were critical issues. Much of the effort and expense of software development went into testing to ensure that the software met its performance requirements. Things had to be demonstrated to happen within certain critical time spans, often in the order of microseconds. The problem of modelling time critical systems is that it is still very much a research topic. Also, for good practical reasons (the training investment, see Obstacle 1) the company has a commitment to MASCOT so MASCOT ACP diagrams were modified to enable timing to be expressed. This 'fix', however, was seen as unsatisfactory.

Obstacle 5: Change.

Specifications are continually changing, at the time of requirements specification, during the process of design and after implementation.

A design will change frequently and radically throughout the project life cycle. For example, initially the requirements will change as specification shows what is practical or affordable. The classic response to this problem is that one should get the requirement specification right first time. However, this misses the point, which is that it is the requirements themselves that change and that they do so in response to the process of building the system (see Quote 7).

In fact in this respect, formal notations may have advantages over their less formal counterparts. Formal notations are designed to be 'compositional' so that changes can be localised and previous work on proofs is not invalidated. In addition the concise form of the notation should allow the designer to pin-point where changes need to be made more easily. Nevertheless much more could be done to facilitate change.

> Quote 7: "The other big thing with formal methods, of course, is that they tend to not really support very well, at this stage, the idea of a dynamic requirement. They tend to be much more, you know, keenly fitting into the ideas of, OK that's the requirement! Now lets think about making that formal — Right? which, in a sense, is the easy bit. If you can get your project to that stage then you're doing very well ... "

3. What is to be Done?

For formal notations to be successful they have to cross the bridge between research in Computer Science and practical commercial systems development. From the point of view of those in industry, much remains to be done before formal notations will be able to help rather than hinder them in their job of software development. The obstacles described above suggest three kinds of work that need to be pursued:

1. Ways of providing guidance in their application within the context of a software development methodology.

2. Developing tool support to automate some of the labour intensive aspects of their use.

3. Developing notations with more specific applications and more 'natural' (to the designer) forms.

One is reminded of previous campaigns for user-centred design. Designers are the users of formal notations. What is required here is some designer-centred design.

Acknowledgement

This research was supported by DTI/SERC grant to the first author.

Theme 2 Discussion Report

For this theme, the discussant introduced the following six issues for discussion by the delegates:

1. Is Rist's definition of plan and schema congruent with any previous ones?
2. Could a system be written that would learn plans and use these to reverse engineer code?
3. How do experts map between their code-level representations and higher-level ones?
4. Can plan-based reverse engineering be integrated with re-engineering?
5. How do other code representations interact with plan-based representations in software comprehension?
6. What impact does the software process model have on reverse engineering?

Four discussion groups were formed. A summary of each of these groups' discussion is reported below.

Group 1

1. The answering of this question requires more interdisciplinary expertise between the Human–Computer Interaction and the Software Engineering communities. We are unfamiliar with tools including the Programmers' Apprentice and Program Analysis Tool, while the Software Engineering community does not incorporate psychological features into tool-based environments. More combined workshops and conferences, cross-fertilization of ideas are needed in this area.

2. In short, this question is proposing a need for inductive machine learning of programming plans and schemas from program instances. However, support tools are unlikely in real environments to have sufficient knowledge of domains, programming languages and constructs etc. In addition current ML techniques are still limited to Blockworlds (see AAAI'91 Proceedings). Effective acquisition of programming plans and schemas will probably require interaction with domain/environment analysts and experts, which unfortunately has proven to be time-consuming and difficult (e.g. Arango, Freeman). However, what choice have we?

3. This question assumed that plans referred to formal plans/schemata held in support tools. Concern was expressed as to whether these 'generic' plans could aptly represent the breadth and appropriateness of the needs which they must meet. The breadth or coverage problem dictates that it is difficult to provide a set of formal plans generic to all plan/program instances, which may vary by application domain features, nonfunctional requirements such as timing etc. Similarly, the appropriateness problem suggests that formal plans will probably require modification to fit domains in which they must be realised or embedded. Plans are unlikely to

fit each instantiation without customisation. The implication from this is the need to support interaction between man and machine during selection, instantiation and customisation of plans.

4. The question implied that reverse engineering may be supported by knowledge structures other than plans. The group was unable to identify other knowledge structures to assist re-engineering of program designs. However, alternatives may exist during engineering of the earlier stages of software development, for instance, the Requirements' Apprentice provides generic domain cliché represented using declarative rather than procedural knowledge.

5. No answer.

6. Reverse and Re-engineering is likely to have an impact in the following areas of the software development process:

   — Complete design rationale be lost, for example the Plain-Old Telephone System of AT&T was developed 20 years ago, however the only software engineer who understood the entire system died leaving considerable 'knowledge holes' during the reverse engineering process.

   — In light of this, reverse engineering can sell specifications and designs back to the software engineering community, thus justifying the role of reverse engineering to the software development community as well as underscoring the importance of developing specifications and designs in the first place during forward engineering. In short, reverse engineering presents us with a lesson to be learnt.

   — Reverse engineering is probably the best way to get around problems of hardware reconfiguration.

   — Reverse engineering of designs and specifications inevitably moves the emphasis of tool and method support up the life cycle to bring the well-documented improvements in software productivity and quality.

Group 2

Our group decided to discuss what the terms reverse and re-engineering mean rather than should mean.

First, two definitions: *Reverse engineering* is to translate from object code to source code. *Re-engineering* is to take source code and other available information and to create complete documentation.

One point made was that too many terms meaning more or less the same thing are in use. For example, words like plan, schema, template and cliché seems to stand for or have the same meaning as the word pattern and are probably used to distinguish patterns of slightly (but not definitely) different nature.

A second point was that the area may benefit much by looking at reverse engineering and pattern matching in other engineering areas, for example electronic circuit recapturing or design rule checking. That is, there are many areas where one is interested in the recognition of patterns and tries to find proper higher level abstractions of these patterns.

Point three, too much attention seems to be paid to the support of procedural languages like Pascal.

This area has some interesting similarities with archaeology, e.g. many clues from many sources; never complete (many pieces will be missing); different perspectives may give rise to different interpretations.

Finally, and partly based on the analogy with modern archaeology, it could be productive to analyze the current use and environment of the reverse or re-engineering object in question and to reconstruct from major functions and habits in use in order to capture the intended functionality of interest.

Group 3

Major Questions addressed by this group:

1. What impact does the software process have on reverse engineering?
2. What are the limits of reverse engineering?

Some Conclusions:

1. We cannot extract from a system any design information which was never put into the system in the first place.
2. There are two major things that can be learned from reverse engineering:
    i. to deal, maintain, and change existing systems;
    ii. by studying difficulties with current systems, what can we learn for our current system building efforts?
3. Major goals for any system building effort should be:
    i. design for change;
    ii. design for evolution;
    iii. design for maintainability.
4. To achieve these goals will create upfront costs in the system development process; to do so, may be difficult to achieve, because the people who have to do the work are not necessarily the beneficiaries of these efforts.
5. A promising approach appears to be the careful recording of the design rationale; claim: extensive recording of design rationale will facilitate the reverse engineering process.
6. With respect to design rationale there are two aspects:
    i. those which were articulated in the original design process but never documented and recorded;
    ii. and those which were overlooked in the original design effort.
7. Interesting examples to think about:
    i. the US phone system running out of area codes (because of the strange design decision that the second digit of the area code had to be a zero or a one);
    ii. the revenge of the year 2,000 for many software products;
    iii. a success story of not minding up-front costs: the "5 years/50,000 miles" warranty of the automobile industry.
8. The appealing aspect of reverse engineering: if it worked, it could be applied to basically all existing programs to extract a conceptual structure behind the system.

Group Four

The state-of-the-art today: All that are available are low-level tools for, e.g. recognising the appearance and use of RECORDS in Cobol. There are no high-level tools available that can perform plan recognition or similar on a large scale. Even if we had a 100,000 cliché library, the potential for plan-based recognition would still be unclear. There is still a large role for human expertise and human intelligence in software tools. Something akin to plan recognition would be an ideal, but we were not sure precisely how far such an approach could be taken in reality.

We felt that plan recognition might be a more feasible approach if it were adopted in tandem with formal methods, so that formal proofs could be made of program correctness. Plan recognition starts with plan libraries, whereas formal specifications can be generated in a bottom-up fashion. But human interaction would be necessary here.

We felt that re-engineering was applied in cases where there had been no software process model used in the development of the system; however, this was not a significant factor in the application of reverse engineering.

We were unsure as to the precise role of clichés and the knowledge that they contained. For example, could two or more clichés have the same 'fingerprint'.

We discussed a case where a software engineer was required to port software from a sequential architecture to a parallel one. Certain parts of the algorithm had to be recognised as non-optimal; this required different parts of knowledge:

1. of the algorithm;
2. of the original programmer's objectives;
3. of the constraints of the original (sequential) computer;
4. of optimising techniques;
5. the range of the input data.

We were not sure how to separate the overall knowledge being used in this example into the different types of knowledge discussed in the five original papers. We felt that code inspection tools, e.g. 'intelligent' browsers, might support such tasks, but there is a lot of human expertise being brought to bear that the software psychology community does not yet understand.

The group's overall feeling was that a technique such as plan recognition represented an important first step in the development of future tools, but we felt that large-scale tools that would have a significant impact in software engineering were not yet on the horizon. At the same time it was felt that people will continue to develop systems in the short term future, irrespective of whether the software psychology community has a useful input. Therefore it was felt to be important to continue to develop theories such as the plan theory of Rist, and to seek practical ways in which these theories could be applied to software engineering tools.

Ray Waddington
AECL Research

Theme 3: Technological Solutions

Theme 3 Introduction

Whereas the previous two themes addressed what is known about human factors in software engineering, this theme (and the next) examine some of the solutions available for improving the lot of software engineers. This theme focusses on tools for software engineering environments ranging from program visualization, through graphical user interface tools, to assisting in task analysis and dialogue specification.

These chapters should be read in conjunction with the previous two themes. Whilst some of the authors in this theme directly address the issues of usability for the software engineer, others leave these issues implicit. The emphasis within many of the discussion groups was on the paradox of the undoubted value of these tools, coupled with concern at how they can be integrated into existing work practices without compounding the software engineering crisis.

The first chapter in this theme by Domingue et al. looks at the issue of software visualization. By trying to provide a common, coherent framework for visualization this chapter is addressing usability issues, in that it provides dimensions and terms for discussing and evaluating systems. As a bonus, they do this in the context of building a visualization system as well, as a demonstration of the value of their classification schema. An issue left unaddressed is that of when visualization systems should be used — they are primarily an aid to comprehension, maintenance and debugging, but their value is only just being assessed (see the chapter by Patel et al. in Theme 2).

The next chapter, by Herczeg, and the following one by Schneider-Hufschmidt, present tools for composing graphical user interfaces. It has been estimated that a major proportion of software engineering time is spent on the design and construction of the user interface — reducing this time, and providing tools which enable interface specialists to perform the task (separately from building the application) should be of major benefit to the software engineering profession. Herczeg's contribution also shows how such a tool can be integrated within a general programming environment, whereas Schneider-Hufschmidt emphasizes more the potential separability of interface design from application construction. This contrast between the two chapters provides an interesting challenge in relation to providing human factors advice about the pros and cons of each approach.

The chapter by Blumenthal provides a more general overview of this topic, reviewing a number of interface design tools, with a particular emphasis on those that provide automatic interface design. A key element of this chapter is the suggestion that knowledge about the context in which the interface will be used is required in the design of the interface. Although Blumenthal presents this in the context of an Artificial Intelligence problem, it is a more general issue — to what extent can all the information required in interface design be brought together at the point of design either in a tool, or in the hands of a designer?

Which brings us to the final chapter in this theme by Monk & Curry, which describes a tool which does not design the interface, but which serves to help in the massive task of information assimilation. Here the emphasis is on providing a usable tool which will help designers to make the right interface choices when using tools like those described in the preceding chapters. In addressing the usability issue, this tool is not a separate framework for reviewing interface choices, but a part of the overall environment and provides a way of dealing with the integration of interface design with application construction.

David Gilmore
Department of Psychology, University of Nottingham

Viz: A Framework for Describing and Implementing Software Visualization Systems

John Domingue, Blaine A Price & Marc Eisenstadt

Human Cognition Research Laboratory, The Open University, Milton Keynes MK7 6AA, UK.

Tel: +44 (0)908 653800

Fax: +44 (0)908 653169

EMail: j.b.domingue@open.ac.uk

In recent years many prototype systems have been developed for graphically visualizing program execution in an attempt to create a better interface between software engineers and their programs. Several classification-based taxonomies have been proposed to describe visualization systems and several general frameworks have been proposed for implementing such systems. In this chapter we provide a framework for both describing existing systems and implementing new ones. We demonstrate the utility of automatic program visualization by re-implementing several existing programming language visualization systems using this framework.

Keywords: program visualization, algorithm animation, CASE, debugging aids.

1. Introduction

1.1. What is Software Visualization?

The tools traditionally used by software engineers to help monitor and analyse program execution have been plain ASCII-text based debugging environments which usually allow the user to trace the currently executing code, stop and start execution at arbitrary points, and examine the contents of data structures. Although they can be understood by experts, these tools have a limited pedagogic value and by the early 1980's the work of Baecker & Sherman (1981) and Brown (1988) showed how algorithms could be animated with cartoon-like displays that show a high level abstraction of a program's code and data. Brown referred to this as 'algorithm animation' since the emphasis was on meaningful graphical abstractions about the high level algorithm underlying a program. Both of these systems proved successful in computer science teaching, but since algorithm animations tend to be custom built (by hand) for specific algorithms, the overhead is too high for use by software engineers working on large projects.

A concurrent development in the mid-1980's was the appearance of systems which displayed graphical representations that were more tightly coupled with a program's code or data and showed more or less faithful representations of the code as it was executing. Although the displays were not as rich as the custom built algorithm animations, these systems were closer to the tools that software engineers might use. These 'program animators' together with the algorithm animators became known as 'program visualization' systems. We prefer the more descriptive term 'software visualization' (Price, Small & Baecker, 1992) which encompasses both algorithm and program visualization as well as the visualization of multi-program software systems. In this chapter we will use the term software visualization (SV) to describe systems that use visual (and other) media to enhance one programmer's understanding of another's work (or his own).

1.2. Classifying SV Systems

One of the first taxonomies of SV was that of Myers (1986; Myers, 1990a) which served to differentiate SV, visual programming, and programming-by-example. In classifying SV systems, Myers used only two dimensions: static vs. dynamic and code vs. data. The first dimension is based on the style of implementation; static displays show one or more motionless graphics representing the state of the program at a particular point in time while animated displays show an image which changes as the program executes. The second dimension describes the type of data being visualized, be it the program source code or its data structures.

The taxonomies that have been proposed since Myers have also used few dimensions, which seems to ignore that fact that there are many styles for implementation and interaction as well as different machine architectures and ways of utilizing them. Price, Baecker & Small (1993; Price, Small & Baecker, 1992) recently proposed a taxonomy which describes 6 broad categories for SV systems: scope, content, form, method, interaction, and effectiveness. Each of these categories has a hierarchy of characteristics, for a total of over fifty dimensions to describe each system. This pragmatic classification system provides a means for comparing the functionality and performance of a wide range of SV systems, but it does not provide a language or framework for implementing new systems. Eisenstadt et al. (1990) described nine qualitative dimensions of visual computing environments which can form the basis of a language for describing SV systems, but these serve only to describe the attributes of systems rather than drive their construction.

1.3. From Taxonomy to Framework and System: "What goes on?"

Taxonomies are useful, but we need more if we are to provide a firm basis upon which to describe SV systems in depth, let alone implement them. A framework for describing SV systems could provide extra leverage by being a little more prescriptive, i.e. making a commitment regarding how to approach the design and construction of SV systems. In fact, it is not a very big step from specifying such a framework to designing a system for building a SV system (SV system-building system). An important difference is that the former activity is merely a paper exercise, whereas the latter activity is intended to lead towards a working tool. Indeed, the latter activity serves as a useful forcing function: it encourages us to build re-usable libraries of software that we believe encapsulate important generalizations about SV system-building. The proof of the soundness of a design built in this way lies in the ability to use it both to reverse-engineer existing SV systems and construct new systems with ease.

By shifting our focus of attention from taxonomy to working system (and its underlying framework), we force ourselves to face the fundamental question of software visualization:

"What goes on during program execution?" There are many different 'truths' or 'stories' that one can tell about the seemingly unambiguous behaviour of an executing program, as convincingly demonstrated (in the case of Prolog) by Pain & Bundy (1987). The choice of a certain story or metaphor to explain how a particular machine, programming language, or program works depends on the culture of the audience, their level of experience, and which points the author wishes to emphasize. Our problem is not how to work out which story to tell, but rather how to enable diverse story-tellers to carry out their craftwork. As in Propp's analysis of folktales (Propp, 1968), we want to understand the commonalities, the invariances, the essentials of a 'story' that differentiate it from random scribblings or random collections of 'sentences', and to do this at a level of abstraction which is meaningful to the community of 'story-tellers' (SV system builders) we are addressing. This means that the 'kernel truths' about memory addresses, registers, and CPU instructions are not necessarily of immediate use to us, because they usually offer too low a level of abstraction.

1.4. Programming Language Visualization vs. Algorithm Animation

Several of the noteworthy SV building systems and frameworks focus on algorithm animation (AA), which means that the animations that they produce are custom designed and each new program requires manual annotation to animate it. Programs are animated in BALSA (Brown, 1988) by adding calls to the animation system at 'interesting events' in the code. TANGO (Stasko, 1990) also animates programs with interesting event calls and it provides facilities for smooth transitions in animations. While producing aesthetically pleasing results, these techniques are not practical for large software engineering projects, which require a more automatic approach.

In Viz we have focussed on supporting the construction of systems which visualize the execution of programming languages. By visualizing a programming language interpreter (or compiler) one also automatically gets a visualization for any program written in that language — thus achieving the automatic goal suggested in (Price, Small & Baecker, 1992). Programming language visualization (PLV) and algorithm animation (AA) overlap, but there are differences in the approach. AA systems typically show a very high level picture of a program's execution and the images that it generates can be far removed from the data structures contained in the program. The animations cover a narrow set of programs (typically a single algorithm). PLVs on the other hand have to deal with any program which can be realised in the language. Thus PLV displays usually have much simpler images than AA displays since they must be highly generalized whereas AA displays can be custom tuned. The problem for an AA is to show the characteristics (signature) of an algorithm as clearly as possible. The problem for a PLV is to allow arbitrarily large execution spaces to be examined in a comprehensible fashion.

Our approach is to concentrate primarily on PLV, but to provide generalizations which are applicable to AA as well. In the rest of this chapter we describe the design of a SV system-building system (and framework) called Viz, which we have implemented as a prototype running in Common Lisp on Sun workstations. Our Viz implementation has already been used to reconstruct three well known PLV systems: an OPS-5 visualization system (based on TRI (Domingue & Eisenstadt, 1989)), a Prolog visualization system (based on TPM (Eisenstadt & Brayshaw, 1988)), and a Lisp tracer (based on the Symbolics tracer). After describing the Viz architecture, we explain how two of these reconstructions were implemented. In order to explore the relationship between Viz's PLV-oriented approach and AA-oriented systems we have also used Viz to implement some of the animations from BALSA (sorting) and TANGO (bin-packing). We conclude with a comparison of the terminology used in BALSA, TANGO, and Viz to describe abstractions and we highlight the advantages of the Viz design.

2. Viz Fundamentals

In Viz, we adopt the 'story-telling' metaphor by considering program execution to be a series of *history events* happening to (or perpetrated by) *players*. To allow our 'story-tellers' (SV system builders) considerable freedom, a player can be any part of a program, such as a function, a data structure, or a line of code. Each player has a name and is in some *state*, which may change when a history event occurs for that player. History events are like Brown's 'interesting events' in BALSA — each event corresponds to some code being executed in the program or some data changing its value. These events are recorded in the history module, which allows them to be accessed by the user and 'replayed'. Events and states are *mapped* into a visual representation which is accessible to the end-user (the programmers who need to use the SV system, not the SV system builder). But the mapping is not just a question of storing pixel patterns to correspond to different events and states — we also need to specify different views, and ways of navigating around them. Before we describe the Viz architecture in detail, let's preview the main ingredients:

- *Histories*: A record of key events that occur over time as the program runs, with each event belonging to a player; each event is linked to some part of the code and may cause a player to change its state (there is also some pre-history information available before the program begins running, such as the static program source code hierarchy and initial player states).

- *Views*: The style in which a particular set of players, states or events is presented, such as using text, a tree, or a plotted graph; each view uses its own style and emphasizes a particular dimension of the data that it is displaying.

- *Mappings*: The encodings used by a player to show its state changes in diagrammatic or textual form on a view using some kind of graphical language, typography, or sound; some of a player's mappings may be for the exclusive use of its *navigators*.

- *Navigators*: The tools or techniques making up the interface that allows the user to traverse a view, move between multiple views, change scale, compress or expand objects, and move forward or backward in time through the histories.

This framework is equally at home dealing with either program code or algorithms, since a player and its history events may represent anything from a low-level (program code) abstraction such as "invoke a function call" to a high level (algorithm) abstraction such as "insert a pointer into a hash table".

3. Viz Architecture

Figure 1 shows the general architecture of Viz. The target system source code is annotated to generate history calls. When the system being visualized is a programming language, hooks into the interpreter or compiler are used to generate history events. As the code executes, the inserted calls cause 'interesting' events regarding players to be recorded in the history module. When the user runs the visualization, the view module reads the history data at the request of the navigator. The view module sets the layout of the history events and sends local coordinates for each history datum through the mapping module, which draws a graphical or textual representation for each event. The screen images are then transformed and presented

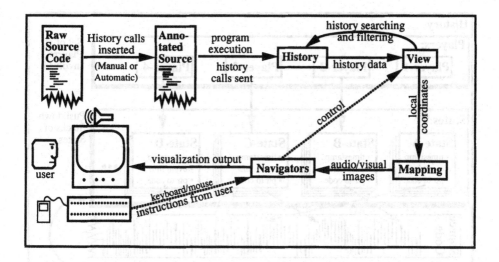

Figure 1: The architecture of Viz

on the screen by the navigator. The user interacts with the visualization using the navigator, which sends control signals to the view module to cause all changes in the visualization, such as panning, zooming, local compression and expansion, and moving forward and backward in time through the program execution space.

3.1. Histories

Histories are the data that form the basis of any visualization and they roughly correspond to what Price, Small, and Baecker called 'content' in their taxonomy. Most SV systems require the visualization designer to manually select the events in the program which will characterize it or show each of its continuous or discrete states. This can be done by inserting explicit instructions in the code or by attaching 'probes' to various data structures (this requires that the language interpreter be modified). The probe method is necessary when one wishes to visualize a programming language itself. It is also possible to have the events automatically selected by using algorithm recognition techniques, as shown by a recent system which recognizes simple programming clichés and produce algorithm animations (Henry, Whaley & Forstall, 1990). This algorithm recognition work has only been successful with a small set of simple programs, however, and thus can not yet scale up to the demands of full-size software engineering visualizations. A simpler approach using a preprocessor to automatically insert event calls into the source code at points related to the language syntax, such as procedure calls and returns, can be used to achieve automatic visualization of programs of any size (Price & Baecker, 1991), but the visualizations tend to display few abstractions.

The first task for the visualization programmer using Viz is to decide what types of events may occur during program execution, which elements in the program will be the players and how the players change state. After defining these, the programmer may insert *create new player* and *note event* calls in the code, which form the interface between a program and its visualization.

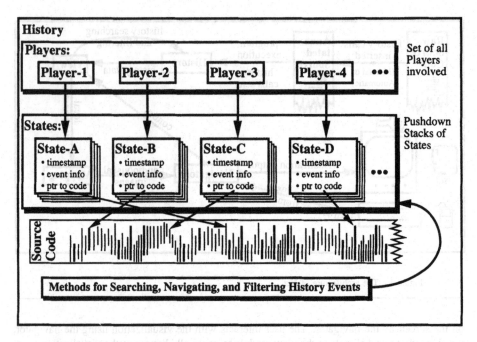

Figure 2: A snapshot of a prototypical history structure

Figure 2 shows a prototypical history structure in the history module. This consists of a set of players and a sequence of history states. Each player has a name, a pointer to its current history state and a pushdown stack of previous states. Each state has a timestamp, a pointer to the appropriate segment of source code and an event structure. As a program executes, new players and history states are created, and existing players are 'moved' into new states, pushing previous states onto a stack. The various states of the players are caused by the different types of events.

The choice of players and event types together with the judicious placement of *note event* calls in code determine the execution model. Currently, we do not advocate any methodology for creating the execution model, except to point out that events are the "things that happen" in a program causing a player or players to move into a particular state.

3.2. *Views*

A view can be thought of as a perspective or window on some aspect of a program or algorithm, with (possibly) many views making up a visualization. A view is a kind of style for laying out the mapped players, so it is possible to have two different views of the same players in order to emphasize different details.

Stasko states:

> "In designing animations with Tango, I quickly discovered the need to
> repeatedly create logical structures of objects such as rows, columns, graphs
> and trees." (Stasko, 1990, pp.233-234)

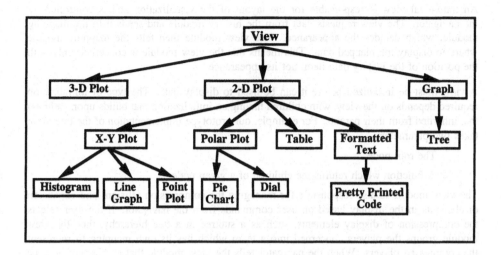

Figure 3: Inheritance hierarchy of views

Stasko addressed this by implementing a package of high level macros. Rather than an add-on or macro package, we see these complex entities as a central part of any visualization. We have observed that the methods or procedures for drawing and managing many graphical visualizations can be characterized by an inheritance hierarchy. For example, if one has a set of methods for drawing a histogram, then many of these methods could be reused for a 'thermometer' display, since a thermometer is just a histogram with one data element. Similarly, if one has a set of methods for managing generalized directed or un-directed graphs then these would form the basis of any tree drawing methods that were required. This has an important implication for the design of a SV system-building system: it means that by implementing the views as a hierarchy with inheritance, new views that are required can be added as new 'child nodes'. Since these new nodes inherit the methods of their parents, a great deal of code reusability is achieved.

Figure 3 shows our initial view hierarchy. The first level is based on the number of spatial dimensions required to draw the display (note that we do not address displays of more than three dimensions, which is beyond the scope of this chapter — see (Feiner & Beshers, 1990) for a good treatment of this). Three dimensional displays of data are still quite rare and are often achieved by mapping onto two dimensions and relying on the ability of the viewer to see the perspective. High speed graphical workstation technology has now made true stereo displays practical and we expect to see SV designers take advantage of both this and virtual reality technology as it becomes better understood.

As the hierarchy indicates, two dimensional displays are the most common and we have implemented a number of methods for several different two dimensional styles. Graphs are a common style for displaying many kinds of data and they usually appear in two dimensions on a workstation screen, but this is a convenience of media: graphs are actually multi-dimensional and the methods required for their management have little in common with the other two dimensional views.

An individual view is responsible for the layout of the visualization and is controlled by the navigator. The view requests data from the history module and sends it to the mapping module, which decides the appearance. The view module then tells the mapping module where to display the mapped data. This means that the view module is concerned only with the position of the history data item, not its appearance.

A view must be initialized before it can be used to display data. The type of initialization required depends on the view, with children having an initialization that builds upon (refines) that inherited from their parents. For example, our prototype implementation of the tree view takes two parameters:

i. The root node.

ii. A function which returns the children of a given node.

The view module is also responsible for managing the compression (elision) and expansion of elements in the display based on user commands from the navigator. If the user selects the compression of display elements, such as a subtree in a tree hierarchy, then the view module groups the players concerned into a team which has its own mapping to represent the compressed players. When the navigator tells the view module that an element is to be expanded, the view disbands the team and displays the individual mappings for the players.

The navigator may also instruct the view module to show a more coarse grained display of the visualization data, perhaps so that long term changes over time are visible or to increase the rate of display. This increase in granularity is achieved by switching to another view which filters the history data.

3.3. Mappings

The goal of a mapping is to communicate the maximum amount of information about a player's state while imposing the least possible cognitive load on the user. Some general advice on the subject of communicating information may be found in Tufte's books (Tufte, 1983; Tufte, 1990), but the problem of finding an effective SV mapping is far more complex. These mappings must communicate large and varying amounts of information to an audience in a very specialized culture. Software engineers do not have a standard notation for communicating about high level abstractions (compared with, say, chemists, who have several internationally recognized notations). Even if a good notation existed for describing computing abstractions, there is still the problem of algorithm animations which often use abstractions that are completely unrelated to computing.

One attempt at solving this problem is the use of graphic mappings that are based on detailed models of how programmers think about programming — for example (Anderson, Farrell & Sauers, 1984). This strategy is promising, but such models focus on programmer's plans rather than on ways of graphically visualizing such plans. With such little guidance, the visualization designer is often left to use intuition along with typographic techniques and graphics to create effective mappings.

In conjecturing a theory of effectiveness of graphical languages, Mackinlay (1986) noted Cleveland & McGill's observation that people accomplish the perceptual tasks associated with the interpretation of graphical presentations with different degrees of accuracy. Using psychophysical results, Mackinlay extended Cleveland & McGill's work to show how different graphical techniques ranked in perceptual effectiveness for encoding quantitative, ordinal, and nominal data. He found that the position of the data item in the x–y plane is ranked first for all three types of data, which is why we separate the view layout from the mappings. The other techniques which may be varied to create an effective mapping are (in decreasing order of effectiveness): colour hue, texture, connection, containment, density (brightness), colour saturation, shape, length (size), angle or slope (orientation), and area (or volume).

A mapping in Viz is attached to a particular type of player, event or state, and view. Multi-method inheritance occurs over the class of entity and view, allowing a Viz user to formulate expressions such as "all entities in view-x are to be displayed as a filled triangle", "entity-y is always displayed as a white circle" and "entity-a is displayed as a circle in tree based views but as a square in all other views". Mappings can be inherited, forming an inheritance hierarchy in much the same fashion as views. Our future work in Viz will create a library of mappings.

3.4. Navigators

In a software visualization, one must provide tools for navigating through both the space (two or three dimensions) and time of the execution history. Brayshaw & Eisenstadt (1991) outline various navigation techniques which we have refined to form the basis of the Viz navigators:

- *Panning*: Moving through the 2-D (or 3-D) space of a view which is larger than the window that it is displayed in.

- *Searching*: Finding an event in the execution space (selectivity).

- *Scale*: Changing the magnification factor (zooming) for a view, including non-uniform scale changes (e.g. fisheye views).

- *Granularity and detail control*: Changing the way in which history events are filtered, which may have the effect of compressing or expanding time or individual elements.

- *Customizable layout*: Allowing the user to alter the display in arbitrary ways (e.g. manually adjusting a complex graph layout to minimize edge crossings).

The Viz navigator module encapsulates the interface between the user and the visualization, although the methods for performing the navigation tasks are found in the view module, thus allowing custom navigation interfaces to be built independently of the task. This also means that when new views are developed the SV system builder must provide a minimum level of navigation functionality for the default navigation tools. For example, we could construct a detail control module for tree based views which would be able to collapse subtrees into a single node.

Our prototype provides a replay panel (see screen snapshots, Figures 4 and 5) for searching, which has buttons for moving to the beginning or end of the animation, single-stepping forward or backward, playing forward, and stopping. Stepping in Viz involves notifying the history and view modules of the change of focus. The history module selects the next appropriate event. Currently, the view module simply redraws the mappings for the old and new focus points. In future versions of Viz we intend to incorporate a smooth animation mechanism similar to that found in (Stasko, 1990). Horizontal and vertical scrollbars are provided for panning while simple zoom in and zoom out buttons provide scaling. The user can select a fine grained view of a data element by clicking on it.

There are many techniques for navigating through large information spaces, e.g. (Mackinlay, Robertson, & Card, 1991), and since many techniques are application specific, we leave specific implementation choices to the individual visualization designer.

	Prolog	OPS5	Lisp	Sort	Bin-Packing
Player	predicate instantiation (goal)	rule	form	data item	data item bin
States	pending goal; succeeded; failed; failed on backtracking; redo-goal	failing to match working memory; firing	unevaluated; evaluated	location	attempting to fit; succeeded; new
Events	call; exit; fail-1st; fail-nth; redo	choose for firing	call; return	assignment of item to cell	attempt-fit succeed-fit new-item
Mappings	▪; ◢; ■; ▪; ■ (colour)	✚ ▪	-> *italic*; <- **bold**	●	▯; ▪; ■
Views (in order of decreasing granularity)	tree: players, players current state; formatted text	table: players vs. cycles, player's state @ cycle formatted text	pretty printed code: player's current state	point plot: players, player's value & current state; formatted text	point plot using rectangles: bin-players and current state

Table 1: Viz description of four example systems

4. Examples Defined in Viz

The descriptions of the three systems that we have implemented using Viz are presented in Table 1 along with the two examples from BALSA and TANGO animations. The table provides a summary of the players, states, events, mappings, and views used in each visualization. Each row represents a distinct Viz entity type and each column represents one of the visualizations. The players row lists the players which can take part in each example. The states row shows the possible states players can enter. The events row shows the events which cause state changes. The mappings row contains, in order, the icon mapping for each state. The views row lists the names of the possible views in decreasing order of granularity. The connection between a view and the history is also shown. We shall now explain the first and second columns in detail.

4.1. A Prolog Visualizer

The Prolog visualizer is based on the Transparent Prolog Machine (TPM) (Eisenstadt & Brayshaw, 1988). TPM uses an *AND-OR* tree representation where the nodes represent goals which are instantiated Prolog predicates, and the arcs represent conjunctions or disjunctions of subgoals.

The players in the visualization are the instantiated Prolog predicates or goals in the proof tree. The events, which are adapted from the Byrd Box Model (Byrd, 1980), are: call (trying to prove a goal), exit (a goal succeeding), fail-1st (a goal failing the first time attempted), fail-nth (a goal having succeeded earlier, later failing on backtracking), and redo (re-attempting to satisfy a goal). There is a corresponding state and mapping for each event type.

The Prolog interpreter takes a list of goals left to prove. When no goals are left the environment is returned. The algorithm, adapted from (Nilsson, 1984), for the interpreter is:

> *If there is nothing to prove then return the environment; else*
> > *if the first-goal-left-to-prove is true, then*
> > > note event: succeed, the goal that was proved, env,
> > > *and prove the remaining goals; else*
> > > note event: goal, first-goal-left-to-prove, env, *and*
> > > create a player for the-first-goal-left-to-prove, *and*
> > > *loop for each clause in the database*
> > > > *if the head of the clause matches the first goal then*
> > > > create a player for each of the subgoals in the clause
> > > > *if we prove the new list of goals (which is the body of the matched clause*
> > > > *appended to the rest of the goals)*
> > > > *then return the new environment else*
> > > > note event: redo, first-goal-left-to-prove, env,
> > > note event: failure, first-goal-left-to-prove, env, *and*
> > > *return failed-to-prove first-goal-left-to-prove.*

In the above, the algorithm is shown in italics while the Viz event calls are shown in plain text.

Figure 4 shows a screen snapshot of the proof for the goal ?- `nephew(Who, ann)` given the following Prolog database:

```
nephew(Person, Uncle) :-
   brother(Uncle, Parent),
   parent(Parent, Person).

nephew(Person, Aunt) :-
   sister(Aunt, Parent),
   parent(Parent, Person).

brother(Sibling1, Sibling2) :-
   parent(Parent, Sibling1),
   parent(Parent, Sibling2),
   male(Sibling1),
   not(Sibling1 = Sibling2).

sister(Sibling1, Sibling2) :-
   parent(Parent, Sibling1),
   parent(Parent, Sibling2),
   female(Sibling1),
   not(Sibling1 = Sibling2).

male(adam).
female(ann).
parent(adam, charles).
parent(baker, adam).
parent(baker, ann).
```

Bearing in mind that atoms beginning with upper-case letters depict variables in Edinburgh-syntax Prolog, the code above defines the nephew relation to hold between its two arguments if the second one is the brother of the first one's parent (in which case we normally refer to that second person as an uncle), or *alternatively* if the second is the sister of the first one's parent (in which case we refer to that second person as an aunt). The brother and sister relations are analogously defined (the 'not' relation keeps a person from being his own brother), followed by five 'facts' about who is male, who is female, and who is a parent of whom. The small window in the snapshot is a fine-grained view of the goal `sister(ann, Parent)` which succeeded with the variable `Parent` instantiated to `adam`.

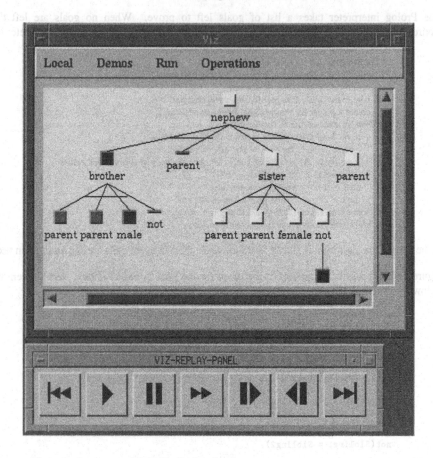

Figure 4: A screen snapshot of the Prolog visualizer

The following table shows the first state in the above example for the query **nephew(Who, ann)**:

type	goal-event
player type	goal-player
player name	**nephew(Who,ann)**
instantiation	

Because history events are invoked by inserting hooks into our own Prolog interpreter, the Viz implementation is straightforward once the machinery for players, views, mappings, and navigators is in place. Even with this straightforward implementation, the functionality is sufficient to deal with non-trivial cases of tricky backtracking and unification (e.g. proof trees with hundreds of nodes and thousands of history steps).

4.2. An OPS-5 Visualizer

The OPS-5 visualizer is based on the Transparent Rule Interpreter (Domingue & Eisenstadt, 1989). The two basic elements in an OPS-5 style language are the rulebase and working memory. A rulebase is simply a collection of rules. In the rule: "rule-10: if it is raining and I am travelling on foot then take an umbrella", 'rule-10' is the name of the rule, "if it is raining and I am travelling on foot" is the antecedent and "take an umbrella" is the consequent. Working memory is a set of facts which can be added to. Our simple language is based on the OPS-5 style match fire cycles. In each cycle a rule is selected to fire from the rulebase. The process of selecting a rule involves finding the first rule whose antecedents match against (i.e. can be found in) the current working memory. Firing a rule adds its consequent to working memory.

The players in the OPS-5 visualization are the rules and the events are: a rule firing, and a rule failing to match against working memory.

The algorithm for the production system is given below:

> *Loop until either halt is signalled or no rules fire*
>   *find a rule to fire*
>   *fire the rule*
>   create a new player for the rule
>   note event: fire-event, new player, current cycle
>   *increment the current cycle number*

The screen snapshot in Figure 5 shows the display for the following set of rules:

rulea	*if (red light)* **then** *(president awake)*
ruleb	*if (red light)* **&** *(president awake)*
	then *(chiefs summoned)*
rulec	*if (red light)* **&** *(president awake)* **&** *(chiefs summoned)*
	then *(hotline used)*
ruled	*if (red light)* **&** *(president awake)* **&** *(chiefs summoned)*
	& *(hotline used)*
	then *(worldwide red alert)*
rulee	*if (red light)* **&** *(president awake)*
	& *(chiefs summoned)* **&** *(hotline used)* **&** *(worldwide red alert)*
	then *(button pushed)*
rulef	*if (red light)* **&** *(president awake)*
	& *(chiefs summoned)* **&** *(hotline used)*
	& *(worldwide red alert)* **&** *(button pushed)*
	then *(%%halt%%)*

These were run with initial working memory `[[red light]]`. Each cross is drawn by the fire-event map. Column 4 is highlighted because it is the current focus in the history. The window inset is a fine-grained view of rule 'rulee' in cycle 4.

The table below shows the first event created:

type	fire-event
player type	rule
player name	rule-a
cycle	0

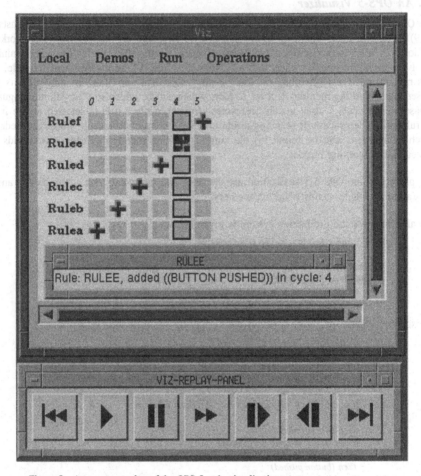

Figure 5:   A screen snapshot of the OPS-5 style visualization system

4.3. Additional Systems

To fully exercise our evolving framework across a range of players, events, states, mappings, and views, we have also used Viz to re-implement the textual visualization provided by the Symbolics Lisp stepper/tracer which uses layout to summarize the execution history of the Lisp evaluator (the Viz implementation actually improves on this by using colour and typography as well). We have also duplicated some of the well known AA examples from BALSA (sorting) and TANGO (bin packing) to show that the system can be used to easily construct custom algorithm animations as well.

5. A Comparison of Viz, BALSA and TANGO Terminology

Although each of the goals of Viz, BALSA, and TANGO are somewhat different, the importance of the pioneering work of BALSA and TANGO is such that a close comparison of terminology

BALSA	TANGO	Viz	Comments
Interesting (Algorithm) Events	Algorithm Operations	Events and Create Players	The BALSA and TANGO terms are virtually identical while Viz events are more general, can be arranged hierarchically, and are designed to relate to the code rather than the algorithm.
Modellers	Image, Location, Path, and Transition	States and Players	In describing a visualization's internal representation, TANGO adds to the BALSA framework by providing 4 abstract data types (geared towards animation); Viz's states and players are program execution level abstractions.
Renderers	Animation Scenes	Mappings and Views	BALSA provides a general mechanism for each view while TANGO provides reusable libraries of animation scenes; Viz discriminates between the actual images that are mapped to the screen and the style in which they are displayed (the view).
		Navigators	BALSA and TANGO don't specify any kind of user interface interactions within the framework, nor techniques for dealing with arbitrarily large programs.
Adaptor and Update Messages		History	The Viz history is a structure for the collection of events, states, and players generated during program execution. The history module includes various searching and filtering functions.

Table 2: A comparison of terminology

is warranted. Viz terminology is designed to allow existing systems to be described as well as implement new ones. Table 2 shows the systems in left-to-right chronological order, mapping the similar terminology across systems where appropriate, and highlighting differences accordingly in the 'comment' column.

6. Conclusions

The main goal in designing Viz was to provide a descriptive mechanism for understanding and explaining the diverse notations and methodologies underlying existing software visualization environments. Our re-implementation based approach is in contrast to the current literature (Eisenstadt et al., 1990; Green, 1989; Green, 1990c; Myers, 1990a; Price, Small & Baecker, 1992) which focusses on cognitive and notational dimensions and practical categories. The amount of effort involved in our approach is of the same order of magnitude as category or dimension based approaches. Each of the example systems was constructed within 1–2 days (this included many extensive alterations to the first version of Viz) and is of the order of 100 lines of code.

By providing a descriptive abstraction for internally expressing the state of an algorithm (players, events, and states) we have augmented earlier frameworks and added to the common language for representing algorithm animation designs. Since Viz provides visualization facilities for programming languages, we have provided a framework for generalized visualization that is applicable to software engineers since it provides visualizations that are automatic and faithful to the execution model of the language. The use of Viz to implement systems which differ widely in terms of their scope, content, form, method, interaction, and effectiveness, suggests that the framework is sufficient to design and implement a wide class of software visualization systems.

Acknowledgements

This research was funded by CEC ESPRIT-II Project 5365 (VITAL) and the SERC/ESRC/MRC Joint Council Initiative on Cognitive Science and Human Computer Interaction (Algorithm Visualization Project). We thank Ron Baecker, Mike Brayshaw, Thomas Green, and Marc Brown for their helpful comments on early drafts of this chapter.

Electronic versions of our papers and software may be obtained by anonymous FTP from hcrl.open.ac.uk.

A Design Environment for Graphical User Interfaces

Jürgen Herczeg

Research Group DRUID, Department of Computer Science, University of Stuttgart,
Breitwiesenstraße 20–22, D-70565 Stuttgart, Germany.

Tel: +49 (0)711 7816 364

Fax: +49 (0)711 780 10 45

EMail: herczeg@informatik.uni-stuttgart.de

Today, building user interfaces for sophisticated applications may be characterized as a design activity that needs powerful programming tools. Many of the existing tools are either too low-level or too restricted. We will describe a layered architecture of object-oriented user interface design tools, comprising user interface toolkits as well as visual programming tools for building, inspecting, and modifying graphical user interfaces interactively. They correspond to different abstraction levels on which user interfaces may be constructed and modified by user interface designers or even end-users. We will further argue that these tools are even more effective when they are integrated within a visual programming environment together with general browsing and tracing components.

Keywords: user interface design, graphical user interfaces, user interface toolkits, user interface builders, construction kits, design environments, object-oriented programming, visual programming.

1. Introduction

With the availability of window systems like the X Window System (Scheifler & Gettys, 1986) on different computer platforms, the use of graphical user interfaces in different application domains is permanently increasing. These systems basically provide a communication protocol for window server and client programs, as for instance the X protocol (Nye, 1990), and low-level programming interfaces, such as XLIB (Nye, 1988), which are open to very different interface styles. Because of their generality these programming interfaces are not appropriate for direct application; they rather form the basis for higher-level tools. Especially for building graphical user interfaces, object-oriented programming techniques proved to be very useful (Barth, 1986). *user interface toolkits* are object-oriented programming interfaces that provide a higher abstraction level. They may be basically characterized as a library of common user interface elements like buttons, menus, or scrollbars, also called *widgets*, which are used as building blocks for graphical user interfaces. Over the last years, numerous toolkits emerged, as for instance the X Toolkit and the various widget sets built on top of it (Nye & O'Reilly, 1990). Mostly, these toolkits are difficult to use and do not provide appropriate means for defining new building blocks, let alone modifying predefined building blocks interactively. On the contrary, they often give up generality in favor of restricting appearance and functionality to a particular interface style, a so-called 'look and feel', e.g. Open Look (Sun Microsystems, 1990) or OSF/Motif (Open Software Foundation, 1990a).

Although object-oriented approaches employed by many high-level toolkits have achieved substantial improvement, constructing user interfaces with toolkits still needs high programming skills. Therefore, building graphical user interfaces for sophisticated applications definitely needs more powerful programming tools. *user interface management systems* (UIMS) denote tools that support the development of user interfaces separately from the underlying applications (Pfaff, 1985). Many examples of UIMS are based on the formal description of user interfaces. Building user interfaces employing graphical visualization and direct manipulation techniques, however, may be rather characterized as a design activity than giving formal descriptions or just program coding. For these kinds of tasks, the idea of *construction kits* and *design environments* raised special interest over the last years (Fischer & Lemke, 1988). Especially in the domain of user interface construction and design, interactive programming tools using visual programming techniques have been successfully employed (Myers, 1990b; Myers et al., 1990). So-called *user interface builders* can be very helpful for building interfaces by means of direct manipulation, especially as far as visual properties are concerned. However, they are typically restricted to a fixed set of predefined interface elements and mostly are very poor when a slightly modified appearance or functionality is required.

We have implemented a layered architecture of interactive tools for building, inspecting, and modifying graphical user interfaces for the X Window System, comprising user interface toolkits as well as visual programming tools integrated in an interactive programming environment. Their design and implementation follow the concepts of the USIT system (Herczeg, 1989), developed by the research group INFORM at the University of Stuttgart, and make them available on a more standardized software platform. These concepts have been further developed towards a design environment for user interfaces.

2. A Layered Architecture for User Interface Design

Figure 1 shows the layered architecture of a user interface design environment for the X Window System. The layers correspond to different abstraction levels on which user interfaces may be constructed and modified (Herczeg, Hohl & Schwab, 1991). The components have been implemented in Common Lisp and CLOS, the Common Lisp Object System.

- XIT is a user interface toolkit for the X Window System based on the lower-level programming interfaces CLX (Scheifler & Oren, 1988) and CLUE (Kimbrough & Oren, 1990). It is composed of two major components:
    - XIT_{low} is a low-level toolkit providing a general framework for building user interface elements.
    - XIT_{high} is a high-level toolkit providing a library of common user interface elements.
- XACT is a user interface builder for constructing user interfaces out of building blocks of XIT.

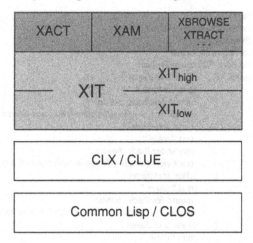

Figure 1: Layered architecture of a user interface design environment

- XAM is an interactive graphical tool for inspecting and modifying user interfaces built with XIT or XACT.
- General programming tools for CLOS, such as XBROWSE and XTRACT, are used to inspect and manipulate object-oriented application programs and their user interfaces at run time.

In the following, we will describe the different system components and how they may be used in an integrated visual programming environment by user interface designers and to some extent even by end-users.

3. The User Interface Toolkit

XIT (X User Interface Toolkit) provides a general object-oriented framework for building graphical user interfaces. Its main design goals are generality, extensibility, and usability. These partly contrary goals have been achieved by separating XIT into a low-level and a high-level toolkit.

3.1. The Low-Level User Interface Toolkit

The low-level toolkit XIT$_{low}$ comprises basic building blocks and general mechanisms for uniformly building and composing arbitrary user interface elements, in the following called *interaction objects*. Figure 2, for example, shows how an interaction object representing a menu for window operations can be defined with XIT$_{low}$. Interaction objects are characterized by the following properties:

- *Structure*: Each interaction object may be composed of other interaction objects (its *parts*) and, conversely, may be part of a compound interaction object (its *parent*). Thus, interaction objects are organized into *part-whole hierarchies*. The parts of a menu, for example, are the menu entries.
- *Geometry*: Each interaction object contains attributes for its *position* (relative to its parent), its *size*, and *layout*. The layout of an object is based on relations between

```
(make-window    'intel
                :view-of a_window_object
                :border-width 1
                :background " white "
                :layouter 'distance-layouter
                :parts '((    :class text-dispel
                              :text "refresh "
                              :mouse-feedback :border
                              :reactivity ((:single-left-button (call :view-of refresh-window ))))
                         (    :class text-dispel
                              :text "totop "
                              :mouse-feedback :border
                              :reactivity ((:single-left-button (call :view-of totop-window ))))
                         (    :class text-dispel
                              :text "move "
                              :mouse-feedback :border
                              :reactivity ((:single-left-button (call :view-of move-window ))))
                         (    :class text-dispel
                              :text "close "
                              :mouse-feedback :border
                              :reactivity ((:single-left-button (call :view-of destroy ))))))))
```

Figure 2:   Creation of a menu with XIT_{low}

its position and size and the position and size of its parts. It is controlled by objects, called *layouters*, which define one-directional constraints between attributes of the interaction object and attributes of its parts — cf. (Barth, 1986; Myers, 1990b). Various layouters producing specific kinds of layout are predefined. In the menu example, a *distance-layouter* is used to position the menu entries one below the other; the size of the menu is determined by the position and size of the entries.

- *Presentation*: Each visual interaction object defines how it is displayed on the screen by general attributes, such as *background* and *foreground* color or *border width*. A compound interaction object is presented by displaying its parts. Basic interaction objects are *text* and *bitmap* elements or graphical elements, such as *lines*, *arrows*, and *rectangles*. They form the leaf nodes of an interaction object hierarchy and are described by specific attributes, such as *font*, *line width*, etc. The entries of the example menu are textual elements, depicting the possible selections. In addition to these customary interface elements, interaction objects presenting *sounds* and *videos* have been included for multimedia applications.

- *Reactivity*: The *reactivity* of an interaction object describes the behavior of the object by mapping user interface *events*, e.g. keyboard input or mouse button clicks, onto *actions* of the underlying application. A menu entry, for example, may trigger an application-specific operation when it is clicked on with the left mouse button. Furthermore, attributes describing feedback behavior are provided.

- *Application Link-up*: Interaction objects may be associated with objects of the application. Thus, user interface and application are represented by strictly separated objects communicating with each other by message passing or function calls, comparable to the *MVC paradigm* (Krasner & Pope, 1988). In the menu example, a selected menu entry sends a message to a window object associated with the menu by the *view-of* attribute.

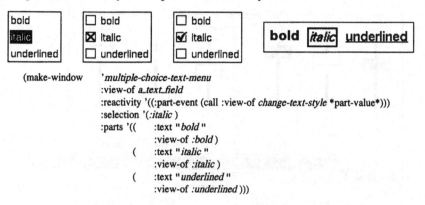

```
(make-window    'multiple-choice-text-menu
                :view-of a_text_field
                :reactivity '((:part-event (call :view-of change-text-style *part-value*)))
                :selection '(:italic )
                :parts '((     :text "bold "
                               :view-of :bold )
                         (     :text "italic "
                               :view-of :italic )
                         (     :text "underlined "
                               :view-of :underlined )))
```

Figure 3: Creation of a multiple-choice menu with XIT$_{high}$

XIT$_{low}$ provides mechanisms for constructing arbitrary components of a user interface. For common interaction objects like menus, however, this toolkit need not be used directly; they are available in higher-level tools built on top of XIT$_{low}$.

3.2. The High-Level User Interface Toolkit

XIT$_{high}$ is a library of predefined, commonly used interaction objects, e.g. *icons, buttons, menus* (including *single-choice* and *multiple-choice menus*), *switches, sliders,* and *property sheets*, as well as building blocks, such as window *titles, scrollbars,* and *decorations*. They have been implemented out of building blocks of XIT$_{low}$. Each interaction object provides attributes to be adjusted for a particular application. Defaults are provided to show up a special 'look and feel'. Figure 3, for example, shows how a multiple-choice menu containing three options to change a text style may be created with XIT$_{high}$. Four different examples are presented how the menu may look, depending on the setting (or defaults) of attributes describing font, layout, or highlighting of selection.

By use of the mechanisms provided by XIT$_{low}$, the predefined interaction objects of XIT$_{high}$ may be modified or combined to more complex objects of a graphical user interface, e.g. dialog windows composed of (editable) text fields, buttons, menus, sliders, property sheets, etc. — cf. Figure 4.

XIT serves as a construction kit for arbitrary user interface elements. XIT$_{high}$ is just one example of a high-level toolkit. Other toolkits with different 'look and feel' or even application-specific tools may be implemented with XIT quite easily.

By strictly separating application objects and interface objects, user interfaces may be developed and tested independently of an application program. Interaction objects of XIT may be created without links to application objects. These links may be established and changed at run time. Thus a user interface may be 'plugged' into a running application. This is one of the important features required for the development of higher-level interactive programming tools for XIT. With XIT, user interfaces in various application domains have been implemented. Some of the largest applications of XIT are the tools described in the following sections.

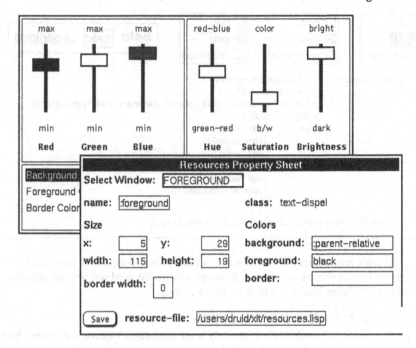

Figure 4: Resource property editor

4. The User Interface Construction Kit

The object-oriented design of XIT (and many related tools) by modularity and reusability substantially reduces the complexity of developing sophisticated graphical user interfaces. However, building user interfaces, even with the help of high-level toolkits, still requires high programming skills and deep knowledge of their functionality.

The design of XIT as an *internal* construction kit providing building blocks and mechanisms for composition suggests itself to be enhanced by an *external* visual construction kit. Especially in the domain of user interface construction, employing visual programming techniques is most natural, since the objects manipulated graphically are identical with the visual objects to be created.

XACT (XIT Application Construction Kit) is a user interface builder for XIT, which lets the user select graphically presented interaction objects and compose them to more complex user interface elements. By means of the metasystem, described below, attributes of the interaction objects involved may be modified. With XACT, a user interface may be constructed separately from the underlying application. At any time, it may be connected to an application to explore its functionality. When the constructed user interface shows the desired behavior and appearance, XIT program code may be generated automatically. Figure 5, for example, shows the construction kit building the user interface of a bitmap editor.

Currently, XACT does not cover all of the functionality of XIT. It only contains the most commonly used building blocks shown in the *Palette* window in Figure 5. For geometrical

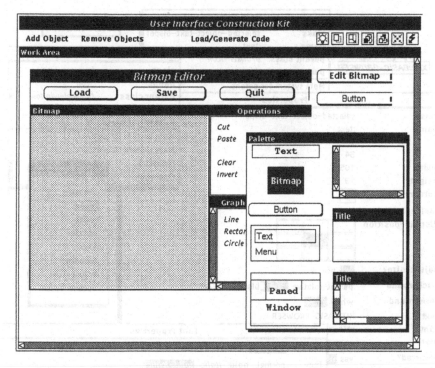

Figure 5: The user interface construction kit XACT

properties, like position, size, and layout of windows, which can be best adjusted by directly manipulating graphical objects on the screen, this construction kit proved to be very helpful, especially for users with poor knowledge of XIT.

5. The User Interface Metasystem

Building a user interface is an iterative design process where a prototypical implementation is incrementally modified. This stems from the fact that very often design flaws are not detected until the user interface is viewed as a whole. Even when the design process is finished and the application is passed to the end user there are still a lot of properties which should be modifiable according to special preferences or needs of the user, e.g. changing the layout of the objects on the screen, or changing font, color, text, or bitmap attributes, or even adding or removing entries of a menu. Instead of anticipating all these needs in the user interface of an application, this functionality should be provided by a separate, application-independent tool.

XAM (XIT Application Metasystem) is a tool for interactively inspecting and modifying user interfaces built by means of XACT or the toolkits of XIT. The metasystem may be invoked for any type of interaction object of XIT, either predefined or user-defined. It presents dialog windows containing menus and property sheets, which are dynamically created for the interaction object in question, i.e. the properties of an object determine the contents of the menus and property sheets. This process is controlled by inheritance of properties defined in

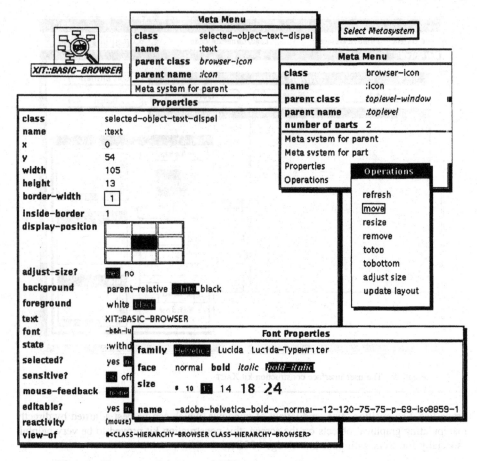

Figure 6: The user interface metasystem XAM

the corresponding object classes. So usually there is no need to extend the metasystem for user-defined interaction objects. However, this can be easily done when an application-specific behavior is required.

Figure 6 shows different components of the metasystem invoked in a running application. The icon corresponding to an application window is inspected and modified. The property sheet for its text part has been invoked to change the font attribute, and the *move* operation is being selected to position the icon on the screen interactively. None of these modifications has been supplied by the application. The metasystem menu invoked for an interaction object provides the following choices:

- Invoke the metasystem for the parent or one of the parts selected from a menu. Thus, the user may navigate through the interaction object hierarchy.

- Change properties of the selected object. Attribute values may be either selected from menus, when a fixed set of possible values is available, e.g. font attributes, or they may be entered by keyboard, e.g. to specify an application function called as the reaction to an event. Alternatively, values may be copied from other interaction objects on the screen by simple point-and-click actions, e.g. to give a text element the font or color of an object already presented on the screen.

Modification of particular properties, such as font, color, layout, or reactivity, trigger the invocation of more specific property sheets, e.g. for describing a font specification by *family*, *face*, and *size* (cf. Figure 6), or for specifying the red/green/blue values of a color by moving sliders (cf. Figure 4).

- Perform operations on the selected object; these may be either general operations, such as moving or resizing a window with the mouse, or object-specific operations, such as adding an entry to a menu.

Each modification performed with the metasystem is immediately applied to the corresponding object, which triggers an update of the presentation on the screen.

XAM is used in combination with XACT to change attributes of newly created interaction objects. When XACT produces program code the current values adjusted by the metasystem are inserted. The metasystem may also be used without the construction kit for inspecting or modifying arbitrary user interfaces built with XIT. This is not only useful for debugging but also for adapting the user interface of an application to specific needs at run time. Because the metasystem mainly works by menu selection and direct manipulation, this may be even performed by end-users — cf. (Fischer & Girgensohn, 1990).

For a set of so-called *resource attributes* of interaction objects, including position, size, border width, color, font, text, bitmaps, etc, a *resource property editor* has been added to the metasystem (Figure 4). Modifications to a user interface performed with this editor can be saved on external files and reloaded, whenever the application in question is used again. Users may thus keep individual versions of the user interface for the same application.

6. An Integrated Visual Programming Environment

XACT and XAM are visual programming tools for designing user interfaces with XIT independently of an application program. Like most graphical user interface building tools, they mainly concentrate on the visual properties of an interface. For sophisticated applications, however, user interface design and the development of the underlying application are tightly interwoven. For establishing links between user interface and application objects, for specifying application functions invoked in response to user interface events, and for updating the user interface according to changes in the application, understanding and managing the application program also plays a crucial part in user interface construction. Object-oriented programming environments like SMALLTALK-80 (Goldberg, 1984) are based on general programming tools for inspecting and modifying user interface objects and application objects uniformly. *Browsers* provide insight into static properties of objects, *tracers* visualize their dynamic behavior. By means of XIT we have implemented general visual programming tools for CLOS:

- XBROWSE is a browsing component including general object browsers, class browsers, and method browsers (Figure 7). It combines text-oriented and graphics-oriented visualization and interaction techniques (Herczeg & Hohl, 1991). For the development of user interfaces, XBROWSE may be used to visualize interaction object hierarchies and links between user interface objects and application objects and to inspect and modify the corresponding object definitions. The browsers in Figure 7, for example, show a part of the class hierarchy of XIT (*Class Browser*), a window

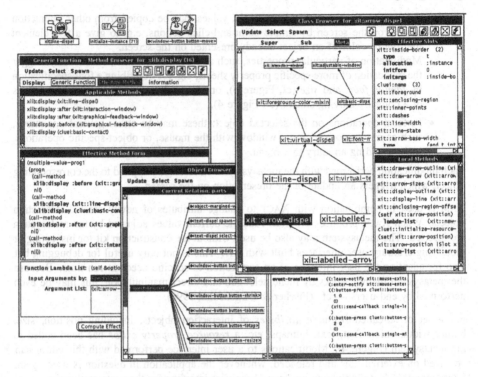

Figure 7:   Browsing tools of XBROWSE

hierarchy for a selected window object (*Object Browser*), and dependencies between different implemented *display* operations (*Generic Function/Method Browser*).

- XTRACT is a general tracing component for generic functions and methods of CLOS. In addition to textual and graphical trace information, it may provide arbitrary visual program animations. For the development of user interfaces, XTRACT may be used to visualize the communication between user interface objects and application objects at run time, e.g. reactivity and update operations.

As a supplement to the user interface programming tools XACT and XAM, general visual programming tools like XBROWSE and XTRACT can play an essential part in the design of user interfaces with XIT. In an integrated visual programming environment, all of these tools could be used simultaneously, invoking each other mutually.

7. Conclusions and Future Work

We have implemented a layered architecture of programming tools for designing graphical user interfaces in an object-oriented programming environment. XIT provides a powerful user interface toolkit for the X Window System, XACT and XAM are visual user interface construction and design tools for XIT. We will further extend the functionality of these tools and integrate them with browsing and tracing components like XBROWSE and XTRACT in a visual programming environment, where we can investigate, how each of these tools may benefit from the others and conversely enhance their application. Another important aspect will be the integration of knowledge-based tools into this environment providing both tool-specific and tool-independent user interface design knowledge.

The construction and design of graphical user interfaces is still a difficult task, demanding major portions of the development time for an application. Releasing the user interface designer from low-level programming tasks and providing him with the tools appropriate for the problem at hand, will enable him to concentrate on more important and even more interesting design tasks, which eventually helps building better user interfaces. Therefore, especially for user interface design, the idea of visual programming environments will play an ever increasing part in the near future.

Acknowledgements

I want to thank Michael Herczeg, who by implementing the USIT system prepared the ground for the implementation of XIT and XAM. I would also like to thank Hubertus Hohl and Matthias Ressel, who substantially contributed to the development of the systems described in this chapter, Michael Wichert, who implemented major parts of the construction kit and the metasystem, and Uta Wollensak, who implemented XTRACT.

Automated Interface Design Techniques

Brad Blumenthal

Department of Electrical Engineering and Computer Science, University Illinois at Chicago, 851 South Morgan, Chicago, IL 60607, USA.

Tel: +1 312 996 2648

EMail: brad@eecs.uic.edu

Keywords: automated interface design, UIMS, metaphors, interface application separation.

This chapter presents a short overview of several systems for automating the design of human–computer interfaces. The sophistication of these systems varies from simple skeletal frameworks for organizing interface entities to systems using extensive knowledge to fully automate the design of interfaces with a variety of styles, emphases and metaphoric characteristics. From the existing body of research, trends for future research in this area are abstracted and extrapolated.

1. Introduction

Over the last few years, the technology for automatically generating user interfaces to computer applications has advanced from its bare beginnings to the point where interfaces to commercial products are being produced entirely automatically (see the bibliography for numerous examples). While these systems have varied considerably in the types of inputs they take and in the kinds of interfaces they produce, the overall trend in this development has been toward systems that are more autonomous and pay more attention to issues beyond the mere appearance and performance of the interface. In particular, automated interface design systems have included components for representing aspects of interface design ranging from the designers's knowledge to features of the real world that might shape the interface. This trend toward adding more ancillary knowledge to the process of automated interface design is leading to interface design systems that are broader in scope and use representations of more than just the application as part of the design process.

The purpose of this chapter is two-fold. First, it provides a survey of the techniques in automated interface design that are available at the present time. This survey examines a number of issues including the progress of input specifications from drawings and demonstrations to specifications of application functionality, the progress of outputs from simple interface devices (such as scrollbars) to complete, functional interfaces, and the other central issues addressed by each system. In addition, this chapter surveys a broad geographical distribution of research efforts. While active research in this area is being pursued in the US, Europe, and Asia, there is a certain amount of isolation between these three communities.

The second purpose of this chapter is to examine the trend in automated interface design toward representing and using more information about the context in which the resulting interface will be used. This additional information is used to cast the design of an interface in terms that are separate from the functionality of the underlying application.

2. Existing Systems

There are a large number of systems described in the literature concerned with automating the design and generation, in whole or in part, of user interfaces for computer applications. It is sometimes difficult to draw a clear distinction between systems that automate interface design and systems that allow end-users to modify the interface. However, for the purposes of this chapter, an automated interface design system will be defined as one that takes some sort of specification from a designer, and uses that specification to create some set of interface components for the end user.

The rest of this section examines various approaches to this problem, beginning with the simplest cases of generating simple interaction techniques, such as buttons, scrollbars and dialog boxes. Next, some approaches to generating complete interfaces to applications are presented, and finally, some extensions to add metaphoric features and other customizations to these interfaces are discussed.

2.1. Representations of Interface Objects and Actions

The simplest systems for aiding in the creation of interface designs do little in the way of automating the design itself. Their primary purpose is to speed the generation of interfaces once the design has been completed. The value of such systems is that they allow designers to prototype and test their ideas rapidly. The simplest of these systems merely provides a set of interface techniques that can be used to create interfaces. The more advanced systems allow the designer to quickly create new techniques.

2.1.1. HyperCard

Perhaps the best known interface design tool is the HyperCard system (Goodman, 1987). It provides the non-programmer with a selection of interface techniques, such as check boxes, radio buttons, scrolling text fields, etc., that can be arranged to present a wide variety of interfaces.

This system further allows the user to specify a large number of states that an application might be in by allowing the user to create any number of 'cards' that can present independent interfaces. Simple behaviors can be implemented by specifying that particular mouse clicks change the state of the application by changing to different cards.

Intermediate users of HyperCard can use the simplified programming language built into the system to produce more complex interface techniques, such as dialog boxes, and more complex behaviors, such as creating new cards at run time. Advanced users can interface HyperCard to such programming languages as C and Pascal to take advantage of their power and flexibility.

By providing the non-programmer with a simple, direct way to produce an interface and simulate a working program, HyperCard represents a first step toward automatically generating a user interface to an application. In particular, features like the dialog that allows a non-programmer to connect a mouse click in a particular region to a particular change of state in the application are a rudimentary form of automatic programming. Although it is conceptually simple and computationally restricted, the framework of explicit application states (cards) and explicit interface entities (buttons and fields) affords a certain amount of automation in the interface creation process.

2.1.2. Generating Dialogues

The next step is to automate the creation of the techniques that HyperCard makes available. There are two parts to this, corresponding to the interface entities that HyperCard provides and the state changing behavior that it embodies. The Scope System addresses the first part by creating new interface entities from a functional specification composed of selections from a pre-defined collection of data objects and functions (Beshers & Feiner, 1989). These data objects specify the 'active variables' in the system which are the ones whose values are displayed. In addition, attributes of these data objects are specified, such as whether they are for input, output, or both.

The behavior of the system is specified by a set of relations between the active variables, again in terms of a collection of relations provided by the Scope System. The resulting functional specification is combined with a number of interface design rules that are specific to the underlying hardware and software to create new interaction techniques.

To see how this allows a designer to create new interface entities, consider the following example. While HyperCard provides an entity that looks like a radio button and allows the (intermediate) user to program radio button functionality into a collection of radio buttons, Scope can be used to specify the behavior of a collection of radio buttons and implement it automatically. Further, Scope can be used to specify and automatically implement 'chinese restaurant menu buttons' that would allow a user to pick (for example) one choice from column A and two choices from column B. Such interface entities could then be stored and reused in other applications.

Similar approaches to creating dialogues from specifications have been explored in the GRADIENT system (Alty & Mullin, 1989) and in the GEGS project (Szwillus, 1987).

2.1.3. Interface Toolkits

The GARNET system takes this approach further by providing a set of tools for specifying a wide range of interface techniques (e.g. different kinds of scrollbars, buttons and collections of buttons, dialog boxes, etc.), constraints and behaviors for these techniques, and appearances of these techniques (Myers, 1989). Like HyperCard, GARNET also provides a framework for combining these techniques into coherent interfaces. In addition, GARNET has interfaces to a wide variety of underlying interface presentation software that allows it to present its interfaces in a number of standard styles (e.g. Motif).

The GARNET tools allow designers to build a wider variety of interface entities and behaviors than Scope by allowing the designer to specify appearances and behaviors in a number of flexible ways, rather than simply choosing from a collection provided by the system. Among other techniques, the GARNET tools allow appearances to be specified by direct manipulation and a variety of system-provided spatial relationships (e.g. various kinds of relative and absolute alignments, orderings, etc.). The USIT system (Herczeg, 1989) provides a similar functionality that allows the construction of graphical and textual interfaces.

In addition, the GARNET tools allow the behaviors of these entities to be specified by demonstration (Myers, 1987); specific mouse clicks, keystrokes, etc., can be connected with specific results, and the GARNET tools can infer the general behavior desired. By contrast, England (1988) has explored the use of augmented transition networks (ATN's) for specifying the behavior of the resulting systems.

By providing direct methods for specifying new interface entities and behaviors, the GARNET tools further automate the process of designing interfaces for applications. However, powerful as they are, these tools are still only concerned with building individual interface techniques. Combining them into coherent, usable interfaces is still left to the designer.

2.2. Constructing Complete Interfaces

The next step then, in automating the construction of interfaces for computer applications, is to use some representation of the application to drive the production of a complete, coherent interface. This section describes three steps toward that goal: a representation for independently specifying an application, an interface, and the interaction between them; a system for generating multiple interfaces to a single application based on designer-imposed constraints; and a system for generating multiple interfaces to multiple applications which includes a system for eliciting new design rules in the context of design problems.

2.2.1. Representations of Applications and Interfaces

In order to automate the generation of application interfaces, it is necessary to separate the functional component of an application from the interface. Although there are some arguments that this cannot be done and some compelling examples supporting these arguments (e.g. response time can be considered part of an interface, but it is inextricably linked to the functional implementation), the existence of a number of successful systems that depend on this separation implies that an adequate separation can be achieved.

One formalism for specifying applications, interfaces, and the interactions between them is the NEPHEW UIMS/application interface (Szekely, 1989). This formalism captures the objects and operations that an application makes available to the user, and provides a bridge between these objects and operations and the 'presenters', 'commands', and 'recognizers', that make up the interface. This bridge between the application and interface provides a language for communicating the dynamic state of the application to the user and the actions of the user to the application. A number of applications and interfaces have been implemented using this formalism, including chess programs, file system interfaces, and icon editors.

By providing a way of separately representing applications, interfaces, and the interactions between them, formalisms such as these pave the way for extending automatic interface construction to entire applications rather than just interaction techniques. The next step is to provide the rules for automating such application interfaces.

By contrast, Hoffner, Dobson & Iggulden (1989) propose an architecture that is based on a series of translations from the underlying programming language to the user's language. This allows the interface to be considered as a means of communication rather than as a collection of objects and techniques.

2.2.2. Arens et al.

The intelligent interface project of Arens et al. (1988) is applied to the task of drawing maps that present information from a naval database about ship and fleet operations in the south Pacific. It uses a relatively simple set of design rules to produce maps and tables that appropriately display the desired information. Although this system designs interfaces for only one application, it demonstrates that a set of design rules can be coupled with designer-supplied constraints to produce a variety of usable, coherent interfaces.

The job of the designer in this system is to specify what information from the data base should be presented and what the priority of each kind of information is. By applying a set of design rules to these constraints, this system can produce a display that combines graphic and textual presentations in a clear, concise way. Altering the information to be presented or the priority of the information causes different interface techniques to be used and different interfaces to be produced.

Although this system has limited applicability, it demonstrates that a variety of coherent, complete interfaces can be generated for the same application by specifying a small number of parameters. However, in addition to limited flexibility, this system also presents designers with the problem of writing the rules for producing the interface. The next section describes a system that addresses this latter problem in the context of design problems.

2.2.3. Wiecha et al.

The work of researchers at IBM's T J Watson research facility has led to a system that not only automates the design of interactive interfaces, but also automates the elicitation of design rules from an interface design expert (Bennett et al., 1989; Wiecha et al., 1989a). One common technique among many automated interface design research projects is to allow the designer to arbitrarily modify the design produced by the automated design system after the system is run (Wiecha et al., 1989b). This combines the autonomy of a rule-based system with the flexibility of systems like GARNET. However, while this increases the flexibility of an automated interface design system, it makes such arbitrary design decisions difficult to capture and record.

The fundamental philosophy behind the work of Wiecha et al. is that the interface produced by the automated design system can be changed however the designer wishes, as long as the designer can supply a rule specifying the change and specifying under what conditions that change should be invoked. Thus, new design rules are elicited in the context of specific interface design problems. By building up the collection of design rules interactively and incrementally, this system has grown to the point where it can adequately design a number of robust, usable systems. It is currently being used to design the interface to an information, reservation, and message delivery system for attendees of the World's Fair in Spain.

While this system exhibits the capability to design commercially viable interfaces, it is difficult to determine just what the contributions of the various rules are to the success of the system. In particular, the design expertise is embedded in a set of essentially procedural rules, rather than a set of declarative models. As a result, changes in (for instance) the desired interface style or the intended user population may have far reaching effects on the rule base. The next step is to explicitly represent aspects of the design process that are independent of a particular application or interface style.

2.3. Representing Outside Influences

There are a number of influences on a design outside of the functionality of the application and the particular interface toolkit used. Among these are the style of interaction chosen, information about the intended users, and real-world objects that might serve as the source for metaphoric features of an interface. However, in order to make a clear, coherent contribution to the interface, such information must be kept separate.

2.3.1. UIDE

The UIDE project includes subprojects addressing the problems of automatically altering the syntax of an interface (Foley et al., 1988), automating the generation of dialogue boxes (Kim & Foley, 1989), and automating the generation of animated help for the user (Sukaviriya, 1989). The foundation of the contributions that the system makes is a rich knowledge representation for the components of an application's functionality.

Taking a single example, the UIDE system has a representation for operations that includes a specification of the pre- and post-conditions of the operation and a representation of what other operations may invoke or be invoked by this operation. For instance, in a program for drawing and manipulating graphic primitives, the operation for moving a graphic around the screen has the pre-condition that there is a graphic to be moved. Its post-condition is that the graphic is in the location specified. It may call on operations to select a graphic and to select a location on the screen. It may be called upon by an operation to copy a graphic (if the copy operation causes the user to select a new location for the new copy).

By using this rich representation for operations, the UIDE system is capable of doing a number of modifications to the interface design. In particular, it can easily modify a 'subject–verb interface' (where an object is picked, and then an action — in this case, select an object then move it), to be a 'verb–subject interface' (where an action is chosen, and then applied to an object — in this case, choose the move action and then select the object to be moved). In addition, the system can determine when pre-conditions of an action have or have not been met and can modify the interface accordingly. For instance, if a 'currently chosen' object is maintained by the application, then the UIDE system can determine that a separate interface action for selecting the object to be moved is unnecessary.

Burgstaller et al. (1989) describe a very similar system for generating dialogue managers. There approach, however, uses a layered architecture that is similar to that developed by Szekely (1989).

By representing and reasoning with these aspects of interface design, the UIDE system can reason about styles of interaction, rather than just designing interfaces. It can thus design a wider range of interfaces and is more amenable to changes and additions in the desired interaction style. However, there are still aspects of interface design that are not captured by this system.

2.3.2. CT-UIMS

The Conceptual Template User Interface Management System (CT-UIMS) uses a frame-based representation of the kinds of data and abstract dialogues that are typical of a wide range of office tasks (Märtin, 1990) — see also (Waldhor, 1989). These dialogues are essentially specifications of the abstract functionality of an application. To produce interfaces for this functionality, a combination of abstract dialogue templates, general presentation rules, and user- and application-specific profiles are used. All of these sources of design knowledge are organized by a single dialogue manager that produces an architecture-independent interface specification. This specification is then passed to an interface generator that instantiates the design on a particular architecture (e.g. the Andrew toolkit or OSF/Motif).

In addition to separating the application functionality from the interface, CT-UIMS separates out the user, application, and architecture specific aspects of interface design into independent modules. This allows the designer to modify the designs produced in an appropriate way by modifying only the appropriate knowledge. In particular, it means that the same interface can be implemented across a wide range of hardware and software platforms without forcing the interface to be redesigned.

2.3.3. MAID

The MAID system (Blumenthal, 1990a; Blumenthal, 1990b; Blumenthal, 1990c) automates the design of metaphoric human interfaces for computer applications. Briefly, a metaphoric interface is one that uses features from the real world to present the appearance and behavior of the objects and operations that a computer application makes available to the user.

Perhaps the most familiar metaphoric interface is the desktop metaphor for operating systems. This interface uses pictures of pieces of paper to represent files, pictures of file folders to represent directories, and animations of putting pictures of pieces of paper into pictures of folders to represent putting files into directories.

MAID separately represents the functionality of an application, the objects and operations that a real-world object presents, and the metaphoric relationship between the application and the real-world object. It then interleaves the application of three distinct sets of design rules to import characteristics of the real-world object into the application, determine what interface entities need to be created to present the objects and operations made available by that application, and to determine the location, appearance, and behavior of those interface entities.

By separating these various sources of knowledge, the MAID system allows a designer to independently specify different applications, metaphors, and design techniques. However, MAID leaves it to the designer to determine what combination will be best for a particular class of users.

3. Trends

There are two important trends demonstrated in the progression of systems presented here. The first is toward greater autonomy on the part of automated interface design systems. These systems are addressing more and more aspects of interface design as development continues: from HyperCard's simple skeleton for specifying and organizing interface entities, to systems for automatically designing entire application interfaces using a pervasive metaphor. The result of this trend is more coherent, complete interfaces. By attending to the entire interface, rather than just parts, an automated design system can insure consistency and coordination across the various components.

The second trend is toward bringing more knowledge to bear on the problem of designing an interface. As automated interface design technology develops, more and more issues relating to interface design are being explicitly represented and used: from simple representations of the set of interface entities available, to representations of interaction techniques, users, and real-world metaphors. The result of this trend is that more innovative interfaces are being developed and more expertise is being stored in automated interface design systems.

4. The Future

Following these two trends into the future suggests two lines of development to pursue. Given that automated interface design systems are covering more and more of the interface, the next step is to use this automated design technology to design *integrated systems*, rather than just computer applications, for addressing tasks. Such systems might include an interactive computer application, but would also need to take into account the organizational and environmental factors that will affect the task. As a result, automated interface design programs would not only have to design application interfaces, but would also have to design the roles of the various people using the application and the environment in which those roles would be conducted.

To revive an overworked example, if an interface design system were given the problem of developing an interface to an automated teller machine, it would not only have to consider the interface to the software, but also the roles of the bank employees who fill the machine (perhaps suggesting two at a time for security) and the environment in which the interface will be used (e.g. if there are other machines nearby, then part of the functionality would be to have a disabled machine make the location of those machines known).

Given that more and more information is being brought to bear on the interface design task, the next step is to add more knowledge about the user, task, and real world to the design process. Explicitly modeling not only the preferences and level of expertise of the user, but also an expected rate of learning would help a system design interfaces that adapted to the user as the user gained expertise. Representing knowledge about the real world where the system operates might produce interfaces that adapt as outside conditions change (e.g. using different presentation styles when a system is to be used in bright sunlight). This last example shows how the two trends might converge to suggest more effective interface designs for the real world.

5. Conclusions

This chapter has presented a fast tour of some of the landmarks in automated interface design, ranging from systems that merely support the creation and specification of simple interaction techniques, to systems that provide coherent, comprehensive interfaces for large applications. The strengths of these systems have been discussed as well as the limitations that they may impose on the design process.

By abstracting from these systems, two trends in automated interface design systems have been identified: the trend toward more coverage and the trend toward more knowledge. The extension of these trends points to interface design systems that take into account not only a computer application, but also the people who will be using that application, the tasks they will be performing, and the environment in which they will be performing those tasks. By adding this knowledge to automated design systems, more effective, comprehensive systems can be built.

There are a number of trade-offs inherent in automating interface design that will be repeatedly confronted as the work progresses. Perhaps the most troublesome is the question of how much the functionality of an application can, or should, be separated from the interface. Despite a number of representations for achieving this separation, there are still compelling reasons to provide the interface with direct access to the underlying application.

Related to this issue is the question of how much manual modification a designer should be allowed to apply to an automatically designed interface. Such modifications make the design opaque by not only introducing human-created code that may not match that created by the system but also by introducing design decisions that may not be clearly elucidated.

The question of how these trade-offs are best addressed and how the trends in interface design will develop is clearly an empirical one. The next generation of automated interface design systems will provide more clues.

Acknowledgements

Support for this work has been provided by the Medical Research Council, UK.

Designing User Interfaces by Direct Composition: Prototyping Appearance and Behavior of User Interfaces

Matthias Schneider-Hufschmidt

Siemens Corporate Research and Development, ZFE ST SN 71, Otto-Hahn-Ring 6,
D-81739 München, Germany.
EMail: msch@zfe.siemens.de

The design of the user interface of interactive systems is one of the major tasks in software engineering. User interfaces tend to be complex software products which reflect specific properties of applications as well as technological properties of the hardware and software used for the realization. The knowledge necessary to design good user interfaces can be divided into three categories: knowledge about the appearance and behavior of user interfaces, knowledge about the design process to create user interfaces, and knowledge about the application. This categorization is reflected in the conceptual models of interactive systems necessary to understand systems during design and usage. An approach called 'Direct Composition' of user interfaces offers the possibility to simplify these conceptual models and thereby the process of user interface design. Within this approach user interface objects comprise aspects of manipulation, visualization, and construction, and can take on different roles according to the models involved. Additionally, this approach offers the possibility of end-user adaptivity for user interfaces.

The structure of this chapter is as follows: Section 1 describes the use of user interface management systems in the interface design process. In Section 2 and 3 we describe the conceptual models relevant for the design process of user interfaces and show how the amount of necessary knowledge can be estimated from these models. Section 4 introduces the principle of direct composition and shows how the amount of important knowledge can be reduced by using this technique. Section 5 summarizes the industrial requirements for user interface design tools. In Section 6 a user interface management system for industrial applications is presented which follows the principle of direct composition.

Keywords: conceptual model, user interface design, direct manipulation, direct composition, dialog model, processing model, interactive system, design environments.

1. User Interface Management Systems

The design of the user interface of interactive systems is one of the major tasks in software engineering. User interfaces tend to be complex software products which reflect specific properties of applications as well as technological properties of the hardware and software used for the realization.

Many efforts have been made to support the software designer during the development of user interfaces. During the last years user interface management systems (UIMS) (Pfaff, 1985) have become state of the art. These systems serve two purposes: they support the software developer during the design of user interfaces (the user interface design system (UIDS) aspect) and they supply a runtime environment necessary to use the developed interface. The development of the user interface includes the definition of the static properties of user interfaces and of their dynamic behavior at the user interface level. One important feature of UIMSs is the strict separation of application and user interface code. This separation allows the independent development of system and interface. However, even with a UIMS the designer has to know the intricacies of the application in order to design an appropriate user interface.

UIMSs offer several important advantages. First, they allow the uniform design of user interfaces for a variety of application systems. This includes the possibility of ensuring a certain style of interaction on the level of the UIMS. Second, they allow the combination of one application system with different user interfaces, either for hardware reasons or to fit specific users' demands. Third, it is possible to prototype user interfaces at a very early stage of the development process to get early user feedback on the quality of design. This prototyping is nearly independent from the existence of the application system. Finally, UIMSs offer possibilities for reuse of existing components of user interfaces in future designs.

Even with the aid of a UIMS, the design of good user interfaces remains a complex task. The knowledge necessary to design user interfaces can be divided into three categories: knowledge about the appearance and behavior of good user interfaces, knowledge about the design process to create user interfaces, and knowledge about the application. Lack of knowledge in any of these categories will result in non-optimal user interfaces. Since it is rarely the case that the software designer is an application expert, serious failures and misconceptions on the level of a system's user interface are to be expected.

A further improvement on the quality of user interfaces can be gained by delivering the user interface design environment to the end-users. They are then able to adapt their user interface both to their working style and specific knowledge, and to changing requirements of the application systems. In this case the burden is moved in part to the end-user. If he wants to adapt his interface, he has to learn how to use the design environment and how to design good user interfaces. This additional learning overhead can be reduced by using a UIMS which incorporates an interaction style called 'Direct Composition' in which each object at the user interface contains information about its own *designability* (cf. Section 4 of the chapter).

Conceptual models of computer systems have been used to estimate the amount of learning effort and knowledge necessary to handle a system with competence. In the following sections we describe the conceptual models relevant to the task of user interface design using different methods and tools. A more detailed discussion of conceptual models and their relevance for the design of UIMSs can be found in (Kühme, Hornung & Witschital, 1991).

2. Conceptual Models of Interactive Systems

One of the most important goals in the design of interactive systems is to overcome the fundamental difficulties humans have in understanding and using computer systems. As one particular aid in solving this problem, the explicit formulation of conceptual models and their integration into the system design process has been proposed. Since Norman published his paper on mental models (Norman, 1983b) several types of conceptual models have been discussed, each one addressing different aspects of system design or usage (Chignell, 1990; Dzida, 1987; Hartson & Hix, 1989; Nielsen, 1986).

The main goal is to design a system that follows a consistent, coherent conceptual design model, so that users can develop their own model of that system which is still consistent with the designer's conceptual model (Norman, 1986; Tauber, 1987).

As a consequence, the main emphasis has been placed on the application of models which look at an interactive system from the point of view of its usage. In the field of user interface design, however, a second point of view has become more and more important. The attempt to separate user interface and application functionality of a system and to develop the resulting parts more or less independently from each other, resulted in new conceptual and architectural models which describe the interaction aspects of a system in more detail. Two of these architectural models are known as the *Seeheim Model of User Interfaces* (Green, 1985) and the *IFIP Model of User Interfaces* (Dzida, 1983).

These models not only serve as basic conceptual models of system interaction and usage, but also explain which elements of the interface part of the system are subject to design (and to what extent) and how they relate to each other (Dzida, 1987). Hence, these models still look at the interactive system as such, but now from an additional point of view, that of user interface design.

The difference between the two aspects, that of system usage and system interface design, becomes most apparent in the case of systems having direct manipulation interfaces (Shneiderman, 1983). Such systems have proven to be very effective in giving the user an insight into the conceptual model on which the interactive system is based. The graphical objects of the interface can be manipulated directly and the impact of these graphical operations on the represented domain objects is visualized immediately. The user feels directly engaged in communicating with the objects of interest and in manipulating them, instead of communicating on these objects with the system or the interface as an intermediary (Hutchins, Hollan & Norman, 1986). Ideally, the user only has to be an expert in the domain of the application. He should not need specialized knowledge and experience about the use of computers or about the software which is managing the dialog with the user. On the other hand, the user interface designer of course needs a conceptualization of the user interface elements under design.

Since the development of good user interfaces is costly and time consuming, software tools and design systems are being developed to support the user interface designer in his work. Many user interface design systems are themselves interactive in nature. They use graphical user interfaces to communicate with their users, i.e. with the user interface designers. As with other interactive applications, the user interface designer should be able to communicate directly with the objects of interest, i.e. with the elements and objects which he combines to form the user interface he wants to design. He should not have to communicate with these objects by using additional design tools.

3. Conceptual Models in User Interface Design

In the interactive process of user interface design, conceptual models for the design process are still playing a minor role. Although the necessity for the modeling of user interfaces in order to understand man machine interaction in principle is acknowledged, cf. for example (Hartson & Hix, 1989), the process of user interface design is only described in terms of representation techniques or from a tool-oriented view.

It is obvious, however, that all considerations of conceptual models for interactive systems hold equally for any interactive design system. Furthermore, there is a need for having a conceptual model of the user interface design process which is easy to understand. In particular, this is indispensable if the end-user is to become more and more actively involved in the user interface design process. The task now is to identify those conceptual models that are relevant in the interactive design of user interfaces.

An arbitrary interactive system can be divided into two parts: one part implements the application functionality, the other implements the user interface of the system. The same holds for the conceptual model of the system. It can be divided into a *processing model* modeling the application aspect and the *dialog model* modeling the interaction aspect of the system. The end-user's conceptual model of the system is not necessarily identical to the conceptual model the system's designer had in mind. The end-user's conceptual model is of major importance for the usability of a system, and the degree of consistency between the interface designer's and the end-user's conceptual model can serve as a measure for the quality of a user interface design. In our context, however, the conceptual model of the user interface designer is of primary interest, i.e. the system's dialog model from an interface designer's point of view.

The use of a tool for the design of user interfaces makes the analysis of relevant conceptual models even more complicated. In addition to the conceptual model of the system and its user interface, we now have to consider the *processing model of dialog design*, which is the processing model of the user interface tools, and the *dialog model of dialog design*, which is the interface model of the tool. The processing model of dialog design determines the degrees of freedom a designer has in manipulating the static appearance and also the interaction techniques of the user interface of a system. The dialog model of dialog design describes the ways in which the designer can interact with his tool in order to develop a user interface.

User interface design systems typically contain a set of generic user interface tools such as form and bitmap editors, object browsers, etc. to design a variety of user interfaces for different applications. Therefore, the dialog model of application systems can be generalized and instantiated to fit specific applications. Again, the dialog model of dialog design can be used to conceptualize the tools and techniques necessary to develop user interfaces.

By means of the different conceptual models described above it is possible to estimate the amount of knowledge necessary for a user interface designer in order to create concrete user interfaces. When using a design system for user interfaces (UIDS), the designer still needs four conceptual models: the model of the application functionality, the generalized model of user dialogs, the model of user interface design, and the dialog model of user interface design. All those aspects may be relevant to a user interface designer and therefore should be understood by him.

One important problem is that in most UIDSs the dialog model of user interface design is inconsistent with the model of dialog design the designer has in mind when developing a user interface. It is possible to reduce the necessary amount of knowledge by matching those two conceptual models, i.e. by ensuring that the dialog necessary to design a user interface is consistent with the conceptual model of the dialog between a user and an application system.

4. The Conceptual Model of Direct Composition

The term *Direct Composition*direct composition stands for the thorough application of the principle of Direct Manipulation to the design and development of graphical user interfaces. It characterizes a fully object-oriented approach to the creation and specification of a user interface without using specialized tools. Direct composition is based on an elementary object model. The conceptual model of a user interface is then represented by the union of the models of all objects of which the interface is composed. The object model contains a model of the object's interactive design, and for this reason each user interface composed by those objects contains a model of its own design.

Again the object model is divided into the *processing model* and the *dialog model*. These models include the models describing the interactive design of an object. More specifically, they describe not only how to design the object's interaction aspect described by the dialog model, but also how to design the object's application aspect described by the processing model. The interactive design of the parts of an object which are used for its own design can be modeled using a recursive approach.

The static appearance and the interactive behavior of objects described by the conceptual model, which is based on the Direct Composition philosophy, can be designed by using purely interactive techniques. New objects can be copied or derived from existing ones and a user interface can be composed directly by using those objects.

As a consequence, each object has exactly one dialog model which is valid for the dialog with the end-user of a user interface as well as for the dialog with its designer. The user interface designer can communicate directly with the objects of his interest, i.e. with the elements and objects which he combines to form the user interface he wants to design. He does not have to communicate with these objects via separate design tools.

The processing model defines different roles for the object and describes the semantics of the dialog depending on the chosen role. A single interaction can cause very different effects on an object according to the role the object takes. The dialog model includes aspects of manipulation, visualization, and construction. An object always encapsulates the union of all interaction techniques needed in all its roles. The role "design of the object itself", mainly needs construction aspects, whereas in the role "dialog with the user of the application" manipulation and visualization aspects predominate.

Objects can change their roles and therefore can be used in the design environment as well as in the runtime environment. Moreover, interactive design and testing is not restricted to a specialized design environment but can also be activated at run time by simply changing the object's role.

If direct composition is used, the conceptual model of some user interface design system is reduced to navigational tools necessary to access the elements out of which the user interface is composed. The processing model of the user interface design environment no longer contains tools for dialog design because all objects in the interface of the design environment and in arbitrary interfaces to be designed contain the means for their own modification and design.

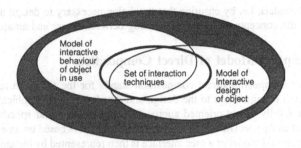

Figure 1:   The object model of direct composition

5. Requirements for User Interface Design Environments

In Section 6 a user interface environment based on the principles of direct composition is described. To understand the design rationale for the system called SX/Tools (Hermann, 1990) it is necessary to give a short overview of the requirements imposed by industrial application areas for this kind of tool. It should be stressed, however, that the requirements discussed here hold for other application domains, such as office automation, with minor shifts of importance.

5.1. Extensibility

5.1.1. Interactive Design of New Widgets

Different areas in production automation, numerical machine control, robot control, etc. have similar requirements regarding the design of user interfaces for computer-based visualization and control applications; the task of the system designer is to develop application specific graphical objects ('widgets').

The prototypical user interface of a system is composed of these application specific visualization objects and 'standard' user interface objects like menus, windows, scrollbars, forms and icons. It is important to note that the prototyping of these interfaces does not end at the window system level. Both the screen layout and the interface to the application using graphics need to be prototyped by the designer. For prototyping the control interface of an assembly line, one might want to combine symbols for robots, cutting tools, drills etc., with menus for selecting operations, dialog boxes for displaying warning messages, or other arbitrary user interface elements. All these elements are combined inside a window into a symbolization of the 'real' assembly line, in order to allow visualization and control of that assembly line through the computer. To take another example, a traffic visualization and control system needs symbols for, traffic lights, detectors, lane markers, etc. These, again, are combined in order to provide a visualization of events happening at some corresponding 'real' intersection.

The application specific graphical objects mentioned above are not just visualization objects. They usually have specific semantics known to the application expert. Moreover, it is necessary to define both their static appearance (the 'graphical' aspect of the user interface) and their dynamic behavior (the 'interactive' aspect).

5.1.2. Interactive Design of Dynamic Behavior

If the definition of the behavior of an interface can be done largely on the level of the user interface itself, most of the prototyping of behavior aspects can be performed without the application system.

The expressive power of the technique and language used for defining dynamic properties is important. The interface designer need not be a computer expert. It must be possible to express the design in terms understandable to application experts. On the other hand, the language for the definition of behavior has to be powerful enough to describe all interaction sequences on the user interface level and with the application system.

Several possibilities exist to support the interactive definition of dynamic properties. Objects receiving messages or events from other objects may be selected by pointing, lists of acceptable messages or events can be displayed in a menu-like style on demand, etc. Another possibility to define behavior of user interfaces is programming by example (Myers, 1990b). It must be possible to simulate the behavior of a user interface without an existing application. Tools for debugging the behavior are essential in a user interface design environment.

5.2. Reusability of Standard Widgets

Just as important as the ability to design new widgets is the reusability of existing, quasi-standardized widgets. Within a flexible design environment it should be possible to use a combination of both interactively designed widgets and 'standard' ones from any existing widget set (e.g. OSF/Motif or Sun's OLIT).

5.3. Openness to New Interaction Media

What today is specifically called 'multimedia' can be considered to become the norm in user interface technology within the next few years. Furthermore, new interaction media and techniques will appear, as well as new tools for interface design coming along with them. In order to avoid 'multi-tool' environments which tend to cause severe consistency problems, future design environments should be open for a full integration of arbitrary interaction media.

This integration has two aspects. First, it must be possible to incorporate into user interfaces all interaction media in a similar way. On the other hand, the design environment itself should make use of 'multimedia' interaction with the designer wherever it is convenient.

5.4. End-user Adaptability

Often the design of user interfaces in an industrial environment is not finished when a system is delivered to the customer (Fischer & Girgensohn, 1990). If the interface of the system is to reflect the structure of the real system, it must be possible to reflect changes in an application at the user interface level. This is only possible if the end-user gets tools for the modification of the system's user interface. By delivering both the application system and the design environment for the user interface, it is possible for the end-users to adapt the user interface to either their personal taste and abilities or to modify the interface to reflect a modification in the structure of the application.

One conclusion of this demand is that the definition of the appearance and behavior of a user interface should not be in the form of program code. First, the end-user cannot be expected to be an experienced programmer or to know the programming language used. If a programming language is used, e.g. for the definition of the dynamic behavior, it should be simple and tools must exist to support the user with the modification or redefinition of the behavior description. Second, the application system and the user interface cannot be recompiled and linked after every modification made by the end-user. Therefore, modifications at the user interface level have to be possible without changing the delivered object code of a system. (An example of end-user modifications which do not affect the code of an application interface is the use of resource-files in the X Window System (Scheifler & Gettys, 1986).)

5.5. Uniform Design Mechanisms

With a UIMS which fulfills the requirements of extensibility, openness, reusability and end-user adaptability as discussed above, there is an increasing need for a uniform construction and design discipline over all parts and levels of an interface. In order to achieve a good learnability and usability of a design environment the design mechanisms have to be independent of several design parameters described subsequently.

Independence of the Interaction Technique. It should not make any difference what is designed, e.g. a push button, a graphical symbol for a traffic light, or a frame for audio/video input/output. Changing static properties or the interactive behavior should work for all interaction objects in a similar way.

Independence of the Granularity of Designed Elements. Constructing a new elementary interaction technique (e.g. a special kind of a menu), an aggregated object (e.g. a robot visualization), or a complete user interface to an application has to follow the same basic principles.

Independence of the Interface Style (Look-and-feel). Switching the style of the interface in construction (e.g. using OSF/Motif widgets instead of those in the SUN OLIT toolkit) should not force the designer to switch between different design techniques.

Independence of the Life Cycle Stage and the Designing Person. The demands for end-user participation in the design process and end-user adaptability of a user interface result in the requirement for design mechanisms that are independent of the stage at which the design is performed. e.g. a user who has participated in the interface design process and thereby has become skilled in some frequently used design mechanisms of course expects the same mechanisms to be available when modifications of the interface become necessary at a later point of time.

Nevertheless, for reasons of system evolution the possibility of reusing existing user interface design tools within such an environment is important. It can be quite meaningful to make use of well known or specialized design tools although they might break the overall uniformity. Ideally, a coexistence of different design tools as well as a smooth, evolutionary change from existing, however inconsistent, tools to a new homogeneous tool environment should be possible.

5.6. Further Requirements

5.6.1. Conforming with Standards

For industrial application it is necessary to follow standards or quasi standards. This has consequences on several levels. First, the implementation language of a UIMS has to be widely used in industrial applications. Currently, C and C++ seem to be the languages of choice for the realization of these systems. Second, the style of interaction should follow some generally accepted user interface style, such as the Motif style ('Look-and-feel') (Open Software Foundation, 1990a). Finally, the user interface description produced with a user interface management system should conform to widely used representation languages, such as the Motif-UIL (Open Software Foundation, 1990b). As a minimum a UIMS should have the ability to interpret user interface descriptions written in those languages and create descriptions in a form that can be interpreted by other tools.

5.6.2. Realtime Support

Industrial applications often impose rather strict requirements for the realtime behavior of automation systems. If it is not possible to guarantee a necessary reaction time in the user interface component of such a system it is necessary to separate the user interface from the realtime dependent parts of an application.

5.6.3. Support for Distributed Applications

Industrial application systems like assembly lines or traffic control systems usually run on different machines, possibly with different operating systems in a physically distributed environment. A user interface management system for these applications has to support a simultaneous interaction with different hosts on a higher level of abstraction than a distributed window system like X does.

Similar requirements hold for applications in the area of computer supported cooperative work (CSCW) where different people in distributed locations share a workspace to solve tasks in a coordinated way.

5.6.4. Security Requirements

In many industrial applications specific requirements are imposed on automation systems, such as security properties or reaction to system malfunctions. In many cases the correct behavior with respect to some given specification or legal document has to be verified or validated. The verification of those properties can prove difficult or impossible for user interface components since they are open to the unspecifiable behavior of users. A well defined application interface can resolve this problem because it is possible to control the influence of user behavior on the interface between UIMS and application.

5.6.5. Separation Between User Interface and Application System.

A strict separation of the user interface and the application system is a requirement for many application areas. Several advantages can be gained by such a separation:

> *Early prototyping of the user interface.* The separation of application and user interface allows the prototyping of the user interface before the application has been fully implemented.

> *Different user interfaces to one application.* A strict separation of user interface and application systems offers the possibility to combine different user interfaces with a single application. This can be necessary if different hardware platforms are to be used for the implementation of the user interface. It also offers the possibility to adapt user interfaces to the personal style of users on a large scale.

> *Generic user interface for several applications.* For different application systems with similar functionality it is possible to give one interface to the users which allows them to handle several applications in a uniform way. In (Brown, Totterdell & Norman, 1990) the user interface to different mail systems is presented as an example for a generic user interface.

> *Evolution from non-graphical to graphical user interfaces.* Existing application systems are often equipped with standard non-graphical interfaces. With the advent of cheap graphics hardware customers want to switch from their old interfaces to new interfaces using graphical abilities of terminals. This evolution can be done smoothly if a clear separation between the interface component and the functional part of the application system exists.

A prerequisite for the separation of user interfaces from application systems is the definition of a sufficiently powerful application interface which maps user actions into application functions and the functionality of the application into surface changes at the user interface.

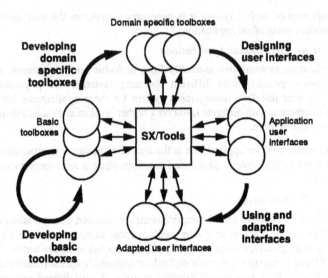

Figure 2:   The SX/Tools interface development process

5.7. *State of Practice*

Most toolkits for the prototyping of user interfaces do not fulfil the requirements stated above; they either allow the prototyping of the window system elements of a user interface (i.e. menus, buttons, etc.) or the definition of interactive graphics, but not the homogeneous handling of the entire user interface. Other requirements, like the definition of the dynamic properties of objects, are only fulfilled rudimentary, or, even worse, cannot be fulfilled at all (e.g. a straightforward end-user adaptability of interfaces).

6. SX/Tools — A User Interface Management System Based on Direct Composition

SX/Tools (S stands for Siemens, X for the X Window System) is a homogeneous extensible user interface management system that is designed for the prototyping of complete user interfaces in different production automation application areas. Thus, it allows evolutionary software development in areas where this is currently not customary. The system may, however, also be used in other application areas such as office automation. In the following sections we describe how far the requirements stated above are fulfilled by this UIMS. It is shown that direct composition plays a major role in meeting many of these requirements.

6.1. *Direct Composition*

SX/Tools follows the principle of direct composition as described above. Each interface object contains all the knowledge necessary for its own design and for its use as part of an application interface.

With SX/Tools, interfaces are built by copying and modifying existing interface components and creating new components composed of them. The interaction process for the design follows a direct manipulation style, i.e. the designer does not have to write code in order to define a user interface, but instead, can concentrate on the ergonomic features of the user interfaces to be designed. Interface components can be collected into so-called toolboxes. Basic toolboxes exist, for graphics, forms, windows, menus, etc. New toolboxes can be created in the same way as new interfaces, namely by interactively copying objects from other toolboxes or interface definitions. Toolboxes, as well as interfaces, can be stored permanently and their contents can be used in later sessions. According to the principle of direct composition, the necessary object management is performed by each object itself.

As illustrated by Figure 2, the direct composition approach implies a uniform interface development process which covers tool development, interface design, and 'on-usage' interface adaptation. The entire process is performed within one and the same environment following the same basic principles. This is in contrast to the conventional approach of separated design and runtime environments (Green, 1985) found in most state-of-the-art UIMSs.

Extensions to SX/Tools can be obtained through further development of basic toolboxes by adding new, interactively designed interaction techniques. Only the most basic techniques (e.g. the handling of new I/O channels) have to be implemented by conventional, although object-oriented, programming. Internally such elementary techniques are encapsulated in classes. Default objects of these classes are used as toolbox representations. For reasons of performance, however, some even more complex interaction techniques are supplied in the same way, i.e. they are programmed, although they could have been composed interactively (e.g. standard menus, buttons, etc.).

The customization of the design environment can easily be accomplished by interactive development of domain specific toolboxes. Figure 3 shows a toolbox designed for interface construction in the domain of traffic control systems. Domain specific toolboxes provide the user interface designer with elements which fit the application's needs through an adequate level of abstraction.

Since direct composition preserves the design mechanisms during the objects' lifetime, end-users are able to adapt SX/Tools user interfaces to their particular needs. They proceed from some standard user interface of an application and use the same interactive design techniques as the designer.

In the following section, some issues of user interface development with SX/Tools are discussed in more detail. It is pointed out what impact the direct composition approach has on each of these aspects.

6.2. Uniformity of Design

In the SX environment, interface elements like menus, buttons, text labels, icons or windows, and graphical objects like lines, polygons, rectangles or circles are handled in a uniform way. The techniques for the definition of interfaces do not change from the screen layout to the graphical representation of system properties. The user interface designer is not forced to use different tools to define the layout and the graphics part of the interfaces. SX/Tools allows the interactive design of static and dynamic properties of user interface objects. While the definition of aggregated objects also can be achieved interactively, a specialization (derivation) of new object classes from existing ones still has to be realized by programming in the current environment.

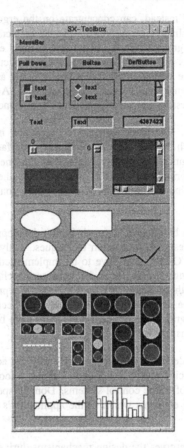

Figure 3: SX-toolboxes contain both standard and application specific interface elements

6.2.1. Definition of Appearance

Static properties are defined in two ways. Properties which can be modified by direct manipulation (e.g. size, position, rotation) are defined using a pointing device. All other properties can be modified using property sheets. The principle of direct composition applies to those property sheets, as well. Each property knows how it can be modified in an optimal way from the user's point of view and uses an appropriate property sheet for its design. There are various property sheets to define, e.g. numbers, texts, selections (1 of many or n of many), or colors. These property sheets can also be adapted to specific hardware and software requirements. For example, the property sheet to define colors may look different on a workstation with 8 colors (simple 1 of 8 selection) than it would look on a machine allowing a large number of colors. In the latter case RGB-sliders could be the appropriate choice. Figure 4 shows a specific property sheet for color selection.

6.2.2. Definition of Behavior

For the definition of dynamic properties of user interfaces (the 'behavior') different techniques have been proposed, among the most commonly used are state-transition-nets, context-free

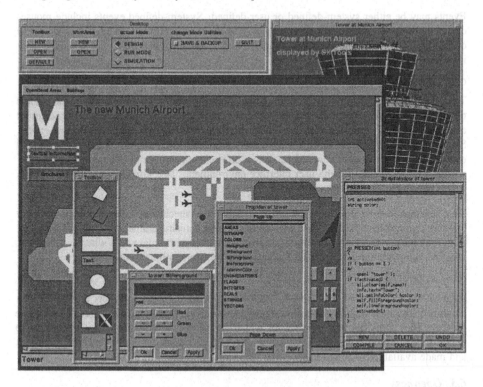

Figure 4: Some elements of the SX/Tools design environment

grammars and event-based techniques. For a discussion of the advantages and disadvantages of these approaches we refer to (Green, 1986). For the development of SX/Tools we have chosen an event-based approach. One of the advantages of this approach is that the reaction to incoming events can be defined locally in the user interface objects, conforming to the principle of object-orientation. The overall behavior of the user interface can then be described by the interplay of the local reactions to incoming events.

For the description of the reaction to incoming events (called scripts) a simple C-like language SX/Talk has been defined (Witschital, 1991). To relieve the user interface designer from the burden of knowing the syntax of this language exactly, SX/Tools provides an interactive, structure-oriented editor for event-definitions (see Figure 4). This can again be seen as an example of direct composition: if the designer wants to define a script of an object, a specific modification tool is instantiated to perform the task for that object. The reaction to an incoming event can be either the modification of local properties, the application of other local scripts or the creation of an event sent to another object of the user interface or application system. Scripts are not compiled and linked into the UIMS-code. Scripts are parsed and a syntax check is performed on their contents. Afterwards, a binary version of the scripts becomes a property of the user interface object in question. This version of the scripts is then interpreted. The reason for this solution is that the user interface need not be compiled and linked after each modification (see above).

Events may be either system-defined or user-defined. System-defined events include mouse-clicks, key-presses and selections in menus. User-defined events can be of any kind. These events are sent to interface objects either from the application system or from other user interface objects.

6.2.3. Specialization

Two styles of extensibility have been realized in the environment. Besides the simple modification of existing objects, more complex objects can be created by *specialization* and *aggregation*. Specialization is usually performed by a user interface design expert. Specialization is a process during which new classes are derived from existing classes and extended in order to create new objects with a different appearance or behavior. It is done by writing additional code for the user interface environment. This also implies that the system has to be rebuilt after these modification.

As a consequence of the direct composition principle, specialized classes inherit not only the normal interactive behavior but also all design mechanisms defined by their superclasses. They may locally specialize these mechanisms due to their particular needs whereas otherwise, with the conventional tool approach, large-scale extensions might be necessary.

6.2.4. Aggregation

Aggregation can be done without explicitly writing code. Existing objects are copied and combined into new objects, so-called *aggregate objects*. These objects behave like simple objects. They also have static properties which define their appearance and it is possible to define scripts which control their behavior. Aggregate objects can be copied into toolboxes and made available for future use.

6.3. Openness

SX/Tools is an *open* user interface design environment. The integration of new interaction media is relatively simple. Although some programming effort is necessary, the integration of audio or video output is not a major problem. Given the necessary hardware, we were able to create interface objects for audio output in less than a day. Certainly, more effort is needed to really integrate these interaction media, but the experiences so far have been encouraging.

The *openness* of the user interface management system extends into the design of the UIMS itself. The designer is free to define some personal environment in which the further use of SX/Tools is performed. The use of domain specific toolboxes containing interactive graphical elements and layout elements is just one example for this possibility. As each object in a direct composition environment contains the information necessary for its own design and use, the same is true for the elements comprising the design environment. This property has the consequence that after the realization of the basic elements of the UIMS (the 'bootstrapping phase'), the entire system can be developed using its own design techniques. Tools necessary in the UIMS for the design of interfaces can be designed in the same way as the interfaces themselves. For example, a file selector window can be composed of a number of text fields, text input fields, list-boxes, and action buttons related by appropriate dynamic scripts. Once its design is finished, it can be used inside the design environment and copied to a user defined toolbox for future use in application interfaces.

Some tools in the environment are used only for the design of application interfaces, not in the interfaces themselves. These tools include the property sheets for the definition and modification of object properties, the editor for dynamic scripts, and browsing tools for the selection of formerly defined interface objects. Figure 4 shows an example screen layout developed with SX/Tools and a set of object specific design tools. For these tools, all the properties of direct composition hold equally. Excluding the basic features they are composed of existing interface objects and are subject to modification by the interface designer.

6.4. End-user Adaptability

Objects in direct composition environments contain the information about their modification *and* their use. These two parts can not be separated easily. Therefore interfaces designed with SX/Tools contain the means for their own modification even after the delivery to the end-user. The user of an application system can modify its user interface using the same techniques and tools as the designer. The interaction techniques employed during the modification of user interface components are the same as the user has learnt from the interaction with the application system itself.

The end-user must be able to *adapt* application system interfaces for several reasons. First, it is possible to create user-specific interfaces reflecting the personal working style and abilities of individual users. Second, modification can become necessary when system requirements change and modifications in the structure of the application systems become necessary. In state-of-art automation systems with the ability of dynamic reconfiguration of automation processes this ability of adapting to new application structures is very important.

7. Implementation Issues

7.1. Object-orientation

SX/Tools has been developed as strictly *object-oriented*. For UIMSs following the principle of direct composition an object-oriented approach is an absolute necessity. The implementation of the system is done in C++. Although this programming language does not offer all the object-oriented features we would like to have for the realization of the system (e.g. it lacks a usable meta-object protocol), it seems to be a reasonable compromise between industrial requirements and quasi standards, and the requirements coming from the design style of direct composition.

7.2. User Interface Standards

The second basis for SX/Tools is the use of the X Window System and UNIX. This decision again reflects our need to follow industrial standards. X is currently being used in many application areas and seems to be a sensible foundation for the design of a UIMS. The style of interaction follows the so-called Motif Look and Feel (Open Software Foundation, 1990a), i.e. by using SX/Tools different user interfaces can be built with a uniform design and interaction technique which is widely used in industrial applications. Due to the decision to conform to these quasi-standards (UNIX, C++, Motif, and X) the environment is highly portable and could be developed for several different hardware platforms in parallel.

Figure 5 shows how the functionality of SX/Tools can be classified in terms of software layers. A specific widget, called 'SX-Widget', serves as a gateway between the two worlds of Xt widgets and SX objects. The SX-Widget allows the mapping of an arbitrary SX object hierarchy into the widget hierarchy as a subtree. From the SX/Tools point of view all widgets, even the SX-Widget, are encapsulated in appropriate classes which are subject to the mechanisms of direct composition. On the other hand, a C programmer has access to SX/Tools by means of the gateway widget. Moreover, the SX-Widget can be used

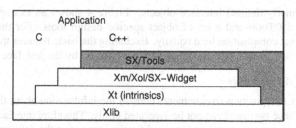

Figure 5: Functional scope of SX/Tools

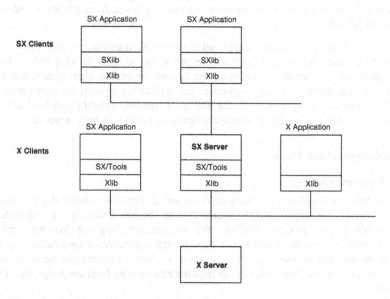

Figure 6: Multiple application interface to SX/Tools

within existing, e.g. OSF/Motif based design environments, if they are configurable in order to handle non-standard widgets. This is due to the requirements of evolutionary system design.

7.3. Multiple Application Interface

The application programmers interface (API) to SX/Tools is based on the communication protocol of the objects involved. Both application and interface objects can be identified by name and communicate with each other via messages. In the case of non-object-oriented applications, messages to the application appear as ordinary events.

At the technical level SX/Tools provides a multiple application interface. First, the application code may be linked to the SX/Tools code as it works with common toolkits. Besides that, SX/Tools offers a client–server architecture similar to the X architecture (see Figure 6). While the figure represents the logical structure of this architecture, the 'SX protocol' is physically built upon the X protocol exploiting the appropriate X mechanisms with regard to the Inter-

Client Communication Conventions Manual, ICCCM (Nye, 1990). This approach offers the possibility of distributing SX applications to any environment which supports the standard X protocol.

Besides the realization of distributed applications, the client–server architecture of SX/Tools allows connection of additional interaction channels to SX/Tools. e.g. the functionality of an audio/video control program can be encapsulated into an object which communicates with this program via the SX protocol. The complete definition of such an object and its communication procedures can be set up interactively according to the direct composition mechanisms.

7.4. State of the SX/Tools Implementation

A prototype of the SX/Tools user interface management system has been implemented. The prototype has been used for the design of user interfaces for automation systems and process control systems. Although the system in its current state still needs an experienced user (e.g. there is yet no help facility), our evaluation of the prototype has been positive. The amount of time required for the design of user interfaces can be cut down considerably and the resulting interfaces show a high degree of homogeneity. The experiences gained during its development and the first use encourage further work on SX/Tools. Current work covers the realization of an SX-based authoring system for CBT and the implementation of a multimedia time-line editor. The next steps in the development of SX/Tools include a complete integration into OSF/Motif, further integration of multimedia techniques, and a thorough evaluation of the ergonomic properties of the UIMS.

8. Conclusions

In this chapter we have argued that interactive design of user interfaces can be realized best in design environments where the dialog model of dialog design is consistent with the dialog model of the user interface to be designed. We have attempted to point out some markedly important requirements of user interface management. In particular, the growing variety of interaction media and techniques as well as the current trend towards a higher degree of end-user participation in the design process of user interfaces have to be taken into account. Thus, a model covering all the aspects of complex interfaces and their design, which are still as simple as possible, is needed.

The principle of direct composition is considered to be such a simple design model which can serve as a basis for appropriate architectures of user interface design environments. The main characteristic of an environment following the direct composition approach is the holistic view of *what* is to be designed, *when* it is designed (i.e. *at which stage* in the development process), and *by whom*.

Although direct composition UIMSs do not fulfil all the requirements mentioned in this chapter, they are an important step towards comprehensive but, nevertheless, easy-to-use user interface design environments.

Acknowledgements

I would like to thank Thomas Kühme for his contribution to this report. He influenced its contents by stimulating discussions and valuable ideas. The members of the SX/Tools team within Siemens Corporate Research and Development made this report possible by creating an excellent system and a challenging working environment.

Dialogue Specification as a Link Between Task Analysis and Implementation

Andrew Monk & Martin Curry

Department of Psychology, University of York, York YO1 5DD, UK.

Tel: +44 (0)904 433148

EMail: AM1@york.ac.uk

Dialogue specification is a way of linking task analysis to an implementation. The approach is illustrated with an example in which a specification of the behaviour of a vending machine is progressively built up by adding rules to a production system. This specification is checked for predictability, reversibility and task fit.

Keywords: dialogue specification, user interface design, task analysis, production systems.

1. Introduction

This research is being conducted in the context of a collaborative project funded by the UK Science and Engineering Research Council and the Information Engineering Directorate. The industrial partners are Data Logic (Harrow) and System Concepts (London). This project is to develop advanced tools and techniques for building new PC-based interfaces to existing mainframe applications.

A graphical user interface (GUI) offers designers much more freedom than the more old fashioned dumb terminal interfaces. This freedom presents new opportunities but it also presents new dangers. We may just be giving them more "rope to hang themselves with". For this reason we aim to build tools and techniques that encourage good design practice. In particular, there should be some way of linking a task model (the product of business analysis, task analysis and job design) to the implementation. We are currently experimenting with the use of a dialogue model to do this. The dialogue model is specified using a modified version of PPS — Propositional Production Systems (Olsen, 1990). This specification abstracts across the detail of presentation and application components but still provides an unambiguous description that can form the basis of implementation. A representation based on a production system was chosen because:

1. Such specifications can be written so that they are relatively easy to read.

2. They can be run or animated when incomplete.

3. They can be subjected to certain analyses and checks that may show up potential usability problems.

This chapter describes how these properties may be used by suggesting an iterative design process. This takes as input an informal design in the form of a task model and some sketches of screens. The output of the process is a precise specification of the various sequences of events open to users that is well designed with respect to the task they have to do.

2. A View of Interface Design

One of the other partners in the project (System Concepts) is developing procedures by which the job of the user can be designed with regard to a well rounded picture of business and ergonomic requirements. This will result in a task model consisting of a hierarchical decomposition and some sample task scenarios. Figure 1 presents a fictional task model for a hamburger vending machine.

The task model is the stimulus for the next informal/creative phase of design in which screen objects are sketched and a rough idea of how they are used is formulated. Figure 2 presents such an informal design for the burger vending example.

The task model and the informal design are the input to the dialogue specification phase. A dialogue specification is developed iteratively. After each iteration the following checks and analyses are done:

1. Is the specification internally consistent (condition names used in the right way etc.)?

2. Can the user achieve all the steps in the task model and task scenarios (or those covered so far) in an efficient way? This is demonstrated by animating the specification.

3. Is the design as developed this far 'predictable' (Monk, 1990) that is, where one input event could have different effects depending on the state of the machine, can the designer make a convincing argument that the user will be able to predict which it will be in each case?

4. Can the dialogue specification deal with all user exceptions (e.g. user decides he doesn't want a drink with his meal after all)? This corresponds to the Monk (1990) concept of reversibility.

5. Can the dialogue specification deal with all application exceptions (e.g. machine out of burgers)?

During this process it will almost certainly be necessary to change the informal design, and possibly even the task model. The final design to be passed on for implementation consists of the refined screen sketches and task model plus a complete dialogue model. Because this was based on a task model and the above checks have been done, it should form a good basis for a usable design. Because it is readable and runnable it is a good way of communicating the design.

3. An Example

A propositional production system, as defined by Olsen (1990), consists of two parts:

1. a representation of the system state space as a collection of conditions that can be set or not set; and

2. rules that work on these conditions.

Task Scenario 1

1. Give me a Huge Burger with everything on it and a large fries.
2. (Anything to drink?)
3. Root beer.
4. (Regular or large?)
5. Regular, please.
4. (That will be $5.40.)
5. Here is $6.
6. Takes change.

Task Scenario 2

1. Large cola please.
2. (Anything to eat?)
3. No thanks.
4. (That will be 75c please.)
5. Here is $1.
6. Takes change.

Task Scenario 3

1. Large cola please.
2. (Anything to eat?)
3. No thanks. Err make that an Orange.
4. (That will be 75c please.)
5. Here is $1.
6. Takes change.

Task Scenario 4

1. Give me a Large Burger with everything on it and a large fries.
2. (Anything to drink?)
3. Regular root beer.
4. (That will be $5.40 please.)
5. Whoops, cancel the root beer.
6. (That will be $4.95 please.)
7. Here is $5.
6. Takes change.

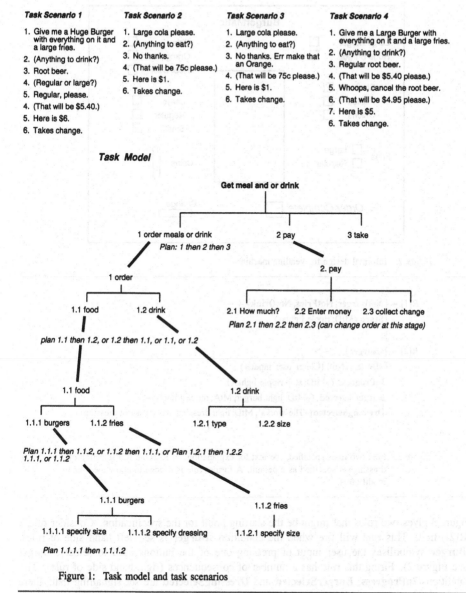

Task Model

Get meal and or drink

1 order meals or drink — 2 pay — 3 take

Plan: 1 then 2 then 3

1 order

2. pay

1.1 food — 1.2 drink

2.1 How much?   2.2 Enter money   2.3 collect change

Plan 2.1 then 2.2 then 2.3 (can change order at this stage)

plan 1.1 then 1.2, or 1.2 then 1.1, or 1.1, or 1.2

1.1 food

1.2 drink

1.1.1 burgers   1.1.2 fries   1.2.1 type   1.2.2 size

Plan 1.1.1 then 1.1.2, or 1.1.2 then 1.1.1, or Plan 1.2.1 then 1.2.2
1.1.1, or 1.1.2

1.1.1 burgers

1.1.2 fries

1.1.1.1 specify size   1.1.1.2 specify dressing   1.1.2.1 specify size

Plan 1.1.1.1 then 1.1.2

Figure 1: Task model and task scenarios

If the conditions on the left hand side of a rule are all set then the rule is said to 'fire' setting all the conditions on the right hand side of the rule. Conditions are used to represent long term system states (e.g. **InProgress** indicates that the system is in an 'order in progress' state as opposed to a 'start' state or an 'order complete' state) as well as more transitory states or 'events' (e.g. **sBurger** indicates that the user has pressed one of the buttons to select a burger).

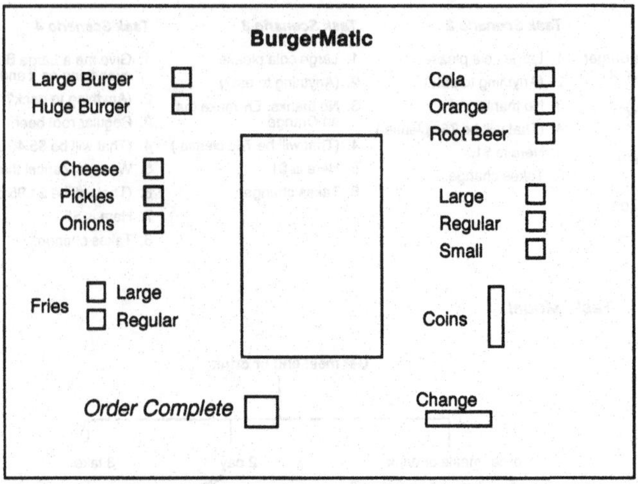

Figure 2: Informal design for vending machine

R[1] ▪ {NotBurger, NotFries, NotDrink} – – >
      {Start(∗MtD: ripple lights∗)
      .};
R[2] ▪ {sBurger} – – >
      {sDone, (∗Null (Clears user input)∗)
      InProgress, (∗MtD: stop ripple lights∗)
      BurgerSelected, (∗MtD: light burger, MtA: request burger∗)
      DressingSelected(∗The works!, MtD: light dressing, MtA: request dressing∗)
      };

Figure 3: First two rules specified, see text for explanation. In R[2] the full selection of
           dressings is specified as a default. A further rule is needed to allow the user to
           modify this.

Figure 3 gives two rules that might be the starting point for the specification. Consider rule 2
(R[2]) first. This rule will fire when the condition **sBurger** is set (left hand side of rule).
sBurger symbolises the user input of pressing one of the buttons used to select a burger
(see Figure 2). Firing this rule has a number of consequences (right hand side of rule). The
conditions **InProgress, BurgerSelected** and **DressingSelected** are set signalling that: there
is an order in progress, a burger has been selected and the default dressing has been specified
respectively.

Conditions can have associated actions which occur as a side effect of setting the condition,
i.e. when they occur in the right hand side of a rule. These take the form of messages to the
display and messages to the application. Thus, for example, when **BurgerSelected** is set a
message is sent to the display to put on a light indicating the burger selected and a message is
sent to the application to start preparing a burger. These actions must be the same whenever
the condition appears on the right hand side of a rule.

$U[1] = F[1] = Selections = \{$sDone, sBurger, sDressing, sDrink, sDrinkSize, sFries, sOrderComplete$\}$;
$F[2] = Burger = \{$NotBurger, BurgerSelected$\}$;
$F[3] = Dressing = \{$NotDressing, DressingSelected$\}$;
$F[4] = Fries = \{$NotFries, FriesSelected$\}$;
$F[5] = Drink = \{$NotDrink, DrinkSelected$\}$;
$F[6] = DrinkSize = \{$NotDrinkSize, DrinkSizeSelected$\}$;
$F[7] = OrderStatus = \{$Start, InProgress, Complete$\}$;
$A[1] = F[8] = OutOf = \{$OK, OutOfBurger, OutOfDressing, OutOfDrink, OutOfFries$\}$;

Startingstate $= \{$sDone, NotBurger, NotFries, NotDrink$\}$;

Figure 4: Fields of mutually exclusive conditions. These represent the state space for the
system. See text for explanation.

R[1] has the effect of setting the order status to **Start** whenever there is no food or drink ordered. The side effect of setting it is to send a message to the display to ripple all the lights on the machine.

Figure 4 presents some conditions for use in these and future rules. Conditions are gathered into mutually exclusive 'fields' so that setting one condition in a field automatically unsets any other. For example, **sDone** and **sBurger** are both conditions in the same field 'Selections'. This means that when R[2] fires, setting **sDone**, **sBurger** is 'cleared' preventing the rule from firing again.

F[1] and F[8] are special fields. Their conditions are set by the user and the application respectively. For this reason they should not appear on the right hand side of any rule. **sDone** is the exception to this. The fields in Figure 4 specify the complete state space at this stage of the design. In addition the conditions that are set initially, when the production system is started, are specified here.

Production systems are good at representing parallel functionality. This makes them particularly suitable for representing the large number of options simultaneously available to the user of a graphical interface. Both Hill (1987) and Olsen (1990) use them for this reason. However, the cost of this power is that they may obscure sequential dependencies. This is particularly true when 'conflict resolution' algorithms are brought into play. Conflict resolution is necessary when more than one rule can fire. The simplest conflict resolution algorithm, and that used here, is to fire the rule with the lowest number. It means the rule writer must sequence the rules to achieve the required behaviour. The effect of this sequencing can be subtle. For example, R[2] in the two rule set of Figure 3 will never fire using this conflict resolution algorithm. R[2] has the purpose of changing **NotBurger** to **BurgerSelected** and so would prevent R[1] from firing after the user has selected a burger (**sBurger**), but at the point where the left hand sides of the rules are evaluated both rules could fire. R[1] comes first and so it will fire, not R[2]. Of course, if the rules were listed in the opposite order there would be no problem. In a specification notation, intended for communicating and reasoning about a design, this kind of hidden sequential dependency is unfortunate.

Rather than attempting some more sophisticated conflict resolution algorithm of the kinds used by Olsen (1990) and Hill (1987), we avoid these hidden sequential dependencies by

R[1] – {NotBurger, NotFries, NotDrink, sDone} – – >
    {Start(*MtD: ripple lights*)
    };

R[2] – {sBurger} – – >
    {sDone, (*Null (Clears user input)*)
    InProgress, (*MtD: stop ripple lights*)
    BurgerSelected, (*MtD: light burger, MtA: request burger*)
    DressingSelected(*The works!, MtD: light dressing, MtA: request dressing*)
    };

R[3] – {sDrink} – – >
    {sDone, (*Null (Clears user input)*)
    InProgress, (*MtD: stop ripple lights*)
    DrinkSelected, (*MtD: light drink, MtA: request drink*)
    };

R[4] – {sDrinkSize} – – >
    {sDone, (*Null (Clears user input)*)
    InProgress, (*MtD: stop ripple lights*)
    DrinkSizeSelected, (*MtD: light drink size, MtA: request drink size*)
    };

R[5] – {sFries} – – >
    {sDone, (*Null (Clears user input)*)
    InProgress, (*MtD: stop ripple lights*)
    FriesSelected, (*MtD: light fries, MtA: request fries*)
    };

R[6] – {InProgress, sOrderComplete} – – >
    {sDone, (*Null (Clears user input)*)
    Complete, (*MtA: Compute bill*)
    };

Figure 5: Extending the rule set

---

insisting that there is no conflict i.e. the designer must specify sufficient context to separate all the rules. Our analysis of the rules in Figure 3 would reveal the conflict described above and the designer would be forced to add a condition 'no input' (**sDone**) as an additional context to R[1] (see Figure 5).

Figure 5 represents the next stage in building a dialogue specification for this application. The small problem with R[1], discussed above, has been fixed and further rules for user selections have been added. There is now sufficient functionality to evaluate the dialogue specification for task fit, predictability and reversibility.

Task fit: By running the production system, following the operations required to achieve Task Scenarios 1 and 2 (see Figure 1), we can see that the dialogue has good task fit. Each of the conceptual steps in the task model corresponds to a single button press and there is no obvious way it could be made more efficient. This is unsurprising given that the dialogue has been designed around these scenarios. However, comparing the input events available to the user at each point in the dialogue with the hierarchical task analysis reveals a potential

$U[1] = F[1] = Selections = \{sDone, sBurger, sDressing, sDrink, sDrinkSize, sFries, sOrderComplete\}$;

$F[2] = Burger = \{NotBurger, BurgerSelected\}$;

$F[3] = Dressing = \{NotDressing, DressingSelected\}$;

$F[4] = Fries = \{NotFries, FriesSelected\}$;

$F[5] = Drink = \{NotDrink, DrinkSelected\}$;

$F[6] = DrinkSize = \{NotDrinkSize, DrinkSizeSelected\}$;

$F[7] = OrderStatus = \{Start, InProgress, Complete, DrinkSizeNeeded\}$;

$A[1] = F[8] = OutOf = \{OK, OutOfBurger, OutOfDressing, OutOfDrink, OutOfFries\}$;

Startingstate = $\{sDone, NotBurger, NotFries, NotDrink\}$;

Figure 6:   Adjusted fields for the rules in Figure 7, DrinkSizeNeeded added to F[7]

---

problem requiring a design decision. As the rules stand a user may start her interaction with the machine by selecting a burger, fries, a drink or a drink size. There is no constraint on the sequence in which the order continues. She could for example order fries in between specifying a drink type and its size. It is decided to constrain the dialogue so that a user is forced to choose a drink size immediately after selecting a drink type. This design decision is justified by the task model which suggests that people will tend to want to choose the size of a drink immediately after choosing its type and because it would cause considerable problems later on if a user forgot to specify the drink size at this point. To achieve this change to the dialogue model the condition **DrinkSizeNeeded** is added to the order status field (see Figure 6) and the context conditions in rules R[2] to R[5] changed (see Figure 7).

Predictability: Having dealt with this problem we go on to consider the predictability of the new specification. Our concern here is that the user should be able to predict the effect of any action they take with the interface. There are two situations that can lead to unpredictability in a system. The first is where an input condition occurs in two rules, so that, the same user action will have differing effects depending on the state of the machine. If this is the case then the designer must assure that the user can predict which effect will occur (which rule will fire) from the state of the display. Each of the input conditions in field 1 occurs in only one rule and so there is no problem here. The second potential source of unpredictability arises when an action is potentially available to a user but the system state makes it ineffective. For example, the buttons for selecting a drink size are only effective when a drink type has been selected (R[4], Figure 7) and when a drink type is selected none of the other buttons are effective until a drink size is selected. If an action is available to a user they should ideally be able to predict when it will be effective and when not. This is the principle behind dimming menu items. In general, the first kind of unpredictability is of more importance than the second as an unexpected response is more likely to be a problem than no response. On this basis it is decided that the potential unpredictability introduced by R[4] can be dealt with by drawing attention to the drink size selection buttons after a drink type selection is made, perhaps by lighting up a border around them. This decision can be incorporated as a message to display for **DrinkSizeNeeded** (see R[3], Figure 7).

Reversibility: This is assessed by considering points in the task model where users may wish to change their minds, as in task scenarios 3 and 4. Examining the rule set in Figure 7 reveals that the dialogue is not reversible. There is no mechanism for cancelling an item on the

$R[1] = \{$NotBurger, NotFries, NotDrink, sDone$\} - - >$
    $\{$Start(∗MtD: ripple lights∗)
    $\}$;

$R[2] = \{$sBurger, $\{$Start, (∗OR∗)InProgress$\}\} - - >$
    $\{$sDone, (∗Null (Clears user input)∗)
    InProgress, (∗MtD: stop ripple lights∗)
    BurgerSelected, (∗MtD: light burger, MtA: request burger∗)
    DressingSelected(∗The works!, MtD: light dressing, MtA: request dressing∗)
    $\}$;

$R[3] = \{$sDrink, $\{$Start, (∗OR∗)InProgress$\}\} - - >$
    $\{$sDone, (∗Null (Clears user input)∗)
    DrinkSelected, (∗MtD: light drink, MtA: request drink∗)
    DrinkSizeNeeded(∗MtD: light border round drink size button∗)
    $\}$;

$R[4] = \{$DrinkSizeNeeded, sDrinkSize$\} - - >$
    $\{$sDone, (∗Null (Clears user input)∗)
    InProgress, (∗MtD: stop ripple lights∗)
    DrinkSizeSelected, (∗MtD: light drink size, MtA: request drink size∗)
    $\}$;

$R[5] = \{$sFries, $\{$Start, (∗OR∗)InProgress$\}\} - - >$
    $\{$sDone, (∗Null (Clears user input)∗)
    InProgress, (∗MtD: stop ripple lights∗)
    FriesSelected(∗MtD: light fries, MtA: request fries∗)
    $\}$;

$R[6] = \{$InProgress, sOrderComplete$\} - - >$
    $\{$sDone, (∗Null (Clears user input)∗)
    Complete, (∗MtA: Compute bill∗)
    $\}$;

Figure 7: Adjusted rules, LHS more specific as to order status

order. Additional rules and user input fields have to be added to do this. These rules must be effective even after the 'Order Complete' button is pressed as Task Scenario 4 suggests that this is precisely when users will want to change their minds when they find out how much the order is going to cost.

This process is continued until there are enough rules to complete all the task scenarios. Further rules are then generated to deal with possible application exceptions (F[8]). At all points the dialogue model can be run and analysed for task fit, predictability and reversibility as above. When the time comes to pass the design on for implementation the ability to run the specification and examine its behaviour is again invaluable, this time for communicating the design.

4. Future Work

At present we are building and analysing dialogue specifications using Mathematica. We are building a dialogue specification tool in Smalltalk/V. We are also exploring ways in which the specification can be directly incorporated into the implementation code (an agent like architecture again in Smalltalk/V).

Of course, the effectiveness of the process outlined can only be demonstrated by using it to design a real application and, in the long run, if it can be encapsulated in such a way that other designers can use it.

Acknowledgements

This work was supported by a DTI/SERC grant to the first author. We are grateful to the other collaborators on this project from Data Logic and System Concepts Ltd.

Theme 3 Discussion Report

The third set of presentations during the workshop was entitled 'Technological Solutions'. Despite the fact that the area of software engineering tools is rather broad, all four presentations focused on user interface design questions. In the first presentation, John Domingue presented a framework and support tools for software visualization for different programming languages. Next, Jürgen Herczeg presented a system which allows the interactive design of user interfaces in a Lisp-based environment. Tim Dudley then talked about the problems which arise due to the fact that in software engineering environments users and developers are identical. The final presentation described industrial requirements for user interface design tools and an approach called Direct Composition for the interactive construction of object-oriented graphical user interfaces.

Obviously, the discussion in the area 'Technological Solutions' was also mainly centered around user interface design questions. The main topic was the impact of end-user modifiability on the design process and the complexity of the resulting systems. The separation of user interface and application, the viability of research results for complex user interfaces, and methods and tools for the design of real-world user interfaces were other issues discussed in the working groups.

In this report I will not try to capture the discussion process of the different groups. I have ordered the contents of the different discussions according to the topics mentioned above and tried to bring the different issues raised in the four groups into a homogeneous order. My own comments are in *italics* to separate them clearly from the groups' results.

The Impact of End-user Modifiability on User Interface Design

By far the largest number of comments was made on the topic of system adaptability. Overall, there was general agreement about the desirability of end-user modifiability in user interfaces. Several open questions, however, remained after the extended discussion.

What Should Be Modified?

One group was concerned that end-users would want to change both the interface and the existing functionality. Users might be more concerned with changing the application functionality than the 'look and feel' of the interface. Since the user interface is supposed to present the functionality of an application system, there needs to be a close relationship between the application functionality and the user interface. In cases where changing the functionality should not be allowed by the end-user, appropriate protection mechanisms have to be installed.

The term end-user modifiability is not clearly defined. The possible range of changes to the functionality and the user interface is large, from simple display modifications to restructuring tasks and the modification of basic functions. The functionality to reach these goals ranges from simple selection of different built-in alternatives to 'real' end-user programming.

What should be modified? Should one be able to change the functionality or simply the appearance? The group felt that the latter was not a problem, but that the former would cause difficulties. Adding 'shortcuts' is OK, but the additions of new functions changes the behavior of the interface and may confuse the user. A possible approach could be to allow a controlled degree of modifiability, e.g. 'minimal modification' or 'restricted flexibility'

Closely connected with the question of what should be modifiable is the increase in the complexity of the system as it is modified over time. A good design would be similar to Le Corbusier's Modulor system in which the 'end-user' could assemble modules as desired but the underlying principles would remain.

Another open question is the complexity of the system as it initially presents itself to the user. Little is known about how increasing the abstraction level, by providing possibilities for modification, will affect the perceived complexity.

Views and Abstractions

An interface presents the user with a view of the underlying functionality of a system. Changing the user interface can be seen as changing this view. If the appropriate abstractions are not built into the underlying application, however, it may be impossible to change the view and hence the interface.

In order to change the underlying system so that the new view can be constructed, new abstractions must be built. If it is not possible to change the underlying application then a shell must be built around the existing application functionality. The shell provides abstractions appropriate for the new view. This is similar to the approach adopted in 'Viz' by John Domingue.

Modification of the user interface leads to a changed environment. The extent to which this is desirable may depend on the nature of the user; for example, the user of a software development environment may require extensive modifiability (e.g. the UNIX user) whereas a less sophisticated user may require less.

If it's Good for Us Then it's Good for Them

If we want user interfaces to be adaptive or customizable, the question arises as to by what means the end-user might achieve the desired modification. In my talk I presented a system which offers the same modification means to both designers and end-users.

One group questioned the validity of this approach. According to their discussion it is not necessarily the case that a good set of tools for modifying the application functionality will be equally good for interacting with the application itself.

Use of the same language for both the development of an application and the use of the application causes another problem. As soon as developers become familiar with an interaction language, they believe that their interaction style is 'natural'. They are therefore more likely to force an inappropriate interaction language on the user.

Separating the languages and tools for user interface adaptation and the use of the application forces end-users to learn and memorize more options and constructs. This might prevent them from modifying the user interface.

Maybe the first statement makes more sense if turned around: if it is good for them it ought to be good for us. Even then, the tools and techniques which support the modification of user interfaces will not be the most appropriate selection for changing functionality. On the contrary, if we want to offer the functionality of the design environment to the end-user, a clear separation of user interface and application functionality is important. We should not expect the end-user to be able to modify the functionality in a consistent way, but he may be capable of performing consistent changes at the interface level.

The second point is certainly well taken. Offering a poorly designed development environment to the end-user will certainly not lead to the desired user interfaces that are easy to modify. Therefore the user interface of the design environment becomes much more important. This is a challenge for tool developers, who have been notoriously bad at designing their own user interfaces.

Who Decides on the Question of End-user Modifiability?

Should it be the end-user or the interface designer/developer? One discussion group came up with the view that a 'rich' interface can provide a degree of flexibility which appears as modifiability.

The necessary flexibility to change a user interface after the system has been delivered needs to be built into the system beforehand. There is no end-user modifiability without the designer's explicit integration of the required functionality.

It is an open question as to whether the end-user is in a position to modify the interface. Is he able to use the tools provided? Does he have to learn the interface in addition to the application?

We need to distinguish between re-allocation of function and actually programming new functionality. While the first should be achievable by the majority of users, the latter certainly requires deep knowledge of the application area and the system design.

What Are the Requirements for End-user Modifiability

A number of requirements for end-user modifiability was mentioned by different discussion groups. The following is a collection of all the different opinions stated.

The system should:

- be able to accept unstructured and inconsistent work (users will not be prepared to undergo training in design);
- change gradually (the user should not have to deal with sudden changes in the task demands caused by modifications);
- not restrict the user's initiative to experiment (the EuroPARC Buttons system was mentioned as a good example of this);
- allow modifications in a domain-oriented language (cf. Gerhard Fischer's chapter in this volume);
- offer a rich variety of restructuring methods, giving the user many possibilities and thereby increasing his sense of enjoyment (HyperCard has many 'loose parts'

which can be jiggled into new structures, giving incidental rewards and a sense of accomplishment to the end-user, even if nothing substantial is achieved);

- give the user tools to allow him to develop an interesting interface (i.e. reward the user for his modification efforts); and

- help the user foresee the consequences of changes.

Is Separation Always a Good Thing?

An underlying assumption of two of the presentations was that the user interface and application can and should be separated. The advantages of a clear separation have been stated. There are constraints, however, which may enforce a tighter connection between the user interface and application. The need and desirability of separating the user interface and application depends on the nature of the problem. If the separation is possible, there are two aspects to be considered:

- That there is a continuum between strict separation and tight interconnection.

- The timing problems and the information bandwidth between the user interface and application impose important constraints on the separability.

It should be noted that the topic of so-called 'application frameworks' for user interface design has not been addressed by the presentations of this day's session. Clearly, the opinions of the inherent value of separation and the advantages of user interface management systems differ widely in the user interface community. We should not expect to find a globally accepted view on this problem.

User Interface Design for Large Systems

The need for a good methodology for user interface design was stated. The available tools support only the implementation phase, not the whole design process. The user interfaces of large systems, in particular, have other qualities other than just screen layout, presentation, and navigation, which can be explored by prototyping approaches. One example of these qualities is consistency of interface behavior.

Tool developers should emphasize the reduction of the cognitive load on the designers. This should apply to all levels at which the designer works. For user interfaces, the levels to be taken into account are the presentation, navigation, task, and behavior level. For larger systems there is a need for methods and tools for structuring complex interfaces. The selection of the appropriate granularity has to be supported.

Capturing design knowledge in the tools can support the design of consistent user interfaces (just as spelling checkers in wordprocessors enforce consistent spelling). The output of those tools should not, however, be restrictive to the designer.

Design tools should support and encourage explorative design. This holds especially in the case of user interface development. Tools should be developed that allow the extraction of design information from the results of this exploration and an assessment of the ergonomic quality of user interfaces.

Composition of user interfaces by graphical means offers many advantages. Still, for the purpose of analysis and conciseness, a textual representation may be desirable.

The general conclusion of the discussion is that the nature of the design process for large and complex user interfaces has not been analyzed and understood thoroughly enough to give us insight into the nature of support, tools, and methods necessary to really help the designer.

Appendix 1: Questions for the Discussion on User Interface Design

The following questions have been proposed for discussion by the working groups:

1. In at least two of the presentations the possibility of user interface adaptation by end-users has been proposed as a possible way of making the user interface design task easier. It seems that it would be interesting to explore how far the principle of end-user modifiability might carry. Where are the principal problems and the main advantages of this approach?

2. One of the 'user-centered requirements for software engineering environments' is, at least in my opinion, that we should try to reserve interesting tasks for the user and do our best to support him with appropriate tools. Less interesting tasks should be automated if possible. Design, both of the application component and the user interface, is one of these interesting tasks: can we infer from this that we should not try to automate user interface design but leave this task to the designer? Isn't the textual specification of user interfaces as input to automated design tools more difficult than the use of appropriate tools would be for the designer? If we automate the development process, what provisions should be made to enable us to change the result if it does not meet our expectations?

3. The third question deals with the problem of 'scaling-up'. Almost everything we have heard during this workshop applies nicely to toy or academic applications. The question of transferring the results to large industrially used systems has not been answered. This remark is also true for most of the talks about user interface design tools. What do we have to change to make our results applicable for non-trivial problems? Which requirements have to additionally be taken into account? What could the final positive effect of our results on large application systems be?

Acknowledgements

I appreciate the help of Rachel Bellamy, Ben du Boulay, Thomas Green, Jürgen Herczeg, Selahattin Kuru, Marceli Wein, Keith Whiteley, and Henk van Zuylen in preparing this chapter. They organized the discussion groups, presented the results, and wrote the reports which were the basis for this article.

Matthias Schneider-Hufschmidt
Siemens Corporate Research and Development

Theme 4: The Impact of Design Methods and New Programming Paradigms

Theme 4 Introduction

This theme was initially intended to look at either: the relationship between the act of programming, the design of the environment and the use of particular design methods; or the use of particular programming paradigms. Questions posed before the workshop were: Are there any general principles which apply across all design methods/all programming paradigms or do software engineering environments (SEE) have to be method or paradigm specific? How might we evaluate the claims made for new methods/new paradigms?

In the event, the speakers interpreted the above quite liberally and, whilst addressing the spirit of the original questions outlined above, the questions themselves were not addressed directly. The first four chapters present and discuss new approaches and/or new techniques in software development (all of which include some aspects of communication) whilst the fifth chapter directly addresses some of the issues related to interdisciplinary communication in the HCI community. The five chapters all focus on the notion of 'paradigm' but from five very different angles; this theme comprises five polemics on very different but very related issues.

The opening chapter by Petre tackles the thorny problem of the term 'paradigm' itself. Side-stepping the debate as to which of the 20 interpretations of the word as used by Kuhn is correct, the chapter investigates how the word is actually used within the systems development community. Whilst confirming that words are labels whose semantics change over time, Petre finds that the term paradigm, as used in software engineering, is a label for a virtual machine with its implied instruction language and programming style. Further, paradigms in software engineering are heavily influenced by cultural interpretation. Indeed, the chapter concludes that, in software engineering, a paradigm is not something that can be defined objectively but only within its cultural context.

The second chapter by Larsson & Vainio-Larsson addresses the issue of system development and requirements for SEE in an industrial setting. The chapter assumes a standard process model of system development (the current development paradigm) and considers the social context (see also the chapter by Strübing in Theme 1) and the consequences for SEE in the light of evidence from real developments. It is determined that early verification and validation of requirements and design ideas is crucial to success and that this is best supported by effective management of documents, particularly specifications. The result is the requirements for an architecture for user-centred SEE, the implied process, and the need to prefer organizational needs over individual user needs.

The next chapter by Fischer also addresses the issue of process but goes further. Indeed, Fischer attacks the very foundation of the current approach to systems development. He believes that the role of computing professionals needs reviewing in the light of their failure to deliver usable systems and their need to re-learn information about the domain for each application. Fischer uses the analogy of the scribes in pre-reformation society; they were the indispensable people who read and wrote all information. With the arrival of (almost) universal education and the ability of (almost) all to read and write, the scribes had to redefine their role; they became teachers or story tellers. Fischer believes that computing professionals need to turn their skills to the production of application generators and frameworks and leave the generation of the actual applications to the domain experts, the people who will actually use the system. The chapter presents the example of JANUS, a system Fischer's group is developing which is an environment in which kitchen designers can define and manipulate graphical representations of things found in kitchens in order to design layouts. Fischer's message is that by identifying the roles and problems properly and by getting the right people to apply their skills to the right part of the problem, systems will improve.

The chapter by Winder moves to a more localized technical issue, investigating the usefulness of the object-oriented paradigm. The chapter addresses the question of whether this is all 'salesmanship' as discussed in Petre's chapter, or whether there is more to it than just hype. The argument is that the object model is a good one for all concurrent systems, that it facilitates the reuse required by systems such as Fischer advocates, and is able to integrate exception handling in a 'natural' way. Whilst recognizing that object-orientation is just one of many useful paradigms, it is argued that it is a step forward in system infrastructure; it may not be a 'silver bullet' but it is exceptionally useful.

The final chapter in this theme, by Green, addresses the issue of why software engineers appear to be willfully ignoring all the work being done in cognitive psychology that is clearly applicable. Green finds that there is some poor as well as some good work emanating from cognitive psychology, but that it is the inability to communicate that is the real barrier. Software engineers themselves contribute to the problem by being prepared to pontificate about psychological and sociological issues based on little or no knowledge of the field. Part of the problem is clearly cultural, software engineering is attempting to be a mature engineering discipline before it has a mature science base; perhaps it should recognize that it is still a craft discipline. Green does not address this particular aspect but focusses on the communication gap between psychology and software engineering, hypothesizing that the use of boundary objects (as a communications interface) and cognitive dimensions (as a metricated language of debate) may facilitate better communication.

Summarizing this theme is difficult for a number of reasons: the chapters are forward-looking and ask more questions that they answer, the questions all needing further investigation; and the different perspectives from which the questions are asked should, perhaps, be left distinct, the different viewpoints being important in understanding the problem. It is clear, however, that language, notation, and communication are at the root of systems development. All the chapters in this theme offer possible ways to increase communication of the right information, between the right people, at the right time.

Russel Winder
Department of Computer Science, University College London

A Paradigm, Please — and Heavy on the Culture

Marian Petre

Institute of Educational Technology, Open University, Milton Keynes MK7 6AA, UK.

Tel: +44 (0)908 653373

EMail: m.petre@open.ac.uk

What contributes to the identification of a paradigm? Advances in technique or reasoning are the usual claims, but marketing and programming culture are two under-explored ingredients. What is 'sold' as revolutionary is often the packaging of ideas that have been pre-figured in practice; the arrival of the 'new' paradigm signals recognition, not revolution. This chapter begins to discuss these neglected notions. It will analyse some of the mechanisms (e.g. choice of particular examples, disparagement of alternatives, claims to 'naturalness') by which the market image of so-called new paradigms is heightened in order to attract adherents. It will observe that discussions about programming languages are often not just about notations, but about how they should be used. The character of a programming culture is not just the definition of its tools, but the received wisdom of its adherents. Evidence and examples will be drawn from a variety of investigations of expert programmer behaviour and from the literature. This is not a call to resist this state of affairs, but to accept that a paradigm may be both more and less than what is presented.

Keywords: programming paradigm, programming culture, programming languages.

1. Introduction: What is a 'Paradigm', Anyway?

'Paradigm' is a wonderful word, carrying authority and boasting a venerable history in 'real' science. Unfortunately, adopted by the computing community, it has become a Humpty Dumpty word, its meaning diluted by creative usage. This discussion will avoid the debate — which will continue happily on networks and electronic bulletin boards all over the world — about what constitutes a 'programming paradigm'. It will discuss instead some interesting, under-considered phenomena (namely, salesmanship and programming culture) associated with things advertised as paradigms. It will consider the issues in terms of *expert* programmer behaviour observed through a number of studies by the author (Petre, 1990; Petre & Winder, 1988).

What the great electronic debates tend to convey is that language designers everywhere aspire to a Kuhnian ideal that paradigms are absolute (Kuhn, 1962): complete and exclusive, dominating and defining every aspect of an approach, a set of eyes through which to view the world. In fact, discussions with expert programmers suggest that programming paradigms:

- evolve, emerging gradually from practice;
- can be interleaved and intermixed, as a problem demands;
- are *reference* models, not strict models of practice; and
- are temporarily artificially important because of the limitations of current environments.

Rather than offering a concise definition of 'programming paradigm' or worrying whether or not some category of language is properly a 'paradigm', this discussion will adopt a loose, pragmatic view (or set of related views) of 'paradigm' as a way of looking at programming, having a range of influence (from small, individual presentation issues, to fundamental differences in approaches to problem solving) and potentially affecting all aspects of programming (e.g. characterizing problems and solutions, reasoning about them, expressing solutions, debugging them).

A 'paradigm' will be taken to be a convenient (if temporary) world view, a way of looking at things, a way of doing things — a decision about what the world is, for the moment. But the sense is of a pair of spectacles rather than of the Kuhnian set of eyes — something one can put on, take off, alternate with something of a different hue, like prescription sunglasses, surround with different frames, even combine into bifocals; not necessarily something incorporated permanently and to the exclusion of alternatives.

The emphasis here will be on paradigms as *reference models*: different models to which to map a solution, and which facilitate different aspects by offering different virtues. Different views of 'paradigm' will be adopted, as convenient, to highlight issues of the selection or restriction of focus, the expression of a programming culture, programming style, providing the basis for communication within a design team, and so on.

2. What Is Programming? What Is a Program? Moving Around in the Space Between Mind and Machine

There is no doubt that programming has developed and improved over the decades. As the concepts and technology of computing have changed, so too has the terminology. New terms emerge. Familiar, basic terms lose their clarity, and arguments (e.g. the lengthy *SIGPLan Notices* correspondence during the mid-1980's on the meaning of 'program') develop to recalibrate the language. This chapter is just one such argument.

Words as fundamental as 'programming' and 'program' have become vague over time, their meanings shifting to accommodate shifts in the purposes of the programming task and of its artefact, the program. A program bridges some portion of the space between the programmer and the machine, each of which has its own priorities and its own peculiar 'circuitry' onto which ideas and communication must be mapped. (cf. Payne (1987) characterizing user and device as 'yoked state spaces'). The shift in the meaning of 'program' reflects its shifting placement within that translation space, as influenced by a number of related evolutionary phenomena:

1. *The shift in relative cost of machines and people*: Whereas, originally, machines were the expensive commodity, good programmers have assumed increasing value, so that whereas early programming strategies economized on computer processing and machine memory, current strategies try to economize on programmer effort.

2. *The notion that programs are read by people*: The sole emphasis on producing machine-readable code soon yielded to the recognition that programs are often read by their human producers (perhaps more often than by the target machines). Notational elements that had nothing to do with efficiency of execution were introduced for the convenience of the programmer. At the extreme, programs were viewed *primarily* as communications to other programmers, with characters like Dijkstra (1976) publishing programs never intended for machine execution.

3. *The shift in the burden of translation (both deciding and describing)*: Originally, the notion of 'program' favoured the machine; the programmer was left to do all the work, both *deciding* what to do and how it should be done and *describing* it in terms convenient to the machine. Developments in programming languages (and environments) have sought to ease the burden of translation. As was argued in (Petre & Winder, 1990), language designers have tried to reduce the apparent translation distance by hiding the machine behind an intermediate computational model, one intended to be more accessible to the user and more compatible with the user's inherent reasoning. Instead of translating solutions into machine operations, the programmer describes the solution in terms of the higher-level model offered by the programming language. The terms of *description* are raised from the machine level nearer to the programmer, via the good offices of the language translator. (In Payne's terms, this is like bringing the device space closer to the user's goal space — albeit only apparently, because actually an additional, intermediate space is yoked: the device space of the language.) Further, in the case of declarative languages, the language implementation assumes some of the burden of *decision* as well; many control or computational issues governing machine behaviour are handled within the language implementation.

4. *The burgeoning of everything*: Computing has been characterized by spurts of 'more, bigger (and smaller), better, faster' in all respects: processors, memory, storage, I/O, communications, languages, applications, users. Not only have languages proliferated, but also various implementations of each language. And, as the capacity of the tools increased, so did the size and the range of problems people tried to address, so that attention shifted from making solutions concise enough to fit on a machine, to making them manageable by a person. (In a typical declarative programmer scenario: "Program too slow?", "Buy a bigger/faster machine.") Complexity control is a persistent requirement, and with it issues about dividing problems up, modularizing solutions, and so on.

5. *The blurring of boundaries between 'program' (and programming language) and environment*: Originally, the program was complete in itself, a full set of instructions. But the increasing sophistication in computing has meant that the boundaries between program, programming language, and environment have become blurred. A program may just stand alone, or it may make use of a few other files or library routines, or it may be inextricable from its environment, which may itself be a cluttered, interconnected collection of programs and other files.

The emergence of various so-called paradigms is tribute to the difficulty of bridging the space between programmers and machines — and the desirability of making best use of each. As phrased elsewhere: "The priorities of programming language development are clear: the translation distance from the user mind to the user language must be minimized; the rest is technology." (Petre & Winder, 1990)

3. Salesmanship

'Paradigm' is one of those wonderful, authoritative words that promises a great deal without making clear exactly what — i.e. the sort of word advertisers love. No wonder it is enmeshed in programming language salesmanship. With the literature full of references to the Kuhnian paradigm, it is unsurprising that 'programming paradigm' is usually accompanied by words like 'revolution' and 'religious conversion', and that the programming language literature is fiercely evangelistic. Cox offers a choice example. His article 'There *is* a silver bullet' not only cites Kuhn but compares the projected effects of object-oriented programming to the industrial revolution:

> "The silver bullet is a *cultural* change rather than a technological change.
> It is a paradigm shift — a software industrial revolution based on reusable
> and interchangeable parts that will alter the software universe as surely as
> the industrial revolution changed manufacturing." (Cox, 1990)

With so much happening in the computing world, i.e. the various population explosions of computers and programmers and publishers, and their accompanying 'information explosion', it's no wonder that promulgators of paradigms tie bells and banners on their progeny in order to make them visible among the rest. It's like a field full of sheep and lambs in the spring: everyone bleating at the tops of their voices while listening for other bleatings that sound familiar.

3.1. Attracting Attention, Investment, and Commitment

Getting over the threshold: New techniques and approaches need to attract attention, investment, and commitment. They need first and foremost to intrigue users enough to convince them to pay the 'entry costs' for playing with the new toy — after which they can hope it will be kept handy in the toy box by virtue of that initial investment and habit, if not from profound interest. The conservatism that makes people slow to adopt new tools operates in favour of those tools adopted even briefly. The most suitable tool is often just the handiest one.

Paradigms need adherents: New techniques and approaches need adherents to keep them alive. Adherents nurture techniques by finding and addressing their shortcomings, by fitting them into real-world contexts, by working through the arguments and issues surrounding their use, by presenting them in public. Adherents become the 'stage mothers' who keep their charges in the spotlight.

The cost of conversion: The problem of entry cost, or initial commitment, persists even after the new product or paradigm has survived infancy. The problem is many-times-multiplied for organizations, where the costs and consequences of introducing a new paradigm are far-reaching — they reach all the way to the marketplace. Proponents must demonstrate that the *costs* of converting are overwhelmingly compensated for by the advantages of the paradigm — e.g. (Yourdon, 1990). One of the issues for organizations is that some paradigm changes can be introduced incrementally and others can't (are there families of upwardly (onwardly) compatible paradigms?). Incremental shifts are easier; converting from C to C++ will cost less than from moving from C to Miranda.

With so much competition, and with survival at stake, it is no wonder that salesmanship is a factor, that proponents are selective, or emphatic, or hyperbolic in their portrayal of a paradigm. The danger is that the bandwagon will be obscured by all those decorative bits of coloured tissue paper, so that people may not know just what they've climbed onto, as Tim Rentsch foresaw for object-oriented programming in 1982:

> "Everyone will be in favour of it. Every manufacturer will promote his products as supporting it. Every manager will pay lip service to it. Every programmer will (differently). And no one will know just what it is."
> (Rentsch, 1982)

3.2. Sales Ploys

A variety of mechanisms are employed to distinguish one paradigm among all others. Here are three examples, with examples:

1. *Choice of particular examples*: A quick scan of the programming language texts on the shelves of a local bookstore shows patterns in the selection of examples:

   > *Functional programming*: Fibonacci series; least common denominator; factorial.

   > *Object-oriented programming*: desk calculator; stack implementation.

   > *Pascal*: eight queens problem; payroll calculations; computing averages; ordinal number-to-day conversion.

   > *Prolog*: family relationships; who-likes-what collections; the farmer, the fox, the goose, and the grain.

   > *C*: operating system calls; reverse polish calculator simulation; directory list manipulations.

   > *Lisp*: animals classification; palindromes; structures built of blocks.

2. *Disparagement of alternatives*: Sneers are rife in the computing culture.

   > "APL — even the name is a contradiction in terms."

   > "Oh, yeah, Forth: 'Non-syntactic language' means 'any shit is possible'."

   > "Basic rots the brain."

   > "Pascal is just plain not suitable for serious programming."

   > "Functional programming? Come back when you're serious about I/O."

   > "Cobol isn't a programming language; it's a way of fooling managers into thinking they can read programs."

3. *Claims to 'naturalness'*: Apparently, naturalness is a universal quality of artificial languages; the literature demonstrates that, for every programming language, there exists some fan who will say it is natural.

   > "Teaching a Miranda-like notation first usually can be done quickly and informally, because the notation is quite natural." (Wadler, 1987)

   > "Many people consider [production systems] a particularly natural way to write programs." (Lesk, 1984)

   > "Logic reconciles the requirement that the specification language be natural and easy to use with the advantage of its being machine-intelligible." (Kowalski, 1982)

> "In OOD [object-oriented design], inheritance provides a convenient mechanism for capturing this natural structure." (Rosson & Alpert, 1991, originally seen 1989)

> "The expressions of predicate logic, while formal and precise, are much closer to natural intuitive thought than are the statements of most programming languages." (Bowen, 1982)

> "The simple structure and natural applicability of lists are reflected in functions that are amazingly non-idiosyncratic." (Abelson & Sussman, 1985)

> "Dividing a problem into objects and defining actions that are 'natural' for those objects actually simplifies programs ... We know that the procedures we call from the high-level code are correct because they match the way we think about the problem." (Kaehler & Patterson, 1986)

Assertions of naturalness acknowledge the desire to bring the machine (that is, the virtual machine) closer to the programmer, to reduce the translation distance between them. Saying that a language or paradigm is 'natural' suggests that it at least doesn't get in the way of solving the problem. Naturalness seems like a reasonable aspiration, even though the unsubstantiated, salesman-like claims are meaningless.

Yet these devices aren't necessarily just salesmanship; they can have a function in *defining* the paradigm as well. The claims made for a paradigm can indicate which factors are of particular importance to it. The sneers made against opposing paradigms can indicate what virtues a paradigm boasts — or what it chooses *not* to address and so dismisses and devalues. The examples chosen as standard can act as a reference set to the reference model, a set of fenceposts marking out the terrain of problem types, solution style, and so on.

4. Paradigms Emerge from Practice

Despite the persuasive salesmanship that associates 'startling, new' programming paradigms with revolution and religious conversion, this chapter suggests that programming paradigms are for the most part unstartling and unrevolutionary. With a few notable exceptions, they typically don't require profound conversion, because they provide a coherent account of something programmers have *already* been hankering after or attempting via less concerted or direct means. What is 'sold' as revolutionary is often the packaging of ideas that have been pre-figured in practice; the arrival of the 'new' paradigm signals recognition, not revolution.

Providing names for experience: The paradigm may provide a vocabulary for unarticulated practice. Consider the notion of 'programming-in-the-large' captured by de Remer & Kron (1976). Their article is cited widely, not because of the module interconnection language which it presented, but because the introductory premise that analysing a system into an interacting collection of modules is essentially different from programming an individual module — and the catchy title they conceived for the premise — resonated with the work that programmers of large systems were doing.

Codification emerging from post-hoc rationalization: This view of a programming paradigm as a codification of evolved practice is not unrelated to the sort of 'post-hoc rationalization' that accounts for the discrepancy between what experts say (especially what they tout) and what they actually do. Notions such as top-down design and the waterfall model of software development are most effective as idealizations or rationalizations, rather than as strict models of practice. Parnas & Clements (1986), for example, make a good argument for faking 'rational' design even though the design process is actually opportunistic, even chaotic. Strictly declarative programming might be viewed as just such a conscious re-assessment instead of a design practice, a rationalized reading which may clarify post-hoc an imperatively-produced program. Extracting the essence out of practice is familiar in Mathematics as well. Mathematicians tidy up proofs before they publish them, removing all the detours and blind alleys travelled during the discovery process.

Robert Floyd described his own form of paradigm codification in his 1978 Turing Award speech:

> "After solving a challenging problem, I solve it again from scratch, retracing only the insight of the earlier solution. I repeat this until the solution is as clear and direct as I can hope for. Then I look for a general rule for attacking similar problems, that would have led me to approach the given problem in the most efficient way the first time. Often, such a rule is of permanent value." (Floyd, 1978)

Floyd uses 'paradigm' as the name for such a rule.

Pre-figuring paradigms: The evidence from expert programmers is that programming paradigms are adopted by people who are working that way already, for example by writing programs in a style other than that of the programming language (e.g. 'structured' assembler, or 'functional' C, a state machine implemented in Prolog). It is common practice among experts working on large projects to build superstructures or intermediate languages customized for the problem domain onto some crude but effective general purpose language. In the study reported by Petre & Winder (1988), one group of experts had built an object-oriented superstructure for C (although without identifying it in those terms; they still viewed 'object-oriented programming' with some scepticism). Another group had written a schematics-encoding language in *Lisp*.

So, although adopting a new paradigm is not an effortless transition, it is not a crisis either. Moreover, for experts, once the paradigm has been learned, the transition is nearly effortless, as will be described below. Paradigms are collected in the expert's 'bag of tricks' like any other tools. They are used as reference models, not strict models of practice. They offer a focus on a problem.

5. A Paradigm Restricts (Focusses)

Despite the salesmanship, the yearnings after naturalness, and the cherished notion that the right programming paradigm will be a panacea that leads programmers consistently to exemplary solutions, finding a globally-general programming paradigm is computing's search for the philosopher's stone. A paradigm provides a simple way of dealing with a complex thing; hence, *restriction* is necessary to the production of a paradigm. A paradigm is a decision about what to see, a kind of formalism, a focus on particular aspects of a problem. It makes some things more accessible by pushing others back. Hence, no one paradigm will suit every problem; no one paradigm will make easier the whole set of problems that people solve with computers.

Expert programmers use a paradigm as a thought-organizer or a discipline. They collect a repertoire of useful paradigms which offers different views, onto which problems can be mapped, and which facilitates different aspects of solution and different virtues. Within this view, it makes sense that a good language should be restrictive — or, that a language *should* be restricted by culture, so that there is an 'acceptance grammar' which is a subset of the language grammar. Conversely, it makes sense that a programmer will also need to escape the restrictions of one paradigm in order to achieve a more complete view of a problem (unless of course the paradigm is a perfect fit).

Sashimi programming: Petre & Green (1990) introduced the need to 'escape from formalism' as an essential part of real-life, professional-level design, necessary to cope with things not accessible within a given formalism. Changing paradigm is a mechanism for escape from one formalism — from one set of constraints or values — into an alternative. Expert programmers employ a conscious change of paradigm in order to re-assess a solution or to gain insight. They indulge constructively in 'sashimi programming': given this collection of unembellished raw morsels, which flavour do I need next?

Sashimi programming is compatible with the evidence that the programmers who perform best are those who have encountered the most programming languages — i.e. whose experience is broadest (Connelly, 1984; Holt, Boehm-Davis & Schultz, 1987) — and with the evidence that experts do not observe language boundaries when constructing solutions but rather borrow useful features across languages or domains (Petre & Winder, 1988). So where does this leave the popular assumption that the first programming language or paradigm marks a programmer indelibly, and especially that someone learning the 'wrong' language first will be corrupted forever? (Just about everyone knows someone who can write Fortran in any language; on the other hand, most, if not all, of the new paradigms have been developed by people whose first programming language was assembler or Basic or Fortran.) That assumption fits the Kuhnian view of paradigm well enough, although the empirical evidence is equivocal. It may simply be a matter of continued narrowness of experience, or of plain bad programming.

6. Programming Culture and Programming Style

So, a paradigm restricts in a particular useful way; it can provide a discipline within which to devise a solution. Yet it is a vain hope that a programming paradigm itself will provoke good code, cf. Flon's axiom:

> "There does not now, nor will there ever, exist a programming language in which it is the least bit hard to write bad programs." (Flon, 1975)

Any programming language or raw paradigm is amenable to interpretation and abuse. As the confusions in the literature demonstrate, what people are discussing is not just a reference model or a language that instantiates it. A programming paradigm does not exist in isolation; it is established within the collective experience of a community of users. The mechanism by which a paradigm is disambiguated, restricted, and refined, by which it is associated with a model of practice and a style of expression, by which particular examples emerge as exemplars, by which its weaknesses are avoided, by which newcomers are introduced to (or indoctrinated into) the wisdom, traditions, and conventions of the paradigm's local community, is programming culture.

6.1. Received Wisdom

Discussions about programming languages are often not just about notations, but about how they should be used. Discussions about programming paradigms are often not just about formalisms, but about how programmers should think. The character of a programming culture is not just the definition of its tools (or its paradigm), but the received wisdom of its adherents.

Programming culture extends from typographical and other conventions of expression (e.g. the tendency of Pascal programmers to use long identifiers versus that of C programmers to use short ones) through restrictions on the interpretation of a paradigm. The restrictions have both advantages and disadvantages; sometimes they guide, and sometimes they constrain.

Consider modelling elementary algebra in an object-oriented style. Under the familiar 'nouns and verbs' interpretation of object-oriented programming, objects are like 'nouns' within which 'verbs' (actions or methods) are defined. Hence, one would define a class of objects which are variables, which contains a method for addition. One would establish instances of that class, say, 'a' and 'b'. So, to model 'a + b', one variable sends a message to another to 'add me to yourself'; the operation is asymmetrical. Alternatively, there is a more appropriate version which retains the symmetry of addition: '+' is itself an object. Although this interpretation is within the capacities of a typical object-oriented language, it is outside the normal cultural restrictions.

Another, more constructive example is the Forth culture. To outsiders, given the language definition alone, Forth appears to be a 'write-only' language. But Forth proponents tout it as an especially 'intelligible' language, because their conventions of use produce a neat structure of definitions which gradually builds up from the messy low-level underpinnings to a surface vocabulary consistent with the problem domain.

Programming culture can be closely and enduringly bound to paradigm. There are plenty of programmers in circulation who grew up in assembly language days who can't write quick-and-dirty solutions in assembler, because the associations of assembler with limited-memory machines (and the culture which that evokes) prompts them to code efficiently.

In the best cases, programming culture enhances and clarifies a paradigm. It can make it easier for novices to absorb and adopt a paradigm. Where the paradigm provides a reference model, the culture can add a model of practice.

6.2. Programming Style: The Contaminated Paradigm

With a few esoteric exceptions, programming is not a 'pure' activity; it is contaminated by unavoidable contact with reality, with the constraints of time and machines and people. The first program most experts write in an unfamiliar language is one that establishes contact with peripherals: printing 'Hello, world'. The operating system impinges on the programmer's view, influencing ways of visualizing system interactions and ways of thinking about what a file is and how it is accessed. And programming exists within a broader culture of people working — often together — to solve problems. Portrayals of a paradigm as a 'programming style' reflect the infiltration of working programming culture into the notion of paradigm. 'Programming style' takes in not only the reference model (the style of thinking) but also a model of practice (the style of working), and an 'acceptance grammar' that shapes an instantiating language to conform to some interpretation of the paradigm (the style of expression).

Local culture and common ground: A local programming culture, within a group or organization, selects from a paradigm and its associated culture (or from a variety of paradigms and cultures) in a way that reflects what the group considers important to its work. It develops a 'house style', a collective style which keeps its projects working and comprehensible. The 'house style' makes cooperation possible within the group by providing a local idiom, a familiar composite style of expression — a basis for communication — as well as a repertoire of approaches to problems. Such working cultures will also reflect insights or novel approaches developed within or by the group. If a group is working on a project over years, chances are it will develop custom tools that will reflect the things the group hasn't found in any adequate form elsewhere: custom languages to support a particular paradigm (perhaps one borrowed from the problem domain); superstructures to support a certain view of the problem; custom library routines that reflect the group's way of dividing up solutions. A local culture makes what it needs. It interprets paradigm and language, establishes conventions of use, and builds tools to embody portions of its expertise. The 'house style' provides a foothold for novices — either to the paradigm or to the particular community — to integrate into the group.

This notion of local programming culture is manifest in the paradigm sub-cultures that spring up. Stanford and MIT each developed a Lisp community with its own interpretation (and implementation) of the underlying paradigm.

7. Individual Style and Variation

One of the most enduring effects in empirical studies of programming is individual variation — e.g. (Curtis, 1981). The variability is not just in experience, or skill, or cognitive style (whatever that may be), but also in what the programmer expects from programming.

Reflective vs. non-reflective programming: Despite the concern of this chapter with expert programmers, most programmers are not expert, and many of those who program professionally do so as something supplementary to their primary of work of engineering, or architecture, or geology, or whatever. They dwell within the language and paradigm of their domain and write programs that conform to or interpret them. These 'part-timers' are like the early programmers, with little or no regard for 'reading' programs. They are usually working independently to write one-off solutions for their own use; if they pass one on, it is as a *tool*, not as a text. New paradigms are interesting only if they are expedient; handiness matters more than elegance to people who are creating quick-and-dirty solutions. They do not *reflect* on their programs.

This 'non-reflective' programming is what distinguishes 'part-timers' from full-time professional programmers, even though they may well spend as much time writing code and may create sophisticated applications within their domains. Other, less professional groups of 'part-timers' are similar in this respect; many spreadsheet users address complex problems, but how many people 'read' a spreadsheet?

The investment in good programming: Another important difference between full-time professional programmers and 'part-timers' is that professionals recognize themselves as existing within a programming culture. It's not just that part-timers tend to work singly. The professional sees the program has having a potential value in itself; the personal 'corpus of programs' contributes to the professional programmer's reputation and identity. The professional has reason to invest in clear, economical, insightful work for its own sake.

To the professional, a program is a communication to another programmer — not just the control of a machine.

Individual style: Whether or not a programmer subscribes to a local culture, individual styles vary. Members of teams can usually recognize who wrote what by the style 'signature' in the code. Green (1990b) writes about programmers with 'neat' and 'scruffy' habits, and about 'the mystique of cryptic programming.' Neats or scruffies may choose languages appropriate to their preferences, or they may impose their personal style on whatever is available. Persistent *individual* style may be a be a better explanation for that Fortran-in-any-language phenomenon that is usually attributed to the permanent effects of first experience.

So, even if the skill and standards of programmers were uniform, their aspirations are not. Paradigms can help smooth differences by providing a common, workable reference model, and cultures can help by promoting shared standards and styles; both can help by minimizing obstacles. But individual differences will persist.

8. Paradigms Don't Solve Problems

What motivates the solution: the programmer or the paradigm? As Brooks so colourfully stated:

> "Sound methodology can empower and liberate the creative mind; it cannot inflame or inspire the drudge." (Brooks, 1987)

The view advanced here that a paradigm can provide a discipline within which to devise a solution is a much weaker assertion than those typically advanced by paradigm proponents: those reflect a conviction that programming languages *influence the sorts of solutions* that programmers will devise and that good languages guide the programmer's thinking (into whatever avenue or paradigm is endorsed by the particular language model). Yet Petre & Winder (1988) found no correlation between programming language styles and solution strategies; on the contrary, strategies volunteered as typical of one paradigm would often be implemented in a language that fit within another.

Error-proneness of languages: In contrast, although a paradigm may not drive people into good thinking, there is some evidence that some *languages* are more error-prone than others, contributing to errors or oversights. For example, in the study cited above (Petre & Winder, 1988), stream-oriented Scheme approaches to various problems caused mishandling of special cases or the failure to include initial elements of a sequence. Ada's abstraction facilities led to complicated, over-generalized solutions which were incomplete. du Boulay & O'Shea (1981) also suggest that different error types may correlate to particular programming languages. Fortran-style parameter passing (by alignment, unchecked) is a situation in which errors can occur easily. Uncontrolled go-to's are a well-known pitfall; people can write spaghetti, and untutored people do (Sime, Arblaster & Green, 1977a).

It may be that we should rate paradigms, not in terms of which is more helpful than another, but rather in terms of which is less obstructive than another.

Problem decomposition and abstraction management: The major problem in programming is not how things are expressed (although that is an issue), but how solutions are conceived. Green characterizes programming as the building and manipulation of information structures.

The hard part — and the one neglected by programming paradigms — is how to decide what structure to impose. Green offers the example of object-oriented programming:

> "Both anecdotal evidence and observational data show ... that programmers have difficulty in deciding which logical entities shall be represented as objects and which as attributes of objects. Object-oriented programming may be effective, but it is certainly not artless: and in that case, it is not natural." (Green, 1990b)

One man's object is another man's attribute.

Part of arriving at a solution is figuring out just what the problem is; many problems are not well-defined. Big solutions require management: identifying a structure within the solution, dividing it up into manageable chunks, and understanding all the implications of one component within a whole system (both the whole program and the program's environment). More recent paradigms have introduced support for building abstractions, but they provide little or no insight into the difficult problems of choosing and managing them. The notion of code reuse doesn't help, because the idea that parts will be 'reusable and interchangeable' (Cox, 1990) assumes too much about solution structure; in fact, it is difficult to build components that are genuinely both useful and reusable. Brooks again:

> "The complexity of software is an essential property, not an accidental one. Hence, descriptions of a software entity that abstract away its complexity often abstract away its essence." (Brooks, 1987)

A great deal of programming is just plain difficult.

9. Conclusion

A paradigm may be both more and less than what is presented. It is more than a 'pure' advance in technique or reasoning, because it is (perhaps inextricably) embedded in a programming culture that can embrace the collective traditions, wisdom, and bigotry of its advocates. It is less than a revolution and less than a panacea, although, added to an expert's repertoire, it can promote insight.

The choice of a paradigm is artificially important now, because the existing environments aren't sufficiently flexible, forcing programmers to choose and adhere to a single paradigm. However, empirical studies that recognize actual design strategies, that investigate the borrowings across domains and paradigms, and that explore the nature of expertise, cf. super designers in (Krasner, Curtis & Iscoe, 1987), will put programming paradigms into perspective.

Ironically, the commercial pressures — especially the need to protect the investment in existing products and tools — that have enforced conformity to a local standard may open the door to multi-paradigm environments; for example, one electronics–CAD vendor is touting an 'open programming language' to make its design tools extensible in a variety of programming languages. Marketing and programming culture are both important ingredients — under-rated and under-explored — in the identification of a paradigm, and will continue to be so. After all, any paradigm is "Generally considered to be good by those who like it".

Software Producers as Software Users

Tony I Larsson[†] & Arja A Vainio-Larsson[‡]

[†]Ericsson Radio Systems AB, Box 1248, S-581 11 Linköping, Sweden.

Tel: +46 13 28 47 34

Fax: +46 13 28 73 70

EMail: eratony@lmera.ericsson.se

[‡]Department of Computer Science, Linköping University, S-581 83 Linköping, Sweden.

Tel: +46 13 28 14 77

Fax: +46 13 14 22 31

EMail: ava@ida.liu.se

Within the framework of a large industrial software development project designers' needs and requirements on software engineering environments have been studied. The study focussed on software designers as being not only software producers but also users of software. The results show that in order to benefit productivity and quality, improvements of the methodologies and tools that support co-work and document traceability are often more essential than many other improvements. In the chapter the concept of user-centered requirements and its implications on design work are developed from a bifocal perspective, the designers' and the potential customers' perspective. From the standpoint that design should be requirement-driven, methodological implications for productive, user-centered software engineering environments are traced and discussed.

Keywords: software engineering, requirement-driven design, design environments, validation, verification.

1. Introduction

In this chapter we focus on software design from two different but related perspectives: software designers as producers of software and software designers as users of software. The industrial environment of software engineering is discussed and design work is viewed as a requirement-driven activity. These requirements are analysed and specified, and corresponding products are implemented, verified and delivered by organizations with the intended purpose of implementing productive system design and marketing processes.

The main task of software designers is to design software systems fulfilling specified requirements. As producers of software, designers must be productive while doing high quality work. As users of software tools, designers will have productivity and quality as well as more individual concerns in mind. These individual concerns may influence designers' job satisfaction, creativity and cooperativeness. Considering that design work often takes place at multiple sites and involves many people, concerns that are related to the motivation, organization and synchronization of human work are indeed very important.

This chapter opens with a short presentation of a software development project study. In subsequent sections the results of this study are discussed with respect to what should constitute necessary requirements for productive and user-centered software engineering environments. The concept of 'user-centered requirements' and its implications on design work are discussed from designers' perspective as well as from potential customers' perspective. The view that design is requirement-driven is developed and the concept of software design environments is extended to include also the effective support and visualization of the linking between information, people and tasks.

2. Background

2.1. Software Engineering Research

From a productivity and quality point of view the software industry (not to speak of its customers) still seems to suffer from unreliable software, overruns, managerial problems, etc. (Buchanan, 1991; Gilb, 1989; Kraut & Streeter, 1990). It is a well known fact that effective coordination among the various efforts involved in software development is crucial for the design of successful systems. Kraut & Streeter (1990) point out some of the characteristics of software engineering that make coordination problems inevitable. These characteristics are:

- *Problems of scale*: Many software projects are too large to be fully understood by individual or groups of designers.

- *Uncertainty*: Software engineering is conceptualized as being a non-routine activity.

- *Interdependencies*: Software components as well as the work of different designers, need to be integrated properly in order for a perfect system to appear.

The proposed solutions to these problems mainly follow three approaches, or support levels:

1. A *tool approach*: Where various tools are developed in order to support the individual tasks of designers.

2. A *methodological approach*: Which is more process oriented and with the aim of providing systematic support for design work.

3. A *formal approach*: Which is oriented towards an automation of the design process.

These approaches are interrelated, a choice on one level thus effects potential solutions on other levels.

2.2. Industrial Software Engineering: A Case Study

Within the framework of an industrial software development project carried out at Ericsson Radio Systems, software designers' needs and requirements have been studied from an industrial perspective where productivity issues were of prime concern (Larsson, 1991). The study was set up to cover a wide range of topics such as design methods and tools, work organization, quality assurance, training, product planning and project control. The results are relevant for large system oriented industries. The product design flow was followed from product planning to application support with major focus on the central parts, i.e. system specification, implementation and test phases (illustrated in Figure 1, where:

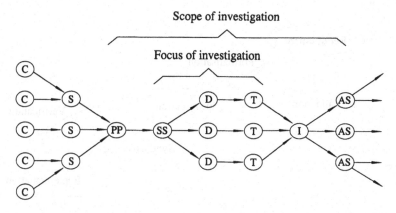

Figure 1: Product design flow

C = customer, S = sales, PP = product planning, SS = system specification, D = design, T = test, I = integration, AS = application support).

In total 25 designers from Canada, England, Ireland, Mexico and Sweden took part in the study. They were chosen in order to represent different roles in the design process including product planning, project management, line management, quality assurance, specification, design and testing. Data was gathered by means of questionnaires, person-to-person interviews, group meetings and examinations of in-house product and project documents as well as design and test manuals.

Ericsson Radio develops cellular radio (mobile telephony) systems for a world-wide market. Different standards partition this market into submarkets located all over the world. Although the development of products is market driven, it is also influenced from the general technology development within and outside the company. Software development takes place at multiple sites (located in different countries). In terms of scale, the products and the development projects are usually large and a hundred to two hundred person projects are common. Product development is based on PCs, workstations and on large mainframe systems and often involves supplements to and modifications of existing products.

In the following sections, results and conclusions from the study will be presented and discussed. Sections constitute main topics with subsections to present the actual requirements for software design environments formulated by the designers themselves.

3. Requirement-driven Design

The designers were asked to define what they mean by quality. A majority answered that: quality is when an implementation conforms to its specification. Thus it seems to be a common opinion that software product quality requires a top-down view on software development.

If quality is also to include customers' satisfaction, the specification must be validated against customers' requirements. The question of how these requirements can be fed into a design process, besides through specification, is not addressed in this study. The purpose here is not to discuss how to formulate such a specification but instead to describe a top-down design

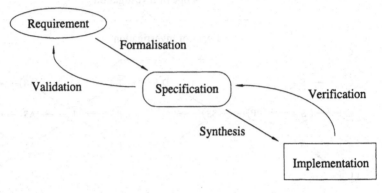

Figure 2: The validation and verification process

process which is driven both by the requirements of designers as well as the requirements of potential customers.

For a discussion of how to involve customers or users directly in the design of a system see (Carter, 1989; Gould, 1988).

3.1. Get Things Right the First Time

In order to improve both quality and productivity there is an increasing interest in trying to get things right from the start and to verify their rightness as early as possible. Designers must thus validate that a specification conforms to customers' requirements as well as the system's implementors having to verify that the implementation conforms to its specification. This process must start in the market analysis, product planning and requirement analysis phases.

The logical linking between implementations, specifications and requirements is controlled by the validation and verification process. As well as satisfying requirements on verifiability and validatability, traceability is important and should be bidirectional. Ideally, validation and verification should be used as quality metrics and be part of an error-prevention strategy. But, in practice, they also function as a debugging mechanism in the detection and location of defects.

Pictured as a dichotomy, the design process may either be strongly oriented towards meeting current needs and requirements of different customers or be oriented towards foreseeing future market opportunities. In the former case (requirement-driven design) the design process must be top-down, since it has largely to be controlled by customers' needs. An implementation thus always has to satisfy a specification or, in other words, a specification must exist before the final implementation. The role of the specification is to prescribe what to implement. Here, the specification has an important bridging function in reducing the conceptual distance between customers, designers and a final implementation. In the latter case (technology-driven design) the design approach is more bottom-up oriented, since future technology and new market opportunities control the design process. In this case, the specification describes what to implement.

4. Designers as Producers

Given the view that the design process is requirement-driven, the input to software designers is a set of requirements associated with different sources (customers) and refined by marketing and product planning personnel. Other sources are national and international standards and documentation of existing systems that usually work as a design base for the required supplementary or modified functionality.

The designers' task is to analyse, partition and refine these requirements. As has already been implied in Section 3 a requirement-driven design process must be top-down oriented. A specification should thus exist before a corresponding implementation can be finalized, i.e. before the requirements are allocated onto components.

Although the design process is top-down, an analysis of the design base (defined by existing as well as new products and technologies) considering the refined and partitioned requirements will proceed more or less concurrently with the specification work. Implementation proposals and subsequent decided and detailed implementations are the outcomes of this work. The designer also has to verify that an implementation fulfills its requirements. Design thus divides into: specification; validation; implementation; and verification tasks (Figure 2). Due to the decomposition process (Figure 3) these tasks are repeated in an hierarchical fashion.

4.1. Shorten the Design Time and Catch Errors Early

A strict top-down design is basically sequential and often saves design resources in terms of the number of man-hours required within a project at the cost of calendar time. From a project planning point of view sequential design approaches usually are easy to implement. In order to speed up the design process and reduce calendar time, a top-down design approach may include concurrent engineering methods. This usually increases the number of man-hours because unnecessary implementation tasks are carried out due to less strict coordination and planning.

In all design work, the need for design loops must be minimized and they should also be kept as short as possible in order to support early error detection. Concurrent engineering methods try to exploit these feed-back and feed-forward loops and enable more effective design processes to be implemented in that requirements and possible implementations are considered concurrently. Concurrency seems to be able to provide a better support for finding technologically optimal solutions. There is, however, always a potential risk that early error detection can be impeded if requirements are implemented without appropriate specification. Therefore, in requirement-driven design early error detection is supported by a repeated validation and verification process. At the same time concurrency is achieved and design time saved by hierarchical problem decomposition. Validation and verification in early design phases aims at preventing long and costly correction loops caused by late error detection (dashed lines), Figure 3.

The 'Spiral model' (Boehm, 1988) claims to be a general approach to software development and enhancement. The model is risk-driven in that it uses risk analysis as the basic transition criteria for progressing between the different design phases. According to Boehm other models (both top-down and bottom-up oriented) are special cases of the Spiral model. The model thus accommodates a majority of the software situations that may arise and:

> "... provides guidance on the best mix of existing approaches to a given project." (Boehm, 1988, p.69)

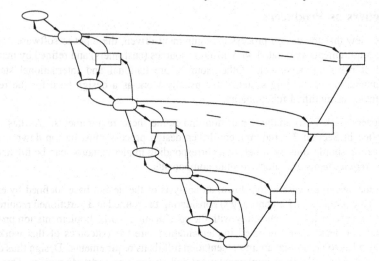

Figure 3:   Requirement-driven design with early error detection supported by a repeated
validation and verification process

Since the model supports successive risk elimination and design refinement, best-mix guidance
can be provided at different stages and in various detail:

> "A risk-driven specification can have varying degrees of completeness,
> formality and granularity, depending on the relative risks of doing too little
> or too much specification." (Boehm, 1988, p.65)

However, projects that apply entrance/completion criteria base these judgements on some
kind of implicit risk analyses. Usually these result in a specification of various requirements.
By advocating an explicit risk-driven approach, different design rationales may become more
clear and obvious. But, as with all models, its success depends on the software designers'
competence to intellectually master the design process and their ability to make reliable
risk assessments using reliable software metrics. Even if these designers had the statistical
knowledge needed, the necessary statistical data must have been gathered by systematic means
and be available when needed.

The design method actually undertaken is always a function of project demands and resources.
Traditionally, software tools have focussed on designers' need of support during program
development whilst software engineering environments reflect a concern for the entire software
life-cycle. These environments support either a specific software engineering methodology or
provide general support and allow various methodologies to be adopted. In order to be able to
work according to a requirement-driven approach the software environment used must at least
effectively support a linking between a specification and its corresponding implementation.

4.2. Formal Specification of Customers' Requirements

A common criticism of the use of formal design approaches is that formal methods only
support routine tasks and not all information admits formalisation. Important but implicit or
tacit information may get lost in the transformation from informal to formal. However, this

is no argument against formalisation per se, instead it is a methodological issue and concerns the application of formal methods. Ideally, any design process can be said to benefit from proper formalisation since this allows designers to concentrate time and effort on those design issues where human knowledge and support are needed explicitly.

Formal methods can at best only support, never substitute for, designers' understanding of the different tasks that the evolving system will provide support for. Since only a minor part of industrial software developers will ever have the opportunity to directly face their users, and since most of them will find that specifications substitute for direct user involvement, these specifications must at least reflect a true understanding of customers' requirements. Customers' or users' true valuations of different requirements, their actual usage of a product and their work practices are arduous to analyse and to specify properly in more formal terms. But in order to provide for productivity and quality, specifications must be validated with regard to completeness and consistency criteria by means of recurrent and systematic user testing, where different perspectives of use are also addressed.

For effective implementation of a design process the software industry must allow for quality and productivity to be made as routine a process as possible. However, design work does not only entail simple redesign and routine work. System development will always involve some amount of human problem solving activities and the best way to control and make effective use of designers' creativity and problem solving capacity is to provide tools that support routine design tasks. Only then can designers concentrate on solving the right problems, i.e. problems for which solutions, or improved solutions, are needed.

A design process must always be kept as open as possible in order to provide for several design alternatives. The design space is reduced and design decisions are frozen successively. In this process, sometimes even on the basis of incomplete knowledge, different requirements have to be balanced. All requirements must be specified in as precise terms as possible but unnecessary restrictions should always be avoided since they effect designers' freedom of work negatively without contributing to the design.

Although the most important requirements are functional, these must often be characterized further by a set of qualitative properties in order to also provide for usability (commonly defined as easy-to-learn, easy-to-use, etc.) which then have to be quantified more precisely in operational terms, for example, by explicit definitions of acceptable or targeted user performances.

Today, validation and verification is, to a large extent, based on the review and inspection of design documents. Designers must thus know the difference between revision and inspection[1] and also know the entrance and completion criteria that actually define the status of different documents. This is important design information since a document's actual status provides a value of the information contained in the document. Other common uncertainties are that the designers have no consistent way of deciding what constitutes a design decision and hence should be made a part of a design document. There is also a resistance to regarding documents as final since changes are then harder to incorporate.

---

[1] Reviews and inspections assess the quality of design documents. Inspections concern single documents which are checked in regard to functional requirements, correctness, etc. Reviews cover a design phase and concern a collection of documents. These documents are checked in regard to their completeness, consistency, etc.

4.3. Let Formal Specification, Validation and Verification Enhance the Design Process

In a top-down design process informal specifications are transformed into more formal specifications and then into implementation descriptions. The validation and verification task follows a similar pattern but goes from validation of formalized requirements to verification of the implementation descriptions (see Figure 2).

Top level specifications are usually described in natural language and low level implementations are described in terms of a programming language. Some companies use more formal notations (commonly state diagrams, data and control flow charts) for parts of the specification in order to bridge between an informal (natural) language and programming languages.

Voices within the software engineering community sometimes say that the move towards high-level languages will make it unnecessary to write elaborate specifications before the actual implementation. The high-level code plus, if necessary, comments is claimed to work also as a specification. In, for example, hardware applications the same language is sometimes used in order to write both the specification and the implementation. It is, however, crucial to note that these describe different aspects of the hardware application and hence have different criteria to fulfill; the specification has to meet human criteria of being clear and easy to understand whilst the implementation also has to describe efficient solutions. Both are thus needed since they cover different design aspects. If these can be expressed within the frame of a common language, the verification process will be simplified.

4.4. Improve Project Statistics and Software Metrics

Project statistics, software metrics and statistical quality control methods should be used more systematically than today in order to improve the project's quality control and assurance routines. An interesting approach that goes quite far in this direction is presented by Cobb & Mills (1990). This approach is part of the cleanroom engineering method which is based on the use of an incremental design pipeline, formalized specification and verification by proof, testing driven by usage statistics and the use of software metrics/statistics as transition criteria for progressing from one design stage to the next.

Levendel (1991) points out the importance of using first-pass pass-rates in order to monitor the product quality achieved at different phases of a design process. By analysing these untampered quality metrics figures it is often possible to identify *design holes* or error intense parts of a design. An elimination of these error clusters has a much larger quality improving effect than traditional elimination of isolated bugs.

4.5. Improve Document Management

Requesting, reading, updating and analysing documents are important parts of the designer's work. This work includes both documents created by other people as well as documents produced or modified by the designer himself. It is important that all designers are provided with the right information and that design documents are updated and requested in a disciplined way. Besides the enabling of effective editing and retrieval routines other important requirements are:

- Traceability between specified requirements and their implementation.
- Support for consistency and completeness checks.
- Support for time schedule, revision status and quality monitoring.
- Support for dependency analysis.

Traceability should be bidirectional; it should be possible to answer the question: "What object implements a requirement?" and also the question: "What requirements does an implementation object support?". All documents, not only formal but also informal text, must be consistent with regard to object, variable, message and attribute names. In fully formalized descriptions, these consistency requirements can of course be formulated more strictly. It should be possible to monitor the actual status and revision information of the documents. Dependency analysis should support the generation of contexts and reflect work dependent objects and their relation to other objects.

Different hierarchies have to be possible for specifications and related implementation units. However, each specification unit or subunit must always be allocated to an implementation unit or subunit at some level. In order to allow for experiments with different implementation structures the design environment should provide the means for simple manipulations of such allocations.

5. Designers as Users

5.1. Individual User Settings

Terms such as user-centered or user-focussed do not necessarily imply individual users but possibly groups of users. This means that a software environment may be user-centered although it does not meet the preferences of each individual user. Generally, a system has the two-fold function of guiding (and thus also controlling) the user's actions according to common requirements and assisting users in carrying out their tasks with as little hindrance as possible. However, occasionally the users' need to adapt system functions to their own personal work style may come into conflict with these requirements of in-house work routines.

5.2. Design as Co-Work

Design work in large companies is, to a great extent, an organized activity involving many individuals, each of whom has to accept established standards for co-work within the organization. These standards should simplify and coordinate the cooperation between individual users and are thus of higher importance than the preferred settings of each single individual. Results from the productivity investigation indicate that the designers felt that improvements of the methodologies and tools that support co-work were more essential than many other improvements. However, since many users want to personalize their design environment, it also is important to identify properties that can be adjusted by the individual user without any disturbances of the co-work in the organization.

Designers working on a common project must share a common view of what they are building in order for different activities to be coordinated easily. A common agreement must, for example, be reached regarding what the software should do, how it should be organized and how it should fit with other systems already in place or undergoing parallel development. (For a further discussion of the importance of different project teams to share a common philosophy see (Lawson, 1990).)

Finally, there are factors outside a system that affect users' ability to do productive work and influence their experiences of system qualities (Vainio-Larsson & Orring, 1990). A system must therefore also be understood and judged in relation to users' organizational setting and work context (Whiteside, 1988).

5.3. Provide Coherent User Interfaces

The present-day design system is negatively influenced by the fact that different tools have been designed at different points in time, by different designers, for different computers and then often moved to new computer equipment. A common tool and environment architecture that provides a proper framework for the design of a coherent user interface and design environment was requested by the designers. Although it is not unproblematic to find such a framework that fits various tools and application situations, uniformity seems to be more important than the provision of optimized but different user interfaces for each individual tool.

Since the design work is carried out at multiple sites and some tools require more or less direct access to large amounts of information, a distribution of the data base is needed. The distribution on physical computers, the use of local coaching, etc., should normally be invisible to the individual designers. Designers must, however, be made aware of time delays when documents are released. As a minimum, information about document releases or changes must be available although the actual document is not accessible.

If the designers are relieved of the task of having to know about physical computers and communication links, their work context may be described by the following architectural elements:

- Design objects.
- Documents (object views) and versions of these.
- Operations (object and view dependent).

Design objects are distinguished by unique identifiers. A set of documents define the design object and each document type defines an object view. All tools should be applicable via a uniform system and provide controlled means of manipulating the content of the different documents. Exactly how document types and operation choices are to be presented and selected — e.g. via menus as well as the way these are accessed and presented — can, to a large extent, be personalized by the user. The style or structure of documents must, however, follow certain standards to simplify information exchange at the document level, at the level of the human–computer interface and between individual designers. In order to enforce the requirement that a certain document style is used, the engineering environment should support the use of templates with predefined standard structure and/or content; thus the template information either prescribes attribute names or values or recommends default attributes or values that can be changed by the individual designer.

5.4. Improve System Reliability and Responsiveness

Organizations' physical locations and sizes change over time and, in order to avoid unnecessary disturbances, it is important to continuously monitor and plan for necessary computer equipment and network improvements.

There are many aspects that must be taken into account if a system is to be good and some of these aspects are more essential than others; they are the '*sine qua non* elements of usability' (Gould, 1988, p.758). If both productivity and usability concerns are to be considered, as has been the case in this study, the importance of different requirements are as illustrated in Figure 4.

The usability of a system is determined by more basic requirements which must be satisfied before higher-level requirements can be satisfactory satisfied at all.

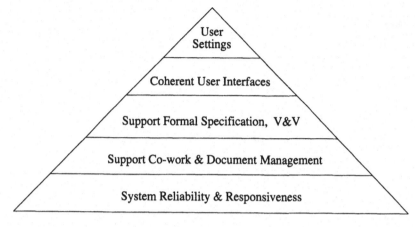

Figure 4: The usability requirements pyramid

6. Summary

In this chapter we have argued that a user-centered software engineering environment must enable design processes that acknowledge both customers' and designers' requirements on design. This calls for a top-down, requirement-driven design process where a specification exists before a final implementation is realized. These specifications have an important bridging function in that they reduce the conceptual distance between customers/users, designers and a final implementation.

Requirement-driven design divides into: specification, validation, implementation and verification tasks. During a design process these are repeated hierarchically. Since design work to a high degree involves the production or modification of various design documents, the design environment must support effective editing and retrieval tasks and enable: bidirectional linking between specifications and their corresponding implementations, multiple implementation hierarchies, consistency and completeness checks, time scheduling, revision status and quality monitoring, as well as dependency analysis.

Present-day design systems are negatively influenced by the fact that different tools have been designed at different points in time, by different designers, for different computers and then often moved to new computer equipment. Although it is not unproblematic to find a framework that fits these various tools and application situations, uniformity seems to be more important than to provide optimized but different user interfaces for each individual tool.

Since design work is to great extent an organized activity where individual designers form part of a work community, improvements of the methodologies and tools that support co-work often are more essential than many other improvements in order to benefit design productivity and quality.

Finally, it is important to remember that design environments only provide a framework for design work. They never substitute the need for careful user-centered analysis and testing or make unskilled or average designers into skilled ones.

Putting the Owners of Problems in Charge with Domain-oriented Design Environments

Gerhard Fischer

Department of Computer Science and Institute of Cognitive Science, University of Colorado, Boulder, Colorado 80309, USA.

Tel: +1 303 492 1502

Fax: +1 303 492 2844

EMail: gerhard@cs.colorado.edu

Domain workers should gain considerably more independence from computer specialists. Just as the pen was taken out of the hands of the scribes in the middle ages, the role of the high-tech scribes should be redefined and the owners of problems should be put in charge.

With this goal in mind, we have developed conceptual frameworks, innovative prototypes and an architecture for integrated, domain-oriented, knowledge-based design environments.

Domain-oriented architectures not only constitute an incremental improvement over current software design practices, but represent a major change to the nature of software development. They reconceptualize our understanding of the proper role of computing as an empowering technology for all of us.

Keywords: problem setting, problem solving, ill-defined problem, languages of doing, incremental problem formulation, owning problems, domain-oriented design environments, high-tech scribes.

1. Introduction

Most current computers systems are approachable only through complex jargon that has nothing to do with the tasks for which people use computers — requiring high-tech scribes (programmers, knowledge engineers) who are able to master this jargon. The role of high-tech scribes should be redefined, eliminating the distinction between programmers and non-programmers as two disjoint classes, and defining programming as the means for users to make computers do what they want them to do, thereby putting the owners of problems in charge. In this chapter, I will: identify problems facing user-centered software engineering environments; describe domain-oriented design environments as systems addressing these problems; and assess to what extent we have succeeded or failed in putting the owners of problems in charge.

2. Problems for Future User-centered Software Engineering Environments

Computing needs to be deprofessionalized. The monopoly of highly trained computing professionals, the high-tech scribes, should be eliminated just as the monopoly of the scribes was eliminated during the reformation in Europe. In order to avoid misunderstandings: This does not mean that there is no place for professionals programmers and professional system designers in the future. It means that the professional computing community should create systems to make computer literacy desirable and achievable. Some of the problems and challenges behind this approach are briefly described in this section.

2.1. Convivial Tools

Convivial tools and systems, as defined by Illich (1973), allow users "to invest the world with their meaning, to enrich the environment with the fruits of their vision and to use them for the accomplishment of a purpose they have chosen". Conviviality is a dimension that sets computers apart from other communication and information technologies (e.g. television) that are passive and cannot conform to the users' own tastes and tasks. Passive technologies offer some selective power, but they cannot be extended in ways that the designer of those systems did not directly foresee. Convivial systems encourage users to be actively engaged in generating creative extensions to the artifacts given to them. They have the potential to break down the counterproductive barrier between programming and using programs.

Unfortunately, in most current computer systems the potential for conviviality exists in principle only. Many users perceive computer systems as unfriendly and uncooperative, and their use as too time consuming. They depend on specialists for help, notice that software is not soft (i.e. the behavior of a system can not be changed without reprogramming it substantially), and spend more time fighting the computer than solving their problems.

2.2. Problems in the Design of Software Systems

The field study by Curtis, Krasner & Iscoe (1988) unveiled the following problems in creating large software systems:

1. the thin spread of application domain knowledge, indicating that the real problem is understanding the problem, not the representation of it as a program;

2. fluctuating and conflicting requirements, requiring that the owners of the problems remain part of the design team and that design in use (Henderson & Kyng, 1991) is indispensable; and

3. communication bottlenecks and breakdowns between designers, clients, and users, requiring representational means, such as "languages of doing" (Ehn, 1988), that can achieve a shared understanding between these groups.

2.3. Beyond Programming Languages: From Supply-Side to Demand-Side Computing

Dertouzous, as reported in (Denning, 1988), argues that the computer science community should operate less on the supply side (i.e. specifying and creating technology and "throwing the resulting goodies over the fence into the world"). More emphasis should be put on the demand side creating computational environments fitting the needs of professionals of other disciplines outside the computer science community. Modern application needs are not satisfied by traditional programming languages that evolved in response to systems programming needs (Shaw, 1989; Winograd, 1979). Most computer users are interested in results, not in programming per se. Shaw (1989) claims that "the major current obstacle

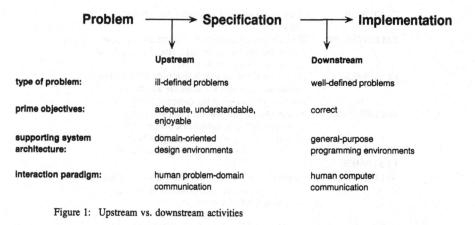

Figure 1: Upstream vs. downstream activities

to widespread, effective exploitation of computers is the inability of end-users to describe and control the computations they need — or even to appreciate the computations they could perform — without the intervention of software experts."

2.4. *Understanding Problems: Beyond Creating Implementations for Given Specifications*

Historically, most software engineering developments (e.g. structured programming, verification methods, etc.) were concentrated on 'downstream activities' (Belady, 1985)). Over the last decade, it has become increasingly obvious that the real problems of software design will be 'upstream activities' (Sheil, 1983) (see Figure 1).

While there is growing evidence that system requirements are not so much analytically specified as they are collaboratively evolved through an iterative process of consultation between end-users and software developers (CSTB, 1990), many research efforts do not take this into account. CASE tools are limited, because they devise more elaborate methods of insuring that software meets its specification, hardly ever questioning whether there might be something wrong with the specifications themselves. One may argue that they provide support after the problem has been solved. A consequence of the thin spread of application knowledge (Curtis, Krasner & Iscoe, 1988) is that specifications often occur when designers do not have sufficient application knowledge to interpret the customer's intentions from the requirement statements – a communication breakdown based on a lack of shared understanding (Resnick, 1991).

2.5. *Integrating Problem Setting and Problem Solving*

Design methodologists, e.g. (Rittel, 1984; Schoen, 1983), demonstrated with their work the strong interrelationship between problem setting and problem solving. They argue convincingly that:

1. one cannot gather information meaningfully unless one has understood the problem, but one cannot understand the problem without information about it (Rittel, 1984); and

2. professional practice has at least as much to do with defining a problem as with solving a problem (Schoen, 1983).

CUSTOMER:	I want to get a couple of heaters for a downstairs hallway.
SALESPERSON:	What are you trying to heat? Is it insulated? How tall are the ceilings? (Remark: They figure out that two of the heaters would work).
CUSTOMER:	The reason it gets so cold is that right at the end of the hallway is where the stairs are and the stairs just go up to this great big cathedral ceiling.
SALESPERSON:	Well maybe the problem isn't that you're not getting enough heat downstairs, maybe your problem is that you're not keeping the heat downstairs. Do you have a door across the stairs?
CUSTOMER:	No.
SALESPERSON:	Well that's the problem. You can put a ceiling fan and blow the hot air back down, or cover it up with some kind of door.

Figure 2: Reconceptualizing a problem: from generating to containing heat

New requirements emerge during development, because they cannot be identified until portions of the system have been designed or implemented. The conceptual structure underlying complex software systems are too complicated to be specified accurately in advance, and too complex to be build faultlessly (Brooks, 1987). Specification and implementation have to co-evolve (Swartout & Balzer, 1982) requiring that the owners of the problems need to be present in the development. If these observations and findings describe the state of affairs adequately, one has to wonder why waterfall models are still alive despite the overwhelming evidence that they are not suited for most of today's software problems.

In our own work, we have conducted an empirical study in a large hardware store to clarify the dependencies between problem setting and problem solving (Fischer & Reeves, 1992). Figure 2 illustrates how the problem setting is changed in an attempt to solve the problem. The customer came to the store to buy a heater. The interaction between the sales agent and the customer led to a reconceptualization of the problem from 'generating more heat' to 'containing heat' redefining the problem itself.

2.6. Why Owners of Problems Need to be in Charge

As the previous example shows, "problems are often dilemmas to be resolved, rarely problems to be solved" (Lave, 1988). Ill-defined problems cannot be delegated (e.g. from clients to professional software designers or professional architects), because the problems are not understood well enough that they can be described in sufficient detail. The owners of the problems need to be part of the problem solving team. Imagine in the above example, the customer would have not gone to the store himself but send someone else with a problem description to buy a heater. This person would have lacked the necessary background knowledge (Winograd & Flores, 1986) as well as the authority to redefine the problem on the fly.

3. Domain-oriented Design Environments

In order to put problem owners in charge, future software environments must be able to interact with their users at the level of the task and not only on the level of the medium. Over the last decade, we have designed and evaluated several prototypes addressing this goal. This section will briefly describe the steps leading towards our current version of domain-oriented design environments as well as one example of such an environment.

3.1. Towards Integrated, Domain-oriented Design Environments

The first step towards creating more human-centered computational environments was the development of general purpose programming environments exploiting the capabilities of modern workstations. While these environments were powerful and functionality rich, they required users to build their systems from scratch. Object-oriented design environments (such as Smalltalk, CLOS, C++) represented an effort to create a market place (Stefik, 1986) for software objects by providing substrates for reuse and redesign at the programming level. Their value is based on the empirical fact (Simon, 1981) that complex systems develop faster if they can be built on stable subsystems.

But domain-independent object-oriented systems are limited in the support they can provide at the problem level. They consist of low-level abstractions (e.g. statements and data structures in programming languages, primitive geometric objects in computer-aided design, etc.). Abstractions at that level are far removed from the concepts that form the basis of thinking in the application domains in which these artifacts are to operate. The great transformation distance between the design substrate and the application domain is responsible for the high cognitive costs and the great effort necessary to construct artifacts using computers.

Domain-oriented construction kits (Fischer & Lemke, 1988) intentionally sacrifice generality for more elaborate support of domain semantics. But construction kits do not in themselves lead to the production of interesting artifacts (Fischer & Lemke, 1988), because they do not help designers perceive the shortcomings of the artifact they are constructing. Artifacts by themselves do often not 'talk back' (Schoen, 1983) sufficiently, except to the most experienced designers. Critics (Fischer et al., 1991a) operationalize the concept of a situation that 'talks back'. They use knowledge of design principles to detect and critique partial and suboptimal solutions constructed by the designer.

3.2. JANUS: An Example

To illustrate some of the possibilities and limitations of these systems, we will use the JANUS system (Fischer, McCall & Morch, 1989) as an 'object to think with'. JANUS supports kitchen designers in the developments of floorplans. JANUS-CONSTRUCTION (see Figure 3) is the construction kit for the system. The palette of the construction kit contains domain-oriented building blocks such as sinks, stoves, and refrigerators. Designers construct by obtaining design units from the palette and placing them into the work area. In addition to design by composition (using the palette for constructing an artifact from scratch), JANUS-CONSTRUCTION also supports design by modification (by modifying existing designs from the catalog in the work area).

The critics in JANUS-CONSTRUCTION identify potential problems in the artifact being designed. Their knowledge about kitchen design includes design principles based on building codes, safety standards, and functional preferences. When a design principle (such as "the length of the work triangle is greater than 23 feet") is violated, a critic will fire and display a critique in the messages pane of Figure 3. This identifies a possibly problematic situation (a breakdown), and prompts the designer to reflect on it. The designer has broken a rule of functional preference, perhaps out of ignorance or by a temporary oversight.

Our original assumption was that designers would have no difficulty understanding these critic messages. Experiments with JANUS (Fischer, McCall & Morch, 1989) demonstrated that the short messages the critics present to designers do not reflect the complex reasoning behind the corresponding design issues. To overcome this shortcoming, we initially developed a static

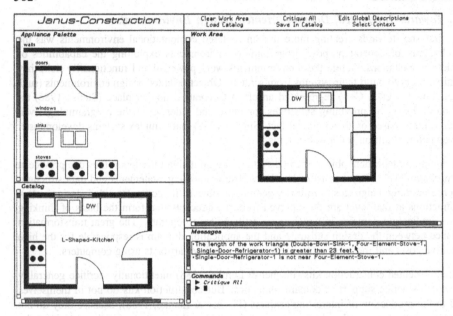

Figure 3: JANUS-CONSTRUCTION: the Work Triangle Critic
JANUS-CONSTRUCTION is the construction part of JANUS. Building blocks
(design units) are selected from the Palette and moved to desired locations
inside the Work Area. Designers can reuse and redesign complete floor plans
from the Catalog. The Messages pane displays critic messages automatically
after each design change that triggers a critic. Clicking with the mouse on a
message activates JANUS-ARGUMENTATION and displays the argumentation
related to that message.

explanation component for the critic messages (Lemke & Fischer, 1990). The design of this
component was based on the assumption that there is a 'right' answer to a problem. But the
explanation component proved to be unable to account for the deliberative nature of design
problems. Therefore, argumentation about issues raised by critics must be supported, and
argumentation must be integrated into the context of construction. JANUS-ARGUMENTATION
is the argumentation component of JANUS (Fischer et al., 1991b). It is an hypertext system
offering a domain-oriented, generic issue base about how to construct kitchens. With JANUS-
ARGUMENTATION, designers explore issues, answers, and arguments by navigating through
the issue base. The starting point for the navigation is the argumentation context triggered by
a critic message in JANUS-CONSTRUCTION. By combining construction and argumentation,
JANUS was developed into an integrated design environment supporting 'reflection-in-action'
as a fundamental process underlying design activities (Schoen, 1983).

But even integrated design environments have their shortcomings. Design in real world
situations deals with complex, unique, uncertain, conflicted, and unstable situations of practice.
Design knowledge as embedded in design environments will never be complete because design
knowledge is tacit (i.e. competent practitioners know more than they can say (Polanyi, 1966)),
and additional knowledge is triggered and activated by situations and breakdowns. These
observations require computational mechanisms in support of end-user modifiability (Fischer

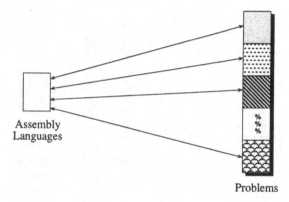

Figure 4: The 1950s: describing problems in the computer's internal language

& Girgensohn, 1990). The end-user modifiability of JANUS allows users to introduce new design objects (e.g. a microwave cooker), new critiquing rules (e.g. appliances should be against a wall unless one deals with an island kitchen), and kitchen designs which fit the needs of a blind person or a person in a wheelchair.

3.3. An Historical Context

Computers in their early days were used to compute. The typical problem at the time was: take a given algorithm and code it in assembly language. The process of programming was totally computer-centered (Figure 4). A large transformation distance existed between the problem description and its solution as a computer program.

High-level programming languages (Fortran, Lisp, Cobol, Algol, etc.) became available in the 1960s. Certain problem domains could be mapped more naturally to programming languages (e.g. algebraic expressions, recursive functions, etc.). While all of the languages remained general purpose programming languages, a certain problem orientation was associated with individual languages (e.g. Lisp for AI, Fortran for scientific computing). The professional computing community started to become specialized:

1. compiler designer (creating programs that mapped from high-level languages to assembly language); and

2. software engineers (creating programs that mapped problems to programming languages).

In the 1970s and 1980s new classes of programs appeared: spreadsheets, query languages for databases, and powerful interactive programming environments. Spreadsheets were successful for three major reasons:

1. they relied on a model and packaged computational capability in a form that the user community was familiar with;

2. they added important functionality (propagation of changes) that did not exist in the non-computational media; and

3. they avoided the pitfall of excess generality: Instead of serving all needs obscurely, they serve a few needs well (Shaw, 1989).

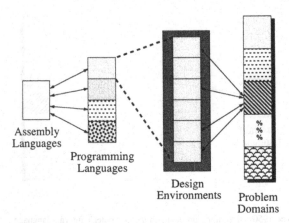

Figure 5: The 1990s: domain-oriented design environments

These types of systems can be considered to be construction kits with limited domain-orientation. In our own work, we demonstrated (Fischer & Rathke, 1988) that the spreadsheet model can be further enhanced by adding additional domain knowledge to it.

By extending construction kits with critiquing and argumentation components, design environments (Figure 5) have the potential to put domain experts (the problem owners) in charge. Computational environments based on design environment architectures lead to a further specialization among computer users: knowledge engineers in collaboration with domain workers create design environments, at least the seeds for them (Fischer et al., 1991b), and domain workers use and evolve the seeded environments.

4. Assessment, Evaluation and Implications

4.1. Is There an Owner or are There Owners of Problems?

So far we used the concept of 'ownership' in a way suggesting that there is 'an owner' of a problem ignoring that realistic design problems are multi-person activities where ownership is distributed. The reason for this is that neither clients, system designers, nor users have a very good idea of what they want a system to do at the outset of a project. Rittel (1984) speaks of 'a symmetry of ignorance' arguing that knowledge for design problems is distributed among many people, and that there is nobody among those carriers of knowledge who has a guarantee that her/his knowledge is superior to any other person's knowledge with regard to the problem at hand. The notion of 'owning' is related to the amount of right, power, authority, responsibility for contributing to the definition of a problem, and how much people are affected by the solution.

By collaborating with an architectural firm, we recently encountered a convincing example illustrating several of the issues discussed in this chapter. The task the firm competed for was the design (and later construction) of the Denver Public Library. The final design competition took place in 1991, followed by construction to be finished by 1995. The City and County of Denver added as a constraint to the design that the library should not undergo major modifications for the first 15 years. While one may argue that the design task is to create a building, the real question is "what is the function of a public library for a large city in the year 2010?" Who is the owner of the problem? The client (i.e. the City and County of Denver, represented by librarians who have love affairs with books as well as 'techies' who think there will be no books around in 20 years), the designers, and/or the customers who will eventually use the library?

In cases where is no single owner of a problem, the communication between all the 'stakeholders' in the problem is of crucial importance. Shared understanding (Resnick, 1991) needs to be created. One way to do this is to develop languages of doing (Ehn, 1988) which create the possibility of mutual learning, thereby establishing a relationship of professional parity between system designers and system users.

4.2. How are Owners of Problem Put in Charge with Design Environments?

The domain-orientation of design environments allows owners of problems to communicate with the systems at a level that is situated within their own world (Fischer & Lemke, 1988; Suchman, 1987; Wenger, 1990). By supporting languages of doing (Ehn, 1988) such as prototypes, mock-ups, scenarios, created images, or visions of the future, design environments have the advantage of making it easier for owners of problems to participate in the design process, since the representations of the evolving artifacts are less abstract and less alienated from practical use situations. By keeping owners in the loop, they support the integration of problem setting and problem solving and allow software systems to deal with fluctuating and evolving requirements. By making information relevant to the task at hand (Fischer & Nakakoji, 1991), they are able to deliver the right knowledge, in the context of a problem or a service, at the right moment for a human professional to consider.

4.3. The Costs of NOT Putting Owners of Problems in Charge

By requiring high-tech scribes as intermediaries, designers are limited in solving ill-defined problems (Simon, 1973). Ill-defined problems cannot be delegated because if they are delegated, situations do not 'talk back' to the owners of the problems who have the necessary knowledge to incrementally refine them. New requirements emerge during development, because they can not be identified until portions of the system have been designed or implemented. Traditional software design methodologies (such as the waterfall model, insisting on a strong separation between analysis and synthesis) have no chance to succeed in such situations. Alternatives approaches, such as methodologies allowing the co-evolution of specification and implementation, are needed (Fischer & Nakakoji, 1991; Swartout & Balzer, 1982).

4.4. Recreating Un-selfconscious Cultures of Design

Alexander (1964) has introduced the distinction between an un-selfconscious culture of design and a self-conscious culture of design. In an un-selfconscious culture of design, the failure or inadequacy of the form leads directly to an action to change or improve it (e.g. the owner of a house is its own builder, the form makers do not only make the form but they lived with it). This closeness of contact between designer and product allows constant rearrangement of unsatisfactory details. By putting owners of problems in charge, the positive elements of an un-selfconscious culture of design can be exploited in the development of software systems. Some of the obvious shortcomings of un-selfconscious culture of design, such as that they offer few opportunities for reflection is reduced by incorporating critics into the environments (Fischer et al., 1991a).

5. Conclusions

Achieving the goal of putting problem owners in charge by developing design environments is not only a technical problem, but a considerable social effort. If the most important role for computation in the future is to provide people with a powerful medium for expression, then the medium should support them in working on the task, rather than requiring them to focus their intellectual resources on the medium itself.

The analogy to writing and its historical development suggest the goal "to take the control of computational media out of the hands of high-tech scribes." Pournelle (1990, p.281, p.304) argues that "putting owners of problems in charge" has not always been the research direction of professional computer scientist: "In Jesus' time, those who could read and write were in a different caste from those who could not. Nowadays, the high priesthood tries to take over the computing business. One of the biggest obstacles to the future of computing is C. C is the last attempt of the high priesthood to control the computing business. It's like the scribes and the Pharisees who did not want the masses to learn how to read and write."

Design environments are promising architectures to put owners of problems in charge. They are based on the basic belief that humans enjoy deciding and doing. They are based on the assumption that the experience of having participated in a problem makes a difference to those who are affected by the solution. People are more likely to like a solution if they have been involved in its generation; even though it might not make sense otherwise.

Acknowledgements

The author would like to thank the members of the Human–Computer Communication group at the University of Colorado who contributed to the conceptual framework and the systems discussed in this article. The research was supported by the National Science Foundation under grants No. CDA-8420944, IRI-8722792, and IRI-9015441; by the Army Research Institute under grant No. MDA903-86-C0143, and by grants from the Intelligent Interfaces Group at NYNEX, from Software Research Associates (SRA), Tokyo, and by the Software Designer's Associate (SDA) Consortium, Tokyo.

Is Object-oriented the Answer?

Russel Winder

Department of Computer Science, University College London, Gower Street,
London WC1E 6BT, UK.
Tel: +44 (0)71 380 7293

Fax: +44 (0)71 387 1397

EMail: R.Winder@cs.ucl.ac.uk

This chapter investigates the object-oriented approach to systems and systems development to see whether this new paradigm is actually an advance or whether the hype surrounding it is based on pure fantasy. A summary definition of the object model is presented along with a summary of some of the features expected of something claiming to be object-oriented. Some computer architectures and programming languages are compared and contrasted with the object model, resulting in the view that, indeed, the object-oriented approach has much to offer. The chapter then goes on to consider some of the issues relating to development environments. Again the object-oriented approach has much to offer. There are, however, a number of problematic issues, both technical and from the point of view of usability, in current object-oriented programming languages and development environments. Thus, whilst the paradigm has much to offer, it is clearly not the answer, only a step in evolution.

Keywords: object model, system architectures, parallel systems, programming model, assertions, exceptions, browsing, searching.

1. Introduction

The history of programming and programming languages has been one of a sequence of answers. When problems were encountered using binary codes to program computers, the introduction of assembler languages was the answer. These languages proved insufficient for the task of general programming so high level languages, such as Cobol and Fortran, were offered as the answer. Again this turned out not to be the case so 'structured' languages, such as Pascal, were introduced as the answer. Yet again this proved fallacious and 'abstract data type' (ADT) languages, such as Ada and Modula-2 were created. It is now being stated that even this answer is not the answer but that object-oriented programming is.

As with all previous answers, there is considerable hype surrounding the term 'object-oriented'. Some people are tending to use it as a synonym for 'good' or 'structured' programming, particularly marketing people. A similar situation to that of a few years ago with the term 'user friendly' is beginning to obtain. The question that must therefore be answered is: Is there any merit in an object-oriented approach to systems development and systems development environments? More bluntly: Is object-oriented the answer?

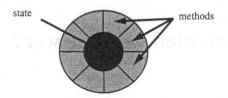
state   methods

Figure 1:   An object

In a sense, the answer to the question must be no; someone will always find problems and propose new approaches. However, all sequences of fashions of this sort have foundations in good sense. The evolution of programming languages summarized above is founded in the need to make programming languages and their in-built computational models (virtual machines) easier for developers to reason about and hence create solutions with. At each stage of evolution the virtual machine is made more complicated, the compilation distance between the programming language and the machine increases and the translation distance between the developers' reasoning language and the programming language decreases (Petre & Winder, 1990).

In this chapter, I will investigate what extra features are introduced in the object-oriented virtual machine to highlight why it has become the next stage of evolution of programming languages. To start, I define the terms as I use them, introducing many of the issues as I go along. I then show that the object-oriented idea can be seen as a unifying concept within computing; that the object-oriented computational model naturally maps to all the computational architectures. I follow this by showing how the concept is applied in programming languages; and how the ideas are implemented. This section of the chapter introduces the fact that the object-oriented approach is evolving even now using the example of the Solve programming language. The next section of the chapter investigates development environments and how the object-oriented approach improves such systems.

2. So What is Object-oriented?

In any discussion of object-oriented ideas, be it in the analysis, design, implementation or the programming environments area, there is a plethora of semantics for the jargon terms used. In order to avoid confusion, I begin by defining my interpretation of the terms.

For me, being object-oriented means adhering to the basic object model as the model of the structure and semantics of a system. This of course begs the question of what the object model is. I will therefore briefly outline my interpretation.

2.1. The Object Model

An object is an item of state (a set of modifiable variables) with a set of operations (methods) that can be invoked. In essence an object is an instantiation of an ADT. The current state of the object represents a value of the type. We can represent an object diagrammatically as in Figure 1.

This direct connection between the object model and ADTs shows clearly that the object-oriented approach is an evolution of the ADT approaches. In the ADT virtual machine, the functions are the active entities operating on passive data items of the relevant type. The object model virtual machine changes the model of control flow: instead of a sequence of function calls acting on passive data items, control flow is a sequence of message passes requesting the action of a method in an object. An object sends a message to another object asking it to undertake a calculation or make a state change: a message is a request by one object for another object to execute a method. The objects, being composed of state, methods and a mechanism for receiving and interpreting messages, become the active entities.

At this level of description of the control flow mechanism, one could argue that there is little or no difference to function and procedure invocation in procedural languages. The distinction becomes clear when analysing the responsibility for interpreting which code to execute. In a procedural language, it is the caller of the function that determines which code is executed. In object-oriented languages, it is the object that receives a message that performs the binding, which is always done at run time.

This distinction can become blurred. Procedural languages that admit dynamic binding of functions, for example C++, can behave very like object-oriented languages with respect to determining which methods are executed. Indeed in C++, the lack of distinction becomes the major bonus of the language; C++ is an abstract data type procedural language with dynamic binding of functions and inheritance, thereby allowing it to be used in an ADT way or what is essentially an object-oriented way.

In implementing this control flow mechanism, object-oriented languages extend the idea of data protection present in procedural languages with ADTs. An object encapsulates state behind a barrier of methods, which in itself is not very different. The benefit lies in the fact that it is the object receiving a message that decides which method to invoke. An object is not able to interfere at all with the state of any other objects, they may only make requests for activity — the client–server model. An object is responsible for the operations on its own state and for ensuring that the state is never inconsistent. Responsibility has been localized, modularity enhanced. Contrast this with procedural languages where any function can operate on any data structure of an appropriate type. In such languages data may be encapsulated but it is not fully protected.

Because of this extra data protection and modularity, object-oriented systems have a better chance of providing an infrastructure supporting full software reuse. The tighter encapsulation permits more full and rigorous testing of the implementation units, the objects, and hence increased confidence in the software. Further, a 'plug-in' approach is better supported by the object-oriented approach. Cox (1986) has dealt with many of these issues and further coined the phrase 'SoftwareIC' to highlight the ability to treat objects in an object-oriented system in a way analogous to the way chips are dealt with in electronic circuit boards.

2.2. Types and Classes

The object-oriented community is still in hot debate as to the meanings of the jargon words type and class, not to mention the terms subtype, supertype, subclass and superclass. Different people use the terms in different ways. Generally though, a type is a label denoting a set of objects all of which have a particular set of methods available, often called a protocol. A type is an abstract concept, it describes what an object can be asked to do; the methods available for invocation by messages from other objects. A class is usually taken to mean an implementation template for objects. A class not only describes what services an object of that class can offer (as with a type) but also how it goes about achieving the actions; the source code for methods are defined. Therefore, a class describes the implementations of the state and the methods.

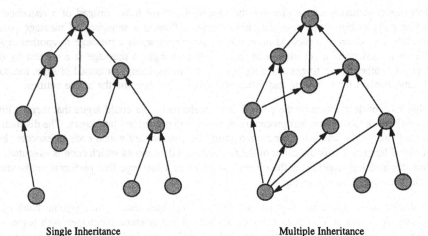

Single Inheritance   Multiple Inheritance

Figure 2:   Varieties of inheritance graph

In Smalltalk (Goldberg & Robson, 1983) and C++ (Ellis & Stroustrup, 1990; Stroustrup, 1991), no distinction is made between types and classes. Newer languages, e.g. Eiffel (Meyer, 1988) and Solve (Roberts, Wei & Winder, 1990; Roberts, Wei & Winder, 1991b; Roberts, Winder & Wei, 1988) enforce the idea of type and class as distinct concepts. In particular the notion of type conformance, rather than strong type checking, is used which impacts on the nature of polymorphism within the language. This, transitively, impacts on the software reuse capabilities of the language. These issues will be followed up later in the programming language section.

2.3. Inheritance

Inheritance is a relationship between types (or classes) that was introduced with object-oriented languages. Languages of other computational models could make use of inheritance but do not. Inheritance defines 'ISA' relations between types. A type has one (or more) supertype(s) and is a named, specialized variant of that type; it is a subtype. This facility can be used in many ways; to construct types in an incremental fashion; to provide a classification scheme for types; and to permit sharing of code. The first two in the list can be seen as the purists approach, the last as the 'hacker's' use.

It is worth pointing out that inheritance in this context is somewhat different to that used in artificial intelligence work. Inheritance in this context is to do with ADT (state and methods) specification. In artificial intelligence work values as well as slots can be inherited. This introduces extra complexity to inheritance which need not be addressed when talking about object-oriented languages.

I indicated above that a subtype could have one or more supertypes. The former case, single inheritance is easier to handle but the latter case, multiple inheritance, is more flexible. Examples of the two varieties of inheritance are shown in Figure 2. Argument rages as to whether supporting multiple inheritance is worthwhile. Advocates of supporting only single inheritance claim that developers do not make use of the multiple inheritance facility even when it is available. The observation, even if true, could be due to the poor implementation

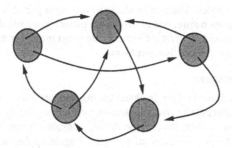

Figure 3: An abstract object system

---

of multiple inheritance in the early languages that supported it. Developers may well have been avoiding an inefficient and/or 'flaky' feature of a language rather than not being able to use it. More work is required on this.

3. Applicability of the Object Model

As part of my argument that object-oriented is indeed a step on from ADT languages, I show in this section the isomorphism between the object model and the various different types of architecture available for supporting computer systems. The claim is that the object model provides a good abstraction (a conceptual model) of the underlying system. This means that the computational model embodied in an object-oriented language admits a good and easy mapping to the way in which the final software system will behave; the translation distance between the developers' conceptual model of the system and the computational model of the object-oriented language is relatively small. The consequence is that developers can gain a good intuitive feel for the system behaviour permitting easier development and most especially easier debugging whenever bugs are discovered in the system.

Although I show the isomorphism, the claims of ease of use are conjecture. Evaluation studies are clearly required to justify the claims.

3.1. Object-oriented Software Systems

At an abstract level an object-oriented system is a collection of objects, each an instance of a type from the inheritance hierarchy, connected by links permitting messages to be sent. One object can only send a message to another if the receiver can be addressed by the sender, i.e. if a reference to the object is accessible.

So if a blob represents an object and an arc a link indicates the reference structure, the potential to pass a message, the diagram in Figure 3 represents a small object system.

3.2. Distributed Systems

A distributed system is a collection of computer systems that communicate with each other over a network (local area — LAN or wide area — WAN). If we represent each of the computer systems as a blob and the network connection by an arc, we can represent a distributed system exactly as in Figure 3.

This is exactly the object model. The isomorphism is very strong in this case. Computers are objects, but of a very complex nature, and networks are pathways by which the computers send messages to each other. Indeed, distributed systems are programmed in highly object-oriented ways already, reflecting the obvious isomorphism.

3.3. Uniprocessor Computers

On the face of it, a uniprocessor is a single object having only one thread of control. However, such a system can be conceptually decomposed in two ways. Firstly, it can be seen as a collection of connected parts; disc drives; tape drives; consoles; terminals etc. all connected via buses or other connections. The diagram of Figure 3 again applies as a description where the blobs represent the physical devices and the links the pathways connecting them. The second decomposition is of the tasks being undertaken. Few uniprocessor systems do not implement multi-tasking at the operating system level[1]. Further, most systems permit tasks to communicate with each other; inter-process communication. The task set can therefore be described with the ubiquitous diagram of Figure 3.

The object model again provides an abstraction of the architecture, in either viewpoint. Indeed, modern operating systems are being developed using object-oriented techniques and languages, integrating the two decompositions described above as a single object system.

3.4. Parallel Computers

A multiple instruction multiple data (MIMD) parallel computer, is a collection of processors, connected by a communications system. This is often a synchronous bus-based system but asynchronous systems are supported in many current system, especially Transputer based ones, e.g. the Parsys SuperNode, the Transtech machines and the Mieko Computing Surface. We can think of this as infrastructure to enable point to point communication. With this interpretation parallel computers are conceptually identical to distributed systems. The differences are many, varied and technical, at a low level. The principal difference is that parallel systems have fast error-free communication, whereas distributed systems have slow error-prone communications.

The upshot here is that MIMD parallel systems can be described with diagrams as in Figure 3, where the blobs are processors and the arcs are the communications connections. Again, a distinct isomorphism with the object model.

For single instruction multiple data (SIMD) machines, such as the AMT DAP, or for vector processors such as the Cray series of computers, the isomorphism with the object model does not hold nearly as well. The difference here is the type of concurrency. In these architectures the communications structure is far more rigid and the processing synchronous. SIMD and vector machines have a level of synchronicity which is not really describable with the object model. Computation does not proceed by one agent sending messages to another, the parallelism is of a much finer grain and internal to the operation of what can only be described as a single object. Object-oriented thus has boundaries of applicability.

3.5. Summary

The object model, at the level of detail given is really just an abstraction for asynchronous concurrency. It is therefore not surprising that there is an isomorphism between the object model and the various machine architectures. Nonetheless, the object model is a good

---

[1] MSDOS is the obvious exception but systems like MS-Windows hide MSDOS under a multi-tasking executive.

abstraction for any asynchronous concurrent architectures. It provides a good model for developers to use when reasoning about machine behaviour.

In summary of this section, the claim is that the object model can be seen as a model, at many levels of abstraction, of computer architectures and that by using the model as the one embodied in our programming language, we can construct systems that are easier to understand and reason about.

4. Object-oriented Programming

The purpose of a programming language is to offer a notation that embodies an understandable virtual machine (programming model) and with which developers can construct useful and usable systems. Two languages, Smalltalk and C++, are usually held up as paradigms of object-oriented languages. The questions that must be answered about the languages are: Are they truly object-oriented? Do they permit object-oriented applications to be constructed? Are they the apotheosis of object-oriented languages?

This section summarizes the position of Smalltalk and C++ then considers a language, Solve, which shows that there are many issues not dealt with by Smalltalk and C++ and that further development is not only happening, it is also essential.

4.1. Smalltalk

The Smalltalk language (Goldberg & Robson, 1983) is certainly object-oriented in that all things in the system are objects, it has an object management system with garbage collection and it implements true message passing. The virtual machine is a very consistent one, however, the implementation of the language is such that is is unreasonable to use it as a general paradigm. For example, it supports only single inheritance[2]. Further, Smalltalk, like Lisp, is an image-based system, it assumes a global shared memory. Thus, whilst it is possible to construct a parallel Smalltalk application, it is difficult, though not impossible, to construct a distributed system as a single Smalltalk application.

Since, like Lisp, Smalltalk is image based, the language and the environment (and hence tools) are integrally related. The Smalltalk language exists only within a programming environment and hence can only really be discussed in the context of the Smalltalk environment. This is good in many ways, in particular, the development tools are always available to the Smalltalk system developer; programming in Smalltalk involves developing classes and methods within a supportive environment. It is intended that developers make use of pre-existing classes (using inheritance) and pre-existing objects within the system (software reuse). Unfortunately, the syntax of the language is something of a problem for some people, especially beginners. More importantly though, the interface of the environment can act as a severe barrier to progress (Pun & Winder, 1988). The browser presents the contents of the system as a linear list of named objects, without an indexing mechanism. Semantic information about an object must be presented through the name or throughout the source code itself. No use made of the implicit graph structures to index the objects. The system has a large surface area and hence a steep learning curve.

A further problem is that the Smalltalk environment is unique to the development of Smalltalk systems. If all problems could be solved in Smalltalk then there is, perhaps, little problem.

---

[2] In fact, Smalltalk partially supports multiple inheritance but as a programming technique rather than as part of the virtual machine. Most Smalltalk users recognize this to be a 'hack' and therefore very rarely use multiple inheritance.

However, some problems are better solved in other languages, languages with different virtual machines. Thus, it is perhaps better to have a factorization between the environment and the particular programming language. A programming environment should support a number of different languages equally. Further, environments need to be more than just programming environments, they need to support all tasks involved in systems development, analysis, design, etc. Whilst, such additions could be made to the Smalltalk environment, they are not. This is indicative of a partitioning of the environment building community into factions as much as it is to do with the inability of Smalltalk to provide an implementation notation for all object-oriented systems.

4.2. C++

C++ (Ellis & Stroustrup, 1990; Stroustrup, 1991) is a procedural language that can be used in a way that appears object-oriented to the developer. What looks like message passing is just procedure call. However, this can be ignored by the developer, the inheritance and dynamic binding features of C++ admit object-oriented interpretation of the virtual machine and hence object-oriented programming, at least at the conceptual level. The conceptual model is not violated by the transformation to a procedural model for execution. C++ allows all classes of object-oriented system to be built; sequential, parallel and distributed. Having said this, it must be added that standard C++ is a language for developing sequential systems. To program concurrent systems requires the use of libraries and an explicit description of the concurrency desired. However, a number of projects are extending standard C++ to deal in an integrated way with concurrency (both parallel and distributed); UC++ at UCL (Winder, Wei & Roberts, 1991; Winder, Wei & Roberts, 1992), Topas C++ at Bull, Concurrent C++ at AT&T are but a few of the projects. One of these will undoubtably become standard C++ and then the language will be able to claim more universal applicability.

Unlike Smalltalk, C++ usually exists as a standalone notation, with compiler, hosted by whatever environment the developer wishes to use. A number of suppliers are moving towards integral environments: In the PC world, Borland C++ and Microsoft C++ are the market leaders, supplying language specific programming environments. In the UNIX world, there are two approaches. A number of suppliers provide language specific environments, e.g. ObjectCenter, but many suppliers are providing framework systems, e.g. SoftBench from HP, SNiFF+ from Take Five, which are not language specific but provide a communications infrastructure in which tools can be embedded. Such mechanisms are also beginning to appear in the PC world on top of the OLE communications standard. Frameworks are beginning to overtake special environments as the mechanism of preference.

There is, currently, one major problem with C++, it is not currently a language that supports incremental compilation. At present a C++ program must be edited and recompiled in total. There are shortcuts, by carefully partitioning the source code and making use of compilation management tools, e.g. make, much of the compilation can be avoided but there must always be a link phase. On very large systems, linking itself can be a very lengthy process, often taking days. The Smalltalk language has a significant advantage over C++ in this respect in that incremental compilation is the only form of compilation supported.

Work on UC++ at UCL is showing that incremental compilation of C++ is possible. By hosting the language on an environment, CoSIDE (Roberts, Wei & Winder, 1991a; Winder, Joly & Kamalati, 1992; Winder, Roberts & Wei, 1992), similar in nature to Smalltalk, many of these problems of C++ compilation can be avoided.

4.3. Solve

It has been argued that Smalltalk and C++, whilst being reasonably object-oriented, do not constitute apotheoses of the style. Indeed, many researchers have developed new object-oriented languages which are more 'pure', particularly people working in the parallel computation area. Eiffel (Meyer, 1988), Pool and Solve (Roberts, Wei & Winder, 1990; Roberts, Wei & Winder, 1991b; Roberts, Winder & Wei, 1988) are examples. Here, I will consider Solve which is an experimental language designed to be both truly object-oriented and truly parallel.

As with Smalltalk, a Solve program is a collection of objects, some are types, others instances of types. Each object is associated with a message reception process which acts as the dispatcher of method processes. In line with the strategy of supporting parallelism in an integral fashion, Solve supports not only object level parallelism but also method level parallelism; unless covered by a monitor to serialize activity, any accepted message creates a parallel method execution. Each object can have many threads executing concurrently. This purity of virtual machine makes Solve able to describe parallel and distributed object systems very directly. The claim is that because of this, Solve is a more evolved object-oriented programming language than Smalltalk or C++.

Solve follows the software engineering paradigm of separate specification and implementation of types. Not only is this done for the usual modularity reasons, it also supports the incremental compilation mechanism and the type conformance (as opposed to traditional strong type checking) system. In a type specification, not only are the operations declared but so are preconditions and postconditions for each operation. Further, domain conditions and behavioural specifications are made in the specification so that users of objects of the type know the sort of error reporting that might occur. These assertion mechanisms are integrated into the language via the exception handling mechanism. Multiple inheritance of types is supported, with all types being parameterizable.

The following is an example specification, for a parameterized stack:

```
Signature Stack(elementType)
SuperTypes (Object)
InstanceOperations
  Monitor
    push : (<someType>) -> <selfType>
           postcondition (pushFailed, internalError)
    pop : () -> <someType>
          postcondition (internalError)
    top : () -> <someType>
          precondition (stackEmpty)
    isEmpty : () -> <Boolean>
  EndMonitor
TypeOperations
DomainConditions
    infeasibleSize
TemporalProtocol
    stackUnderflow
      satisfies tr
      inwhich $a
      iff $a!send(pop) <= $a!send(push)
End
```

The source code for each method, the assertions and the exception handlers are presented in the implementation section. The example given below is a little overcomplicated in order to show features of the language.

```
Implementation Stack(someType)
Includes (Object)
InstanceSection
    Local storage <List(someType)> := ()
    Export Const push <Method((someType), selfType)> :=
    [
        ( element <someType> )
    |
        storage<--atInsert(1, element) ;
        => self
    ]
        postcondition (
            bizarrePush [ self'<--top()<--eq(element) ]
            wrongSize [ storage'<--length()<--subtract(1)<--eq(storage<--length()) ]
        )
    Export Const pop <Method((), SomeType)> :=
    [
        Let value <SomeType> := storage<--atValue(1) ;
        storage<--atDelete(1) ;
        => value
    ]
        postcondition (
            wrongSize [ storage'<--length()<--add(1)<--eq(storage<--length()) ]
        )
    Export Const top <Method((), SomeType)> :=
    [
        => storage<--atValue(1)
    ]
        precondition (
            stackEmpty [ self<--isEmpty()<--not() ]
        )
    Export Const isEmpty <Method((), Boolean)> :=
    [
        => storage<--length()<--gt(0)
    ]
TypeSection
DomainSection
    infeasibleSize [ storage<--length()<--ge(0) ]
LinkSection
    Handles postcondition::bizarrePush With pushError
    Handles postcondition::wrongSize With internalError
    Handles postcondition::noMemory From Object::new With memoryFault
    Handles precondition::stackEmpty With emptyStackError
    Handles domain::infeasibleSize with negativeStackSize
    Handles temporal::stackUnderflow with protocolError
HandlerSection
    Local Const pushError <Method((), Void)> :=
    [
        self<--pop() ;
        self<--dispatcher~toclient(pushFailed)
    ]
    Local Const internalError <Method((), Void)> :=
    [
        self<--dispatcher~debug()
    ]
    Local Const memoryFault <Method((), Void)> :=
    [
        System<--wait(400) ;
        self<--dispatcher~retry(2) ;
        self<--dispatcher~toclient(pushFailed)
    ]
    Local Const emptyStackError <Method((), Void)> :=
    [
        self<--dispatcher~toclient(stackEmpty)
    ]
    Local Const negativeStackSize <Method((), Void)> :=
    [
        self<--dispatcher~toclient(infeasibleSize)
    ]
    Local Const protocolError <Method((), Void)> :=
    [
        self<--dispatcher~toclient(stackUnderflow)
    ]
End
```

This integration of assertions, exceptions and message passing means that Solve systems can be made self-validating at run-time. This gives more confidence that the program will not simply crash in unusual situations, an absolute necessity for safety-critical systems. The addition of such features to object-oriented programming notations is therefore part of the next stage in development of the notations. Smalltalk and C++, because they do not support them at all, are clearly superseded in the development thread of object-oriented programming languages.

Following the strategy of Smalltalk, the Solve language is directly associated with a environment, CoSIDE (C++ or Solve Interactive Development Environment) (Roberts, Wei & Winder, 1991a; Winder, Joly & Kamalati, 1992; Winder, Roberts & Wei, 1992). This allows us to permit the syntax of the Solve language to contain considerable redundancy, the environment not the developer is responsible for doing much of the text construction of a Solve program.

Although CoSIDE is currently a programming environment it is not language specific, it supports both Solve and C++. This is possible because the objects being created are describable in both notations. By adhering to the object model, all programming language descriptions of the system become different syntactic representations of the same basic set of objects. There is semantic difference however, why else would there be different notations? Solve objects have integral behavioural specification, C++ objects do not. Further, the different notations separate specifications and implementations to different extents, either aiding or hindering incremental compilation.

Systems like CoSIDE can be extended to deal with other notations, in particular the graphical notations used in analysis and design. Work currently being undertaken at UCL into the 'Object Factory' are showing that any notation can be used to construct object systems, simply providing different views on the overall system.

This integration of views on the system, from analysis diagrams to source code, is a different approach to information integration in development environments from that of the frameworks. In frameworks, the integration mechanism is implemented as a communication between tools. In the environment approach, the tools are constructed on top of and within the communications system. Only time will tell which turns out to be the standard method. Hopefully, only technical rather than socio-politco-economic considerations will make the decision.

4.4. Summary

Smalltalk and C++ are essentially programming languages (with environments) of the 1980s. Without them the object-oriented approach would probably not have got off the ground. They are not, however, the languages of the future.

With the lessons learnt from Smalltalk and C++, new languages are being developed which extend the features available in the object system, progressing the development of the notion of object-orientation. The features introduced by these languages in terms of the support environments is showing that by being object-oriented, the environments can be more functional, more efficient and hence more likely to be successful.

Future object-oriented programming languages will certainly need better support for type and class specification and especially the relationships between them, as well as supporting better object behaviour specification. Object-oriented analysis (OOA) and design (OOD) methods will have important and significant input here. The notations used in OOA and OOD methods are being derived from the way in which solutions are being developed in the real world rather than being a simple reflection of the object model. They are introducing into the object paradigm the modelling concepts required in solutions, concepts which need to be reflected in the object-oriented programming languages of the future.

Object-orientation in programming is not, however, the total answer. As Petre & Winder (1988) have shown, problems tend to have solutions which 'naturally' fit with the virtual machine of certain classes of language. The solution to a particular problem will best be described by one particular class of language. Object-oriented languages are appropriate for a large class of problems, particularly concurrency problems. Prolog is nice for describing relationships and facts. OPS5 is nice for describing rules and actions. In supporting the tasks and reasoning of the developer, particular computational models should not be forced on the solution of any problem.

The real summary is that we need multi-style solution capability supported by the environment. Also, we musn't forget that the choice of implementation language impacts on the analysis and design techniques and that a multiplicity of these are also required. Being object-oriented may not be the only way to program but for relevant problems, and environments is one of those, it is a significant way forward. Object-oriented environments permit the multiplicity of styles that is required to provide a proper tool base for the problem solver.

5. Development Environments

The above has shown that an object-based architecture for an environment is probably necessary. The questions left are multitudinous, the following are but two: What should the interface be like? What is the toolset that should be provided? These two are not unconnected.

It goes without saying that the environment should support the developer in their tasks. This requires tools to support analysis, design, implementation, testing, debugging, verification and validation. The environment must have editors, compilers and debuggers integrated together. Rather than seeing the notations manipulated by these tools as providing different information contributing to the totality of information about the system, they should provide different views on the same information. The developer interacts with the system mainly through editors and/or browsers, these are the most crucial tools of the environment.

5.1. Editing

Consider the manipulation of programming language notation. Editors used to be text editors with little or no support for the developer correctly entering the tokens of the language. In C++ for example, 'while' is a single token that happens to be represented by 5 letters. The developer has to ensure, if they are using a text editor, that they spell the word correctly. They only find out about errors when using the compiler, the editor gives no real support.

Recently, editors in popular programming environments have allowed the various classes of token of a language to be colour coded, see for example the Borland C++ environment. By reflecting aspects of compilation of the language in the editor, certain classes of error can be limited as the program is entered. Such features are not, however, new. Syntax directed editors (SDE) have been available for years. Such editors include the compiler for the language directly, the result of compilation being the parse tree of the program. This is, in effect, the ultimate in incremental compilation. There are significant HCI problems associated with incremental compilation at this level which is why systems such as Smalltalk and CoSIDE use a courser grain of compilation unit. However, interest in SDEs is picking up, particularly as more and more notations become graphical in nature.

5.2. Browsing and Searching

Another issue is that of finding reusable components within a system. Traditionally, the unit of reuse is the function library. Such libraries have been documented through reference manuals. Developers had to search through permuted indexes to try and find the relevant function. This was, of course, not always done and much unnecessary replication has occurred, the Not Invented Here (NIH) syndrome. Some replication of activity is beneficial, a given reusable component may be better or worse that another implementation of the same functionality or the functionality may be subtly different. The current state is, however, that replication far outstrips necessity.

With object-oriented systems, the basic problem is essentially the same. How should class and object libraries be documented and reused. With the rise of the use of environments to support development, the problem has in fact subtly shifted. As well as requiring documentation on libraries which are included at compile time, information is required on the classes and object forming the environment and all that is in it; since the system is being developed within an environment, reuse can be made of other parts of the system and parts of the environment itself (which would contain the library of reusable components). The editor and/or browser used by the developer to construct their system needs to support searching of the system to support reuse.

Object systems tend to be a flat address space of names, such a space is not easy to search. This is particularly true as the searching must be syntactic, on the name, rather than semantic. Finding things that are stack-like is fairly easy since very few people disagree with using the label 'stack' for things that are stack-like and people do not use the label 'stack' for things that are not stack-like. However, consider trying to find, in a C++ environment, a function to convert a string representation of an integer value into a machine representation of an integer value; would you have though of looking up 'strtol'?

Smalltalk does not really provide any useful insights here. It does partition the name space of classes by introducing the notion of category but the name space is still flat and must still be searched syntactically, by name. How can reuse be made if people cannot appreciate extant sub-systems.

Work is being done in this area, for example, the Cognitive Browser (CogBrow) (Green et al., 1992; Green, Gilmore & Winder, 1990; Green et al., 1992), a collaborative project between MRC-APU at Cambridge, Department of Psychology at Nottingham and Department of Computer Science at UCL. CogBrow is an interface hosted on CoSIDE (Roberts, Wei & Winder, 1991a) for searching classes and objects within an object system. The work focusses on two aspects of searching, trying to embed semantic and syntactic information about the class or object in the index and trying to support developer defined (and possibly very transient) indexes on the system. The goal is to develop means of assisting program construction and comprehension through explicit representation of cognitive macro-structures; to investigate the usability of different types of perspective (e.g. episodic versus semantic, how it works versus what it does) as comprehension aids for large program structures. On a more implementation oriented note, the project is investigating whether the graph structures within the system map to developers' cognitive structures and whether developers' cognitive structures can be instantiated as an index on the object system.

The implementation strategy is to avoid the Smalltalk user interface model and make the graph structures explicit in the representation of the system. Object use relationships and class inheritance relationships are available explicitly to the developer. Presenting the inheritance graph is not in itself particularly new, presenting object use relationships is. Further, CogBrow will allow developer defined graph structures to be defined and displayed. For example, a time ordered display of all the objects I amended this afternoon. Such a display can be important for backtracking through edits and often design alterations.

Such explicit use of the embedded graph structures supports not only development but also learning of the system. Exploratory investigation of the space of classes and objects is supported, enabling developers to discover more about the system, to extend their knowledge of what it is possible to reuse and hence supports reuse of those components.

Providing support for semantic searching of the classes and objects has been somewhat less successful. The original intention had been to use assertions (preconditions, postconditions, domain conditions and trace conditions), as available in Solve and to a lesser extent Eiffel, to define the semantics of the code. For various reasons this turned out not to be as fruitful a direction as originally anticipated, principally because no realistic notation for composing semantic queries could be envisaged. It seems then that semantic searching, whilst still considered essential for future environments, requires a step forward in notations.

5.3. Management Tools

Finally in this section, it is important to support the process of system development as well as the tasks of system development. Not only does this mean supporting the integration of the tools within the environment, it means supporting the management of development. For single developer activities, this may just mean supporting access to all the documents comprising the system but most systems are developed by teams. This means supporting both multiple people working on the same documentation, i.e. all the locking and revision management required, and also the management of the people.

In the CASE environment and IPSE world this has often meant creating mechanisms for controlling the documentation and people doing the development. Clearly, dictatorial systems are not the way forward, the management regime embedded in the environment must support rather than control. Pert charts, GANTT charts, etc. are still useful tools and should be supported in the development environment, connected directly to the rest of the system so that the information being used and recorded is accurate. Such tools should however, be informative rather than controlling. Implementing the environment in objects makes such systems easier to envisage conceptually and to implement.

5.4. The End of Traditional Programming Languages?

The level of integration of all the information regarding a system implied by the above section, plus the Smalltalk and CoSIDE(Object Factory) experiences of programming environments raises the question: Where does the programming language stop and the environment begin? Also, are traditional programming notations and evolutions of them, the way forward?

In a system where the analysis and design documentation is as integral as the programming language, the notations used in the documents become part of the programming notation. Thus, if such an integrated environment supported the Schlaer/Mellor system, their notation for describing systems becomes part of the notation that actually constructs the system. This idea is the one core to the Object Factory. Such systems are, by definition, multimedia environments and will almost certainly be object-oriented in architecture.

6. Conclusion

Having addressed many, but possibly not all, of the issues, I must now decide whether I have been able to answer the question: Is object-oriented the answer? I believe that I have shown that object-oriented approaches are useful, that being 'object-oriented' is perhaps the next step on from being 'structured'. The problem is, of course, that the question is faulty. Looking for absolute answers nearly always fails:

> 'Forty-two!' yelled Loonquawl. 'Is that all you've got to show for seven and a half million years' work?'
>
> 'I checked it very thoroughly,' said the computer, 'and that quite definitely is the answer. I think the problem, to be quite honest with you, is that you've never actually known what the question is.'
>
> 'But it was the Great Question! The Ultimate Question of Life, the Universe and Everything,' howled Loonquawl.
>
> 'Yes,' said Deep Thought with the air of one who suffers fools gladly, 'but what actually is it?'
>
> A slow stupefied silence crept over the men as they stared at the computer and then at each other.
>
> (*The Hitchhikers Guide to the Galaxy*, Douglas Adams, Pan, 1979.)

In the programming domain: Object-oriented programming can be useful since it extends the ADT idea by insisting on very specific data protection ideas via message passing. The object-oriented approach admits an efficient program level description of concurrent (parallel and distributed) systems due to the unity of model between the software and the underlying physical system.

In the environments domain: Object-orientation supports multi-style systems and the management of them. Object-oriented environments and software libraries are useful since they promote easy understanding and hence good reuse of software. It is therefore a good integrating model for system implementation.

The issue of object-oriented analysis and design has not been addressed in detail here but must be useful since it allows us to work in terms of models of the real world and models of the system being developed with easy mappings to object-oriented implementations.

Object-orientation is generally a good idea; it is *an* answer on the evolutionary road, it is not *the* answer.

Acknowledgement

Thanks are due to Graham Roberts for commenting on drafts of this chapter.

Why Software Engineers Don't Listen to What Psychologists Don't Tell Them Anyway

T R G Green

MRC Applied Psychology Unit, 15 Chaucer Road, Cambridge CB2 2EF, UK.

This chapter centres on two observations. First, although software engineering environments are among the most interesting and enterprising products created by software engineers, they frequently contain features seen by psychologists and cognitive ergonomists as usability blunders. On the face of it, this problem stems directly from the second problem, which is that software engineers pay little or no heed to empirical results obtained by cognitive ergonomists and psychologists, even where directly relevant. These two problems have been seen by some (including the author) as exasperating failings on the part of software engineers. I here suggest a different interpretation, which I hope does better justice to software engineers and to the realities of science. In many cases, hard-to-use software engineering environments should be viewed not as failed systems but as successful experiments, which have shown that a particular computational model or style is inadequate. Thus, the first problem is not the engineers' problem but the psychologists' misappreciation (at least to some extent), while the second problem demonstrates not wilful deafness but the absence of a workable communication path. Evidently, improved communication is badly needed. Many ways have been suggested to improve knowledge transfer, but most can be dismissed as unsuitable. My suggestion is that a distinct, semi-formal framework of concepts (such as 'cognitive dimensions of notations') should be consciously adopted as a 'boundary object', accessible to software engineers from one side and to cognitive ergonomists and psychologists from the other side.

Keywords: cognitive dimensions, transfer of knowledge, cognitive ergonomics, psychology, software engineering environments, sociology of science.

1. Introduction

Originally I was going to describe all the wonderful insights that psychologists could offer to software engineers, especially about the psychology of programming. But on reflection I decided that all that had been done before; so instead, I would ask about why there was no visible effect. Do psychologists have anything to say about software engineering environments? Are they saying it in the right places? Do software engineers care? Can the state of things be improved?

I want to make three points:

1. Many software engineering environments have usability problems which are very obvious in hindsight and should have been obvious beforehand.

2. These usability problems are crossly condemned by psychologists, but software engineers view them more complacently; perhaps they see their activities in a different light.

3. If we want to improve the situation we have to look at the 'transfer paths' — the mechanisms for achieving shared understanding of activities and for disseminating knowledge in a usable form.

Of course, a lot of the software engineer's activity deals with topics where cognitive psychology has no obvious input. My concern is not with the many aspects of specification and design that are purely technical. Nor am I concerned with the details of human–computer interaction, which is essentially concerned with how information is exchanged between people and/or computers.

My concern is with *designing information systems that support the activities people really engage in.* (This is an activity that has been dubbed 'cognitive ergonomics'.) In this chapter, I shall concentrate on the design of software engineering environments (SEEs). There are exciting, if difficult possibilities in this area, and because the designers are their own customers or users they have a better understanding than usual of the user's problems.

By the way, this chapter is full of sweeping generalizations. I will try to defend them if challenged, of course, but I think I ought to point out that when I say 'software engineers do this' or 'cognitive psychologists do that' I do not mean each and every one of them.

2. Are the Psychologist's Goods in Demand?

2.1. 'Professional-quality' Evidence Not Used

A casual flick through my bookshelves reveals that cognitive scientists are not making much inroad into the realms of software engineering, at least as evidenced in the textbooks. Shu (1988) describes a wide variety of visual programming languages and makes strong claims both about visual languages in general, and about particular languages; yet she cites virtually no empirical evidence except the experiment by Cunniff, Taylor & Black (1989). That experiment was based on only 6 programs in a flowcharting notation, together with an unspecified larger number of Pascal programs, all written by students. Not only is this far too small a sample for serious conclusions to be drawn, but also it turned out that in the variable of interest, the frequency of different types of 'conceptual bugs', the two languages were essentially identical. Thus, Shu's basic premise that visual languages are superior to textual ones is based on a single small study, investigating very few of the possibilities, which actually failed to achieve statistically significant results. Yet there exist well-controlled, extensive, and highly professional studies, such as that by Curtis et al. (1989) — which reached journal form in 1989 but had been widely available well before that date.

So much for Shu; what else do we find? In the 25 chapters of the Bennett (1989) collection of papers on software engineering environments, Adelson & Soloway (1985) is almost the only experiment cited. They report that software designers benefit from prior experience in the domain for which the design is intended, a not unexpected finding. (Indeed, Johnson's (1989) chapter in that volume draws on a wide range of human–computer interaction literature, but since Johnson is a well-known HCI specialist the chapter can hardly be regarded as an example of a software engineer drawing on the psychology literature.) Sommerville's collection (Sommerville, 1986) makes still less reference to such work. The Fenton (1991) text on software metrics actually includes a chapter on experimental design, yet apart from one rather poor experiment cited in that chapter empirical methods make little showing, even though to confirm or refute his armchair analyses of 'complexity' Fenton could easily have turned to experimental evidence — some of which is summarized in readily available form by Curtis (1989b). Somerville's text on software engineering (Sommerville, 1989) is unusual, ahead of the pack in that he explicitly considers sociological and organizational implications, but still the work of cognitive psychologists and ergonomists has not found a niche. And so on.

2.2. 'Amateur-quality' Evidence is Worrying

Maybe worse is the variable standard of published research in journals for software engineers. Some of it, to be sure, is excellent stuff by any standards; such as the extensive set of studies by Curtis et al. (1989), already mentioned. Other studies are problematic both in depth of thought, experimental design, and proper scholarship — that is, reference to earlier studies to gain a fuller understanding of one's own work. Two that have recently crossed my path are by Kudo et al. (1989) and Scanlan (1989). Others include the well-known studies on so-called 'software science', whose foundations have been picked apart by others before me.

Such a degree of variability shows, as nothing else can, that the journals have not yet identified a strong refereeing tradition for them to call upon; the mark of a problematic area. On the other hand, these studies at least show that some software engineers evidently do want to know the things we cognitive psychologists think we are telling them. One of the problems is evidently that what we psychologists say isn't reaching their ears.

3. Critiquing Some SEEs: Usability in Hindsight

None of this would matter if software engineers could do perfectly well on their own in designing usable systems. They certainly don't always. In fact, software engineers have a long history of producing systems which are strange and gawky in ways which are perfectly comprehensible and could readily have been foreseen. To illustrate this I need to give some examples. At the end of this section I will ask whether the criticisms are as valid to software engineers as they are to cognitive psychologists.

- *Software engineering environments frustrate human planning.* Certain classes of program support environment require programmers to state the overall structure before descending to the details. This is difficult, and it is all too likely that programmers will need to go back and revise, especially when the structure has to be presented declaratively while the subsequent details are presented as an imperative style. The imposition of a top-down construction style is unnecessary, caused by a misapprehension of how problem-solving really works. There are many instances of this problem.
  Crookes et al. (1985) describe a speech-input system for Pascal dictation. Pascal, however, is not a suitable language for use in a dictation system, because many decisions (such as what identifiers, types, and procedures to declare) must be made prematurely. If one can write the program down and then read it aloud Pascal is quite a good choice, but for 'hands-off' programming, as envisaged by Crookes et al., it is nearly impossible. (Try it. Dictate a program for any simple task, such as reversing an array of integers in place, taking care that your utterances are likely to

be recognizable by a speech-driven compiler. You are not allowed to work out the program on paper and then read it, you have to dictate it, without making notes first.) Another example was reported by Détienne (1990b) in her experiments evaluating an object-oriented software development system, 'O₂', in which programmers were required to build the declarative part of their programs (the statement of the object hierarchy) before they could start on the imperative part (the definitions of methods). As a result, they frequently discovered, when they came to the imperative part, that their objects were incompletely worked out.

These are examples of *premature commitment* (Green, 1989). I believe the designers should have seen the difficulties coming; and that, if they had asked cognitive ergonomists, the problem would have been easily foreseen.

- *Software engineers have not produced an effective definition of 'size'*. An old argument, this: How big should a programming language or environment be? The most celebrated controversy was over the size of Ada, between Ichbaiah (chief designer of Ada, a big language) and Hoare (proponent of Pascal, a small language). Hoare (1981) insisted that Ada was too big, both technically, for implementors (which is not our concern) and cognitively, for users (which definitely is our concern). Ichbaiah responded by asserting that:

> "The human mind has an incredible ability to understand structure.
> ... When you judge something, the complexity is not in the details
> but in whether or not it is easy to infer details from major structural
> lines. From this point of view I consider Ada to be very simple."
> (Ichbaiah & Anon, 1984)

Here we have a clear example of an assertion about cognitive psychology. Why aren't we in there giving evidence?

- *SEEs are based on formal structures, not on cognitive structures*. Early structure-based editors were based solely on strict syntactic structure, making no concessions to users' mental representations at a semantic or lexical level. They did not arouse whole-hearted enthusiasm from users because their method of abbreviating text hid parts of the code on a purely syntactic basis, rather than in terms of meaningful wholes such as 'slices' (Weiser, 1982; Weiser & Lyle, 1986) or 'plans'. This would give rise to situations like this:

```
sum := 0 ;
for j:=1 to 100 do
    begin
      ......
      ......
    end ;
writeln(sum) ;
```

All the material of interest is hidden inside the ellipsis. Because the structured editor uses pure syntax to determine its information hiding, there is no way to see those statements that affect the value of sum without also seeing all the other statements in side the loop body. In other words, the ellipsis is pretty well useless as an abbreviation technique. The problem here is that simple syntax-based ellipsis does not recognize *interleaving of plans*; more generally, although quite a bit is known about what programmers know (Brooks, 1990), no use whatsoever is made that material in the vast majority of SEEs.

- *SEEs are designed for creating software but not for redesigning it.* Just one example from many. The UNIX filestore has a huge problem of *hidden dependencies* (Green, 1989; Green, 1990c), such that it is impossible to know whether a given 'dot file' (such as `.alias` or `.spare_vacation_message`) is somehow in use. As a result, one's filespace slowly silts up with files that are probably 'fossils', i.e. documents which are almost certainly no longer in use but which *may*, just possibly, be invoked by other documents. They could almost certainly be thrown away but one dare not, because one day some rarely-used script might crash if it can't find its data file. (The problem also exists at the system level in UNIX; each time new software is installed, it adds a few more potential fossils.) Smalltalk and other object-oriented languages can contain many other cases of long-range hidden dependencies; changes to a class are inherited by all its children, grandchildren, etc., potentially causing serious consequences later. (Come to that, so do spreadsheets.)

- *SEEs are not usually proofed against well-known sources of human error.* Early programming languages were notorious for the possibilities of making catastrophic errors by simple mistypings, such as leaving out a comma or mis-spelling an identifier, which could only be detected at run-time when something noticeably strange happened. *Plus ça change*: today Prolog has just the same vulnerability to mis-spelt identifiers, as have many expert systems (Ward & Sleeman, 1987). Many other types of human error are encouraged by existing SEEs. Yet a huge literature on human error exists (Reason, 1990), together with specific applications to computing environments (Norman, 1983a).

- *SEEs are not tested against reality.* We seem to be hearing a lot about 'process environments', several of which are described in Bennett's collection. Two of these, the Integrated Software Production Environment IPSE 2.5 (Warboys, 1989) and the Eureka Software Factory (ESF) (Dewal & Kelter, 1989) make extensive use of the notion of a user's *role*. There is, in both cases, an extensive deployment of technical vocabulary. For instance, Warboys outlines role modelling:

  > "A process model for management support can be created by
  > instantiating the *Managing* Role class, with a Terms of Reference
  > as input. The *Managing* instance co-ordinates a network of Roles,
  > which together define and execute a Model for the Goal. Most of
  > its activities are therefore instantiating other Roles, or taking part in
  > Interactions. In order to satisfy the Goal, a *Managing* Role creates
  > three other Roles." (Warboys, 1989, p.325)

  which deal with Technology, Logistics, and Administration. Overall, the 'Process Control Engine', says Warboys:

  > "...is cognisant of the process itself and is thus able to provide
  > the appropriate working environments at the appropriate times."
  > (Warboys, 1989, p.321)

All the papers on process modelling are devoted to architectural or mathematical structures; that is, not a single one of them that I have seen is in any way tested against reality. Many socio-organizational questions are raised. What are 'roles' *really* like? How will the formal structure imposed by the process model be related to the informal structure of the organization, and who will carry responsibility for management catastrophes — the local manager or the model-builder? We know that the 'model' that is built for any particular process will be a satisficing model, as simple as can be got away with. What will happen when such a model runs up against the politics of processes, against determined efforts to use access to information and availability of actions as a means of control? In what way can its authors claim that the model can be 'cognisant of the process'? It will have available to it the skimpiest possible representation, but people's actions will be determined by their mental pictures and their social relationships. Many cognitive questions are raised too; the notion of a fixed Goal conflicts with many design theorists, for example Cross (1984), who see goals as *evolved* (rather than specified) not to mention with field studies (Curtis, Krasner & Iscoe, 1988) reaching the same conclusion. Why have the process engineers gone this far without looking in close detail at what really happens and demonstrating that their device can model it? A better approach might surely be to support flexible goal assignments in cooperative problem solving (Fischer, 1987; Fischer et al., 1992).

In the absence of any kind of reality checking, it seems to me inevitable that the system will turn out to contain serious difficulties of an organizational type.

4. What's the Problem?

The previous section described several cases of poor usability. The evidence needed to build better systems was already available when they were built. Why was there a problem?

4.1. Failures or Successes?

The cognitive psychologist or ergonomist sees these cases in one way: those optimistic technologists have rushed off and built something, only to discover that they have done it wrong, yet again. The problem is not that the idea is not potentially good; it's that the purity of the idea has run away with the technologists. In many cases, matters could easily have been remedied by putting in a few fixes to help users with the difficult bits.

But the software engineer, I suspect, sees these cases in a different way. The systems are experiments. They are not 'failures' because they are hard to use — in fact, if anything they are 'successes'. When a system is hard to use, a particular model has been shown to be imperfect. The only way to do so (as seen by the software engineer) is by real-life trial. An improved model will be generated in due course, based on improved understanding and analysis of the problem.

In short, I suspect that systems seen by cognitive people as being seriously flawed are not necessarily seen as problematic at all by software engineers, because their criteria are different. The cognitive ergonomist wants a system that genuinely does the best it can for its users, while the software engineer wants to try out a model.

4.2. Is There a Scaling-up Problem?

No. Good laboratory research scales up. For example, the Arcturus structured editor (Standish & Taylor, 1984) employs exactly the same template-based programming building techniques that were investigated by Sime, Arblaster & Green (1977b). Criticism of large search problems in Smalltalk and other large systems, and worry about unanticipated consequences of small changes, echoes precisely the vocabulary of 'hidden dependency' etc. in the cognitive dimensions framework (Green, 1989). The mass conversion to perceiving design as an exploratory and opportunistic process was first reported as a result of laboratory studies (Siddiqi, 1985). The difficulty of getting declarative portions right was demonstrated by Hoc (1981).

4.3. Inability to Recontextualize

Technologists are not noted for reading the literature, and so results in the literature vanish from sight. With the rise of visual programming, there have been excited claims that it is more 'natural', etc. But visual programming languages are just another notation, and I thought Bill Curtis and his team, and Max Sime and *his* team, had got that all sorted out — see Curtis (1989b) for a good review of this area. "But all those old studies were on textual languages: surely visual programming languages are different!"

The problem is that not everybody can see the resemblance between one situation and another, so that results established in the first situation need to be re-interpreted for the other. All notations highlight some information at the expense of obscuring other information; that was the principle that arose from the text-based work. There is no single 'superlative' notation. But it seems to have been necessary to demonstrate that principle all over again for the visual programming world (Green et al., 1992). It should, in future, be available and ready for application when another new technological possibility is developed. But will it be?

4.4. Different Perceived Needs

One answer seems to be that although software engineers spend a great deal of time making detailed comparisons of languages and environments, that's not what they want psychologists to deliver. They may quite possibly spend all day talking about Structure and Function, but what they want to be told by psychologists is how to do Good Design. My experience has repeatedly been that software engineers impatiently dismiss all the detailed evidence that psychologists proffer them. They hanker to be told how to teach their pupils and apprentices how to create a good design first time, every time. Who could blame them for that? But psychologists do not believe that good design can be produced so simply. Although we can certainly point to some mistakes not be repeated, we are not in a position to tell software engineers how to do good engineering!

4.5. Train-spotters and Basket-weavers: The Perils of Enforced Separation

Software engineers publish in different journals, are evaluated by different criteria; their hope is to have solved a problem by creating a practicable, generalizable, effective and clean solution. They chose their career and have become successful because they like deep, clean insights. Psychologists, in contrast, hope to produce an analysis that synthesizes the known literature and contributes to understanding, supported by empirical tests; while ergonomists hope to produce a system that supports the users. The gap between the software people and the cognitive people is nearly insurmountable, save in mutual respect (sometimes). It is made worse when attempts to create interdisciplinary collaboration are seen as failures to meet the criteria of one's own kind. Thus, research on programming expertise may be dismissed by computer scientists as being no addition to computer science's achievements, and by psychologists as failing to further our understanding of fundamental psychology.

At the highest levels, the aims of software engineers and cognitive psychologists are reasonably close. But practice on the ground is very different, where enforced separations engender sneers, such as "strong typing is for weak minds" — none of your careful assessments of pros and cons, when to use and when to avoid a technique. "Train-spotters" versus "basket-weavers" are the war-cries in one department I know of to describe the systems people and the human-oriented people respectively.

4.6. Will it Pay?

This is a *Grrr!* question. At a recent workshop, a software engineer insisted that his only criterion for assessing what psychologists had to offer was, would it save him money in development? To his ears, that was no doubt perfectly reasonable. To my ears, it was a case of double standards. The software engineering community sinks vast sums into systems such as CASE tools, based on collective delusions about the nature of the design process. The community ought to be interested in refining its beliefs and bringing them nearer reality. To ask an expert on thought processes to give a financial estimate of the value to be gained from refining software systems is obviously a piece of evasiveness.

5. Paths to Collaboration

What routes are available by which knowledge from two distinct areas can be brought together?

I was brought up to believe that science was a dispassionate and impartial search for knowledge and understanding; that every scientist sedulously combed the literature as often as possible and attempted to synthesize all relevant findings. After twenty-five years of active scientific research I still feel regret for that lost first love, the dispassionate researcher. But it took me a long time to understand just how wrong this model is. I imagined, for many years, that the steady accumulation of relevant research results would somehow reach and influence everyone appropriate. Computer scientists and software engineers were creating languages, environments, and applications; bit by bit they would start to incorporate more and more research results from the cognitive literature.

The fact of the matter, of course, is that this *osmosis* model of knowledge transfer is wildly inaccurate. In the earlier part of the chapter I gave enough illustrations to show that a steady accumulation of relevant results in one culture does not necessarily percolate through to another culture. If you wish to influence people you must make yourself and your research visible. You must engage in 'salesmanship' — one of the dirtiest words in the lexicon, to my erstwhile young ears.

Depressingly, a more realistic model is the *jewel in the mud*; the single research result which sticks out from one culture and is cited, well or badly, by many researchers in other cultures. The best-known example in software psychology is Miller's (1956) 'magical number 7 plus or minus 2', a classic of experimental psychology in the information-processing paradigm, destined to be widely used and misused in support of all sorts of diverse suggestions about software design (Coad & Yourdon, 1990; de Marco, 1979). Sometimes it was clear that researchers had not understood Miller's paper, probably had not even read it, and were simply aping the fashion. We want no more of that style of knowledge transfer than has to borne. (To be fair, though, all of us interdisciplinary boffins have to do the best we can in absorbing ideas from other cultures and we daily risk misunderstanding the work we cite.)

Then we have the *new wave* model of knowledge transfer. I tend to think of the contrast between the Keep Fit movement in Britain and the Aerobics movement. Keep Fit classes had become somewhat grey and unalluring. Along comes Aerobics, with jazzier dress, louder music, and a new wave of jargon. The real differences between the aims and styles of Keep Fit and Aerobics were greatly exaggerated by the welter of inessential stylistic differences, and with it comes a brash, proselytizing style: "all that tired old stuff misses the point, we've got something much better". There are plenty of examples of 'new wave' routes to knowledge transfer around. In our domain, the well-known work of the ethno-methodologists could be seen in those terms; they present an exaggerated division between cognitivist approaches and sociological approaches, they take little notice of existing traditions of organizational psychology, and they cheerfully suggest that cognitivist techniques and questions should be replaced by sociological or ethno-methodological ones.

A point to notice is that 'new wave' movements not only pose the question differently *but they also define the type of answer*! It is very difficult to counter a new wave enthusiast by saying "Yes, but we already have a lot of that knowledge, it just looks different." The fact that it looks different is sufficient to rule it out. The wheel can be re-invented countless times if it is presented each time with sufficient surface differences and plenty of razzmatazz, plus a genuinely new insight or two.

The *demonstration* model is a route that is less likely to succeed but which conforms better to the ideals of scientific progress. In this model, a group of researchers from different backgrounds sets out to show what might be achieved if they tried hard to understand each other. From several examples of groups trying this approach, I shall only pick out a few representatives: the 'cockpit' project, aiming to help expert electronics designers to 'steer' a design process making use of various automated aids (Colgan, Rankin & Spence, 1991); the Plymouth Engineer's Design Assistant, another electronic design environment making explicit use of cognitive models of design (Baker et al., 1991); a programme of investigations into cognitive aspects of reuse of software (Sutcliffe & Maiden, 1990a); and finally the 'Cognitive Browser' project which is a direct attempt to improve usability of object-oriented environments by incorporating more knowledge into the system in a usable form (Green et al., 1992; Green et al., 1992).

The details of these projects are not so important as their group structures. Each of them is built from a combination of different specialists, who are having the usual difficulties in finding publishing outlets which will bring visibility in all the different background disciplines. The same research therefore has to be presented in various places wearing a variety of hats and costumes — now as applied cognitive psychology, now as advanced design engineering. This can be a bit enervating, but a more serious problem is that the work must meet each audience's standards of acceptability. Unless the engineering is good, software engineers will be less than impressed; likewise with the cognitive psychology and, where relevant, the circuit analysis tools. It is for that reason that the demonstration model is a perilous route to transfer — the need to impress several very different groups of consumers.

In the *organizational* model, a 'usability' stage is deliberately introduced into the design process. This method can only be used where the design process is fairly well-specified and self-conscious, but in practice many software engineering organizations do indeed use 'design methodologies'. Walsh, Lim & Long (1989) give a good account of how one such methodology, Jackson Structured Design (JSD), could be adapted to include an explicit user interface specification stage, and claim that they will be able to overcome the obvious problem that "for human factors and JSD to be successfully integrated, contributions from both need to be appropriately timed and structured". These developments are very welcome, although we shall have to wait awhile to measure their success. But approaches which are limited to formalized design methodologies are not really what I am looking for. I want to transfer knowledge, not to find a way to blend the efforts of different specialists.

Lastly, there is the *compulsory education* model. All software engineering students should be made to learn something about — aah, that's the catch. What could they possibly learn, in a smallish fragment of their course, that would really be useful? There now exist a fair number of texts on HCI for interface design, but what about the problems raised by my critiques? There might be scope to show students how to evaluate a system from its users' point of view, and possibly even to show them how to find routes into the jungle of relevant literature, but there is no serious possibility of making them cognitive specialists. That's not what their lives are about.

6. Conclusion: We need Semi-formal Approaches to Recontextualization. How about 'Cognitive Dimensions'?

None of the transfer models strikes me as our solution. So what are we to do? Here's a suggestion.

Star (1989) discusses similar problems of cooperation between diverse groups of actors, and the tension between divergent viewpoints and the need for generalizable findings. (Her analysis is complex and probably contains important bits that I missed.) She demonstrates the need for formalization as a way of cleaning up the mess and allowing diverse groups to communicate, and introduces the idea of 'boundary objects' which are accepted by all the diverse groups, although possibly seen differently. Star & Griesemer (1989) discuss the role of boundary objects in allowing communication between amateurs and professionals in the zoological field. In their sense, boundary objects are things like classification systems which can be used by both groups, although to the amateur zoologist a classification system has a rather different status than to a professional.

Following up this kind of idea, it seems to me that what we are looking for is a moderately formal means of description that can be applied to significant components of a SEE. This description is the equivalent of Star's boundary object. On one side, it can be used by software engineers as a summary of the design, from one viewpoint. On the other side, it can be used by cognitive people as an index into relevant literature. Between them, it can be used as a method of 'recontextualization', in which the solutions to problems can be re-applied in different contexts.

This is where my 'cognitive dimensions' framework (Green, 1989; Green, 1991) comes in. We can use terms such as 'hidden dependencies' to characterize a system such as UNIX or a spreadsheet closely enough to make it clear that will suffer from similar difficulties. Many systems suffer from high 'viscosity' — that is, to achieve a single domain-level goal, many system-level actions are needed. And so on. In Green (1991), I showed a possible route to formalizing these terms. These techniques are far from fully worked out, but the aim is to create a simple, semi-formal, comprehensible means to recognize the similarities between different information structures, in order to assist the process of recontextualization.

I am not going to plug the details of my framework here. For one thing it still needs a lot of work, and for another, that would take another paper. But I do want to plug the idea of cognitive dimensions (or any similar framework) *as a boundary object*. Because the framework is not too informal, it can appeal to the clean-living software engineer; and because it does not suppress too much mess, it does not appal the cognitive psychologist.

How would it work? An example: a cognitive psychologist could do research on how the design process is affected by viscosity. The research might well show that when high viscosity makes undoing design decision is difficult, users will frequently explore only one design possibility — the 'depth-first' problem described by Curtis (1989b) and others.

Likewise, software engineers can apply the dimensions framework to their designs. They might conclude ruefully that their design for a SEE will prove highly viscous and so they had better do something about it. If they want to know more about the effects of viscosity, the relevant literature should be readily available, accessed by the keyword. On both sides thus is honour gained, and neither of us ever had to learn too much about the other one's discipline.

This, then is my final conclusion. If we are to transfer knowledge, a necessary first step is to create and propagate a 'boundary vocabulary' consciously designed to interface between software engineering and cognitive ergonomics. Then psychologists and ergonomists will be able to say something useful, and software engineers will be able to hear it, to understand it — and to request something better and more useful.

Theme 4 Discussion Report

Dispatches from the Front or a Lab Rat's Thoughts on Mazes

1. Introduction

The following is not intended to put across a piece of research work or to report facts. Rather, it is to express some opinions about what I consider important in the design of software engineering environments. As a consequence, it doesn't have the usual structure of the papers accompanying it.

There are two main sections: The first lists what I consider to be the principal tasks that a software engineering environment should address, and is deliberately vague in order to cover a lot of ground quickly. The second section goes into more detail about specific implementation features that seem valuable to me as a potential user. This paper was presented as one of a set of discussions, and so the questions that I raised and a summary of the replies that were garnered during the subsequent discussion round it off.

Who am I to be offering these opinions? Well, I have been a practising software developer for about fifteen years, a professional one for about ten, and I now run a software consulting company with my partner. Following my introduction by her to the psychology of programming community some years ago, I have become concerned that the interests of the professional development community are represented among those people whose ideas may end up shaping the systems we use in the future.

The following two sections refer to a 'Putatively Ideal Programming Environment'. In order to make writing about it easier, I'm going to refer to it by the name 'PIPE'.

2. Tasks to be Facilitated

By a strange coincidence, all the tasks that would be facilitated by my PIPE start with the letters 'co'. Consequently, I've called it the 'costar'[1] list.

> *Construction.* First and foremost, my PIPE exists to help me build things. This includes editing, compiling, debugging and profiling.

> *Communication.* Software, and the process of its construction, involves many kinds of communication:

---

[1] Based on a UNIX shell filename pattern that would match files named after the items in the list, and pronouncing the '*' character 'star'.

- with colleagues (directly, during the process of development; or indirectly, via the software itself);
- with managers;
- with customers and users;
- with computers;
- with myself, even, via the software I build with it.

Co-operation. Software development is rarely done by individuals in isolation; co-operation is almost always involved somewhere in the process. This is related to communication, but is more about the provision of tools that allow people to work together on something, which goes beyond just being able to exchange information about it. It includes planning and budgeting, where appropriate (it isn't just managers who do this).

Correctness. I need to know that I've built what I intended to. This implies a way of reconciling the actual and the intended artefacts.

Completeness. I need to know when to stop building, because to continue would be a waste. Additionally, I need to be able to predict when I'm likely to stop for planning purposes, and so being able to find out what's done and what's outstanding is of value.

Consistency. Not just between parts of a system that are designed to interface, but between different abstractions of the system that describe the same logical constructs, and between the work product of people and standards they are meant to follow.

Concealment. Software systems contain so many 'parts', and can be regarded in so many different ways, that it is essential to be able to hide most of the system most of the time just in order to get any work done. A variety of de facto limitations (from screen size and resolution through to human perceptual limitations) operate here anyway, but it's always handy to be able not only to construct ad hoc views of system components, but also to be able to juxtapose them in arbitrary ways to make visual comparisons.

Complexity Control. One of the reasons why software systems are becoming harder to build is because computer companies keeping upping the technical ante to generate new business, and customers keep buying it, in more than one sense. So the core of your application might be just accounting (to mention a boring-but-common example), but by the time it's been wrapped in vendor independence, stuffed with standards compliance, shot through with internationalisation, been made network-aware, client-serving and object-oriented, then dunked in a bucket of acronyms before having a graphical front end nailed on for good measure, its own programmers wouldn't recognise it. The point being, all this cruft adds to the complexity of the product, and since I probably used third-party products for all these 'details' (because I wanted to finish the program before I retire), I now have an unpredictable variety of interfaces to sort out.

Comprehension. Because I need to understand what I'm doing. This breaks into comprehension of the problem and of the solution.

Conceptualising. Sometime I need to create things that haven't existed before, so tools to help with this are valuable.

3. Desirable Features

Suppose the Software Fairy granted me n wishes, where n was not too small. What would I use those wishes to ask for in my PIPE? Well, in no particular order, and conveniently ignoring the need to trade things off against each other (after all, these are wishes), I'd like:

Multi-language, Multi-paradigm Support. In these days of heterogeneous networks, client–server architectures and integrated systems, it's becoming difficult to imagine the construction of any non-trivial piece of software that doesn't involve multiple languages and multiple programming paradigms. When I say languages, I don't just mean obvious ones like C or SQL or Lisp, but fiddling little ones like command-line interpreters, pattern matching languages, grammars, communication protocols and user interface dialogues; English and other national languages (for documentation, of course, but a lot of messages, prompts and comments could do with being spelling- and grammar-checked[2]); even languages I find it necessary to invent to get a job done. And because the different languages usually end up mixed up together, it's not good enough to be able to handle only one of them at a time, my PIPE must be able to handle them together with the minimum of prompting from me about which one is which (although this will sometimes be necessary).

For example, one project for a current client involves: an object-oriented system design; two main procedural implementation languages (the Bourne shell and ANSI C); a variety of smaller accessory languages in various UNIX system commands (awk, grep, sed, ...); a declarative definition for building the system (make); and event-driven servers controlling stateful objects in the file system and communicating through a custom language (defined with yacc and lex) over TCP/IP with program execution, command-line and full-screen user interface clients. And this is a fairly simple system!

Comprehensibility, Predictability. When using my PIPE, I need to be able to understand what it is presenting to me; no "what does that mean?", "where is it getting that from?" or "why is it doing that?" When time is money (and it usually is to someone in this business), time spent scratching my head is money wasted.

I also need to be able to predict the behaviour of my PIPE, so that when I'm building something with it, I'm building what I think I am.

Both of these require that I come to understand my PIPE, which will certainly require some effort on my part. However, if I could spread that effort out over a period, and be able to learn piecemeal, it would encourage me to make it. If I could leverage my knowledge of existing systems, it would be more encouraging still. Of course, it helps the most to have a PIPE that is actually understandable in the first place. Probably the cheapest way to make my PIPE understandable is to provide its entire source code along with it, and available for browsing from within on demand.

Programmability, Extendibility, Automation. It's as preposterous to suggest that a single programming environment could meet the needs of all programmers as it is to suggest that a single programming language can meet them. Consequently, my PIPE should allow itself to be customised and extended.

Being programmable is an esoteric feature of most computer applications, but this rule is specifically inverted for programmer's applications, since programmability is (by definition) what programmers expect. But being programmable isn't enough, because of the need to handle situations that the original developers didn't anticipate,

---

[2] vi under HP-UX can display: "1 characters, 1 lines, 1 more files to edit"

so my PIPE is also extendible by allowing new capabilities to be added after the fact. A special case of programmability is automation of repetitive tasks, and this is as valuable to programmers as macros are to any other application.

Self-documenting, Prompting, Marlene Mode. The entire set of documentation for my PIPE should be available within my PIPE, including the means to amend the documentation where appropriate. This includes being able to make personal annotations, and the ability to repair actual defects in the documents themselves. I should be able to call up documentation and help appropriate to the context I'm in and to the tasks I'm performing.

When I'm learning how to use some new gadget or feature, I should be able to get a helping hand from my PIPE in the form of prompts, hints or whatever is appropriate. I should also be able to say, "I vant to be alone", and completely avoid the documentation and help if I so wish — I hold on to helping hands; they don't hold on to me (for a good example of how not to do this, see Omnis 7 for the Macintosh).

Visibility. As noted in the item on 'concealment' above, being able to make choices about what is visible to the programmer is of value. This applies not just to the artefacts being constructed by the programmer, but to the tools used in the construction. In short, I don't just want to be able to drive my PIPE, I want to be able to look under the bonnet and see how the engine works.

Customisability. Because the backgrounds and preferences of the individual users will be different, my PIPE should be customisable. It should be possible to alter user interface behaviour, of course, but it should also be possible to alter task-related parts of the system too, such as what happens whenever an object is visited.

Self-applicability. We have to build and maintain this system using something, so why not the PIPE itself? This is not the stereotypical academic stunt of writing a language's compiler in the language itself (which tends to lead to the erroneous conclusion of universal applicability), but rather a test of the power of the environment (it'll be complex, so if it can't maintain itself, it probably can't maintain anything else useful either).

Easy Context Switching. In too many programming environments, one is either stuck in a single type of dialogue with the system (such as entering code or drawing state diagrams), or the overhead of switching from one mode to another is prohibitive. Since humans find it quite easy to switch contexts when working, it seems that the least their tools can do is not impede the process.

Undo Everywhere. Okay, I admit it, sometimes I push the wrong button or type 'Yes' when I mean 'No'. Extensive research leads me to believe that I am not alone in erring[3]. My PIPE would be understanding, and would let me recover from just about any stupid action. (Note that an 'Are you sure? Y/N' interface is not an acceptable substitute for an 'Oops!' button.)

Good Interactive Performance. This doesn't mean that everything should happen in the blink of an eye; rather that timely feedback should be the order of the day. In addition, though, common interface actions (like window creation) should be faster than uncommon ones (like building a garage)[4].

---

[3] "To err is human; to forgive, beyond the scope of the operating system." Anon.
[4] I guess this rules out the X Window System, then. Just kidding, MIT!

Control Over Asynchronous Events. I don't expect that every action I begin should have to run to completion before I start something else (for example, I shouldn't have to wait until the compiler finishes before I can edit some documentation). So it's natural that I should be able to run processes asynchronously ('in the background'). However, once I start something running independently, I should be able to get it under control again if I want to. Foreground versus background shouldn't be a once-only choice.

Lab Notebook. There should be a set of notes that I can access, maintained by my PIPE, that I can browse and add to, but not modify or delete. These notes should be time-stamped and linked to the context I was in. This 'lab notebook' should be accessible easily to encourage me to make notes at any time. This is analogous to the real lab notebooks maintained by engineers to capture random ideas and thoughts as well as specific task-related work.

Integration of Documentation. One of the banes of any engineering manager's life is getting the engineers whom she manages to keep the documentation current. One of the banes of the engineers' lives is maintaining documentation as separate items from the engineered objects. With physical objects such as buildings and computers, this is understandable, but with software there is no excuse, at least in theory. In practice the logical separation of most documentation systems from the software systems they describe is a barrier to maintaining both in sync. My PIPE would have integration of documents and software to the extent that document templates in house-standard form could be derived from software, and the details linked to software components. This would allow the system to highlight to the programmer which of the two could need attention following a change in one. Of course, automatic documentation (i.e. deriving the design rationale, requirements, and system specification from the code) is not implied by this, since I consider this impossible in any practical sense.

Configuration Management. In most models of the software development process, the phase after testing is glibly called 'maintenance'. Given its dominant position in the resource consumption of the software development process, it perhaps should be called: 'the most expensive mess you've ever been in, and you can't get out now, ha, ha, ha. 'In order to help control the cost of 'maintenance', my PIPE would contain features to nominate configured items (such as software components, libraries, compilers, documents, product lists, and almost anything else that could possibly change). Then access to the configured items would be tracked and individuals made accountable for changes to them; auditing tools would allow any particular program to be interrogated about its identity and known associates; version control would be applied ubiquitously to ensure that changes didn't go unnoticed, and that previous versions could be recovered; and release control would make it possible to know what went where, when.

Non-directed Work. Most work done in a day relates to specific tasks at hand, but some doesn't. Sometimes I have an idea to solve a problem on something I know I'll be working on next week, and I just want to whip up a little program to try it out. Sometimes a colleague calls to ask my advice on how to do something and the result is the need to prepare some snippet of code. And sometimes I have a spare half-hour, and I want to refresh your memory about some programming technique. So my PIPE would allow me interrupt whatever I was working on at the time and work on something completely unrelated for a while. arbitrary work order with consistency checking I am unaware of a single programmer who develops software strictly in the order that textbook authors find convenient to explain. Environments that attempt to force such orders on the development process fail (either they fall into disuse, or they get subverted). My PIPE would let be build systems in any reasonable order, and provide help with consistency and completeness.

Host Independence. The computing world is moving towards vendor-independence; my PIPE should be a portable PIPE.

Backward Compatibility. Unfortunately, my PIPE doesn't predate all the software in the world, so if it is to be useful, it must accommodate the needs of that software. This does not mean that it need be constrained by what was thought sufficient five or ten or twenty-five years before; but it must be capable of accepting that software and either working with it or (better) bringing it up to the new standard.

Object Trading. My PIPE doesn't stand alone in the world either. To be useful, it must be able to exchange information with other packages and environments. So it must be able to export its objects to others, and import theirs. A variety of standards, both de facto and de jure, already exist for this kind of thing, and one of the most widely followed is plain ASCII text. Where practical, it should be possible to obtain a representation for any kind of object in plain text form (it's theoretically possible for any object anyway).
Note that it would be silly to require that my PIPE work with such representations internally, but it would be pompous to assert that such representations were unnecessary, because ...

Leveraging Existing Tools. ... by not having them, you would be denying the ability to work with a wide range of existing tools, and there isn't any sense in requiring the wholesale re-invention of perfectly adequate toolsets.

Advisory Constraints. I want my PIPE to tell me when I attempt something dubious or unconventional or known to be a source of error. But unless there are overriding reasons to the contrary, I want to be able to say: "damn the engines, full speed ahead!"

Measurement. Static and dynamic analysis of production programs are valuable features of my PIPE, because they let me compare the program with the specification, with other similar programs and with expected system performance criteria. Of course, the statistics need to be useful (counting semi-colons is almost as useless as counting sheep), but software metrics is slowly becoming more valuable and so should be supported. In addition, profiling of running programs is almost essential these days, where the software often threatens to drown the hardware[5].

Testing. More and more testing is becoming automated today, and this trend will increase in the future as the ratio of programmer cost to computer cost continues upwards. This means my PIPE must provide support for automatic testing of software, including capturing of test results and comparison against predetermined standards.

Aesthetically Appealing to Programmers. If I don't like using my PIPE, then I probably won't, and that would be a waste of the effort that went into its construction.

Fun. I'd like to have a little fun with my PIPE occasionally. I'm only human, after all.

---

[5] My 25 MIPS workstation can often take five seconds to copy a piece of text between two different windows. My simple-minded analysis reveals that copying 25 characters costs 125 million CPU instructions, or 5 million instructions to copy one byte.

I realise that the above is only a PIPE-dream[6], but parts of it are already apparent in systems available today (the UNIX timesharing system, the GNU Emacs, HP SoftBench, and the integrating sub-system beneath Microsoft Windows)[7].

4. Discussion Questions

These are the questions I presented at the workshop, and brief notes on the responses that they provoked.

1. *Are the problems of programming in the small a subset of programming in the large in such a way that one set of tools can be used along the software complexity scale, or must we have different tools for different places?*
   There seemed to be no clear answer to this, although my intuition leads my to believe that the answer is: 'maybe'.

2. *What are the areas where technological solutions are appropriate, versus non-technological ones (managerial, political, organisational, etc.)?*
   The predominant response to this was: 'better education of engineers'. Unfortunately, this may only impact a relatively small percentage of the development community at any one time, and those who have least immediate influence (new entrants into the profession). A subsidiary topic that arose was about the quality of CS education, and the need to include something in the courses that make it clear that CS isn't everything.

3. *Is there an Esperanto that can be used to facilitate communication between software engineers and psychologists? (Note: by Esperanto, I meant universal second language, not replacement first language).*
   The general attitude here was: Cognitive Dimensions of Notations (Green, 1989; Green, 1990c; Green, 1991), although some bright spark suggested that 'better abstractions' would help. Gee, thanks.

4. *What are the best places to concentrate development effort to make the biggest improvements in software engineering in the next few years?*
   For some strange reason, no-one seemed to discuss this. For what they're worth, I think the greatest potential benefits will come from the greater availability of integrating frameworks that set policy on things, cutting down the number of trivial decisions needed by the programmer to get any work done, and the proliferation of special-purpose toolsets for use within these frameworks that provide acceptable canned solutions to problems (the most prominent example at the moment is Microsoft Visual Basic). These may be the first useful manifestations of Brad Cox's 'SoftwareICs' (Cox, 1986); unfortunate that they only appear on IBM PCs, but hopefully this will change.

Frank Wales
Grep Ltd

---

[6] Groan.

[7] I specifically exclude the Apple Macintosh from this list, because writing professional quality software on the Mac is a balls-aching task, and this is not because it's a WIMP environment, but because the Mac was conceived as a stand-alone user-centred machine, and few concessions have been made to accommodate the needs of the software developer.

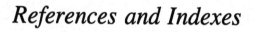

References and Indexes

References

Abelson, H & Sussman, G J (1985), *Structure and Interpretation of Computer Programs*, MIT Press.

Adelson, B (1981), "Problem Solving and the Development of Abstract Categories in Programming Languages", *Memory and Cognition* 9, pp.422–433.

Adelson, B (1984), "When Novices Surpass Experts: The Difficulty of a Task May Increase with Expertise", *Journal of Experimental Psychology: Learning, Memory, and Cognition* 10 (3), pp.483–495.

Adelson, B & Soloway, E (1985), "The Role of Domain Experience in Software Design", *IEEE Transactions on Software Engineering* SE-11 (11), pp.1351–1360.

Adelson, B & Soloway, E (1988), "A Model of Software Design", in *The Nature of Expertise*, M T H Chi, R Glaser & M J Farr [eds.], Lawrence Erlbaum Associates.

Alexander, C (1964), *The Synthesis of Form*, Harvard University Press.

Alexander, H (1987), *Formally-based Tools and Techniques for Human–Computer Dialogues*, Ellis Horwood.

Allard, F, Graham, S & Paarsalu, M E (1980), "Perception in Sport: Basketball", *Journal of Sports Psychology* 2, pp.14–21.

Allard, F & Starkes, J L (1980), "Perception in Sport: Volleyball", *Journal of Sports Psychology* 2, pp.22–33.

Alty, J L & Mullin, J (1989), "Dialogue Specification in the GRADIENT Dialogue System", in *People and Computers V*, A Sutcliffe & L Macaulay [eds.], Cambridge University Press, pp.152–168, Proceedings of HCI'89.

Anderson, J (1983), *The Architecture of Cognition*, Harvard University Press.

Anderson, J R (1987), "Methodologies for Studying Human Knowledge", *Behavioral and Brain Sciences* 10, pp.467–505.

Anderson, J R, Farrell, R & Sauers, R (1984), "Learning to Program in Lisp", *Cognitive Science* 8, pp.87–129.

Arens, Y, Miller, L, Shapiro, S C & Sondheimer, N K (1988), "Automatic Construction of User-interface Displays", in *Proceedings of the 7th National Conference on Artificial Intelligence*, USC/ISI, pp.808–813.

Atwood, M E & Ramsey, H R (1978), "Cognitive Structures in the Comprehension and Memory of Computer Programs: An Investigation of Computer Program Debugging", US Army Research Institute for the Behavioral and Social Sciences, Va: Alexandra, Technical report (TR-78-A21).

Bachman, C (1988), "A CASE for Reverse Engineering", *Datamation* July.

Baecker, R M & Marcus, A (1990), *Human Factors and Typography for more Readable Programs*, ACM Press.

Baecker, R M & Sherman, D (1981), "Sorting Out Sorting", Narrated colour videotape, 30 minutes, presented at ACM SIGGRAPH'81.

Baker, K D, Ball, L J, Culverhouse, P F, Dennis, I, Evans, J St B T, Jagodzinski, A P, Pearce, P D, Scothern, D G C & Venner, G M (1991), "A Psychologically-based Intelligent Design Aid", in *Intelligent CAD Systems III*, P J W ten Hagen & P J Veerkamp [eds.], Springer-Verlag.

Barth, P S (1986), "An Object-oriented Approach to Graphical Interfaces", *ACM Transactions on Graphics* 5 (2), pp.142–172.

Basili, V & Mills, H D (1982a), "Understanding and Documenting Programs", *IEEE Transactions on Software Engineering* SE-8, pp.270–283.

Basili, V R & Mills, H D (1982b), "Understanding and Documenting Programs", *IEEE Computer* October, pp.18–37.

Basili, V R & Selby, R W (1987), "Comparing the Effectiveness of Software Testing Strategies", *IEEE Transactions on Software Engineering* SE-13, pp.1278–1296.

Belady, L (1985), "MCC: Planning the Revolution in Software", *IEEE Software* November, pp.68–73.

Bellamy, R K E & Carroll, J M (1990), "Redesign by Design", in *Proceedings of INTERACT'90 — Third IFIP Conference on Human–Computer Interaction*, D Diaper, D Gilmore, G Cockton & B Shackel [eds.], Elsevier Science (North-Holland).

Bellamy, R K E & Gilmore, D J (1990), "Programming Plans: Internal or External Structures", in *Lines of Thinking*, K J Gilhooly, M T G Keane, R H Logie & G Erdos [eds.] #2, John Wiley & Sons.

Bennett, K (1993), in *The REDO Compendium: Reverse Engineering for Software Maintenance*, H J van Zuylen [ed.], John Wiley & Sons.

Bennett, K H [ed.] (1989), *Software Engineering Environments: Research and Practice*, Ellis Horwood.

Bennett, W E, Boies, S J, Gould, J D, Greene, S L & Wiecha, C F (1989), "Transformations on a Dialog Tree: Rule-based Mapping of Content to Style", in *Proceedings of the ACM SIGGRAPH Symposium on User Interface Software and Technology*, pp.67–75.

Beshers, C M & Feiner, S K (1989), "Scope: Automated Generation of Graphical Interfaces", in *Proceedings of the ACM SIGGRAPH Symposium on User Interface Software and Technology*, pp.76–81.

Bisseret, A (1990), "Towards Computer-aided Text Production", in *Cognitive Ergonomics: Understanding, Learning and Designing Human–Computer Interaction*, P Falzon [ed.], Academic Press, pp.213–230.

Bloomfield, H & Ormerod, T C (1991), "Using Theories of Designer Behaviour to Develop a Design Support System", in *Contemporary Ergonomics*, E J Lovesey [ed.], Taylor & Francis.

Blumenthal, B (1990a), "Incorporating Metaphor in Automated Interface Designs", in *Proceedings of INTERACT'90 — Third IFIP Conference on Human–Computer Interaction*, D Diaper, D Gilmore, G Cockton & B Shackel [eds.], Elsevier Science (North-Holland).

Blumenthal, B (1990b), "Replaying Episodes of a Metaphoric Application Interface Designer", University of Texas Artificial Intelligence Lab, Austin, TX, USA, PhD thesis.

Blumenthal, B (1990c), "Strategies for Automatically Incorporating Metaphoric Attributes in Interface Designs", in *Proceedings of the 3rd User Interface Software and Technology Workshop*, Snowbird, Utah, USA.

Boehm, B W (1988), "A Spiral Model of Software Development and Enhancement", *IEEE Computer* 21, pp.61–72.

Bohner, S A (1990), "Technology Assessment on Software Re-engineering", Contel Technology Center, 15000 Conference Center Drive, PO Box 10814, Chantilly, Virginia 22021-3803, USA, Report Number CTC-TR-90-001-P.

Bonar, J & Liffick, B W (1990), "A Visual Programming Language for Novices", in *Principles of Visual Programming Systems*, S-K Chang [ed.], Prentice–Hall.

Booch, G (1986), "Object-oriented Development", *IEEE Transactions on Software Engineering* SE-12 (2), pp.211–221.

du Boulay, B & O'Shea, T (1981), "Teaching Novices Programming", in *Computing Skills and the User Interface*, M J Coombs & J L Alty [eds.], Academic Press.

Bowen, K A (1982), "Programming with Full First-order Logic", in *Machine Intelligence 10*, Hayes, Michie & Pao [eds.], Ellis Horwood, pp.421–440.

Bower, G H, Black, J B & Turner, T J (1979), "Scripts in Text Comprehension and Memory", *Cognitive Psychology* 11, pp.177–220.

Bowerman, M (1982), "Starting to Talk Worse: Clues to Language Acquisition from Children's Late Speech Errors", in *U-shaped Behavioral Growth*, S Strauss [ed.], Academic Press, pp.101–145.

Bowers, J M (1991), *Studies in Computer Supported Cooperative Work*, Elsevier Science (North-Holland).

Bratko, I (1990), *Prolog Programming for Artificial Intelligence*, Addison Wesley.

Brayshaw, M & Eisenstadt, M (1991), "A Practical Graphical Prolog Tracer", *International Journal of Man–Machine Studies* 35 (5).

Breuker, J (1991), "Learning Construction Problem Solving", in *Proceedings of the International Conference on the Learning Sciences, Evanston, IL*, Birnbaum [ed.], AACE.

Brna, P, Pain, H & du Boulay, B (1990), "Teaching, Learning and Using Prolog", *Instructional Science* 19 (4–5).

Brooks, F (1987), "No Silver Bullet: Essence and Accidents of Software Engineering", *IEEE Computer* 20 (4), pp.10–19.

Brooks, R (1983), "Towards a Theory of the Comprehension of Computer Programs", *International Journal of Man–Machine Studies* 18, pp.543–554.

Brooks, R (1990), "Categories of Programming Knowledge and their Application (Introduction to Special Issue)", *International Journal of Man–Machine Studies* 33 (3), pp.241–246.

Brown, D, Totterdell, P & Norman, M (1990), *Adaptive User Interfaces*, Academic Press, Computer and People Series.

Brown, D C & Chandrasekaran, B (1989), *Design Problem Solving, Knowledge Structures and Control Strategies*, Pitman.

Brown, M H (1988), *Algorithm Animation*, MIT Press.

Buchanan, D (1991), "Figure–Ground Reversal in System Development and Implementation: From HCI to OSI", in *Proceedings of the Conference on Human Jobs and Computer Interfaces*, Tampere, Finland, pp.339–358.

Burgstaller, J, Grollmann, J, Kapsner, F (1989), *A User Interface Management System for Rapid Prototyping and Generation of Dialog Managers*, Elsevier Science (North-Holland).

Bush, E (1985), "The Automatic Restructuring of Cobol", in *Proceedings of Conference on Software Maintenance 1985*, pp.35–41.

Byrd, L (1980), "Understanding the Control Flow of Prolog Programs", in *Proceedings of the Logic Programming Workshop*, S Tarnlund [ed.], pp.127–138.

Byrne, R (1977), "Planning Meals: Problem-solving on a Real Database", *Cognition* 5, pp.287–332.

CSTB (1990), "Scaling Up: A Research Agenda for Software Engineering", *Communications of the ACM* 33 (3), pp.281–293, (Computer Science and Technology Board).

Campbell, R L (1989), "Developmental Levels and Scenarios for Smalltalk Programming", IBM T J Watson Research Center, Yorktown Heights, NY, IBM Research Report.

Campbell, R L (1990), "Developmental Scenario Analysis of Smalltalk Programming", in *Proceedings of CHI'90: Human Factors in Computing Systems*, J C Chew & J Whiteside [eds.], ACM Press.

Carroll, J M (1990), "Infinite Detail and Emulation in an Ontologically Minimized HCI", in *Proceedings of CHI'90: Human Factors in Computing Systems*, J C Chew & J Whiteside [eds.], ACM Press, pp.321–329.

Carroll, J M & Campbell, R L (1989), "Artifacts as Psychological Theories: The Case of Human–Computer Interaction", *Behaviour & Information Technology* 8 (4), pp.247–256.

Carroll, J M & Carrithers, C (1984), "Training Wheels in a User Interface", *Communications of the ACM* 27, pp.800–606.

Carroll, J M & Kellogg, W A (1989), "Artifact as Theory Nexus: Hermeneutics meets Theory-based Design", in *Proceedings of CHI'89: Human Factors in Computing Systems*, K Bice & C H Lewis [eds.], ACM Press, pp.7–14.

Carroll, J M & Rosson, M B (1985), *Usability Specifications as a Tool in Iterative Development*, Advances in Human–Computer Interaction #1, Ablex.

Carroll, J M, Thomas, J C, Miller, L A & Friedman, H P (1980), "Aspects of Solution Structure in Design Problem Solving", *American Journal of Psychology* 93 (2), pp.269–284.

Carter, K (1989), "Methods for Designing with Users", in *Proceedings of the UMIST Workshop on Sociology of Software Design*.

Castell, A M (1986), "Human Factors in Technical Design: A Solution-driven Problem?", Department of Human Sciences, Loughborough University, UK, MSc Thesis.

Chase, W G & Simon, H A (1973), "Perception in Chess", *Cognitive Psychology* 4, pp.55–81.

Chignell, M H (1990), "A Taxonomy of User Interface Terminology", *ACM SIGCHI Bulletin* 21 (4), pp.27–34.

Chikofsky, E J & Cross, J H (1990), "Reverse Engineering and Design Recovery: A Taxonomy", *IEEE Software* 7 (1), pp.13–18.

Clark, H (1977), "Bridging", in *Thinking: Readings in Cognitive Science*, P N Johnson-Laird & P C Watson [eds.], Cambridge University Press.

Coad, P & Yourdon, E (1990), *Object Oriented Analysis*, Yourdon Press (Prentice–Hall).

Cobb, R & Mills, H (1990), "Engineering Software under Statistical Quality Control", *IEEE Computer*, pp.44–54.

Colgan, L, Rankin, P & Spence, R (1991), "Steering Automated Design", in *Proceedings of Artificial Intelligence in Design '91*, J Gero [ed.], Butterworth–Heinemann.

Conklin, J & Begeman, M L (1988), "gIBIS: A Hypertext Tool for Exploratory Policy Discussion", in *Proceedings of CSCW'88*, Portland, Oregon.

Connelly, E M (1984), "Transformations of Software and Code May Lead to Reduced Errors", in *Proceedings of INTERACT'84 — First IFIP Conference on Human–Computer Interaction*, B Shackel [ed.], Elsevier Science (North-Holland).

Cordy, J R, Eliot, N L & Robertson, M G (1990), "Turing Tool: A User Interface to Aid in Software Maintenance Task", *IEEE Transactions on Software Engineering* 16 (3), pp.294–301.

Cox, B J (1986), *Object Oriented Programming: An Evolutionary Approach*, Addison Wesley.

Cox, B J (1990), "There *is* a Silver Bullet", *Byte* October.

Crookes, D, Murray, E, Smith, F J & Spence, I T A (1985), "A Voice Input Programming System", in *People and Computers: Designing the Interface*, P Johnson & S Cook [eds.], Cambridge University Press, Proceedings of HCI'85, Norwich, September.

Cross, N [ed.] (1984), *Developments in Design Methodology*, John Wiley & Sons.

Cunniff, N, Taylor, R P & Black, J B (1986)), "Does Programming Language Affect the Type of Conceptual Bugs in Beginners' Programs? A Comparison of FPL and Pascal", in *Studying the Novice Programmer*, E Soloway, J C Spohrer [eds.], ACM Press, (Reprinted in this volume from the original which appeared in Proceedings of CHI'86: Human Factors in Computing Systems, M Mantei & P Orbeton.

Curtis, B (1981), "Substantiating Programmer Variability", *Proceedings of the IEEE* 69 (7).

Curtis, B (1986), "By the Way, Did Anyone Study Any Real Programmers?", in *Empirical Studies of Programmers: 1st Workshop*, E Soloway & S Iyengar [eds.], Ablex, pp.256–262.

Curtis, B (1989a), *Software Reusability Volume 2: Applications and Experience*, Addison Wesley.

Curtis, B (1989b), "Five Paradigms in the Psychology of Programming", in *Handbook of Human–Computer Interaction*, M Helander [ed.], Elsevier Science (North-Holland).

Curtis, B, Krasner, H & Iscoe, N (1988), "A Field Study of the Software Design Process for Large Systems", *Communications of the ACM* 31 (11), pp.1268–1287.

Curtis, B, Krasner, H, Shen, V & Iscoe, N (1987), "On Building Software Process Models Under the Lamppost", in *Proceedings 9th International Conference on Software Engineering*, pp.96–103, March 30 – April 2, Monterey, CA , USA.

Curtis, B, Sheppard, S, Kruesi-Bailey, E, Bailey, J & Boehm-Davis, D (1989), "Experimental Evaluation of Software Documentation Formats", *Journal of Systems and Software* 9, pp.167–207.

Curtis, B, Sheppard, S B, Milliman, P, Borst, M A & Love, T (1979), "Measuring the Psychological Complexity of Software Maintenance Tasks with the Halstead and McCabe Metrics", *IEEE Transactions on Software Engineering* SE-5, pp.96–104.

Davies, S P (1989), "Skill Level and Strategic Differences in Plan Comprehension and Implementation", in *People and Computers V*, A Sutcliffe & L Macaulay [eds.], Cambridge University Press, pp.487–502, Proceedings of HCI'89.

Davies, S P (1990a), "The Nature and Development of Programming Plans", *International Journal of Man–Machine Studies* 32, pp.461–481.

Davies, S P (1990b), "Plans, Goals and Selection Rules in the Comprehension of Programming", *Behaviour & Information Technology* 9 (3), pp.201–214.

Davies, S P (1991a), "Characterizing the Program Design Activity: Neither Strictly Top-down nor Globally Opportunistic", *Behaviour & Information Technology* 10 (3), pp.173–190.

Davies, S P (1991b), "The Role of Notation and Knowledge Representation in the Determination of Programming Strategy", *Cognitive Science* 15, pp.547–572.

Davies, S P (1992), "Reconstructing the Design Process: Differences between Observed and Described Behaviour in a Software Design Task" (In preparation).

Denning, P (1988), "Awakening", *Communications of the ACM* 31 (11), pp.1254–1255.

Détienne, F (1989), "Une Revue des Etudes Psychologiques sur la Compréhension des Programmes Informatiques", *Technique et Science Informatiques* 8 (1), pp.5–20.

Détienne, F (1990a), "Expert Programming Knowledge: A Schema-based Approach", in *The Psychology of Programming*, J-M Hoc, T R G Green, R Samurçay & D J Gilmore [eds.], Academic Press, pp.205–222.

Détienne, F (1990b), "Difficulties in Designing with an Object-oriented Language: An Empirical Study", in *Proceedings of INTERACT'90 — Third IFIP Conference on Human–Computer Interaction*, D Diaper, D Gilmore, G Cockton & B Shackel [eds.], Elsevier Science (North-Holland), pp.971–976.

Détienne, F (1991a), "Reasoning from a Schema and from an Analog in Software Code Reuse", in *Empirical Studies of Programmers: 4th Workshop*, J Koenemann-Belliveau, T Moher & S P Robertson [eds.], Ablex, pp.5–22.

Détienne, F (1991b), "Reusing Solutions in Software Design Activity: An Empirical Study", *ACM SIGCHI Bulletin* October.

Détienne, F & Soloway, E (1990), "An Empirically-derived Control Structure for the Process of Program Understanding", *International Journal of Man–Machine Studies* 33 (3), pp.323–342.

Dewal, S & Kelter, U (1989), "Role-based Requirements Definition for Software Factories using Reusable Requirements Package", in *Software Engineering Environments: Research and Practice*, K H Bennett [ed.], Ellis Horwood.

Dichev, C & du Boulay, J B H (1989), "An Enhanced Trace Tool for Prolog", in *Proceedings of the Third International Conference, Children in the Information Age*, Sofia, Bulgaria, pp.149–163.

Dijkstra, E W (1976), *A Discipline of Programming*, Prentice–Hall.

Doane, S, Pellegrino, J & Klatzky, R (1990), "Expertise in a Computer Operating System: Conceptualization and Performance", *Human–Computer Interaction* 5, pp.267–304.

Domingue, J & Eisenstadt, M (1989), "A New Metaphor for the Graphical Explanation of Forward Chaining Rule Execution", in *Proceedings of The 11th International Joint Conference on Artificial Intelligence*, pp.129–134.

Downs, E, Clare, P & Coe, I (1988), *Structured Systems Analysis and Design Method*, Prentice–Hall.

Dzida, W (1983), "Das IFIP-Modell für Benutzerschnittstellen", *Office Management*, pp.6–8.

Dzida, W (1987), "On Tools and Interfaces", in *Psychological Issues of Human Computer Interaction in the Work Place*, M Frese, E Ulich & W Dzida [eds.], North-Holland, pp.339–355.

Egan, D E & Schwartz, B J (1979), "Chunking in Recall of Symbolic Drawings", *Memory and Cognition* 1, pp.149–158.

Ehn, P (1988), *Work-oriented Design of Computer Artifacts*, Almquist & Wiksell International.

Eisenstadt, M & Brayshaw, M (1988), "The Transparent Prolog Machine (TPM): An Execution Model and Graphical Debugger for Logic Programming", *Journal of Logic Programming* 5 (4), pp.1–66.

Eisenstadt, M, Brayshaw, M & Paine, J (1991), *The Transparent Prolog Machine*, Intellect.

Eisenstadt, M, Domingue, J, Rajan, T & Motta, E (1990), "Visual Knowledge Engineering", *IEEE Transactions on Software Engineering* 16 (10), pp.1164–1177.

Ekardt, H-P, Hengstenberg, H & Löffler, R (1988), "Subjektivität und die Stofflichkeit des Arbeitsprozesses", in *Hochschule — Beruf — Gesellschaft*, G Gorzka [ed.], pp.13–51.

Ellis, M & Stroustrup, B (1990), *The Annotated C++ Reference*, Addison Wesley.

England, D (1988), "Graphical Prototyping of Graphical Tools", in *People and Computers IV*, D M Jones & R Winder [eds.], Cambridge University Press, pp.407–420, Proceedings of HCI'88.

Essink, L J B (1986), "A Modelling Approach to Information System Development", in *Information Systems Design Methodologies: Improving the Practice*, T W Olle, H G Sol & A A Verrijn-Stuart [eds.], Elsevier Science (North-Holland).

Feiner, S & Beshers, C (1990), "Worlds within Worlds: Metaphors for Exploring n-Dimensional Virtual Worlds", in *Proceedings of The ACM SIGGRAPH Symposium on User Inteface Software and Technology (UIST)*, ACM Press, pp.76–83.

Fenton, N E (1991), *Software Metrics: A Rigorous Approach*, Chapman & Hall.

Finkelstein, A (1989), "Not Waving but Drowning: Representation Schemes for Modelling Software Development", in *Proceedings of 11th International Conference on Software Engineering*, IEEE CS Press.

Fischer, G (1987), "Cognitive View of Reuse and Redesign", *IEEE Software* July, pp.60–72.

Fischer, G & Girgensohn, A (1990), "End-User Modifiability in Design Environments", in *Proceedings of CHI'90: Human Factors in Computing Systems*, J C Chew & J Whiteside [eds.], ACM Press, pp.183–191.

Fischer, G, Girgensohn, A, Nakakoji, K & Redmiles, D (1992), "Supporting Software Designers with Integrated, Domain-oriented Environments", *IEEE Transactions on Software Engineering* (To appear).

Fischer, G & Lemke, A (1988), "Construction Kits and Design Environments: Steps Toward Human Problem-domain Communication", *Human–Computer Interaction* 3 (3), pp.179–222.

Fischer, G, Lemke, A C, Mastaglio, T & Morch, A (1991a), "The Role of Critiquing in Cooperative Problem Solving", *ACM Transactions on Office Information Systems* 9 (2), pp.123–151.

Fischer, G, Lemke, A C, McCall, R & Morch, A (1991b), "Making Argumentation Serve Design", *Human–Computer Interaction* 6 (3-4), pp.393–419.

Fischer, G, McCall, R & Morch, A (1989), "Design Environments for Constructive and Argumentative Design", in *Proceedings of CHI'89: Human Factors in Computing Systems*, K Bice & C H Lewis [eds.], ACM Press, pp.269–275.

Fischer, G & Nakakoji, K (1991), "Making Design Objects Relevant to the Task at Hand,", in *Proceedings of AAAI-91 (Ninth National Conference on Artificial Intelligence)*, AAAI Press/MIT Press, pp.67–73.

Fischer, G & Rathke, C (1988), "Knowledge-Based Spreadsheet Systems", in *Proceedings of AAAI-88 (Seventh National Conference on Artificial Intelligence)*, Morgan Kaufmann Publishers, pp.802–807.

Fischer, G & Reeves, B N (1992), "Beyond Intelligent Interfaces: Exploring, Analyzing and Creating Success Models of Cooperative Problem Solving", *Applied Intelligence* 1 (Special Issue Intelligent Interfaces), pp.311–332.

Flon, L (1975), "On Research in Structured Programming", *ACM SIGPLAN Notices* October, pp.16–17.

Floyd, R W (1978), "The Paradigms of Programming", *Communications of the ACM* 22 (8), pp.455–460.

Foley, J, Kim, Won Chul, Kovacevic, S & Murray, K (1988), "The user interface design environment", Department of Electrical Engineering and Computer Science, George Washington University, Technical Report GWU-IIST-88-4.

Foster, J R (1990), "Proceedings of the Third Annual Workshop on Software Maintenance", Durham.

Fowler, C J, Macaulay, L, Castell, A M & Hutt, A (1989), "An Evaluation of a Human Factors Based Requirements Capture Methodology", in *People and Computers V*, A Sutcliffe & L Macaulay [eds.], Cambridge University Press, Proceedings of HCI'89.

Frohlich, D M & Luff, P (1989), "Conversational Resources for Situated Action", in *Proceedings of CHI'89: Human Factors in Computing Systems*, K Bice & C H Lewis [eds.], ACM Press.

Gero, J (1991), "Foreword", in *Exploration and Innovation in Design: Towards a Computational Model*, D Navinchandra, Springer-Verlag.

Gilb, T (1989), "Software Project Management for the 1990's", in *Proceedings of Focus World '89*, pp.1–23.

Gilmore, D J (1986), "Structural Visibility and Program Comprehension", in *People and Computers: Designing for Usability*, M D Harrison & A Monk [eds.], Cambridge University Press, Proceedings of HCI'86.

Gilmore, D J (1990a), "Expert Programming Knowledge: A Strategic Approach", in *The Psychology of Programming*, J-M Hoc, T R G Green, R Samurçay & D J Gilmore [eds.], Academic Press, pp.223–234.

Gilmore, D J (1990b), "Models of Debugging", in *Proceedings Fifth European Conference on Cognitive Ergonomics ECCE-5*, Urbino, Italy.

Gilmore, D J & Green, T R G (1984), "Comprehension and Recall of Miniature Programs", *International Journal of Man–Machine Studies* 21, pp.31–48.

Gilmore, D J & Green, T R G (1987), "Are 'Programming Plans' Psychologically Real Outside Pascal?", in *Proceedings of INTERACT'87 — Second IFIP Conference on Human–Computer Interaction*, H-J Bullinger & B Shackel [eds.], Elsevier Science (North-Holland), pp.497–503.

Gilmore, D J & Green, T R G (1988), "Programming Plans and Programming Expertise", *Quarterly Journal of Experimental Psychology* 40A, pp.423–442.

Goguen, J A & Tardon, J J (1979), "An Introduction to OBJ: A Language for Writing and Testing Formal Algebraic Program Specifications", in *Proceedings Specification of Reliable Software*, IEEE, pp.170–189.

Goldberg, A (1984), *Smalltalk-80, The Interactive Programming Environment*, Addison Wesley.

Goldberg, A & Robson, D (1983), *Smalltalk-80: The Language and its Implementation*, Addison Wesley.

Goodman, D (1987), *The Complete HyperCard Handbook*, Bantam Books.

Gould, J (1988), "How to Design Usable Systems", in *Handbook of Human–Computer Interaction*, M Helander [ed.], Elsevier Science (North-Holland), pp.757–789.

Gray, W D & Anderson, J R (1987), "Change-episodes in Coding: When and How do Programmers Change their Code?", in *Empirical Studies of Programmers: 2nd Workshop*, G Olson, S Sheppard & E Soloway [eds.], Ablex, pp.185–197.

Green, M (1985), "Report on Dialogue Specification Techniques", in *User Interface Management Systems*, G E Pfaff [ed.], Springer-Verlag, pp.9–20, Proceedings of the Workshop on User Interface Management Systems held in Seeheim, FRG, November 1-3, 1983.

Green, M (1986), "A Survey of Three Dialogue Models", *ACM Transactions on Graphics* 5 (3), pp.244–275.

Green, T R G (1977), "Conditional Program Statements and their Comprehensibility to Professional Programmers", *Journal of Occupational Psychology* 50, pp.93–109.

Green, T R G (1989), "Cognitive Dimensions of Notations", in *People and Computers V*, A Sutcliffe & L Macaulay [eds.], Cambridge University Press, pp.443–460, Proceedings of HCI'89.

Green, T R G (1990a), "Programming Languages as Information Structures", in *The Psychology of Programming*, J-M Hoc, T R G Green, R Samurçay & D J Gilmore [eds.], Academic Press, pp.117–138.

Green, T R G (1990b), "The Nature of Programming", in *The Psychology of Programming*, J-M Hoc, T R G Green, R Samurçay & D J Gilmore [eds.], Academic Press, pp.21–44.

Green, T R G (1990c), "The Cognitive Dimension of Viscosity: A Sticky Problem for HCI", in *Proceedings of INTERACT'90 — Third IFIP Conference on Human–Computer Interaction*, D Diaper, D Gilmore, G Cockton & B Shackel [eds.], Elsevier Science (North-Holland), pp.79–86.

Green, T R G (1991), "Describing Information Artifacts with Cognitive Dimensions and Structure Maps", in *People and Computers VI: Usability Now!*, D Diaper & N Hammond [eds.], Cambridge University Press, Proceedings of HCI'91.

Green, T R G, Bellamy, R K E & Parker, J M (1987), "Parsing and Gnisrap: A Model of Device Use", in *Empirical Studies of Programmers: 2nd Workshop*, G Olson, S Sheppard & E Soloway [eds.], Ablex, pp.132–146.

Green, T R G, Gilmore, D J, Blumenthal, B B, Davies, S & Winder, R (1992), "Towards a Cognitive Browser for OOPS", *International Journal of Human–Computer Interaction* 4 (1), pp.1–34.

Green, T R G, Gilmore, D J & Winder, R (1990), "Towards a Cognitive Browser for OOPS: The Program as a Rich Information Structure", in *Proceedings of "Intelligent Access to Information Systems" Conference*, GMD-IPSI, Darmstadt, 1–2 November.

Green, T R G, Winder, R, Gilmore, D J, Davies, S P & Hendry, D (1992), "Designing a Cognitive Browser for Object-oriented Programming", *AISB Quarterly* 81, pp.17–20.

de Groot, A D (1965), *Thought and Choice in Chess*, Mouton.

Grudin, J (1991), "CSCW: The Convergence of Two Development Contexts", in *Proceedings of CHI'91: Human Factors in Computing Systems (Reaching through Technology)*, S P Robertson, G M Olson & J S Olson [eds.], ACM Press.

Guindon, R (1990a), "Knowledge Exploited by Experts During Software System Design", *International Journal of Man–Machine Studies* 33 (3), pp.279–304.

Guindon, R (1990b), "Designing the Design Process: Exploiting Opportunistic Thoughts", *Human–Computer Interaction* 5, pp.305–344.

Guindon, R & Curtis, B (1988), "Control of Cognitive Processes during Software Design: What Tools are Needed?", in *Empirical Studies of Programmers: 1st Workshop*, E Soloway & S Iyengar [eds.], Ablex, pp.263–269.

Guindon, R, Krasner, H & Curtis, B (1987), "Breakdowns and Processes during the Early Activities of Software Design by Professionals", in *Empirical Studies of Programmers: 2nd Workshop*, G Olson, S Sheppard & E Soloway [eds.], Ablex.

Hale, D P & Haworth, D A (1991), "Cognitive Processes in Software Maintenance", *Journal of Software Maintenance* 3, pp.85–106.

Harandi, M T & Ning, J Q (1990), "Knowledge-Based Program Analysis", *IEEE Software* 7 (1), pp.74–81.

Harel, D (1988), "Statecharts: A Visual Formalism for Complex Systems", *Science of Computer Programming* 8, pp.231–274.

Hartson, H R & Hix, D (1989), "Human–Computer Interface Development: Concepts and Systems for Its Management", *ACM Computing Surveys* 21 (1), pp.5–92.

Hatley, D J & Pirbhai, I (1987), *Strategies for Real Time System Specification*, Dorset House.

Hayes, J R & Flower, L S (1980), "Identifying the Organization of Writing Processes", in *Cognitive Processes in Writing*, L W Gregg & E R Steinberg [eds.], Lawrence Erlbaum Associates.

Hayes-Roth, B & Hayes-Roth, F (1979), "A Cognitive Model of Planning", *Cognitive Science* 3, pp.275–310.

Henderson, A & Kyng, M (1991), "There's No Place Like Home: Continuing Design in Use", in *Design at Work: Cooperative Design of Computer Systems*, J Greenbaum & M Kyng [eds.], Lawrence Erlbaum Associates, pp.219–240.

Henry, R R, Whaley, K M & Forstall, B (1990), "The University of Washington Illustrating Compiler", in *Proceedings of The ACM SIGPLAN '90 Conference on Programming Language Design and Implementation*, ACM Press, pp.223–233.

Herczeg, J & Hohl, H (1991), "Building Browsers for the Common Lisp Object System", in *Proceedings of EastEurOOPe'91, Conference, Tutorials and Exhibition on Object-oriented Programming*, pp.27–36.

Herczeg, J, Hohl, H & Schwab, T (1991), "XIT — A Multi-Layered Tool for User Interface Design", in *Human Aspects in Computing: Design and Use of Interactive Systems and Work with Terminals*, H-J Bullinger [ed.], Elsevier Science (North-Holland), pp.678–683.

Herczeg, M (1989), "USIT: A Toolkit for User Interface Toolkits", in *Designing and Using Human–Computer Interfaces and Knowledge Based Systems*, G Salvendy & M J Smith [eds.], Elsevier Science (North-Holland), pp.605–612.

Hermann, R (1990), "SX/Tools — Externe Architektur Spezifikation", Siemens AG, Internal Paper.

Hill, R D (1987), "Event–Response systems: A Technique for Specifying Multi-threaded Dialogues", in *Proceedings of CHI+GI'87: Human Factors in Computing Systems and Graphics Interface*, J M Carroll & P P Tanner [eds.], ACM Press, pp.241–248.

Hoare, C A R (1981), "The Emperor's Old Clothes", *Communications of the ACM* 24, pp.75–83.

Hoc, J-M (1981), "Planning and Direction of Problem Solving in Structured Programming: An Empirical Comparison between Two Methods", *International Journal of Man–Machine Studies* 15, pp.363–383.

Hoc, J-M (1988a), *Cognitive Psychology of Planning*, Academic Press.

Hoc, J-M (1988b), "Towards Effective Computer Aids to Planning in Computer Programming: Theoretical Concern and Empirical Evidence Drawn from Assessment of a Prototype", in *Working with Computers: Theory versus Outcomes*, G C van der Veer, T R G Green, J-M Hoc & D Murray [eds.], Academic Press.

Hoc, J-M, Green, T R G, Samurçay, R & Gilmore, D J [eds.] (1990), *The Psychology of Programming*, Academic Press.

Hoffner, Y, Dobson, J & Iggulden, D (1989), "A New User Interface Architecture", in *People and Computers V*, A Sutcliffe & L Macaulay [eds.], Cambridge University Press, pp.169–189, Proceedings of HCI'89.

Holt, R W, Boehm-Davis, D A & Schultz, A C (1987), "Mental Representations of Programs for Student and Professional Programmers", in *Empirical Studies of Programmers: 2nd Workshop*, G Olson, S Sheppard & E Soloway [eds.], Ablex, pp.33–46.

Hutchins, E L, Hollan, J D & Norman, D A (1986), "Direct Manipulation Interfaces", in *User Centered Systems Design: New Perspectives on Human–Computer Interaction*, D A Norman & S W Draper [eds.], Lawrence Erlbaum Associates, pp.87–124.

Ichbaiah, J & Anon (1984), "Ada: Past, Present and Future. An Interview with Jean Ichbaiah", *Communications of the ACM* 27, pp.990–997.

Illich, I (1973), *Tools for Conviviality*, Harper & Row.

Ince, D & Andrews, D (1990), *The Software Life Cycle*, Butterworth.

Jackson, M A (1986), *System Development*, Prentice–Hall International.

Jakobs, P (1993), in *The REDO Compendium: Reverse Engineering for Software Maintenance*, H J van Zuylen [ed.], John Wiley & Sons.

Jeffries, R, Turner, A A, Polson, P G & Atwood, M (1981), "The Processes Involved in Designing Software", in *Cognitive Skills and their Acquisition*, J R Anderson [ed.], Lawrence Erlbaum Associates, pp.255–283.

Johnson, P (1989), "HCI Models in Software Design: Task-oriented Models of Interactive Software Systems", in *Software Engineering Environments: Research and Practice*, K H Bennett [ed.], Ellis Horwood.

Johnson-Laird, P (1989), *Foundations of Cognitive Science*, MIT Press.

Jones, C B (1986), *Systematics Software Development using VDM*, Prentice–Hall.

Kaehler, T & Patterson, D (1986), "A Small Taste of Smalltalk", *Byte* August, pp.145–159.

Kamada, T (1989), *Visualizing Abstract Objects and Relations*, World Scientific.

Kant, E (1985), "Understanding and Automating Algorithm Design", *IEEE Transactions on Software Engineering* SE-11 (11), pp.1361–1374.

Kaplan, C A & Simon, H A (1990), "In Search of Insight", *Cognitive Psychology* 22, pp.374–419.

Karmiloff-Smith, A (1979), "Micro and Macro Developmental Changes in Language Acquisition and Other Representational Systems", *Cognitive Science* 3, pp.91–118.

Karmiloff-Smith, A & Inhelder, B (1974), "If You Want to Get Ahead, Get a Theory", *Cognition* 3, pp.195–212.

Katz, I R A (1991), "Assessing Transfer of a Complex Skill", in *Proceedings of the 13th Annumal Meeting of the Cognitive Science Society*, Lawrence Erlbaum Associates, pp.775–779.

Kellogg, W A (1989), "Extracting Psychological Claims from Artifacts in Use", IBM Internal Report No. 67052.

Kim, Won Chul & Foley, J D (1989), "Don: User Interface Presentation Design Assistant", George Washington University, Technical Report.

Kimbrough, K & Oren, L (1990), *Common Lisp User Interface Environment*, Texas Instruments Inc, Dallas, TX.

Klahr, D (1982), "Nonmonotone Assessment of Monotone Development: An Information Processing Analysis", in *U-shaped Behavioral Growth*, S Strauss [ed.], Academic Press, pp.63–86.

Koenemann, J & Robertson, S P (1991), "Expert Problem Solving Strategies for Program Comprehension", in *Proceedings of CHI'91: Human Factors in Computing Systems (Reaching through Technology)*, S P Robertson, G M Olson & J S Olson [eds.], ACM Press, pp.125–130.

Kowalski, R A (1982), "Logic as a Computer Language", in *Logic Programming*, K Clark & S-A Tarnlund [eds.], Academic Press, pp.3–16.

Krasner, G E & Pope, S T (1988), "A Cookbook for Using the Model-View-Controller User Interface Paradigm in SMALLTALK-80", *Journal of Object Oriented Programming* 1 (3), pp.26–49.

Krasner, H, Curtis, B & Iscoe, N (1987), "Communication Breakdowns and Boundary Spanning Activities on Large Programming Projects", in *Empirical Studies of Programmers: 2nd Workshop*, G Olson, S Sheppard & E Soloway [eds.], Ablex, pp.47–64.

Kraut, R & Streeter, L (1990), "Coordination in Large Scale Software Development", Bellcore report.

Kudo, H, Sugiyama, Y, Fuj, M & Torii, K (1989), "Quantifying a Design Process Based on Experiments", *Journal of Systems and Software* 9, pp.129–136.

Kühme, T, Hornung, G & Witschital, P (1991), "Conceptual Models of the Design Process of Direct Manipulation User Interfaces", in *Human Aspects in Computing: Design and Use of Interactive Systems and Work with Terminals. Proceedings of the HCI International '91, Stuttgart, FRG*, H-J Bullinger [ed.], Elsevier Science (North-Holland), pp.722–727.

Kuhn, T (1962), *The Structure of Scientific Revolutions*, The University of Chicago Press.

Lange, B M & Moher, T (1989), "Some Strategies of Reuse in an Object-oriented Programming Environment", in *Proceedings of CHI'89: Human Factors in Computing Systems*, K Bice & C H Lewis [eds.], ACM Press, pp.69–73.

Larsson, T (1991), "Productivity CMS88: Project Status and Proposed Actions", Ericsson Radio Systems document, SL/OM-91:080.

Lave, J (1988), *Cognition in Practice*, Cambridge University Press.

Lawson, H (1990), "Philosophies for Engineering Computer-Based Systems", *IEEE Computer* December, pp.52–63.

Lehman, M M & Belady, L A (1985), *Program Evolution*, Academic Press, APIC Studies in Data Processing No. 27.

Lemke, A C & Fischer, G (1990), "A Cooperative Problem Solving System for User Interface Design", in *Proceedings of AAAI-90 (Eighth National Conference on Artificial Intelligence)*, AAAI Press/MIT Press, pp.479–484.

Leplat, J & Hoc, J-M (1983), "Tâche et Activité dans l'Analyse Psychologique des Situations", *Cahiers de Psychologie Cognitive* 3 (1), pp.49–63.

Lesk, M (1984), "Programming Languages for Text and Knowledge Processing", in *Annual Review of Information Science and Technology 19*, M Williams [ed.], Knowledge Industry Publications, pp.97–128.

Letovsky, S (1986), "Cognitive Processes in Program Comprehension", in *Empirical Studies of Programmers: 1st Workshop*, E Soloway & S Iyengar [eds.], Ablex, pp.58–79.

Letovsky, S & Soloway, E (1985), "Strategies for Documenting Delocalized Plans", in *Proceedings of Conference on Software Maintenanace 1985*, pp.144–151.

Levelt, W J M (1981), "The Speaker's Linearisation Problem", *Philosophical Transactions of the Royal Society 295*, pp.305–315.

Levendel, Y (1991), "Improving Quality with a Manufacturing Process", *IEEE Software* March, pp.13–25.

Leventhal, L M (1987), "Discourse Rules in Program Comprehension: Emergence of a Construct Affordances Rule?", in *Proceedings of INTERACT'87 — Second IFIP Conference on Human–Computer Interaction*, H-J Bullinger & B Shackel [eds.], Elsevier Science (North-Holland), pp.297–302.

Littman, D C, Pinto, J, Letovsky, S & Soloway, E (1986), "Mental Models and Software Maintenance", in *Empirical Studies of Programmers: 1st Workshop*, E Soloway & S Iyengar [eds.], Ablex, pp.80–98.

Longworth, G & Nicholls, B (1986), *SSADM Manual, Version 3*, NCC.

Lundeberg, M, Goldkuhl, G & Nilsson, A (1978), "Systemeering.

MacLean, A, Young, R M & Moran, T P (1989), "Designing Rationale: The Argument behind the Artifact", in *People and Computers V*, A Sutcliffe & L Macaulay [eds.], Cambridge University Press, Proceedings of HCI'89.

Mackinlay, J (1986), "Automating the Design of Graphical Presentations of Relational Information", *ACM Transactions on Graphics* 5 (2), pp.110–141.

Mackinlay, J D, Robertson,, G G & Card, S K (1991), "The Perspective Wall: Detail and Context Smoothly Integrated", in *Proceedings of CHI'91: Human Factors in Computing Systems (Reaching through Technology)*, S P Robertson, G M Olson & J S Olson [eds.], ACM Press, pp.173–179.

Maibaum, T (1986), "Role of Abstraction in Program Development", in *Information Processing*, H Kugler [ed.], IFIP.

Malhotra, A, Thomas, J C, Carroll, J M & Miller, L A (1980), "Cognitive Processes in Design", *International Journal of Man–Machine Studies* 12, pp.119–140.

de Marco, T (1979), *Structured Analysis and System Specification*, Prentice–Hall.

Märtin, C (1990), "A UIMS for Knowledge Based Interface Template Generation and Interaction", in *Proceedings of INTERACT'90 — Third IFIP Conference on Human–Computer Interaction*, D Diaper, D Gilmore, G Cockton & B Shackel [eds.], Elsevier Science (North-Holland).

Martin, J (1991), *Rapid Application Development*, Macmillan.

Martin, J & McClure, C (1985), *Diagram Techniques for Analysts and Pogrammers*, Prentice–Hall.

Mayer, R E (1989), "Human Nonadversary Problem Solving", in *Human and Machine Problem Solving*, K J Gilhooly [ed.], Plenum.

McCabe, T (1976), "A Software Complexity Measure", *IEEE Transactions on Software Engineering* SE-2, pp.308–320.

McClure, C (1989), *CASE is Software Automation*, Prentice–Hall.

McKeithen, K B, Reitman, J S, Rueter, H H & Hirtle, S C (1981), "Knowledge Organization and Skill Differences in Computer Programmers", *Cognitive Psychology* 13, pp.307–325.

Meyer, B (1988), *Object Oriented Software Construction*, Prentice–Hall.

Miller, G A (1956), "The Magical Number Seven Plus or Minus Two: Some Limits on our Capacity for Information Processing", *Psychological Review* 63, pp.81–97.

Monk, A F (1990), "Action–Effect Rules: A Technique for Evaluating an Informal Specification against Principles", *Behaviour & Information Technology* 9, pp.147–155.

Monk, A F & Wright, P C (1991), "Claims, Observations and Inventions: Analysing the Artifact", *ACM SIGCHI Bulletin* January.

Myers, B A (1986), "Visual Programming, Programming by Example, and Program Visualization: A Taxonomy", in *Proceedings of CHI'86: Human Factors in Computing Systems*, M Mantei & P Orbeton [eds.], ACM Press, pp.59–66.

Myers, B A (1987), "Creating User Interfaces by Demonstration", University of Toronto, Toronto, Ontario, Canada, PhD thesis.

Myers, B A (1989), "Encapsulating Interactive Behaviors", in *Proceedings of CHI'89: Human Factors in Computing Systems*, K Bice & C H Lewis [eds.], ACM Press, pp.319–324.

Myers, B A (1990a), "Taxonomies of Visual Programming and Program Visualization", *Journal of Visual Languages and Computing* 1 (1), pp.97–123.

Myers, B A (1990b), "Creating User Interfaces Using Programming by Example, Visual Programming, and Constraints", *ACM Transactions on Programming Languages and Systems* 12 (2), pp.143–177.

Myers, B A, Giuse, D A, Dannenberg, R B, Zanden, B Vander, Kosbie, D S, Pervin, E, Mickish, A & Marchal, P (1990), "Garnet: Comprehensive Support for Graphical, Highly Interactive User Interfaces", *IEEE Computer* 23 (11), pp.71–85.

Mynatt, B T (1990), "Why Program Comprehension is (or is not) affected by Surface Features", in *Proceedings of INTERACT'90 — Third IFIP Conference on Human–Computer Interaction*, D Diaper, D Gilmore, G Cockton & B Shackel [eds.], Elsevier Science (North-Holland), pp.945–950.

Navinchandra, D (1991), *Exploration and Innovation in Design: Towards a Computational Model*, Springer-Verlag.

Newell, A & Card, S (1985), "The Prospect for Psychological Science in Human–Computer Interaction", *Human–Computer Interaction* 1, pp.209–242.

Newell, A & Simon, H A (1972), *Human Problem Solving*, Prentice-Hall.

Nielsen, J (1986), "A Virtual Protocol Model for Computer–Human Interaction", *International Journal of Man–Machine Studies* 24, pp.301–312.

Nijssen, G M & Halpin, T A (1989), *Conceptual Schema and Relational database Design: A Fact-Oriented Approach*, Prentice-Hall.

Nilsson, M (1984), "The World's Shortest Prolog Interpreter?", in *Implementations of Prolog*, J A Campbell [ed.], Ellis Horwood, pp.87–92.

Norman, D A (1983a), "Design Rules Based on Analyses of Human Error", *Communications of the ACM* 26, pp.254–258.

Norman, D A (1983b), "Some Observations on Mental Models", in *Mental Models*, D Gentner & A L Stevens [eds.], Lawrence Erlbaum Associates.

Norman, D A (1986), "Cognitive Engineering", in *User Centered Systems Design: New Perspectives on Human–Computer Interaction*, D A Norman & S W Draper [eds.], Lawrence Erlbaum Associates, pp.31–61.

Nye, A [ed.] (1988), *Xlib Reference Manual*, The Definitive Guides to the X Window System #2, O'Reilly & Associates, Inc.

Nye, A [ed.] (1990), *X Protocol Reference Manual*, The Definitive Guides to the X Window System #0, O'Reilly & Associates, Inc.

Nye, A & O'Reilly, T (1990), *X Toolkit Intrinsics Programming Manual*, The Definitive Guides to the X Window System #4, O'Reilly & Associates, Inc.

Olle, T W, Hagelstein, J, McDonald, I G, Rolland, C, Sol, H G, van Assche, F J M & Verrijn-Stuart, A A (1988), *Information Systems Methodology: A Framework for Understanding*, IFIP Working Group 8.1.

Olsen, D R (1990), "Propositional Production Systems for Dialog Description", in *Proceedings of CHI'90: Human Factors in Computing Systems*, J C Chew & J Whiteside [eds.], ACM Press, pp.57–63.

Open Software Foundation (1990a), *OSF/Motif Style Guide*, Prentice–Hall.

Open Software Foundation (1990b), *OSF/Motif Programmer's Guide*, Prentice–Hall.

Ormerod, T (1990), "Human Cognition and Programming", in *The Psychology of Programming*, J-M Hoc, T R G Green, R Samurçay & D J Gilmore [eds.], Academic Press, pp.63–82.

Pain, H, Brna, P & du Boulay, B (1991), "Teaching, Learning and Using Prolog", *Instructional Science* 20 (2–3).

Pain, H & Bundy, A (1987), "What Stories Should We Tell Novice Prolog Programmers?", in *Artificial Intelligence Programming Environments*, R Hawley [ed.], John Wiley & Sons, pp.119–130.

Parker, J & Hendley, B (1987), "The Universe Program Development Environment", in *Proceedings of INTERACT'87 — Second IFIP Conference on Human–Computer Interaction*, H-J Bullinger & B Shackel [eds.], Elsevier Science (North-Holland), pp.305–309.

Parnas, D L & Clements, P C (1986), "A Rational Design Process: How and Why to Fake It", *IEEE Transactions on Software Engineering* SE-12 (2), pp.251–257.

Patel, M J, du Boulay, J B H & Taylor, C (1991a), "Prolog Tracers and Information Access", in *Proceedings of The First Moscow HCI'91 Workshop*.

Patel, M J, du Boulay, J B H & Taylor, C (1991b), "Effect of Format on Information and Problem Solving", in *Proceedings of the Thirteenth Annual Conference of the Cognitive Science Society*, Chicago.

Payne, S J (1987), "Complex Problem Spaces: Modelling the Knowledge Needed to Use Interactive Devices", in *Proceedings of INTERACT'87 — Second IFIP Conference on Human–Computer Interaction*, H-J Bullinger & B Shackel [eds.], Elsevier Science (North-Holland).

Pea, R D & Kurland, D M (1984), "On the Cognitive Effects of Learning Computer Programming", *New Ideas in Psychology* 2, pp.137–168.

Pennington, N (1987a), "Stimulus Structures and Mental Representations in Expert Comprehension of Computer Programs", *Cognitive Psychology* 19, pp.295–341.

Pennington, N (1987b), "Comprehension Strategies in Programming", in *Empirical Studies of Programmers: 2nd Workshop*, G Olson, S Sheppard & E Soloway [eds.], Ablex, pp.114–131.

Pennington, N & Grabowski, B (1990), "The Tasks of Programming", in *The Psychology of Programming*, J-M Hoc, T R G Green, R Samurçay & D J Gilmore [eds.], Academic Press, pp.145–162.

Petre, M (1990), "Expert Programmers and Programming Languages", in *The Psychology of Programming*, J-M Hoc, T R G Green, R Samurçay & D J Gilmore [eds.], Academic Press, pp.103–115.

Petre, M & Green, T R G (1990), "Where to Draw the Line with Text: Some Claims by Logic Designers about Graphics in Notation", in *Proceedings of INTERACT'90 — Third IFIP Conference on Human–Computer Interaction*, D Diaper, D Gilmore, G Cockton & B Shackel [eds.], Elsevier Science (North-Holland), pp.463–468.

Petre, M & Winder, R (1988), "Issues Governing the Suitability of Programming Languages for Programming Tasks", in *People and Computers IV*, D M Jones & R Winder [eds.], Cambridge University Press, Proceedings of HCI'88.

Petre, M & Winder, R (1990), "On Languages, Models and Programming Styles", *The Computer Journal* 33 (2), pp.173–180.

Pfaff, G E [ed.] (1985), *User Interface Management Systems*, Springer-Verlag, Proceedings of the Workshop on User Interface Management Systems held in Seeheim, FRG, November 1-3, 1983.

Pirolli, P L & Anderson, J R (1985), "The Role of Learning from Examples in the Acquisition of Recursive Programming Skills", *Canadian Journal of Psychology* 39, pp.240–272.

Polanyi, M (1966), *The Tacit Dimension*, Doubleday.

Pournelle, J (1990), *BYTE* September.

Price, B A & Baecker, R M (1991), "The Automatic Animation of Concurrent Programs", in *Proceedings of the 1st International Workshop on Computer–Human Interfaces*, ICSTI, pp.128–137.

Price, B A, Baecker, R M & Small, I S (1993), "A Principled Taxonomy of Software Visualization", (Submitted for review).

Price, B A, Small, I S & Baecker, R M (1992), "A Taxonomy of Software Visualization", in *Proceedings of the 25th Hawaii International Conference on System Sciences*, IEEE Computer Society Press, II, pp.597–606.

Projektgruppe Automation und Qualifikation (1987), *Widersprüche der Automationsarbeit: Ein Handbuch*.

Propp, V (1968), *Morphology of the Folktale, 2nd ed*, University of Texas Press.

Pun, W & Winder, R (1988), "The Smalltalk-80 Browser: A Critique", Department of Computer Science, University College London, RN/88/8.

de Queiroz, R & Maibaum, T (1989), "Abstract Data Types and Type Theory: Theories as Types", *Zeitschrift für Mathematische Logik und Grundlagen der Mathematik*.

Ratcliff, B & Siddiqi, J I A (1985), "An Empirical Investigation into Problem Decomposition Strategies used in Program Design", *International Journal of Man–Machine Studies* 22, pp.77–90.

Reason, J (1990), *Human Error*, Cambridge University Press.

de Remer, F & Kron, H H (1976), "Programming-in-the-Large Versus Programming-in-the-Small", *IEEE Transactions on Software Engineering* SE-2 (2), pp.80–86.

Rentsch, T (1982), "Object Oriented Programming", *ACM SIGPLAN Notices* 17 (9), pp.51–57.

Resnick, L B (1991), "Shared Cognition: Thinking as Social Practice", in *Perspectives on Socially Shared Cognition*, L B Resnick, J M Levine & S D Teasley [eds.], American Psychological Association, pp.1–20.

Rich, C & Waters, R C (1990), *The Programmer's Apprentice*, ACM Press.

Rich, C & Wills, L M (1990), "Recognizing A Program's Design: A Graph-parsing Approach", *IEEE Software* 7 (1), pp.82–89.

Richards, D D & Siegler, R S (1982), "U-shaped Behavioral Curves: It's Not Whether You're Right or Wrong, It's Why", in *U-shaped Behavioral Growth*, S Strauss [ed.], Academic Press, pp.37–61.

Rist, R S (1986), "Plans in Programming: Definition, Demonstration, and Development", in *Empirical Studies of Programmers: 1st Workshop*, E Soloway & S Iyengar [eds.], Ablex, pp.28–47.

Rist, R S (1989), "Schema Creation in Programming", *Cognitive Science* 13, pp.389–414.

Rist, R S (1990), "Variability in Program Design: The Interaction of Process with Knowledge", *International Journal of Man–Machine Studies* 33, pp.305–322.

Rist, R S (1991a), "Models of Routine and Non-routine Design in Programming", in *Proceedings of the Workshop on AI in Design, 12th IJCAI*, Sydney, Australia.

Rist, R S (1991b), "Knowledge Creation and Retrieval in Program Design: A Comparison of Novice and Experienced Programmers", *Human–Computer Interaction* 6, pp.11–46.

Rist, R S & Bevemyr, J (1991), "Automated Plan Analysis in Programming", Centre for Computing Sciences, University of Technology, Sydney, Technical Report 91.2.

Rittel, H W J (1984), "Second-Generation Design Methods", in *Developments in Design Methodology*, N Cross [ed.], John Wiley & Sons, pp.317–327.

Roberts, G, Wei, M & Winder, R (March 1990), "Workpackage 10 Evaluation and Final Report of the SPAN (ESPRIT 1588) Project: The Solve Object Oriented Programming System for Parallel Computers", Department of Computer Science, University College London, TR/92/7 (SPAN-WP10-Deliverable-28).

Roberts, G, Wei, M & Winder, R (April 1991a), "CoSIDE Design and Implementation", Department of Computer Science, University College London, COOTS-UCL-19.

Roberts, G, Wei, M & Winder, R (November 1991b), "The Solve System", in *Object Oriented Programming: The Next Step*, Bruce Anderson [ed.], BCS, Proceedings of the Workshop OOPS-30: The Next Step, March 1990.

Roberts, G, Winder, R & Wei, M (1988), "The SPAN Object Oriented Framework", *OOPS!* September 1988, pp.24–30.

Robertson, S P, Davis, E F, Okabe, K & Fitz-Randolf, D (1990), "Program Comprehension beyond the Line", in *Proceedings of INTERACT'90 — Third IFIP Conference on Human–Computer Interaction*, D Diaper, D Gilmore, G Cockton & B Shackel [eds.], Elsevier Science (North-Holland), pp.959–963.

Robertson, S P & Yu, C-C (1990), "Common Cognitive Representation of Program Code across Tasks and Languages", *International Journal of Man–Machine Studies* 33, pp.343–360.

Rochfeld, A & Tardieu, H (1983), "MERISE, An Information System Design and Development Methodology in Information and Management.

Rosson, M B & Alpert, S R (1991), "The Cognitive Consequences of Object-oriented Design", *Human–Computer Interaction* 5, pp.345–379.

Rotenstreich, S (1990), "Enhancement Through Design Transformations: A Retroactive Case Study", *Journal of Software Maintenance* 2 (4), pp.193–208.

Saariluoma, P (1991), "Perceptual Differences in Expertise in Chess", in *Proceedings of International Conference on Expertise*, Aberdeen University, August.

Sacerdoti, E (1974), "Planning in a Hierarchy of Abstraction Spaces", *Artificial Intelligence* 5, pp.115–135.

Sacerdoti, E D (1975), *A Structure for Plans and Behavior*, Elsevier Science (North-Holland).

Scanlan, D (1989), "Structured Flowcharts Outperform Pseudocode: An Experimental Comparison", *IEEE Software* September, pp.28–36.

Scheifler, R W & Gettys, J (1986), "The X Window System", *ACM Transactions on Graphics* 5 (2), pp.79–109.

Scheifler, R W & Oren, L (1988), *CLX: Common Lisp X Interface*, Texas Instruments Inc, Dallas, TX.

Schmidt, A L (1986), "Effects of Experience and Comprehension on Reading Time and Memory for Computer Programs", *International Journal of Man–Machine Studies* 25, pp.399–409.

Schoen, D A (1983), *The Reflective Practitioner: How Professionals Think in Action*, Basic Books.

Scholtz, J (1989), "A Study of Transfer of Skill between Programming Languages", University of Nebraska, Lincoln, NE, USA, Unpublished dissertation.

Scholtz, J & Wiedenbeck, S (1990), "Learning to Program in Another Language", in *Proceedings of INTERACT'90 — Third IFIP Conference on Human–Computer Interaction*, D Diaper, D Gilmore, G Cockton & B Shackel [eds.], Elsevier Science (North-Holland), pp.925–930.

Scholtz, J & Wiedenbeck, S (1992), "The Use of Unfamiliar Programming Languages by Experienced Programmers", in *People and Computers VII*, A Monk, D Diaper & M Harrison [eds.], Cambridge University Press, pp.45–56, Proceedings of HCI'92.

Schönpflug, W (1986a), "External Information Storage: An Issue for the Psychology of Memory", in *Human Memory and Cognitive Capabilities, Mechanisms and Performance*, F Klix & H Hagendorf [eds.], Elsevier Science (North-Holland).

Schönpflug, W (1986b), "The Trade-off between Internal and External Information Storage", *Journal of Memory and Language* 25, pp.657–675.

Schussel, G (1990), "The Promise and the Reality of AD/Cycle", *Datamation* September.

Schwanke, R W, Altucher, R Z & Platoff, M A (1989), "Discovering, Visualizing, and Controlling Software Structure", *ACM SIGSOFT Engineering Notes* 14 (3), pp.147–150.

Segal, J, Ahmad, K & Rogers, M (1989), "Using Systematic Errors to Investigate the Developing Knowledge of Programming Language Learners", Artificial Intelligence Group, University of Surrey, UK, Technical Report TR289.

Shah, V & Waddington, R (1991), "Concurrent Programming Plans: Real or Imaginary?", Poster presented at the Fourth Empirical Studies of Programmers Workshop, New Brunswick, NJ, USA.

Shank, R C & Abelson, R P (1977), *Scripts, Plans, Goals and Understanding*, Lawrence Erlbaum Associates.

Shaw, M (1989), "Maybe Your Next Programming Language Shouldn't Be a Programming Language", in *Scaling Up: A Research Agenda for Software Engineering*, Computer Science and Technology Board [ed.], National Academy Press, pp.75–82.

Sheil, B A (1983), "Power Tools for Programmers", *Datamation* February, pp.131–143.

Shneiderman, B (1980), *Software Psychology*, Winthrop Publishers.

Shneiderman, B (1983), "Direct Manipulation: A Step Beyond Programming Languages", *IEEE Computer* 16 (8), pp.57–69.

Shneiderman, B & Mayer, R (1979), "Syntactic/Semantic Interactions in Programmer Behavior: A Model and Experimental Results", *International Journal of Computer and Information Sciences* 8 (3), pp.219–238.

Shu, N C (1988), *Visual Programming*, Van Nostrand Reinhold.

Siddiqi, J I A (1985), "A Model of Program Designer Behaviour", in *People and Computers: Designing the Interface*, P Johnson & S Cook [eds.], Cambridge University Press, Proceedings of HCI'85, Norwich, September.

Siddiqi, J I A & Ratcliff, B (1989), "Specification Influences in Program Design", *International Journal of Man–Machine Studies* 31, pp.393–404.

Sime, M E, Arblaster, A T & Green, T R G (1977a), "Structuring the Programmer's Task", *Journal of Occupational Psychology* 50, pp.205–216.

Sime, M E, Arblaster, A T & Green, T R G (1977b), "Reducing Errors in Programming Conditionals by Prescribing a Writing Procedure", *International Journal of Man–Machine Studies* 9, pp.119–126.

Simon, H A (1962), "The Architecture of Complexity", *Proceedings of the American Philosophical Society* 106, pp.467–482.

Simon, H A (1973), "The Structure of Ill-Structured Problems", *Artificial Intelligence* 4, pp.181–200.

Simon, H A (1981), *The Sciences of the Artificial*, MIT Press.

Simplício, F (1991), "Modelling Software Specification Understanding", Imperial College of Science, Technology and Medicine. Department of Computing, Research Report 91/28.

Smith, S L & Mosier, J N (1986), "Guidelines for Designing User Interface Software", USAF Hanscom Air Force Base, MA, USA, Technical Report ESD-TR-86-27.

Soloway, E (1986), "What to do Next: Meeting the Challenge of Programming-in-the-large", in *Empirical Studies of Programmers: 1st Workshop*, E Soloway & S Iyengar [eds.], Ablex, pp.263–268.

Soloway, E, Bonar, J & Ehrlich, K (1983), "Cognitive Strategies and Looping Constructs: An Empirical Study", *Communications of the ACM* 26, pp.853–860.

Soloway, E & Ehrlich, K (1984), "Empirical Studies of Programming Knowledge", *IEEE Transactions on Software Engineering* SE-10 (5), pp.595–609.

Soloway, E, Ehrlich, K & Bonar, J (1982), "Tapping into Tacit Programming Knowledge", in *Proceedings of CHI'82: Human Factors in Computing Systems*, ACM Press, pp.52–58.

Soloway, E, Ehrlich, K, Bonar, J & Greenspan, J (1982), *Direction in Human–Computer Interaction*, Ablex.

Soloway, E, Ehrlich, K, Bonar, J & Greenspan, J (1984), "What do Novices Know About Programming?", in *Directions in Human–Computer Interaction*, A Badre & B Shneiderman [eds.], Ablex, pp.27–54.

Soloway, E, Pinto, J, Letovsky, S, Littman, D & Lampert, R (1988), "Designing Documentation to Compensate for Delocalized Plans", *Communications of the ACM* 31 (11), pp.1259–1267.

Sommerville, I [ed.] (1986), *Software Engineering Environments*, Peter Peregrinus Ltd (Institute of Electrical Engineers).

Sommerville, I (1989), *Software Engineering (3rd edition)*, Addison Wesley.

Spivey, J M (1988), *The Z Notation: A Reference Manual*, Prentice–Hall.

Spohrer, J C, Soloway, E & Pope, E (1989), "A Goal/Plan Analysis of Buggy Pascal Programs", in *Studying the Novice Programmer*, E Soloway & J C Spohrer [eds.], Lawrence Erlbaum Associates, pp.355–400.

Spurr, K & Layzell, P [eds.] (1990), *CASE on Trial*, John Wiley & Sons.

Standish, T A & Taylor, R N (1984), "Arcturus: A Prototype Advanced Ada Programming Environment", in *Proceedings of the ACM SIGSOFT/SIGPLAN Software Engineering Symposium on Practical Software Development Environments*, P Henderson [ed.], ACM Press.

Stanley-Smith, C (1993), in *The REDO Compendium: Reverse Engineering for Software Maintenance*, H J van Zuylen [ed.], John Wiley & Sons.

Star, S L (1989), "Layered Space, Formal Representations and Long-distance Control: The Politics of Information", *Fundamenta Scientiæ* 10 (2), pp.125–155.

Star, S L & Griesemer, J R (1989), "Institutional Ecology, 'Translations' and Boundary Objects: Amateurs and Professionals in Berkeley's Museum of Vertebrate Zoology, 1907-39", *Social Studies of Science* 19, pp.387–420.

Stasko, J T (1990), "The Path-transition Paradigm: A Practical Methodology for Adding Animation to Program Interfaces", *Journal of Visual Languages and Computing* 1 (3), pp.213–236.

Stavy, R, Strauss, S, Orpaz, N & Carmi, G (1982), "U-shaped Behavioral Growth in Ratio Comparisons", in *U-shaped Behavioral Growth*, S Strauss [ed.], Academic Press, pp.11–35.

Stefik, M (1981), "Planning with Constraints (MOLGEN: Part 1)", *Artificial Intelligence* 16, pp.111–140.

Stefik, M J (1986), "The Next Knowledge Medium", *AI Magazine* 7 (1), pp.34–46.

Strauss, S & Stavy, R (1982), "U-shaped Behavioral Growth: Implications for Theories of Development", in *Review of Child Development Research*, W W Hartup [ed.], The University of Chicago Press, pp.547–599.

Stroustrup, B (1991), *The C++ Programming Language (2nd edition)*, Addison Wesley.

Strübing, J (1993), "Subjektive Leistungen im Arbeitprozeß: Eine empirische Unleisuchung von Arbeitsstilen in der Programmierarbeit" (Opladen).

Suchman, L A (1987), *Plans and Situated Actions*, Cambridge University Press.

Sukaviriya, P (1989), "Coupling a UI Framework with Automatic Generation of Context Sensitive Help", George Washington University, Technical Report.

Sun Microsystems [ed.] (1990), *OPEN LOOK Graphical User Interface Application Style Guidelines*, Addison Wesley.

Sutcliffe, A G & Maiden, N A M (1990a), "Software Re-usability: Delivering Productivity Gains or Short Cuts", in *Task Analysis for Human–Computer Interaction*, D Diaper [ed.], Ellis Horwood.

Sutcliffe, A G & Maiden, N A M (1990b), "Software Re-usability: Delivering Productivity Gains or Short Cuts", in *Proceedings of INTERACT'90 — Third IFIP Conference on Human–Computer Interaction*, D Diaper, D Gilmore, G Cockton & B Shackel [eds.], Elsevier Science (North-Holland), pp.895–902.

Swartout, W R & Balzer, R (1982), "On the Inevitable Intertwining of Specification and Implementation", *Communications of the ACM* 25 (7), pp.438–439.

Szekely, P (1989), "Standardizing the Interface between Applications and UIMS", in *Proceedings of the ACM SIGGRAPH Symposium on User Interface Software and Technology*, Williamsburg, VA.

Szwillus, G (1987), "GEGS: A System for Generating Graphical Editors", in *Proceedings of INTERACT'87 — Second IFIP Conference on Human–Computer Interaction*, H-J Bullinger & B Shackel [eds.], Elsevier Science (North-Holland).

Tauber, M J (1987), "On Visual Interfaces and Their Conceptual Analysis", in *Visualization in Programming*, P Gorny & M J Tauber [eds.], Lecture Notes in Computer Science #282, Springer-Verlag, pp.106–123.

Taylor, C, du Boulay, J B H & Patel, M J (1991), "Outline Proposal for a Prolog "Textual Tree Tracer" (TTT)", School of Cognitive and Computing Sciences, The University of Sussex, UK, Cognitive Sciences Research Paper-177.

Tufte, E R (1983), *The Visual Display of Quantitative Information*, Graphics Press.

Tufte, E R (1990), *Envisioning Information*, Graphics Press.

Turski, W & Maibaum, T (1987), *The Specification of Computer Programs*, Addison Wesley.

Ullman, D, Dietterich, T G & Staufer, L A (1988), "A Model of the Mechanical Design Process Based on Empirical Data", *AI EDAM* 2, pp.33–52.

Ullman, D, Staufer, L A & Dietterich, T G (1987), "Toward Expert CAD", *Computers in Mechanical Engineering* 6 (3), pp.56–70.

Vainio-Larsson, A & Orring, R (1990), "Evaluating the Usability of User Interfaces: Research in Practice", in *Proceedings of INTERACT'90 — Third IFIP Conference on Human–Computer Interaction*, D Diaper, D Gilmore, G Cockton & B Shackel [eds.], Elsevier Science (North-Holland), pp.323–327.

van't Veld, S F N (1990), *16 Methoden voor Systeemontwikkeling (16 Methods for Systems Development)*, Tutein Nolthenius.

Visser, W (1987), "Strategies in Programming Programmable Controllers: A Field Study on a Professional Programmer", in *Empirical Studies of Programmers: 2nd Workshop*, G Olson, S Sheppard & E Soloway [eds.], Ablex, pp.217–230.

Visser, W (1988), "Giving up a Hierarchical Plan in a Design Activity", INRIA, Research Report No. 814.

Visser, W (1990), "More or Less Following a Plan during Design: Opportunistic Deviations in Specification", *International Journal of Man–Machine Studies* 33 (3), pp.247–278.

Visser, W (1991a), "The Cognitive Psychology Viewpoint on Design: Examples from Empirical Studies", in *Proceedings of Artificial Intelligence in Design '91*, J Gero [ed.], Butterworth–Heinemann.

Visser, W (1991b), "Evocation and Elaboration of Solutions: Different Types of Problem-solving Actions. An Empirical Study on the Design of an Aerospace Artifact", in *Proceedings of COGNITIVA'90: At the Crossroads of Artificial Intelligence, Cognitive science and Neuroscience*, T Kohonen & F Fogelman-Soulié [eds.], Elsevier Science (North-Holland).

Visser, W & Hoc, J-M (1990), "Expert Software Design Strategies", in *The Psychology of Programming*, J-M Hoc, T R G Green, R Samurçay & D J Gilmore [eds.], Academic Press, pp.235–247.

Voss, J F, Greene, T R, Post, T A & Penner, B C (1983), "Problem-solving Skill in the Social Sciences", in *The Psychology of Learning and Motivation*, G Bower [ed.] #17, Academic Press.

Wadler, P (1987), "A Critique of Abelson and Sussman: Or why calculating is better than scheming", *ACM SIGPLAN Notices* 22 (3).

Waldhor, K (1989), "Creating Advanced User Interfaces using a Knowledge Based Approach", in *Designing and Using Human–Computer Interfaces and Knowledge Based Systems*, G Salvendy & M J Smith [eds.], Elsevier Science (North-Holland), pp.869–876.

Walsh, P, Lim, K Y & Long, J B (1989), "JSD and the Design of User Interface Software", *Ergonomics* 32, pp.1483–1498.

Walz, D, Elam, D, Krasner, H & Curtis, B (1987), "A Methodology for Studying Software Design Teams: An Investigation of Conflict behaviors in the Requirements Definition Phase", in *Empirical Studies of Programmers: 2nd Workshop*, G Olson, S Sheppard & E Soloway [eds.], Ablex.

Warboys, B (1989), "The IPSE 2.5 Project: A Process Model Based Architecture", in *Software Engineering Environments: Research and Practice*, K H Bennett [ed.], Ellis Horwood, pp.313–331.

Ward, P T & Mellor, S J (1985), *Structured Development for Real Time Systems*, Yourdon Press (Prentice–Hall).

Ward, R D & Sleeman, D (1987), "Learning to Use the S.1 Knowledge Engineering Tool", *Knowledge Engineering Review* 2 (4), pp.265–276.

Weiser, M (1982), "Programmers Use Slices When Debugging", *Communications of the ACM* 25 (7), pp.446–452.

Weiser, M (1984), "Program Slicing", *IEEE Transactions on Software Engineering* SE-10 (5), pp.352–357.

Weiser, M & Lyle, J (1986), "Experiments on Slicing-based Debugging Aids", in *Empirical Studies of Programmers: 1st Workshop*, E Soloway & S Iyengar [eds.], Ablex.

Weltz, F & Lullies, V (1983), "Das Konzept der innerbetrieblichen Handlungskonstellation als Instrument der Analyse von Rationalisierungsprozessen", in *Arbeitspolitik*, U Jürgens & F Naschold [eds.], pp.155–170.

Weltz, F, Lullies, V & Ortmann, R G (1991), "Softwareentwicklungsprojekte als Prozeß der Konfliktverarbeitung", in *Software für die Arbeit von morgen*, Projektträger Arbeit und Technik [ed.].

Wenger, E (1990), "Toward a Theory of Cultural Transparency: Elements of a Social Discourse of the Visible and the Invisible", Information and Computer Science, University of California, Irvine, CA, Dissertation.

Whiteside, J (1988), "Usability engineering: Our Experience and Evolution", in *Handbook of Human–Computer Interaction*, M Helander [ed.], Elsevier Science (North-Holland), pp.791–817.

Whiteside, J & Wixon, D (1985), "Developmental Theory as a Framework for Studying Human–Computer Interactions", in *Advances in Human–Computer Interaction*, H R Hartson [ed.], Ablex, pp.29–48.

Wiecha, C, Bennett, W, Boies, S & Gould, J (1989a), "Generating Highly Interactive User Interfaces", in *Proceedings of CHI'89: Human Factors in Computing Systems*, K Bice & C H Lewis [eds.], ACM Press, pp.277–282.

Wiecha, C, Boies, S, Green, M, Hudson, S & Myers, B (1989b), "Direct Manipulation or Programming: How should we Design Interfaces?", in *Proceedings of the ACM SIGGRAPH Symposium on User Interface Software and Technology*.

Wiedenbeck, S (1986a), "Organization of Programming Knowledge of Novices and Experts", *Journal of the American Society for Information Science* 37, pp.294–299.

Wiedenbeck, S (1986b), "Beacons in Computer Program Comprehension", *International Journal of Man–Machine Studies* 25, pp.697–709.

Wiedenbeck, S (1986c), "Processes in Computer Program Comprehension", in *Empirical Studies of Programmers: 1st Workshop*, E Soloway & S Iyengar [eds.], Ablex, pp.48–57.

Wiedenbeck, S (1991), "The Initial Stages of Program Comprehension", *International Journal of Man–Machine Studies* 35, pp.517–540.

Winder, R, Joly, G & Kamalati, A (1992), "Applications in CoSIDE", *OOPS Messenger* 4(2), pp.215–216, (Poster paper presented at OOPSLA'92).

Winder, R, Roberts, G & Wei, M (1992), "CoSIDE and Parallel Object Oriented Languages Poster and Extended Abstract", *OOPS Messenger* 4(2), pp.211–213, (Poster paper presented at OOPSLA'92).

Winder, R, Wei, M & Roberts, G (1991), "Harnessing Parallelism with UC++", in *Proceedings of ECUG91 Conference*, pp.101–114.

Winder, R, Wei, M & Roberts, G (Nov 1992), "UC++: An Active Object Model for Parallel C++", Department of Computer Science, University College London, RN/92/115.

Winograd, T (1979), "Beyond Programming Languages", *Communications of the ACM* 22(7), pp.391–401.

Winograd, T & Flores, F (1986), *Understanding Computers and Cognition: A New Foundation for Design*, Ablex.

Witschital, P (1991), "SX/Tools Dialogbeschreibungssprache", Siemens AG, Internal Paper.

Young, R M & Barnard, P J (1987), "The Use of Scenarios in Human–Computer Interaction Research: Turbocharging the Tortoise of Cumulative Science", in *Proceedings of CHI+GI'87: Human Factors in Computing Systems and Graphics Interface*, J M Carroll & P P Tanner [eds.], ACM Press, pp.291–296.

Yourdon, E (1989), *Modern Structured Analysis*, Prentice–Hall International.

Yourdon, E (1990), "Auld Lang Syne", *Byte* October, pp.257–264.

Yu, C-C & Robertson, S P (1988), "Plan-Based Representations of Pascal and Fortran Code", in *Proceedings of CHI'88: Human Factors in Computing Systems*, E Soloway, D Frye & S B Sheppard [eds.], ACM Press, pp.251–256.

van Zuylen, H J (1993), in *The REDO Compendium: Reverse Engineering for Software Maintenance*, H J van Zuylen [ed.], John Wiley & Sons.

Author Index

Keyword Index

NATO ASI Series F

NATO ASI Series F

Including Special Programmes on Sensory Systems for Robotic Control (ROB) and on Advanced Educational Technology (AET)

NATO ASI Series F

NATO ASI Series F

NATO ASI Series F

Including Special Programmes on Sensory Systems for Robotic Control (ROB) and on Advanced Educational Technology (AET)

Vol. 94: Logic and Algebra of Specification. Edited by F. L. Bauer, W. Brauer, and H. Schwichtenberg. VII, 442 pages. 1993.

Vol. 95: Comprehensive Systems Design: A New Educational Technology. Edited by C. M. Reigeluth, B. H. Banathy, and J. R. Olson. IX, 437 pages. 1993. *(AET)*

Vol. 96: New Directions in Educational Technology. Edited by E. Scanlon and T. O'Shea. VIII, 251 pages. 1992. *(AET)*

Vol. 97: Advanced Models of Cognition for Medical Training and Practice. Edited by D. A. Evans and V. L. Patel. XI, 372 pages. 1992. *(AET)*

Vol. 98: Medical Images: Formation, Handling and Evaluation. Edited by A. E. Todd-Pokropek and M. A. Viergever. IX, 700 pages. 1992.

Vol. 99: Multisensor Fusion for Computer Vision. Edited by J. K. Aggarwal. XI, 456 pages. 1993. *(ROB)*

Vol. 100: Communication from an Artificial Intelligence Perspective. Theoretical and Applied Issues. Edited by A. Ortony, J. Slack and O. Stock. XII, 260 pages. 1992.

Vol. 101: Recent Developments in Decision Support Systems. Edited by C. W. Holsapple and A. B. Whinston. XI, 618 pages. 1993.

Vol. 102: Robots and Biological Systems: Towards a New Bionics? Edited by P. Dario, G. Sandini and P. Aebischer. XII, 786 pages. 1993.

Vol. 103: Parallel Computing on Distributed Memory Multiprocessors. Edited by F. Özgüner and F. Erçal. VIII, 332 pages. 1993.

Vol. 104: Instructional Models in Computer-Based Learning Environments. Edited by S. Dijkstra, H. P. M. Krammer and J. J. G. van Merriënboer. X, 510 pages. 1993. *(AET)*

Vol. 105: Designing Environments for Constructive Learning. Edited by T. M. Duffy, J. Lowyck and D. H. Jonassen. VIII, 374 pages. 1993. *(AET)*

Vol. 106: Software for Parallel Computation. Edited by J. S. Kowalik and L. Grandinetti. IX, 363 pages. 1993.

Vol. 107: Advanced Educational Technologies for Mathematics and Science. Edited by D. L. Ferguson. XII, 749 pages. 1993. *(AET)*

Vol. 108: Concurrent Engineering: Tools and Technologies for Mechanical System Design. Edited by E. J. Haug. XIII, 998 pages. 1993.

Vol. 109: Advanced Educational Technology in Technology Education. Edited by A. Gordon, M. Hacker and M. de Vries. VIII, 253 pages. 1993. *(AET)*

Vol. 110: Verification and Validation of Complex Systems: Human Factors Issues. Edited by J. A. Wise, V. D. Hopkin and P. Stager. XIII, 704 pages. 1993.

Vol. 111: Cognitive Models and Intelligent Environments for Learning Programming. Edited by E. Lemut, B. du Boulay and G. Dettori. VIII, 305 pages. 1993. *(AET)*

Vol. 112: Item Banking: Interactive Testing and Self-Assessment. Edited by D. A. Leclercq and J. E. Bruno. VIII, 261 pages. 1993. *(AET)*

Vol. 113: Interactive Learning Technology for the Deaf. Edited by B. A. G. Elsendoorn and F. Coninx. XIII, 285 pages. 1993. *(AET)*

Vol. 114: Intelligent Systems: Safety, Reliability and Maintainability Issues. Edited by O. Kaynak, G. Honderd and E. Grant. XI, 340 pages. 1993.

Vol. 115: Learning Electricity and Electronics with Advanced Educational Technology. Edited by M. Caillot. VII, 329 pages. 1993. *(AET)*

NATO ASI Series F